The Vampire Lectures

The Vampire Lectures

LAURENCE A. RICKELS

UNIVERSITY OF MINNESOTA PRESS

MINNEAPOLIS · LONDON

Frontispiece: "Untitled," 1995. Photograph by Nancy Barton.

Published by the University of Minnesota Press
111 Third Avenue South, Suite 290
Minneapolis, MN 55401-2520
http://www.upress.umn.edu

Library of Congress Cataloging-in-Publication Data

Rickels, Laurence A.
    The vampire lectures / Laurence A. Rickels.
       p.   cm.
    Includes filmography.
    Includes bibliographical references.
    ISBN 0-8166-3391-6 (alk. paper). — ISBN 0-8166-3392-4 (pbk. :
alk. paper)
    1. Vampire films — History and criticism.   2. Horror tales — History
and criticism.   3. Vampires in literature.   I. Title.
PN1995.9.V3R53   1999
791.43'675 — dc21   99-30570

Printed in the United States of America on acid-free paper

The University of Minnesota Press is an equal-opportunity educator and employer.

11 10 09 08 07 06 05 04   10 9 8 7 6 5 4

Contents

IN MY PREFACE

I started pumping up this corpus called *The Vampire Lectures* in 1986 on the campus of the University of California, Santa Barbara, somewhere between the airport and the beach, or in other words or worlds, somewhere between the middlebrowbeat Back East and the Teen Age on the Coast. It was my new curricular offering, a course load of auto-stimulation, which I made a point of injecting into the student body's circulation system, their curriculum vitae, in order to catch them where they breed. And I had time. All the time of the transference was on my side. Because it was not, not right away, an instant hit; the student body was slow on the intake. "Vampirism in German Literature and Beyond" doubled as intro to psychoanalytic theory: the vampire located on the margin of the psychoanalytic treatment of mourning sickness, where it is as much a symptom as an example, was advanced to the front of the class.

On Halloween eve 1987 the student newspaper ran an interview with me that began with the question of how I came to a topic of study that some might consider "morbid." My answer back then:

> I guess it begins with an interest in Freudian psychoanalysis and the impression I have, which is the basis for all my research, that the issue of mourning is the most vulnerable point of articulation in psychoanalytic theory. So this is what I've pursued throughout, and vampirism, haunting, all these morbid manifestations are frequent analogies for mourning and aberrant mourning in psychoanalysis. On the sidelines of that proper pursuit, I necessarily acquired all this marginal knowledge, and I figured, Why not switch perspectives a little bit, in the usual move of seeing the marginal as somehow more central than it had seemed to be, and address vampirism within psychoanalysis more directly. In the course we're set to do right now I allow vampirism and the technical media and psychoanalysis to occupy interchange-

able places; one isn't necessarily marginal with respect to the other; they converge in one thought experiment.

So the class that right away drew attention but not yet the crowds tried to convey psychoanalytically conceived themes or topics of mourning and melancholia or technology and haunting via the host of cultural phenomena or symptoms served at our media mass. What I find encouraging about the outrageous success of the class, especially since 1995, and now I am talking body count, is that I at no point anticipated or compromised with student-consumer expectations. I believe I never gave in to the desire for paraphrase-o-rama explanations (a desire that most likely gets projected onto students, for their edification or identification, by mediocre professors) not even or especially not in the form of reading assignments, required or recommended. We always encountered our words and thoughts directly. No explanations, please.

The class was always way more about the theoretical issues I placed on the conveyor belting out of my pedagogy than it ever was just another imitation-cool sampling of sensationalisms. When I started offering the course in the 1980s, I would always attract, just by title alone, over one hundred fun-seeking students who after my first lecture had pre-selected or -shrunk themselves into a smaller body of twenty or so. The course was an inside hit with students who were way cool or otherwise in the ready position for post-punk Freudianism. Soon the more hip college guides were singling it out (in the midst of best pizza parlor and best beer joint) as the local curriculum highlight. That core group built up over the years, presumably by work of mouth, the support grouping of the transference, such that when I offered the course in fall 1997, over six hundred students were stuffed, like teens crowding into a phone booth, inside an auditorium with a seating capacity of five hundred.

All modern discursivities have mixed their analogies and metaphors with occult figures. It may shock you to pay attention to the many references in so many more works of literature, philosophy, and social and natural science to what is strictly monstrous, ghostly, and already literally (*monere*) or unconsciously all the show and to what that warning shout is all about. But in our in-class showdown and tell-all we could discern that these ghosts, vampires, werewolves were jamming the intersection between technology and the unconscious.

Excavation is required, even in the psychoanalytic discourse, although here at least the dotted lines for the dig are also already given by three small or narcissistic differences: projection, the work of mourning, and the work of analogy. I gave these lines in my first book, *Aberrations of Mourning:*

> Only by tapping into the separate places occupied by Freud's theory of ghosts and his theory of pathological mourning can we begin to discern that which remains outside by substituting for mourning: the audio and video broadcasts of improper burial—analyzed in *Totem and Taboo*—which are transmitted via the crypts which—as set forth in "Mourning and Melancholia"—those who are incapable of mourning must build inside for the unmourned and, hence, undead. Projection is the doubly missing link between melancholia and phantom possession. . . . The point of conjunction between "Mourning and Melancholia" and "The Taboo upon the Dead" that has been thus excluded nevertheless returns via certain sets of analogy, which in turn invite the theories of projection and incorporation to conjoin by plugging into the technical media. (17, 18)

Opened up along these lines, Freud's science serves not only as a kind of owner's manual to our inside-out technologization but also as master of the university of discourses. Marxism can werewolf its occult figures down with gusto, but what it throws up there in occult analogy is still way more symptomatic than instructive or even, shall we say, performative. The occult force that is with techno-consumer cultures drove Marxists to acknowledge Freud behind their man, especially during the thirties when the countermovements of unconscious politics were so spectacularly on the rise. But Marxism did not give a whole lot back to psychoanalysis, not even in exchange value: commodity fetishism and ideology, for example, represent a subtraction in range and precision from what Freud had to say about fetishism and group psychology. When I first started teaching at UC Santa Barbara, a campus underpass bore the wonderfully reformulated or misremembered slogan, anyway it was a lapsus, sprayed against the wall of grammar: WORKERS OF THE WORLD

UNITE! YOU HAVE NOTHING TO LOSE—EXCEPT YOUR WHIPS! In passing let me just point out, like a guide in a tour bus, that in group-psychological culture there is the sadomasochistic couplification of drives that gets off first before the Marxian class pairs start walking down the aisle. Our graffiti artist could not get around being on location.

Marxism does not put through the connection between its occult identifications and technology (with media technology at the front of the line of reception). The Heidegger reception, by contrast and fine-tuning, can, with great raffinesse, tune in an essence of technology that is all about a certain ready positioning and framing, one that is not necessarily itself technological. But just the same, it too skips or symptomatizes a double beat, that of the occult and melancholia. Marxist social studies and whatever brand of existentialism do not provide a reception area for the dead or undead, nor do they instill or install our community spirits, our ghosts.

The occult, as we know it, dates from the onset of technologization, which by the eighteenth century was literally part of socialization (via the printing press and its assignment of reading knowledge). But the occult makes its comebacks by each time hitching its partings to yet another new techno-mediatic invention. The occult, discontinuously enough, is the afterimage of every media-technological innovation. First, the Before Picture: just look at the self-entitlement of our mass media sensurround. The fantasy content of technologization is immortalizing, replicational, doubling, or narcissistic on an upbeat only. The allure of the vampire does overlaps with this happy-face intake of what is going down technologically or as technology. But where there is a positive overcoming of long distance, it is still the loss of the long distant, our dead or even undead, that just has not, not by a long shot, been overcome or even addressed. The occult fantasy analyzes the techno fantasy and, inevitably, points to the missing place of the death cult inside techno culture. The vampire, the incarnation of mediatic powers across long distance, always also goes down, originally or in some other place, for the body count of missing persons either on his own person or in the reception area of his victims and fans.

Both beats, the up one and the down or dead one, at the same time cover the Teen Age, another name for the techno and occult era I am trying to address up front. I am pushing to the front of reception—also the reception of my own more studied and formal works—the background analogy work that has been the occult line (since the eighteenth century at the latest). The techno connections are rewired in the wake of this push forward of an occult chorus line with the vampire cheerleading us on.

In the 1987 student-newspaper interview, I tried to tell them where the ghosts in Bram Stoker's *Dracula* come from:

> This rapport between the occult and the technical media, which reaches such a high point with the end of the nineteenth century, continues to this day. The terms shift. Obviously the telephone is not uncanny as it had been before, and the various contours of the death cult shared by the occult and the technical media are always shifting. Since the introduction of the telegraph, we have referred to the people in seances receiving the ghostly messages as mediums. And now, in California, how do we refer to them? We call them channels or channelers. We're still tuning in both telecommunications and communications with the dead.... Obviously the range of haunting, the range of our rapport with the dead, and there has always been a rapport with the afterlife, is going to reach as far as our senses extend. What are technical media if not extensions of our senses? Whenever the senses are extended again, they invite another kind of phantom rebound. These figures Shirley MacLaine talks to or through are, you know, as old as the hills. There's no new development there; but they come from newer parts of our sensorium, which is always being expanded.

Where else could my Freudo-vampiric intervention have taken place if not at the modern university, the institution that arose to the occasion of the Teen Age, the heartbeat-later fleshing and flushing out of the emerging techno externalizations of what Freud would analyze as internal psychic mechanisms. The Teen Age, as the first techno culture, the first line of metabolization of the pressures of technologization in language and in groups, is the reception that the discourses crowding the corridors of the university in every sense contain. Even the lip-synching pun power of teen languages represents the first defense against and connection with the techno pressures that are upon us. Adolescence as discursive event, as the creation or replication of idiom, the master mixing of all the overheard sensurround voices jamming in mass media culture or in the borderline states of psychosis, becomes the rehearsal or repetition both of artistic discourse and of theoretical jargon.

In my second book, *The Case of California*, I sent the origin of the Teen Age, as we know it, to the corner of the university classroom. In range of Freud's reading and writing, Stanley Hall (the American host of Freud's first visit to America) postulated a so-called adolescent psychology of conversion:

> Hall's historicizing reading of conversion focuses on an era of its invention—as American fad—which also lends its era to current TV Evangelism. According to Hall's cultural rereading, adolescence was only recently invented—in the eighteenth century—around the society-wide interchangeability (interchargeability) of religious conversion and its model or analogue, pubescent sexuality. (166)

> Beginning in the eighteenth century the modern university and college provided crisis centers and support groups for the new invention of adolescence. The modern educational institution, which TV has increasingly monitored and replaced, was originally the channel of a controlled release of teen passion—the impulse and problem of our epoch. The placeholder of these institutionalizations was mass conversion, in which the releases of a dangerous adolescent interiority were redistributed—new and improved—via the group. (165)

The university was designed to generate and contain the group psychology, conversion psychology, and fandom of adolescents. Now, given that assignment, there are, basically, two ways to go about it. There is the fast-food, fit-of-the-hit (or -tit), doubling-for-nothing approach: give them what they already know and leave them there, feeling good about themselves. And then there is the approach that is styling with the transference, a dynamic that will outlast not only the time frame of each class session but even, and by years, that of the completed course. To learn what you do not think you already know or what you do not think the paraphrasing other knows takes all the time in the word, in the encounter with the word or thought that is uncontrollably, futurally other.

Why California? In the 1987 interview I put myself and my Californian interlocutor on location:

> Why is California the site of most of these manifestations? . . . California is the primal habitat of the technical media. So of course, we would be in the best position to receive phantoms. Good phantoms, like Shirley MacLaine's, but also the bad ones. That is where the issue of child abuse comes in. This is really how we're being haunted now, all over America, but particularly in California. These images on milk cartons, on postcards and so on, these shadowy images, already ghostly images of missing children, where do these ghosts come from? Childhood appears in a state of ghostly disappearance.

Adolescence can be seen from both sides now, because it has extended into the Before and the After, and its ever expanding central experience is college. I take this role call, somewhat glumly, at one point in *The Case of California*: "The Californian learns from the pack, frat or group of friends how to get a charge out of socialization—how to feel good about himself and party and have fun. (College in California has no higher purpose than to sponsor and promote this native pedagogy.)" (165). On the outside there is happy face—but on the inside there is suicide. Let my teen graffiti perform an answer to the question, Why California?—one that is as dumb and unforgettable as god and dog: turn "smiley" upside down and you can see a vampire's blood-dripping fangs.

　　In the rush of my exposure to the third-string show business that is academia at its best (or worst), I noticed one day that a student was taping my lectures. I could not resist the temptation to see those vampire tapes transcribed. The 1987 interview was titled, as though on one loop with the tape recording of Anne Rice's vampire or, indeed, of my own in-class commentaries, "Interview with the Vampire Professor." The taped origin of *The Vampire Lectures* guaranteed, however, that there would be no rush to get them out. The horror of the taped voice, of the one double that always comes life-size, is a special feature of Stoker's *Dracula*. But even after the special someone with Mina Harker's typing skills could be found, the traces of liveness in the transcription, the record of oedipedagogical overkill, promoted a schedule of repress release that kept the document a long time beaming up into the public, published sphere. Beyond this sensurround of literary reference, the attraction of the tapes—ready-mades cast up out of the unconscious—was a self-reflexive one. It is the essence of melancholia, I mean the essence of technology, that has been along for the writing of *The Vampire Lectures* from the start of the tape. Through transcriptions the taped voice became a resource, something held in reserve, a kind of fuel for the endless recycling and revisioning of the text. But reserve fuel is not endless: what gets recycled runs on unacknowledged empty. It is the economy of melancholia, a war economy of stored, rationed, and synthesized resources that must close ranks around every reserve, push back the specter of disappearance of all fuel or energy, and go for the total victory that in turn can only recuperate everything in infinite recycling. For one long haul during a leave of absence, I tried to watch and take in, inscribe, every vampire, werewolf, mummy, horror, slasher, splatter, and science fiction film or TV show ever made. And at the same time, I attempted a parallel universal: I tried sinking my teeth into the popular corpus of horror and sci-fi literature. But even in this leave of my senses, I knew better. There is no object to incorporate in fast food. Even as I was thinking that I might just catch up soon with the body of my work of unmourning, a catch would present itself, the melancholic catch in the throat of my manic orality: there were ever more horror shows coming down the reassembly lines of mass culture. It could only have been a project that would end up complete, at least in itself, once I was out of the way. Its discovery unfinished after my death was the only way for it to go and stop in the mode of completeness. What would have stopped dead in the tracks of interminability would have been another Winchester haunted house, the mansion in San Jose that the gun-money widow kept on building and rebuilding to mislead the vengeful dead into missing their mark. Like watching TV or VCR around the clock, the widow's endless project, always just one heartbeat ahead of her projections, kept her immortal. But the eternal or internal safety zone she mobilized was between the rock-hard crypt of her unmourned, unacknowledged loss of a beloved child and, the hardest place of all, the vengeful projective rebound of phantoms, not only victims of those that Winchester had rifled with but even her little one, trying to make it back home to root for their destruction.

In the lectures sometimes a movie will come up for air waves of public analysis. In the original version of *The Vampire Lectures* (four times the current length) the ready-made status of the transcribed lectures had somehow provoked in me all-out supplemental efforts on the better behalf of a kind of ruinous totalization. I included burial-plot summaries of so many fictions that in class had remained unread, unread. I kept a record of redescriptions (which, as in therapy, are implicit interpretations) of all the other film and TV resources, and kept the running record below the main lecture text, an underworld on every page. It was reminiscent of the nonstop cinema running beneath the top text in *Kiss of the Spider Woman,* in which the prisoner who lives on rough trade with cell mates as "vampire" is captive audience to his (and the author's) internal and eternal cinema. But then I started to play my own project closer to the transference, returned to the closure or context coming right out of the allegorical tension between the in-session materiality of the transference and the shorthand of its psychoanalytic theory, and thus arrived finally at a happier medium.

Only on occasion do the words from your lecturing sponsor get displaced by the upward mobility of some part of the original underworld when it has just been time out for a clip. These redescriptions, which of course never really were a happening event in session, do, however, represent just a few of the many inserts that were always one part visual self-evidence and big part transferential material that the students were prepared to receive or process in certain but diffuse ways. Given the one to one thousand ratio of picture to words, the book just cannot represent the fast clip of the lectures, or how, by association, portions of a lecture were shot straight from a clip. Also left out of the book are the occasional student interventions, which represent in these large group sessions a tall ordering about of the resistance. But in time the few who shorted out would become, of course, my minions.

When *The Case of California* appeared in 1991, my small but compact in-group of student fans would tell me that they totally admired the way I could capture in my writing my way of speaking in class. And yet the book was, to that date, my most writerly and deliberate, even belabored, work. Already upon finishing teaching the vampirism class for the first time, a student commented that what she had loved about my lectures was that what I had to say was so personal, so grounded in my own experience and history. Even when it is theory, it is all about me. Even when it is rewriting to the max, it is the record of my voice. The receiving area of the transference is a highly constructed and hallucinatory space.

While I have included the primal reading list backing my lectures, I do not provide a footnote-by-footnote commemoration of my sources. I admit up front that these lectures recycle what is original about other books, including my own. So, a word from this book's frame of reference, my series on unmourning. The first time around, in *Aberrations of Mourning,* I turned around the building or *Bildung* blocks of "German" culture to read off from the back the ingredients of unmarked, unmourned graves. This book's influence on *The Vampire Lectures* is not least but the most lasting. It took the second book in the series, *The Case of California,* to look into the bicoastal synchronization of the mass of murder or merger in the Teen Age between Germany and California. I gave this state the status of a concept or philosopheme, one closely associated with adolescent or group psychology in Freud's thought, and named it, simply but subtly, "California." It is where all that's fair, no longer love and war, goes down and out as friendship and suicide. I discovered out West, then, on the unconscious side of one conceptual continuum, the bare disguise of mass-media death cults from here to Germany. For the third try, *Nazi Psychoanalysis,* I took the California project on group or adolescent psychology back to a more direct hit or fit of continuity: to all the double fronts of military psychology, war neurosis, espionage, and psychological warfare in which all the master discursivities of modernity took such a controlling interest.

Much of the writing that has been pulled up for this book is not the kind I usually stand by. It is on standby: between reading/writing and the propagandistic talking of teaching. But even in this context of compromise where accessibility is supposed to be the free gift that comes with readership, I have to say that here too I do not pray at the lip service given in memory of received ideas. In time I finally grew accustomed to the canned or rather "uncanned" quality of this document. I guess I am trying to say that what I hate about this book, I mean what I love about it, is that it comes via the other and is inescapably my own. The as-live reconstruction of the lectures could not get around some of the embarrassing mistakes in judgment that "were there." But: what if there are a few howlers? Ahh, listen to them! They are the children of the night.

LECTURE ONE

What is a historical fact? It is after the fact. With vampirism, in any event, history comes after to give definition to an unformed body of symptoms. If one could scan, on rewind, the facts and rumors circulating as vampirism, at any given time or over time — in real time — what we would find before us is the polymorphous confusion of activities and desires that go down and out and under the name of vampirism. There are many, many ways in which one can become a vampire, many ways in which one can exercise one's vampirism. And there are many different parts of the body where the blood can be sucked.

But there are also histories of vampirism. The most prominent history is the one Bram Stoker ended up with in the course of writing *Dracula*. He worked the archives at the British Museum to open a coherent historical account of vampirism to back his novel. But up front, in his own real-time zone, Stoker wrote a spy novel about female sexuality and group psychology that is more about the vampire being replaced by us than it is, over time, about the ongoing history of vampirism.

In our time Anne Rice's *Vampire Chronicles* opens another account (at the vampirism blood bank). Like Stoker's double take, Rice's chronic approach works both time zones at once. It is an account of The Vampire: The Legend over time. But it also draws from the joint account vampirism opens up here, now, and always between self and other. The vampire is us. We have a history, but we don't want to be history. Because now we know (with Rice) what it is like to be the vampire and that we like the vampire. We would like to be different — like the vampire we like — to be like.

In medieval Europe—at the time of the Middle-Ages crisis—a working definition of vampirism was already current, the one, you know the one, that the Christian church came up with to put down sinners. This medieval take first fixed the focus on the vampire. The vampire was by definition a dead person who, since not eligible for proper Christian burial in hallowed ground, was on the rebound.

And finally—for there are four coherent (but largely nonsuperimposable) histories of vampirism—there was the one (a good one) developed in the eighteenth century. That was the time when professors at German and French universities began addressing an outbreak of vampirism sighted back East and reported in the newspapers and journals out West.

If you were to hit the books on vampirology and vampirism, you would be struck by how, at any given time, always different sets of people were suddenly coming under suspicion of being candidates for becoming vampires. But just the same, the selection criteria for going vampiric tended to revolve each time around the hostilities of the in-group against whatever was already on the outside. That is why vampirism can be found where it was forgotten: in the corner of history-making events. Released from where it was cornered, vampirism can be followed (bouncing-ball style) as the other history or the history of the other—as a psychohistory of projection. As one historian of vampirism puts it:

> People who are different, unpopular or great sinners are apt to return from the dead. It may be merely a corollary of this rule that in Eastern Europe alcoholics are regarded as prime candidates for revenants. Löwenstimm gives accounts from Russia of people who were unearthed merely because while alive they were alcoholic. (Barber, 29)

Vampires Anonymous covers the excluded—and already haunted. The alcoholic's literalized intake of inspiration (or spirits) covers identification with some absent (and thus haunting) other. Simply put (deep down inside), the alcoholic has pickled some loss (often the corpse of the loss) that cannot be acknowledged as lost. By the eighteenth century (the opening era of our institutionalization, technologization, and unconscious remote control) the corpses of Madame de Staël's parents could be kept pickled in alcohol inside glass jars.

That is why, in Bulgaria, you can get back your deposit when you bottle a vampire who is thus disposable. Cornered by the hunter armed with a picture or *Eikon* of some saint, the vampire cannot but enter the bottlefield saturated, on the inside, with the vampire's favorite food. "Having no other resource, he enters this prison, and is immediately fastened down with a cork, on the interior of which is a fragment of the *Eikon*. The bottle is then thrown into the fire, and the vampire disappears forever" (cited in Summers, 208).

But it was another literalizer of inspiration or dictation, the suicide, that was the candidate for a vampire's comeback most likely to succeed culture by culture and time and again. The suicide is always the one checkout guaranteed to return with a vengeance; he just plain forgot to take his nearest and dearest with him. The suicide was refused proper burial service in local churchyards: not only to double (antibody-style) the impropriety of the suicidal act but also to keep the suicide, who was bound to come back, confused and out of it. They didn't want him finding his way back to the family setting. That is why the suicide was buried at the crossroads outside town: faced with a four-way choice, chances were the zombie wouldn't make the right one.

Bulgarian accounts of vampirism put robbers, arsonists, prostitutes, and treacherous bar maids on schedule to return as vampires. The seventh child, the child born with teeth, with a split lower lip, an extra nipple, covered with hair, with red caul or birthmark: the checkout list is enormous. Sex with your grandmother can get you there. But the best warranty comes, of course, with the vampire's bite — in the neck, on the nipple, or between the eyes. An animal flying or leaping over a corpse can put departure into reverse. If your shadow was stolen during your lifetime, you must come back from the grave — as you also must if your brother was a sleepwalker. But the people around you (for example, in Romania) were on the lookout for the chance to steal your shadow. They stole the show by driving a nail through the head of the shadow you cast on a wall. It was the surefire way to quake-proof the building. So back then and there (we will unpack this later on, but here it is right now as decontextualized headline) catastrophe preparedness was in the special interest of the group the vampire was out to make. But for now let's continue with the hysteria of vampirism.

To die in childbirth bonds motherhood to vampiric return; to die pre-baptism puts baby in the rebound position. Whosoever suckles a second time—after having already been weaned—is a double sucker for afterlife. Still in Hungary (still hungry!) the stillborn illegitimate off-spring of parents, who were in their own time bastards too, are bound to spring back. The wicked or excommunicated person, the perjurer, apostate, the person who died under a curse, and the person (often the same person) who was buried without proper rites, were each in turn up for finalist entry as the corpse that could not decompose or stay at rest.

If we look at this wide spread of possibilities, we can conclude that vampirism not only serves the exclusion of the different (a kind of double exclusion of whatever is already on the margin), but that it also always covers the need to mourn. That the vampire is someone who was buried improperly also meant, still to the point, that this special someone was not mourned properly. In many countries the view was real popular that anyone who died alone, because there was no one around to care for him in his fatal illness, was bonded to his own return. The Gypsies also reckoned that a person whose solo dying went without seeing was bound to be back. That is why bachelors were so feared when they died. With vampirism it's mourning that's at stake.

So on the one hand there is a kind of political trajectory to vampirism, and on the other we can fold out a trajectory that begins at home, the one that originates with mourning the dead other. To give a final example: when several family members died rapid-fire in Hungary, it was believed that the first to go had not been put to rest once and for all but was now, in the meantime, a vampire back from the grave to claim his dearly beloved. The claim had to be staked.

There are out there still, uncontained by the four coherent but non-superimposable histories and definitions of the vampire, countless examples from every culture's legend reserves of goners returning from death to suck the blood of the living. We will be addressing the blood drive in a moment (a topic that will spill over into antiquity and thus also outside the four-way intersection of histories within which we have taken up position, like the improperly buried suicide). But the issue of the return ticket was seen first (and this is the explanation that satisfies some humanist types) in the natural cycle of the seasons. The problem with this comfort by analogy is that it covers life and death but does not sustain any specific life or life span. But you (or your ego) are not impressed by the trend nature sets for life's continued existence. You and your ego just don't want to go. (And this is where the techno phantasm of the double, the mirror and—on the other side—the uncanny takes off.) But let's stay with Freud on the life or death issue.

Your unconscious cannot conceive of your own death. Thus there is no problem with our own death; at bottom we just do not believe in it: we know we will always bounce back like comic-strip or cartoon figures. Thus Freud is able to argue that there is no such thing as fear of death. Fear of death—as in fear of flying and related panic states—only covers for or displaces another fear, a fear of retribution or punishment brought to us by the internalized parent we once wished dead. "You wanted a dead parent? Go ahead and *be* the dead parent."

In the young-child's-eye view (which in the adult continues to beam up from the unconscious) our own life is indestructible. His majesty the baby is a control freak who thinks he is all-powerful. He likes to play presence/absence with himself and others, now by making himself appear and disappear at will in front of a mirror, now by thinking that his wish is his command. It is what Freud called omnipotence of thoughts. Little one treats mother like the robot and blow-up dolly she becomes at the psycho end of nondevelopment or total regression. But it is inevitable: there *will be* frustration of the infant's fast-food demand for mother and breast. But rather than surrender the primal belief in the omnipotence of his thoughts, little one decides that if she is not here when he wants her, it is because he wished her gone (and that means: a goner). So, inevitably, one of the first applications of omnipotence of thoughts is the death wish. And omnipotence of thoughts (with the death wish at the front of the line) forms one syndication not only with the magical belief systems of so-called primitives but also with our own technological inventions. And what crowds *this* line of development (or non-development)? Countless death-wish casualties, both the direct-hit targets and the victims of their own backfire.

While the image of the vampire slobbering blood over the exposed throat of the victim obviously attracts the kind of Freudian reading that is strictly sexological (the kind the old guy, Freud, less "Freudian" than his pop-psychological following, dismissed as "wild"), the crude specificities of the vampire as a corpse that has come back to life invite another Freudian perspective: the cryptological one that brings into focus our continuing relations with the dead—not with death, then, but with the dead. There is a death that we cannot ignore, that we must conceive, and that is the other's death. It is always the other's death that cannot be circumvented or overlooked. And like mourning and melancholia, vampirism always emerges displaced with regard to the other's death: the dead or missing other.

The *Oxford English Dictionary* entry for *vampire* gives the definition established by the eighteenth century: the vampire is "a ghost (usually of wizard, heretic, criminal, etc.) that leaves his grave every night and sucks the blood of sleeping persons." Inside this eighteenth-century-contemporary habitat of the vampire, we find that a good part of the design goes way back in primal time: blood sucking, our premier and oldest legacy, was practiced in the first place on sleeping persons. All the bodily fluids of certain sleeping bodies were up for grabs: sex with afterlife figures was just a variation on the same score or fix. In the word *nightmare,* as in its German counterpart, *Alptraum,* we find left over and deposited from primal time the great notion of a goblin or little monster, a succubus or an incubus, that visits you at night while you are sleeping and settles down on your chest to disturb your breathing, suck out your breath, or suck your blood. As far back as we can go (and we are going all the way), the nightmare has been received as visitation at night by some spirit, whose ghost appearance was contained in just a bad dream.

The vampire was only one in a long list of creatures that could disturb one's rest — or rest in peace. In his book *On the Nightmare* psychoanalyst Ernest Jones links vampire, werewolf, witch, and sorcerer to the
original goblin figures of bad dreams. Backed up by these phantom visitations admitted into dreaming, Jones associates this phantom or nightmare realm in its entirety with issues of sexual repression and release.
But even after we have kept up with Jones and given in to the protective
impulse to gender and couplify illicit or vampiric impulses at their origin (via the succubus and incubus), we will find that we must first be
sure we know what is being sucked and what or who exactly is doing
the sucking.

The blood and the life have been given a long-standing equation.
In the Greek underworld, the spirits of the departed could only speak —
and thus once more put through the direct connection with life — after
they had been granted a drink of blood. And Christ's blood is one of
the all-time greatest guarantees of eternal life. But issuing from Christianity's main symbol (and from its mass appeal), there emerged in the
Middle Ages blood-healing beliefs identified with the cult of the Virgin
Mary. Physicians prescribed the blood of virgins as a cure-all, one that
celebrated the mass of murder: girls were slaughtered for the magic substance taken from them sometimes with, sometimes even without, their
family's consent or profit.

In *Andy Warhol Presents Dracula,* Paul Morrisey presents Warhol presents
Dracula as a clothes horse, I mean, corpse, of course, one that paints his hair
on twice a day and washes it all off at night. His sister is crypt-ridden. The
Count only has a few weeks left of out-patient mobility. He needs virgin
blood. Italy is religion-bound to produce virginity for the making of mar-
riages. He puts sister in coffin and goes, he says, with her blessing. "Our
family will continue." The Count's assistant, Anton, soaks up the blood spilled
in a traffic accident with a loaf of bread — the host that's the most — and
brings the wound-enriched bread in off the street to the Count. The dead
girl was twelve or thirteen years old. The Count confirms everything was in

working order:"She was pure." Count and Anton target a family of girls. The father is a name taster who loves "Dracula"; he swirls it around, gargles with it, compares it to wine. The Count, who is looking to wed one of the daughters, looks pale to the girls, who can talk:"But he's a vegetarian, they all do." He tries the first candidate's blood and detects the lie or lay behind her claim to purity. It makes him sick. Dalessandro plays estate stud who bullies and satisfies the two "bitches." His anti-feudalism is part of his sex appeal. It is a class tension or attraction that cannot be straightened out, according to the Count:"Dreaming about a change in the order of things?" "Not dreaming, waiting.""I've heard that before."

The Count's second try with the next daughter makes him throw up more than his hands. "The blood of these whores is killing me!" Dalessandro's comment on the sidelines:"There's something slimy about the Count. I don't think he wants marriage, he wants something else." But the youngest daughter is still intact. She breaks away from the taking of a blood count. Dalessandro:"That Count who was going to do so much for the family is a vampire. Throwback to religious perverts from the Middle Ages. He needs to suck the blood of virgins to stay alive." When it comes to staying alive, the youngest needs to lose her virginity, fast. The quickie is in, over, and out. The Count slurps the blood off the floor from the busted hymen. The tramp sisters are now the lesbian slaves of the Count. The eldest daughter, a Fellini geek named Esmeralda, who was previously engaged and thus never entered anyone's thoughts for the running, joins the group portrait. But this virgin is too late for the taking by Dalessandro or Dracula."He lives off of people, he's no good and never was." Dalessandro takes an ax to the Count, cuts off, count them, two arms. Esmeralda throws herself on the stake too to pale by comparison.

Roman Polanski's *The Fearless Vampire Killers* presents the perfect peristaltic reversal of the projection charges of vampire history. What gets dredged up is every stereotyping of vampirism, right down to the still current ranks of the vampire's association at projection central (Polanski gives us the Easern European's unbiased view): the Jew, the first in the movie to become the next vampire, who also bears a reference to Freud's Wolfman case; the homosexual, the Count's "sensitive" son; the bubble-bathing child-woman, whose spot of blood on the leftover tub foam marks vampirism as her menstrual changeover into the woman her parents dread, and who leaves the film as the ultimate carrier of vampirism to the rest of the world.

There is a miniaturist polish to the movie's look that is cuddly, dusty, dead cute. But what polishes the tiny enshrinement off is a backflow of blood from Charles Manson's mass murdering back in California. I am talking about the mass of Sharon Tate's murder. The transmitter of vampirism's future was at the same time the only one to die, really die. Almost a snuff film. When home movies are for the survivor, then snuff's enough. The doll came out on top, top of the mourning to you, together with those undigested pieces of vampirism reception thrown up over the top, onto the screen of projections. The undead, I mean unborn, did not die with her, Polanski saw to that, but was desperately sexualized and reanimated for recognizable and treatable scenarios of abuse, regression, cry for help, one that only your director knows by art of Hollywood. Underneath it all, the babe, the mother inside the wife, was still alive, raised to adolescence by the time the director tried to install but at the same time stall the final cut.

Back to the history lesson, the lessening of pain over time. Phantoms too, it was commonly believed, required blood; that's how they pretended to come alive, that's how they spoke. Another belief current in early Christian culture was that a phantom would invade living persons to put them on. Since the ghost had no mouth, no teeth, no body of his own, he invaded and put on the body of some living person, someone who was suddenly (and to his own amazement) doubled over with the desire to suck blood. You will come to know this transfusion in the mode of what Freud addressed, the first time he took up ghostbusting, as the transference.

But even in ancient Greece and Rome there were bloodsucking evil ghosts: in Greece the *Lamiae* and, when in Rome, the *Striges*. The *Lamiae* were corpses of loose women who were back to devour children or suck the blood of little ones until they died. This kind of intensification of the mother/child relation is an important ingredient in the makeup of vampires (for example, in Stoker's novel). The *Striges*, who could assume the shape of birds, were also on the loose at night out to suck children dry. By law the Romans were forbidden "to leave the dead exposed to the claws of *Strygae* or *Lamiae*" (cited in Ronay, 7). That is why already in ancient Rome a college of clairvoyant priests was established for the training of the first ghostbusters in the war against vampirism. Beginning with their foundation on up, institutions "were there," researching and destroying vampirism, which had to be held up outside in some place other than where it was being held down. But we know better, right here and now in this institutional setting. Our acronym tells all. UCSB: UC Sucks Blood.

Back in the Christian context: we can make out the vampire among all the other occult figures crowding the target range of the Inquisition. However, in the Middle Ages, witches and sorcerers largely took the vampire's place. In the Renaissance, witches and heretics were the most popular stars of persecutory attention. In the sixteenth and seventeenth centuries werewolves were at high risk: between 1520 and the mid-seventeenth century thirty thousand cases of lycanthropy (the official term for werewolfdom) were investigated by the church. The investigation always took one form or one direction. It was believed that the one and only way to be sure that someone was a werewolf was to uncover his one telltale sign or symptom. The werewolf, even when he had assumed normal human shape, still wore on the other side, the inside — his skin was reversible — the hairiness of the wolf. The only way to determine a case of lycanthropy was, thus, to skin the suspect; as you can imagine, most people preferred confessing that they were total werewolves and going for the stake rather than submitting to the reversible-skin lie-detector test. So by the later Middle Ages, by the time of the Inquisition (which, by the way, malingered on until the middle of the nineteenth century), the vampires were lost in the crowd they made, the in-group of occult types. It was home, home on the target range.

But by the Inquisition's late and latest phase, by the eighteenth century, the time of secularization, the beginning of the modern age, our age, the time when the university as we know it here and now—the institution—was invented, the vampire had reemerged, and with redoubled force.

But the vampire legend as we think we know it begins with Stoker, who charted Dracula's lineage all the way back to the fifteenth-century Prince of Walachia, nicknamed "Vlad the Impaler" because his favorite means of taking no prisoners was to, press the pause button, round up the losers and then, press play, have them all impaled on larger-than-life stakes (which I understand is a very slow and painful way to go). Vlad, who was also known as Dracula, "son of Dracul," a real son of a name that means "dragon," was kept busy defending his territory against Saxon traders who had been moving in on the wide open spaces of Eastern Europe. The history (the hysteria!) of Europe has always covered for the West making a move on the East. What is Back East, however, comes into focus as a potential total threat to the West, the kind of threat that requires preemptive strikes. So the Saxon merchants returning from the spot they were in with Vlad the Impaler, who had scored against them, Big Time, came up with chapbooks (which were up there, ahead of their time, with comic books) featuring Vlad the Impaler: monstrous Eastern European subhuman. And Vlad was represented (in these eyewitness reports) as someone who could at any moment invade the West. Ever since the printing press has been with us, journalism has been there too. Here is one of the eyewitness reports sent back to Germany, where it was consumed by a new crowd of readers: "He robbed the St. Jacob Church and set fire to the outskirts of the town. And early next day he had women and men, young and old, next to the same church impaled and had a table put in their midst and partook of breakfast with great appetite" (cited in Ronay, 76). If not vampirism, certainly cannibalism at one remove. Vlad, who is by now a cornerstone of the vampire legend, gives two directions or directives that continue to govern histories of vampirism: first off, his legend coincides with the invention of a technical medium, the printing press; he is the phantom of a new medium—that is a novelty or news item that will return when

we look at Stoker's novel (which is all about the latest gadgets, the gramo-
phone and the typewriter, for example, at least as much as it is about
vampirism). The second feature, which we are here already attending
to, is the way in which vampirism figures in a projective kind of way.
Even as I attack Eastern Europe, it is the East that threatens to attack the
West; it is not we who are actively colonizing (and in effect cannibalizing) the East: it is the East that is packed with the animals and subhu-
mans whose drive Westward we must stop in our tracks back East. The
threat, embodied, for example, as vampirism, always comes from the
East (from Eastern Europe, for example), even when at all times it is
the West that is doubling over with the hunger.

Our next historical supermodel—the Hungarian countess, Elisabeth
Báthory—walked to the end of her runaway blood-bathing contest in
1611. Now that she had the verdict she had done it all, but with a conviction. Let the court record show: she was "a blood-thirsty and bloodsucking godless woman caught in the act in her castle" (cited in Ronay,
94). Her official biographer, a certain Michael Wagner, who wrote at
the end of the seventeenth century (which is when her case was first made
available to inquiring minds just in time for the first epidemic outbreaks
of vampirism in Eastern Europe), tries to catch her in his headlines:

> Elisabeth was wont to dress well in order to please her husband, and
> she spent half the day over her toilet. On one occasion, her chamber-
> maid saw something wrong with her headdress, and as a recompense
> for observing it, received such a severe box on the ears that the blood
> gushed from her nose, and spurted unto her mistress's face.
>
> When the blood drops were washed off her face, her skin appeared
> much more beautiful: whiter and more transparent on the spots where
> the blood had been.
>
> Elisabeth, therefore, formed the resolution to bathe her face and
> her whole body in human blood so as to enhance her beauty. This
> monster used to kill her luckless victim and the old women caught
> the blood in which Elisabeth was wont to bathe at the hour of four in
> the morning. After the bath she appeared more beautiful than ever.
>
> She continued this habit after the death of her husband in the
> hope of gaining new suitors....
>
> She caused, in all, the death of 650 girls...; for murder and blood-
> shed became with her a necessity. (cited in Ronay, 95–96)

To get with this program of skin conditioning, the Countess was already following the logic of magic, which is always about like producing like either by direct imitation or by reversal. Indeed, she had always been happy to reach out and touch her enemies long-distance by destroying their images or by tainting their garments voodoo-style with fatal substances.

The most important gadget inside her household or economy of magic reversal (the economy of getting even) was of course the mirror; it had been the main scanner set up in her ongoing war against decay.

Right from the start, cross my heart, the mirror made important connections with the other realm. It has always opened onto the other place: the reversed world of the dead. To this day when we wear a mourning costume of black in place of lighter colors, or white instead of all black, as the case may be, we perform a final act of reversal that separates us from the departed one, who, just the same, stays in touch, always just a mirror stroke of reversal away.

According to local customs in Transylvania, mirrors were covered up or turned around against the wall in the house where someone had just died. How else could you stop the spirit behind the mirror from holding on to the departed's soul, which, thus on hold, must recall the corpse. It was this spirit behind the mirror, mirror on the wall to which Countess Báthory sacrificed the blood of virgins. The spirit was taking her looks away; it had to be bribed, paid off, paid protection so that it would stop and maybe even return the looks it had already ripped off. The narcissism that holds on to the body cannot but grow uncanny. That is why it is forced to split off from itself and release the emergency projection of the body as machine. This is the psycho version of an inevitable shift from the direct hit of narcissism to its displacement, which runs on (and runs for the cover of) omnipotence of thoughts, the death wish, magic, technologization. The contraptions of torture that are already and always in the service of reducing the body (inside and out) to sheer visibility build the machine around the parasurgically slashed body. "One method, as documented by the court records of the time, was to 'put a terrified naked girl in a narrow iron cage furnished with pointed nails turned inward, hanging it from the ceiling and sitting beneath it enjoying the rain of blood that came down'" (Masters, 87).

But this body cage, which puts the skeleton on the outside, or this automatic sprinkler, which externalizes the blood that no longer flows inward, gets new and improved in the Countess's machine maid that is a specific kind of maid, a "made in Germany." Please hold on to this origin of the automaton sliding into woman's place; it is an origin that lies in advanced stages of the vampiric impulse of mass murder, stages of adjustment away from the uncanny all the way to the totally psychotic (which is the way to go when your libido is no longer in a relationship with the outside world). "Another little gimmick was 'an automat beautifully made by a German clock-smith, which was shaped like a girl and covered with red hair, and wearing red teeth torn from the mouth of some servant; the robot would clutch anyone that came near it in a tight embrace and then transfix them with a series of sharp points that came out of her metal breasts. The blood ran down into a channel so that it could be collected, warmed over a fire and used for the Countess's bath'" (Masters, 87).

From vampiric hunger through Frankensteinian bodybuilding and mummy rewind, we will continue to prepare for that cutting up or technologization of the body (of one's relation to the mother's body) that already gives away the primal preview of the horror movie genre.

I remember when *The Return of the Living Dead* was first released. The sales pitch and motto was: "Just when you thought it was safe to be dead." That is the uncanny threat to afterlife that got the attention of the Western Europeans now faced with the undead epidemic taking over Eastern Europe. Over and out.

The period of publication of Countess Báthory's murders at the end of the seventeenth century (the family had done time trying to conceal the records) converged with the onset of this turn-of-the-eighteenth-century vampirism epidemic. This, the first manifestation of vampirism to make it into the virtual real time of legal, medical, military information-gathering, supplied our only evidence that vampirism might be a happening sort of thing that can be witnessed and investigated on location. In its 1693–94 issue the French journal *Mercure galant* gave the epidemic the kind of coverage it needed to spread:

> The vampires appeared after lunch and stayed until midnight, sucking the blood of people and cattle in great abundance. They sucked through the mouth, the nose, but mainly through the ears. They say that the vampires had a sort of hunger that made them chew even their shrouds in the grave. (cited in Ronay, 15)

That is why, during the first half of the eighteenth century, there was a matching upsurge of scholarly interest in vampirism (which thus coincided with the foundation of the modern university). There were, beginning around 1728 and in the course of maybe fifteen years, as many as forty treatises on vampirism researched and published at German and French universities. These scholars had not witnessed vampirism but were responding, in scholarly fashion, to the long-distance communications of on-location journalism. So, after a slight delay (or repress release), the university, pressed into the service of ghostbusting, tested the documentation that had been collected now for almost twenty-five years. In their respective dissertations on vampirism Dom Calmet in 1751 and Zopfius in 1733 described to the point what was at stake:

> Men who have been dead for some considerable time ... issue forth from the graves and come to disturb the living, whose blood they suck and drain. (cited in Summers, 27)

> Vampires issue forth from their graves in the night, attack people sleeping quietly in their beds, suck out all their blood from their bodies and destroy them. They beset men, women, and children alike, sparing neither age nor sex. Those who are under the fatal malignity of their influence complain of suffocation and a total deficiency of spirits, after which they soon expire. (cited in Summers, 1)

These academic treatises were based on the "we were there" histories featuring run-ins with vampires, say, back in Hungary:

> It is now fifteen years since a soldier, who was quartered in the house of a Haidamack peasant, upon the frontiers of Hungary, saw as he was at table with his landlord, a stranger come in and sit down by them. The master of the house and the rest of the company were strangely terrified but the soldier knew not what to make of it. The next day the peasant died, and upon the soldier's inquiring into the meaning of it, he was told that it was his landlord's father, who had been dead and buried for over ten years, that came and sat down at the table and gave his son notice of his death.
>
> In consequence of this, the body of the spectre was dug up and found to be in the same state as if it had been just dead, the blood like that of a living person. The Count de Cabreras ordered its head to be cut off and the corpse to be buried again.
>
> He then proceeded to take depositions against other spectres of the same sort, and particularly against a man who had been dead over thirty years, and had made his appearance several times in his own house at meal time. At his first visit he had fastened upon the neck of his own brother and sucked his blood; at his second, he had treated one of his children in the same manner, and the third time, he fastened upon a servant of the family; and all three died instantly.

Upon this evidence, the count gave orders that he should be dug up; and being found like the first, with his blood in fluid state as if he had been alive, a great nail was driven through his temples and he was buried again. The count ordered a third person, who had been dead for over sixteen years, to be burned; and he was found guilty of murdering two of his own children by sucking their blood. (cited in Ronay, 18–19)

Now I could quote endlessly from the stockpile of reports of real-life encounters with vampires. They always started with rumors that would circulate among the villagers about a particular dead person who was said to have returned. The officials would then go to the grave, dig up the corpse, and determine whether it had shown sufficiently advanced signs of decaying: if not, it was beheaded or burned or the heart was removed. There were countless investigations that went all the way to digging up suspects, and as the eighteenth century progressed, this preoccupation with vampirism gathered momentum and shifted into automatic: the rest, the remains, of any old dead Freemason, Jew, or heathen were routinely disturbed and desecrated.

There were also available at the same time countless extra measures that could be added to personalize your mourning ceremonies. Freud brought us the ambivalent take on mourning rituals: they reflect less our reverence for the deceased than our all-out fear of the dead. So, if you had the slightest suspicion that your dearly departed was going to return as a bloodsucker, you would, after the corpse had been removed, remove the threshold of your house, so that the zombie would no longer recognize it upon his return; or the coffin could be carried out feet first so the corpse would not be able to watch, record, and play back the tape all the way back to the house. There were many how-to manuals that advised you, for example, to put stones in the mouth of the corpse to keep it from biting and gnawing itself first, then everyone else; or sod could be placed over the corpse's torso up to the chin to keep it from eating itself up (and out of the grave). Originally and always the cross at the grave served the preventive, not the commemorative, purpose.

It is the societywide preoccupation with checking out once and for all that doubly marks the beginning of our modern reception of vampirism. Once the epidemic had reached its high points, vampire courts run by Imperial Army officers were opened throughout the Austro-Hungarian Empire. These courts already gave at the office more than their share of eyewitness reports up for interpretation out West. On location, they had the right to delay the burial of suspected corpses for up to seven weeks. By then the corpses in question would have kept too supple or ruddy for their survivors' own good.

By the eighteenth century vampirism had become synonymous with contagious disease. Circulation was the newly discovered order of the day. With it came notions of contagion and quarantine that would in time set up passport controls between states but led right away to the move to segregate what was dead from the living. We saw the concept of circulation first in the late seventeenth century (and thus just in time to witness that convergence of phantasms we have been unpacking). That is when circulation was discovered, in the first place deep down inside the economy of our own blood supplies. A certain vampire stench had been sniffed out for centuries as the whiff of a contaminant that would be spreading soon as the plague. The memento-mori smell, which found its double and antibody in what garlic had to offer, announced and accompanied the plague before there was a concept of circulation of air. Already in one twelfth-century account, a lecherous husband, recently returned from the grave, terrifies his hometown:

> For the air became foul and tainted as this fetid and corrupting body wandered abroad, so that a terrible plague broke out and there was hardly a house which did not mourn its dead...no sooner had that infernal monster been...destroyed, than the plague...entirely ceased, just as if the polluted air was cleansed by the fire which burned up the hellish brute who had infected the whole atmosphere. (cited in Farson, *Vampires, Zombies, and Monster Men*, 26–27)

Here, too, numerous reports (dating from the end of the seventeenth century to the late eighteenth century) could be cited in which the plague afflicting a town was transferred to the charge of vampirism, and the termination of the plague was bound to the cure or staking of a vampire. There is always some contagious, cureless disease around that blasts through systems of defense and takes over systems of circulation.

Circulation supplies the blood drive the same way substitution, according to Freud, serves the psychic economy that is into life. The vampiric alternatives to circulation and substitution are, point by point, recycling and incorporation.

Be patient, be a patient: it will take time to work these connections; soon, you will see, we will be working them to death.

It's true: vampirism found in psychoanalysis its ultimate match and maker. On Freud's first visit to America there was a moment, so the rumor or legend goes, when he just had to turn to Jung and, while their ship entered New York harbor, cried out (into the wind): "We bring them the plague and they do not know it." Psychoanalysis is the antibody that doubles and contains vampirism. And we will find in the Stoker novel (and in the films based on that novel) that the Van Helsing figure, who is the one who comprehends vampirism and contributes most toward recognition of the vampire's threat, is the representative of psychoanalytic interventions.

Now, the two discoveries that Freud made, and the two rules of ghostbusting that will guide us, let roll direct lines to vampirism. Rule number one: morbid dread always signifies repressed sexual wishes. Rule number two: in the relation of the hypnotized medium to the hypnotist, as in the relation, say, of the group to the leader, it is the seemingly powerless partner, the hypnotized medium, for example, who does all the work. The hypnotist, like the vampire, is a kind of phantom projection produced by the medium's desire to be possessed, controlled, vampirized. And in an aside Freud adds that we can recognize in this hypnotized medium the group of one, the portrait that really becomes us.

Remember, beginning with Stoker's novel, as in the films that followed from the novel, the vampire can enter a home or household by invitation only. No vampirism without the desire to be vampirized.

But what about the actual eyewitness evidence of the corpses, the casualties, both dead and undead, of the vampirism epidemic? Premature burial was a big contributor to the reportable belief in vampirism. If someone taken for dead who had been only in a comatose state was then brought back to consciousness (by accident, perhaps through some grave-robber's intervention, or by awakening on one's own during a wake), the witnesses were so sure that the person was returning from the dead. And even if you remain in your coma, the body taken for dead of course lives on.

Montague Summers was convinced that in the United States in the 1920s, on average one premature burial per week was reported. And that is *reported* (you can imagine how many went — down — unreported). Frantz Hartmann counted seven hundred instances in his neighborhood alone at the end of the nineteenth century. Philip Rohr, in 1679, admitted that vandals robbing a coffin shortly after burial may have been confronted with the horror: the struggles to escape from the casket might explain the distorted features, the stressed position, and the blood. Herbert Mayo, in 1851, advised that the so-called Belgrade vampires "were simply alive in the common way or had been so for some time subsequently to their interment; that, in short, they were the bodies of persons who had been buried alive, and whose life, where it yet lingered, was finally extinguished through the ignorance and barbarity of those who disinterred them" (cited in Summers, 177). But another study of vampirism argues that premature burial, which I will come back to in a heartbeat, cannot account for the majority of the cases reported at the turn of the eighteenth century. Those giveaway signs of vampiric existence — the ruddiness and healthy bloatedness of the corpse, the loss of old and the growth of new skin and fingernails, the blood around the mouth, nostrils, and ears — could check in, with facility, with medical explanations other than the actual living on of the body buried alive, either mercifully punctuated for a period by a coma or, exclamation point, by a captive attentiveness to one's predicament.

The candidates for vampiric afterlife were, after all, those who had, more often than not, died instantly, like suicides or even stroke and heart failure fatalities. To the unconscious, instant or sudden death (indeed described as an "attack" that claims victims) looks like murder. But (and we are back to the medical reality-check) the corpses in question in fact decay only very slowly, especially, of course, if they have been buried in the winter. The corpse of one who died suddenly will in the natural course of decomposition produce a virtual light show of special effects: the way in which the instant corpse decomposes promotes the gravitation of blood to the mouth, the bloating of the body, the seeming growth of new skin (which in fact reflects a slippage of skin that reveals raw, not new, skin and nails). However, on the level with phantasm (which is where vampirism gets off), premature burial (the directest hit of what Freud would call the uncanny) continues to hold the first place when it comes to our reception of the vampire.

In the eighteenth century death or the dead got a new image. This period of secularization and return to classical models punctuated, in a split of the second position, the terminal closure of a Christian past suddenly too dark to follow or let in. In Germany, for example, Gotthold Ephraim Lessing wrote an influential essay on the way the ancients had represented death. He argued that the skeleton that had been the real popular image of death (the way to go) in Christianity did not go beyond that immediate setting: the ancients represented death as the twin brother of sleep, as something attractive or just average, as being, like sleep, a natural. But at the same time Lessing admitted an uncanny consequence of the doubling of sleep and death that had gone — down — without saying.

The eighteenth century chose to naturalize death according to classical models. The ongoing allegorization of death that conceived life societywide (and graveside) as a kind of terminal for waiting around for the better life to come was dropped — into the unconscious. But in the meantime, up front, graves had to be relocated; no longer were the dead to be kept inside the polis; they had to be moved to the suburbs, again following the example of antiquity. In Paris alone some fifty thousand corpses had to be exhumed. In the course of this relocation or resettlement project, abundant evidence of premature burial was encountered. Now it was discovered that sleep had in fact been the double of death and that on the other side of this doubling many had awakened inside the graves to experience their own deaths the only way, it turns out, that is available: at once postmortem and yet "live." This is the primal scene or portrait of vampirism: the corpse with bloodied mouth and nails, whose contortions of clawing, of banging on the lid, of struggling to get out complete the picture.

Institutions of death watch and death certification were now required. The dread of premature burial inspired new and improved coffins fitted with gadgetry designed for those who just might find themselves too quickly buried and would require a means to signal their distress to those aboveground. In Vienna in the nineteenth century a specially designed morgue featured couches containing special metal plates and levers that could pick up the slightest movement in a body and transmit to a control room an electric bell-ringing signal that warned that there was still life left. Beginning in the eighteenth century, everyone wants one last (outside) chance to get out of the crypt. Last call, even or especially for the dead. By the end of the nineteenth century, at the latest, the last will and testament regularly packed the proviso that the body not be buried until the heart had been pierced. With the dread of premature burial one could no longer be certain that the dead *were* dead or dead *enough*. There emerged, then, in our modern secular era, in the new cleaned-up place of death's representation, an uncontrollable blending of boundaries between life and death. Death was growing uncanny: unburiable, unframeable, unrepresentable, unmournable.

I would like to close this survey of the burial plots of the vampire phantasm by getting us back onto the projective track of our histories of vampirism. What follows is the preview of what is coming soon. Projection covers a phase of mourning. The vampiric phantom is a projection; its crypt goes down with the mourner's identification with the deceased. Projection alternates with identification; together these at once psychic and mediatic mechanisms create the sensurround of haunting. It is the death wish (which overlaps with the ambivalence inside identification) that releases the projection and animates the dead. The death wish (which refers not to some conception of our own death but to what's the big idea of the other's passing) gets wished on the same person we also loved. Once this nearest and dearest in fact goes, the death wish, which cannot be acknowledged up close, gets projected onto the corpse, now a vengeful undead out to get the survivor.

When projection goes political, it produces paranoid episodes whether as jealousy or as all-out persecution of the other. We are alienated from (horrified by) the group we persecute (and if only by living in a society that is persecutory in its organization). This alienation or persecution cannot but be extended to the grave. Haven't we heard of desecration of tombs and effacement of their inscriptions animated by the same hatred that cannot get satisfaction even when the despised other should already be, by all appearances, dead and gone?

In 1935 Theodor Adorno argued in a letter to Walter Benjamin that it is always recent history that is primal time or prehistory and is thus conjugated with — jump-cut — catastrophe. This set of disjunctive responses within a recent past sets the mirror stage of identification and projection, which we will be tuning in down the course of lectures, from the vampiric setting of responses within the one on one to their group syndication as acting out in front of the TV set. Stay tuned to the recent primal past of a target-ranging and double-barreling of projection that switches sights or channels from the other sex, to the other race, to the other orientation.

What we see in *Blacula* is a whiting out of tensions between races by displacement of an unreflected thrust of projection onto the gay antique dealers (the only interracial couple in the film) who buy up the contents of Dracula's castle for big resale profits in Los Angeles, where such leftovers are the "crème de la crème of camp." The happy campers also bring back for reanimation the coffin of Blacula, African prince made over as vampire in the eighteenth century by the Count himself, who name-called the guest he turned into a ghost in earshot of his own name. It was not so much that the Count was racist, but he just could not bear any talk about the evils of slavery. The black vampire prince is locked up to starve for an eternity while his beloved bride, who starves for the short run but for real, gets enrolled in the reincarnation plan of immortality. Her reincarnation is waiting for him in California, where he finds her soon after he consummates his first vampiric act by taking out or taking in the interracial gay couple. There are integration tensions along for law enforcement that get control released over the dead gays. When the black gay corpse disappears, one white cop asks the black doctor down the color divide: "Who'd the hell want a dead faggot?" When two white cops on drive-by patrol spot the undead black antique dealer in the cruisy part of town, the emergency shutdown of their sameness bounces back: "Hey, take a look at that fag. Isn't that the one?" "How can you tell, they all look alike." The bouncing balling of displacement can be followed up close when the black doctor tries to call his white police colleague on racist negligence. The police report on the missing gay corpse also got lost: "Strange how so many sloppy police jobs involve blacks." "You're getting paranoid, Schafer [the partner] wasn't black." When the white colleague speculates that Panther activity may be involved in these vampiric acts, the black doctor straightens out full circle, jerk! "Come on, Jack, don't cop out. Two faggot interior decorators? Panthers?" At the close, focus shifts to the unmourning plot or spot Prince Blacula finds himself in. *Blacula's* phantasmatic participation in a gay legacy of epidemic vampirism that comes, via Transylvania, from Africa keeps all the projections grounded in the plot of unmourning that can come to an end for the black but straight couple. Blacula cannot bear to live again only to lose his bride twice. The unbearable begins to happen when a white cop closes his eyes to aim at Blacula and shoots the reincarnation by his side. Blacula is thus forced to turn her into a vampire in the race against the flatline. But when the vampire hunters open the coffin and find the vampire bride, she gets the stake. Blacula goes up into the light and puts himself out.

In Stoker's novel when Count Dracula blocks his three brides from vampirizing Jonathan Harker right away or first thing, he gazes upon the male object and assures the frustrated brides in the same breath that he, the Count, too can love. So, is yet another kind of orientation at stake here? Why not! But the same-sexiness of vampires and vampire hunters alike comes down to technology compatibility (which is always good news) of all the nonreproductive modes of being that are into replication. The new woman cheerleads the way to a new model of group-psychological or technological replication away from the vestigial organization of reproduction. The same-sex tie-on is next in line or, more like it, already between the lines.

LECTURE THREE

One way to go when reading Stoker's *Dracula* is to look at the novel as an allegory-of-capitalism exclusive. This one reading distributes shares of one investment characterizing all the other reading options. What comes up in fact for alle-gory in Stoker's novel is circulation, from blood to money, of course—but that does not cover the whole range. What else circulates? Letters circulate; the postal service is a system of circulation. Any transportation network aims to be a system of circulation. Whenever we take a trip, whenever we send out a letter, whenever we sign our life insurance policy, whenever we engage in any of these systems or contracts of circulation, we always assume that something is going to come back: something is going to arrive and something will return. It is this belief in the returns on our investments in circulation or substitution—it is the complete system of these beliefs—that vampirism inhabits and threatens.

So with reference to one circulation system, you will recall that the soon-to-be vampire hunters first come into all kinds of money. These are rich young men. And they " 'spend it so freely' " (376). But Dracula donates too: as he flees after a run-in with the vampire hunters, he spills not blood but "a stream of gold" (324).

Now, the money one comes into has been delegated by the dead. There is a lot of recent death in this novel: right away the only parents to lay claim on the vampire hunters are on their way out. Other fathers and mothers have gone without saying, are doubly missing, or were never even around to get lost in the first place. Van Helsing's metabolism is grief stuck: Arthur Godalming is the dear double of his dead son. This one example, I am sure, releases a great many others. And these after-images and aftershocks bodybuild the figure or phantasm of Count Dracula, who admits—we hear Dracula speak so infrequently in this novel and here is a bit or byte of his voice—"my heart, through the weary years of mourning over the dead, is not attuned to mirth" (24). By his own account, then, the vampire Count is a specter of endless mourning. And how will that fit into systems of circulation? It is a perfect fit in fact, because successful mourning observes economic principles in the extended sense. Mourning, if it works out, promotes that circulation of life, desire, living on that is based on substitution. Vampirism's recycling take on (or intake of) circulation shuts down substitution (which presupposes and admits loss or lack) and goes instead for incorporation of the irreplaceable relation that goes under, hidden away and preserved inside the sealed-off crypt.

In Greek *oikos*, or economy, also means household. The vampire enters the households or economies within which the standards or norms of living on are guarded and guaranteed. And the novel makes the point—and this is precisely Renfield's role, he embodies this double point—that the vampire never is a trespasser, never makes a forced entry, but is always invited into the household and into the economy by a desire to be vampirized that is already in place on the inside (253). There has to be a correspondence of consumer desires between the vampire and the vampirized for there to be an entry, a crossing over (or, for that matter, an economy). It is a total invitational.

Now I want to start the trip. Whenever we are booked on a journey in literature, what are we in fact in for? Journeys in literature are double-booked as spiritual quests. Quest for what? Always for the self. But it is always through something else, some other (something or other) that we search for ourselves; it is only through the detour that takes us away from ourselves that we have a chance of getting there.

Fast-forwarding now to the end of my point, which we can fill in as we drive it deeper: in Stoker's novel self-surfing does not stop short with the imagination—with art, religion, or nature—but goes all the way with the vampire. And through a series of deaths, undeaths, and killings (that is, mournings), the modern group is born again out of the Eastern bloodbath of vanquished vampirism.

How does one get over and back to oneself? Experience (including art appreciation and nature worship) would be one way to go. Education is a kind of formalization or institutionalization of the experiences one has. The university is that extension of the family that takes us somewhat outside the family unit or unity, somewhat on a trip. But the trip I am talking about really begins when you think you know it all, when you are no longer working on it, when you think you have finished.

Let's begin at the beginning of the Stoker novel with Jonathan's journey to Transylvania, which starts out as the straightforward accounting of a business trip but then becomes the diary of someone who is tripping out. The trip to Transylvania parallels and lubes the reader's entry into the novel; Jonathan is our delegate throughout. Clearly Jonathan undergoes a few turnarounds, a few transformations, a few shell shocks. He who was a tourist becomes a witness to horror, terror or terrorism, a confused and frightened witness, indeed an innocent-bystander victim of this horror, this terrorism. And so he becomes disoriented, everything about his world has been turned around and opened up, and he begins opening a margin account of madness. This Eastern blockage of and resistance to an itinerary forced to turn around, inside out, is referred to as a whirlpool of the imagination — and it leaves Jonathan wondering if he is about to lose it.

If Jonathan Harker is both stand-in for the reader and a kind of Everyman, a kind of representative of Western man, then we observe a vaster backfire than the one brought on by his own overexposure to the East. The primal East is somehow more than this hypercivilized representative of late-nineteenth-century Victorian society can take or stand for.

Let's retrace some of the steps on the way to this transformation. I said that Jonathan starts out as the Anglo-American tourist "doing" Transylvania in a couple of days. He fills his journal with all sorts of little facts and observations about the scenery and the friendly natives and their cuisine, noting even recipes and so on. One gets the sense that he is acquiring a touristic taste for Transylvania. And this zone that had hitherto been out of reach is going to be, by the end of the novel, swallowed by the West and, following the swallowing, left behind as the West's tourist trap. Indeed the closing scene or shot of the vampire hunters' return to Transylvania to enjoy a kind of class reunion one year after the Count's death or murder is crowded with every indication that what had once been a primal zone is now a safe place for souvenir stands to advertise prefab recollections. It's all so fab-you-less.

At first contact with the East, Jonathan's sense of duty gives him shelter; he has this mission to accomplish, and that gets him there. But all this gets turned around. The trip changes. It changes direction. It becomes spiritual, or let's say it becomes haunted, horrifying, and it takes on all kinds of confusing meanings for him. By the end of the novel, the whole notion of duty comes to be redefined, as we will see, with the emergence of a new group psychology out of the showdown with vampirism.

The switchover begins counting down during Jonathan's solo trip in the carriage across the Borgo pass. Increasingly he wonders if reality is not becoming "a sort of awful nightmare," (13) and if a kind of paralysis of fear has not already started to set in. So when he first arrives at the castle and meets the English-speaking Count, he is greatly relieved: he thinks he is back home or in a Holiday Inn. Pleased to be in the Count's company, Jonathan is back in business. He willingly enters the vampire's territory and even adopts the night existence of the Count. But in a flash or flashback Jonathan realizes just what the Count embodies. The vampire's threat thus emerges as soon as Jonathan begins to feel at home with it. (Home is where the uncanny is.) Soon he looks out the window and sees the Count make his skin crawl, dressed up in Jonathan's own travel suit, crawl down into town to steal babies.

But this is when another trip also begins. Because what happens when he senses that "safety and the assurance of safety" (37) have disappeared? He feels locked in. His letters are no longer able to get out and circulate; there is no longer any communication with the outside. Assurance or insurance no longer circulates, nor can it substitute in the name of a survivable death. What now can be admitted is the underlying phantasm that is always also along for the insurance drive. Your own double will collect the proceeds from a death with which you originally negotiated as though on behalf of future generations. Jonathan turns around and faces the inside of the castle; for the first time, then, he turns inward, and, of course, this castle into which he journeys, which he explores, is also at the same time the external view of his own psychic insides.

But what does he find in this castle that is also inside him? It belongs inside the room he penetrates and explores: it is a room where "in old times possibly some fair lady sat to pen her ill-spelt love letter" (37). And this is where he is going to encounter the Count's vampire brides, only to count among them one eidetic recollection. This is very important. Also that Dracula saves him or, on the other side of ambivalence, intervenes at that point, precisely as a father, is another given in Stoker's novel, to which we must give importance. So, at the end of this trip into the interior, he encounters a room (and we will unpack the contents of it in a moment); it's some kind of secret that he encounters in the course of his forced entry upon self-analysis, and it is going to be a secret that will help us gain access to or through those excesses of vampirism, or of becoming vampire, which also involve "the new woman."

The first time around Jonathan is no winner; he does not score against vampirism on his own. But he does survive, and he does make it back to England with the information that gets the vampire hunt going. And it was because Jonathan was without the protection of the law — *outside* the protection of the law — that he could turn to lights! action! But then it is the group that his wife, Mina, cheerleads that will reclaim the projection that his solo trip repress-released.

It is the formation of the group, the formation of a united front of vampire hunters, that, filled to the social-allegorical level, becomes a main content of Stoker's novel. That is why the family pack can only be found missing (that is, near-missing). It is true that everyone talks about marriage, right from the start. Indeed, the Count too has his brides, but there is no parental guidance.

Where did all the parents go in Stoker's *Dracula*? Beginning with Morris and Seward, we can say that there is no mention of any prior blood relation whatsoever; they simply lack any kind of close relation (in either direction, both Before and After family pictures). Mina and Jonathan also have no blood relation backing them. Instead there is Jonathan's employer and benefactor, who indeed — in death — becomes a surrogate father when he leaves them his inheritance (Mina will say, "it seems as though we have lost a father"). Arthur's father is still around at the start of the novel, but he is already mortally ill; he exists only to exit. And, more to the point, his illness takes Arthur away from Lucy's side, where he should have stood on standby; he leaves his fiancée that much more vulnerable to attack. Another family connection on its way out also makes it easier for the vampire to reach Lucy. How does Lucy finally become available for final vampirization by the Count? Lucy's mother drops dead — on Lucy, who is thus pinned in place for the final attack in the series. The parents are only around to drop dead and get in the way, to open the way to the vampirization of their children in the season finale. So there is a real void and avoidance in the place of parents; either the parents are not there, or they might as well not be, or it would be best if they were gone. It is into this place (and this is perhaps the crisis that precedes the novel) that two powerful father figures enter: Van Helsing is the good father, Dracula the bad primal father who threatens the sons. What is his threat to the sons? Van Helsing declares it; Dracula says it point blank and in a frenzy when he confronts the vampire hunters: he will have all the women and keep them to himself, and the sons will have none.

Even though the good father, Van Helsing, arrives too late to save Lucy (because her good was just too damaged when she took the fall), he does redeem her. And he unites all the orphaned and overspecialized children over her mourned — twice murdered — body. If at first the one is just a scientist, the other one just a lawyer, then, going with the blood flow of Lucy's staking, they follow Van Helsing, who is a scientist but also a scholar of the occult, all the way into a new native habitat where the unconscious and technology meet. Stoker's research for the novel went beyond getting to know the primal past of vampirism (the one he was at the same time inventing) but extended into a societywide search for every kind of new gadget or new intellectual phenomenon that had controlling interest at the time. And, indeed, psychoanalysis (which he was real interested in) could be seen as offering another way of knowing everything. At one point we learn that Van Helsing was even Jean-Martin Charcot's student in Paris. Charcot, who, of course, was also Freud's teacher, was one of the first psychiatrists to recognize the psychosexual basis of hysteria or neurosis. The cure he initiated, which Freud also tried out (but then dropped), was hypnosis. Remember, Van Helsing is able to help in the struggle against vampirism by hypnotizing the victim of the Count's infection. And he also knows how to listen; he is the first one to listen to Lucy's nightmares and not just push them aside— back into the inside—as "mere" dreams. He listens to them as the ventriloquated truth of her illness. So, he takes literally the phantasms she relates, not because they have any empirical existence, but because they rule her through a kind of remote control. That is, of course, a psychoanalytic insight: it does not matter whether remembered scenes of traumatization were fantasized or not, not once their ensemble starts repeating or rehearsing on automatic. It does not matter whether the fantasy corresponds to fact; if it is doing a number on you or inside you, it exists. Freud concluded that only his own discovery of the unconscious and the invention of gadgets of live transmission (his example is the telephone) had made it possible to comprehend such occult mechanisms as telepathy. In other words, only psychoanalysis understands vampirism in the context it shares with technology or unmourning. Psychoanalysis and vampirism are rival sciences of the undead.

What is it about Dracula as father figure that is so dreadful? Remember, Lucy represents the original bond. She is the one who unites the hunters right from the start; they share that accumulating interest in Lucy that compelled them all to become her suitors. But even though each member wants to marry her, no one in the group gets to do it. Although they are symbolically (and after the fact, under Van Helsing's analysis) married to her through the blood transfusions offered to save her from her vampirization, in fact only Dracula possesses her—and, by blood proxy, them too. So what if it is only through vampirization. He possesses Lucy and brings about her death, which is at the same time her rebirth as vampire, of course, but also, in a more open season, as a woman with a proposition to make her man.

And what do the former suitors see then when they track down the newest bride of Dracula? They see Lucy strolling through the cemetery wearing the bloody lip gloss of Countess Báthory, with more blood spilling down her long death robe, and she is holding a child to her breast, not to nurse but to devour or suck dry. The sexual threat of the blonde, deposited between the lines by Lucy's proposal in triplicate, and projected onto a bigger-than-life screen, scream, and barely under the covers of her vampiric lust, must be sublimated. The Christian mass in which blood sacrifice gets consumed at the symbolic remove of wine is shot through the person of Lucy as the three-way freeway of transfusions while the vampire's desublimation of this mass or group sucks out the blood it also recycles.

At Lucy's big comeback the men refer to her as this "nightmare of Lucy" (225). She is not just some vampire; she is at the same time still recognizably Lucy. She is not suddenly something else; she is Lucy *and* she is a vampire. She is the nightmare of Lucy, the doubling and dividing of her person on her own person.

Lucy's second death is the first murder that will lead to something new. How is the group formed over Lucy's undead body? By breaking all the rules, by going all the way—outside or against the law—to kill the vampire. They are as outside the law as vampirism can get. What vampirism gives these good-citizenship losers is the outside chance of moving beyond the no-longer tamper-proof enclosures of individualism, the couple, and the family pack toward their new techno regrouping: group of one for all, all for group of one.

So this is the trip? The first trip, remember, took Jonathan into his own interior where his sanity was no longer secure. The second trip takes the band of men into a kind of primal past, which is where vampirism is at, but it is also the place where a new order begins rising up over Lucy's doubly dead body. Something completely new is being created here (although, as with Frankenstein's monster, the component pieces of the new belong to corpses). And how do we know that Stoker is completely attuned to this newness of his enterprise? The alliance Stoker makes with technology gives the creators of the new order their license. So, when you reach the end of the novel, you will have seen, and we will get to why this is so important, that the typewriter (and Mina's being a typist) provided the keys to the success of the group's mission (or transmission). Throughout that final trip, which takes them all the way to Transylvania and which will ensure their victory, Mina carries a traveling typewriter on her lap. On the other final trip when, at the very end, in the afterglow of their having conquered vampirism, they celebrate reunion on the anniversary of Dracula's staking, we see her holding in her lap no longer the traveling typewriter but now a child—the first promise of a future in the novel—a child bearing up under all the names of the vampire hunters (dead or alive). Where there is technologization and gadget love, that is where group psychology will be too. The one investment in reproduction in the novel has been made by the group through the couple.

The group always reserves mega-ambivalence for the couple, which is always the couple of parents just walking away together, withdrawing into the master bedroom, away from little masturbating group-of-one. But the group has no reproducing plan of its own. Group psychology meets vampirism not only over the wavelengths of long distance but also in the regime of replication, the extended plan of reanimation of the long distant. Reproduction, the fixation on one material meaning of her body, makes over little sister as the makeshift compromise formation between the group and the couple. She's become a long way, baby, the way between the reproductive couple and the group spirit of replication, which is also woman's birth or rebirth right. Even or especially as mother, woman takes sides with the melancholic retention span or ban against what is so short and uneasy about the substitutions requested in the order of reproduction.

By the end of *Dracula,* the couple has been overcome as sole model of reproduction, substitution, or mourning. Instead a techno compatibility with replication and all the other group structures or phantasms that the vampire hunters have plugged into has been brought to consciousness in Stoker's update on the occult medium as technical medium.

When we talk about technology and media technology in particular, we are walking the thin line of frequency that, between the lines, improves upon — and extends — letter writing. While the writing of letters, the mailing of letters, the first postal system (which has to be as old as history, as old as writing itself), while all these long ways already double as primal media technologies, beginning in the late nineteenth century, the time of Stoker's novel, it is electricity that brought us completely new and improved devices that illuminated, cut across, and amplified the long distance already in place inside letter writing, inside the sending of letters. We once more cut our losses, which then doubled along the edge of contact to cut all proximity with distance.

Terence Fisher's *Horror of Dracula* was the first movie version to include any of Stoker's gadgets. But it gets stuck in the groove of audiorecording, while the video freeze-frame still belongs, one, to a maternal corpse that will not decompose beyond old age and, two, to the photograph of Jonathan's bride-to-be. It is Lucy this time around: all the names and positions get swapped for all the other ones in the course of the filmic reception of Stoker's *Dracula,* a by-product or outer-corpus experience of the vampire-hunting group's metabolism of mutual admiration and identification without a cause or leader.

Like one of those 3-D stereovision cards, the photo is given twice, once on each side of a collapsible frame: when Van Helsing arrives looking for Jonathan, he finds this superimposable frame empty. He misses Lucy Holmwood in stereo: the photo is now the traveling shot of the vampire's comparison-sucking for avenging and replacement of the bride Jonathan staked. Jonathan was defeated by the Count, however, because he was too slow on the outtake and gazed too long upon the vampire bride he put to rest in one piece, one that did not turn, turn to dust or skeleton but simply into an old dead woman. When in the Count's absence Van Helsing breaks into the vault that now also contains an undead Jonathan, the staked old woman has stayed where she was, uncovering no advance of decomposition, even in the meantime, beyond the bottom-line transformation of bride into mother-in-law.

Back in the tracks of the vampire's shot in the darkroom, Van Helsing hears the voice of his own mastery cut off from the other's live reception: while we see him reading his source or note books, we listen to the dictaphonic record of his own voice, the audio instruction he gave Jonathan. The first gadget from Stoker's novel to make it to the screen is introduced as voice-over, over the intended recipient's doubly dead body.

On the ongoing record that Van Helsing next continues, the scenes in which women are seen to facilitate the grope of the vampire's desire are ambiguated. The victims do not want the first or even further contact, but at the same time they crave it: "similar to addiction to drugs."

Soon the confrontation or demonstration scene in the cemetery shows undead Lucy going for the little girl, but then, when she sees Arthur, her bro, she thinks it best to proposition incest. Van Helsing's interventions follow on schedule, and Lucy is given a peace of their mind. Van Helsing now holds the floor or the transference for his how-to instructions on busting "the undead, as we call them." The call of the un, the prefix of repression Freud diagnosed in his essay on "The 'Uncanny,'" marks dead and undead as synonymous, as reemerging each in the other's personal space or face where both were to have been forgotten.

But now that we call them un, the focus can be fixed on two sites of transgression, one located in the social or social-studies register, the other belonging in the home. At the border crossing in Ingolstadt (the university town of Dr. Frankenstein's studies), the address of the coffin traveling from Klausenburg to Karlstadt was, in keeping with the line or law of good boundaries, recorded. But in the meantime Mina has been summoned by deceptive invitation to the same address, the place of work of J. Marx, Mortician.

> A late arrival of the orientation via the orient that the English were giving themselves with the projective trajectory that brought us Stoker's *Dracula*, this cinematic reference to a certain Marx in Karlstadt, the mortician housing the un, follows out a division in intellectual labor between an external world that is socially classed and the internal place of the heart bait. Once more in the meantime Dracula has switched registers from Marx to Freud and taken up his new hiding place right down in the basement of the Holmwood home. The in-house blood communions between Count and Mina indeed go unnoticed until it is too late to drive the point home. But as morning cuts off the house from the network of night and doubles the contours of a crypt back onto the house, Van Helsing need only open drapes and let in the light for mourning to take its place. Everyone is watching as this second decomposition passes beyond the old woman's arrest in passing.

OK. So where were we? We were talking about trips. Remember that the means of transportation always traveled the same routes, took the same time, same space, as letters. Letters and carriages and horses, what have you: they all followed the same paths, the same methods and logic.

A kind of internal epigraph: there is a quote from the Gottfried August Bürger poem "Lenore" in the opening pages of *Dracula* (10); the line that we hear, "Die Todten reiten schnell," informs us that "the dead ride" — or, let's go ahead and say it, "write" — "quickly." The poem addresses a case of undeath brought on by a survivor unable to let go of her lover who ended up part of some war's body count or missing in action. But in no time he rides (writes) back from the war zone of his missingness. But this riding/writing has always been conjugated with death. This union was never not an issue when it came to writing. There was always talk of dead letters and living thoughts. And if it is not living thoughts, then it is living speech. Speech and thought were always awarded the rewards of being somehow alive, the award of frequent real time traveling. Writing got the charges of being in league (the big league) with death. But writing also gets a charge out of surviving the impressions of a moment. What would have survived if writing had not been around for the saving? Every piece of writing survives death because it is signed, sealed, and delivered. Every piece of writing is a letter, a letter sent to survive the limitedness or one-sidedness of your big moment.

To fast-forward again: if this new group formation of doubles and replicates is able to conquer vampirism at or as its living end, that is because this new body, which comes complete with all the new media technological devices plugged right up into all orifices or outlets, is more vampiric than even vampirism itself.

A primal view of the novel is given in Stoker's story "Dracula's Guest," which was split off from the novel right from the start: the posthumously published "story" is the deleted original opener of *Dracula*, in which the "Lenore" line was first given at point of peril and rescue, inscribed on the crypt that gives the narrator shelter in the midst of the reawakening of the dead. This is where the cables of occult and technological media intersect. The first opener belongs to a narrator and not to the web of journal-keeping gadget lovers. Stoker's decision to technologize the very discourse of the novel — to suspend disbelief between the fanglike markers of citation while thus at the same time never departing from the recycling of opinion — would preempt this voice-over.

Stoker also originally headlined his vampire novel up there with the Faust tradition: "Dracula's Guest" opens with Jonathan's stopover in Germany on Walpurgis Night. On his guided tour of Munich's environs he resists itinerary and schedule and ends up stuck in a village of the dead, off the main drag down from a suicide's grave at the crossroads. He makes it to the main tomb, spectacularly grounded or wired by a large metal stake crossing through it (220):

COUNTESS DOLINGEN OF GRATZ
IN STYRIA
SOUGHT AND FOUND DEATH,
1801

On the back of the tomb of the suicide the narrator finds, suddenly written large in an "oriental" alphabet, the ingredients of the package deal between the dead and the media (221):

THE DEAD TRAVEL FAST

At this point, "with a terrible shock," Jonathan finally gets the message that it is indeed Walpurgis Night: "when . . . the devil was abroad—when the graves were opened and the dead came forth and walked" (221). The stormy night that raises a broad or she-devil and assorted zombies corners Jonathan in this graveyard of a suicide. But then a lightning bolt jolts down the stake into the tomb and convulses the dead or only sleeping woman in "a moment of agony" (222). But whose agony is it, anyway? Another electrotransmission, one that the occult contraption rudimentarily copies, namely, the telegraph, has also been turned on. The closing lines of the excised opener give up the ghost in "Dracula's Guest": "From a distant country had come, in the very nick of time, a message that took me out of the danger of the snow-sleep and the jaws of the wolf" (226). The Count's telegram, which Jonathan finds partic-ularly uncanny in its neck-to-neck timing across long distances, sends in a posse to his rescue. On the occult wavelength or tele-path, a " 'wolf— and yet not a wolf' " (224) was in the meantime already covering Jona-than, protecting his heart and jugular from deep freeze or from seizure by the jump-started dead. Upon rescue we find Jonathan suspended by the citation, the summoning, of some primal scene—as we will be see-ing, it was Stoker's—a scene of standing upright:

> As yet my tongue refused its office, and I was perforce silent. I must have fallen asleep; for the next thing I remembered was finding my-self standing up, supported by a soldier on each side of me. It was al-most broad daylight, and to the north a red streak of sunlight was re-flected, like a path of blood, over the waste of snow. (224)

His insupportable return to infancy comes complete with a view, broad-side, of a maternal flow of blood over a waste, I mean a waist, that is frigid. Jonathan has been reduced by cryogenic conditions to the lack of motor coordination that characterized the first seven years of Stoker's life (which Stoker would return to by fainting dead away on at least one occasion in his adulthood, as though to punctuate, puncture, and sus-pend yet another scene as primal). But Jonathan has been saved by a two-band frequency, at once occult and media-technological, that, let me give it to you for now only in shorthand, control-releases the reani-mation of the mother tongue.

LECTURE FOUR

(New) Woman   Vampirism   Mourning
                Media Technology
                Psychoanalysis

Here is the master map of our thought experiment while we work it on
out through *Dracula*. I want you to think of these three items in the
middle as somehow interchangeable or competing sciences, institutions,
and perspectives. Each of these rival perspectives is asserting itself with
regard to this double object: woman, on one side, and a certain relation
to mourning or, if you prefer, corpse disposal, on the other.

In his essay "The Psychoanalysis of Ghost Stories" Maurice Richardson gives his blurb on the Dracula novel: "Mina is saved and Lucy avenged
by a noble, brotherly band led by Van Helsing." Apart from Van Helsing, who represents the good father, this setup recalls the primal horde
as introduced by Freud in *Totem and Taboo*: the brothers band together
against the father who has tried to keep all women to himself. Dracula's
connection with his victims is incestuous. He is the father vampirizing
a daughter. But that conclusive primal scene that brings Mina so close
to complete vampirization, in which we see her being suckled by Dracula, is clearly a mother-and-child reunion. No matter how you turn it,
there is something incestuous going down when one creates a vampire.

You get the basic scenario: Freud creates in *Totem and Taboo* a myth
or an allegory of the history or development of each and every psyche,
which he broadcasts or extends over time as a kind of evolutionary history of society. But even if it does not make historical or empirical sense,
Freud's point is always that it makes primal sense. So, Freud says, in the

40

beginning the first social order was the horde (here we are joining Darwin), which was originally ruled by the primal father or the chief, who indeed did keep all women to himself and thus extended his rule over his sons to get them where they breed; he either castrated them or cast the extras out as exiles. Only once he grew too old to get it up to kill or drive out any more remotely possible rivals did a youngest son come into the top-man position. Now, what happens over time is that the exiled sons or brothers band together and return to kill the primal father. But as soon as they kill him, they do what comes naturally: they devour him, and as they devour the primal father, they also maternalize him; the body they feed on now nurtures them, which is to say that as soon as they kill and devour the detested father, they double over with indigestion and ambivalence overload, and thus they find that they must also mourn him, that they are already mourning him. They set him up as an ideal father, as a friendly ghost. And to avoid the relentless return of a bad scene (like, it's obscene), they agree among themselves that there will no longer be any sexual union among members of the same family. They set up the first incest taboo, or the law of exogamy, which says that you go outside the family to find your special friend.

This is the beginning of the law, according to the psychoanalytic myth program. There is no other law than the incest law that comes complete with the corollary prohibition against patricide. Why is this so important? It is important because the incest law or taboo guarantees that substitution will be the order of the day. One must by law find substitutes for what one cannot, by the same law, have and hold. So, from this legal point on out, all desire, all socialization, and so on will be based on substitution and not on a direct hit or fit.

That is the program that governs desire; I can't get no satisfaction. That is the law, and that is what the incest taboo turns on. But also notice that in cannibalizing the murdered father, we also created, in a more bearable higher sphere of ambivalence, the mourned or mournable father. This father guarantees, as the model for every corpse or loss at our disposal, that whoever goes can be let go, can be put to rest, and can be substituted for. The mourned, mournable dead father would guarantee that even right in the face of death, substitution will continue to keep the loss of all our others replaceable and mournable. The father embodies death right from the start, but the death he inoculatively embodies or anti-bodies is the one that is survived together with the inheritance of his name and the takeover of his legacy. All this is part of a prescription all set to go down in every one of us; we all tune in the voice of conscience that Freud calls superego, the internalized mournably dead father down under, the inside-out transmitter of the law with a primal band length ranging from self-recrimination to public opinion (and back again). Over the dad's body paternal and maternal ingredients get mixed into the happy hour of mournability. The unmournable connection, the corpus of the mother, will not be gagged on in all its purity. To put it in shorthand and store it for future decoding: the dad inside us promotes fast food over the mother tongue's unmediated dictation or incorporation.

To mourn, one must kill the dead; only what we murder can we mourn properly or successfully. So on pages 171–73, we have the strange scene or juxtaposition in which, you remember, when Lucy dies (the first time around), she becomes a mortician's vampire: she has never been more beautiful. The mourners visit her corpse's Forest-Lawn-style layout: "The undertaker had certainly done his work well, for the room was turned into a small *chapelle ardente*. There was a wilderness of beautiful white flowers.... We both started at the beauty before us.... All Lucy's loveliness had come back to her in death" (172).

On the preceding page the mortician says, "She makes a very beautiful corpse, sir. It's quite a privilege to attend on her. It's not too much to say that she will do credit to our establishment!" What is Van Helsing's reaction on the next page? It seems so out of place. At first Seward thinks that it is merely a question of an autopsy, and then Van Helsing says: "I want to operate, but not as you think. Let me tell you now but not a word to another. I want to cut off her head and take out her heart." And that, in terms of what we have been saying right now, is what every one of us must do if successful mourning is to take place over the other's dead body.

I recently read an essay that argues that all the brides surrounding Dracula seem to observe an incest taboo: vampirization is so short-lived. The vampire has to keep coming after new victims. What we could call the vampire's sexuality transpires only in the course of vampirization; once that is over, the vampiric wounds close; remember, on Lucy's neck, once she is a vampire, she needs no further outlet for another vampire's desire to plug into. But what that really means is that incest would seem to be the law when it comes to vampirism. We will return to this reversal of the law of Oedipus when we get into Anne Rice's genealogy of bloodsucking.

Freud's parable is supposed to give the good news in the consumer's guide to substitution. But substitution is precisely what vampirism cannot admit; instead a kind of doubling on contact takes over (over each incest victim's undead body). No substitutions please.

To get back to the reading of the novel that we began earlier: any surface reading of the novel is going to be pretty clear-cut about the novel's higher purpose. Dracula is destroyed; Mina is cleansed, redeemed; the vampire hunters, the boys, are triumphant. This lets roll a whole series of parallel readings: the spirit from the East is defeated, the spirit of the West is saved, and the corruption of the West, of Lucy Westenra, is avenged, reversed (even God—Godalming—is on our side). The bad father has been killed, the good father triumphs, the mother has been cleansed and restored to her sons. In other words, she has gone and washed that man, the father, right out of his heir. But these Oedipal readings, at least or at best on the surface, may even be decoys set up in the way of and on the way to a quite different kind of reading.

The first question we have to ask is, what is Lucy's function in all this? What is her role? Well, within the setup of the whole novel, she *has* to go. *She* made the sons or brothers into rivals. The murder or redemption of Lucy indeed unites the sons or brothers once they realize, after the fact, that they all gave her their blood transfusions and thus are, after all, blood-bonded via her dead and doubly off-limits body. She caused couple trouble for the boyfriends.

Lucy's role as the one who has to go (who has to be helped *out*) also brings us back to that room or scene in the castle. Remember we had at one point left Jonathan cut off from the outside, unable to send letters via the post or the past to the outside. He is all alone with his identifications. Turning toward the castle's interior, and thus at the same time moving inside himself, he enters a room in which he imagines some fair lady's dead-letter office. It is in this post of noncirculation or non-substitution, remember, that Jonathan encounters the brides of Dracula.

Why is this scene the place to which both Lucy and Mina must be assigned? Why is this the rehearsal or repetition of episodes that turn on Mina and Lucy? If the novel could be broken down into two big blocks or episodes, we would say that it covers two vampirizations or seductions: the one that does Lucy in, and the other one from which Mina must be rescued. The first episode, the journey to Transylvania, is a kind of prologue to the rest that sets the trend Lucy and Mina must follow. Jonathan's journey into madness overlaps with and parallels the Lucy story. Once Lucy's vampiric syndication has been shut down, Jonathan returns as shell-shock victim with nurse-wife, or Sister Mina, in attendance.

Because of this interconnection—I am talking the big one driven between Lucy and Mina—one has the sense that these episodes model each other, or that one is the retake of the other, or in fact, getting to the figures themselves, that Lucy and Mina are together two aspects of one person, or of one problem. What does it mean when we encounter a figure that can only appear in a doubled or divided way? It means that the figure in question is so threatening to your psychic balancing acts and therefore so repressed that a direct connection has become impossible but must be staggered or delayed through all that doubling and dividing. It also means that this figure is undergoing emergency operations that are phobic in their staying power: the doubling that divides also divides and conquers. But how to win the peace, the rest in peace? When will it all rest in one piece?

We saw how much conspired to help Lucy out, to place her out there alone in the zone of unprotectedness where the vampire's wish was her command. The vampire hunters repeat this ambivalent operation in the Mina story: even though she has been chief organizer of the information-gathering band, the men suddenly decide that she can only be protected by being left out of the planning stages of the showdown with vampirism. Left behind in the asylum she is easy prickings under the Count's fangs. Some logic compels her abandonment, contamination, humiliation so that the men can reclaim her, as the object of their protection and projection, through rescue and redemption.

So, back to the room in the castle. Harker goes there against the Count's orders. He receives one rule during his stay in the castle: he is told never to leave the guest suite. Dracula continues: let me warn you with all seriousness, if you leave these rooms, do not by chance go to sleep in any other part of the castle. Not sleeping around (in the castle) is the one house rule in Castle Dracula. But as soon as the law gets issued, we see Jonathan quickly rush to transgress it—two seconds later he is asleep in another part of the castle. Remember, Dracula comes to his rescue. Now forget about whether Dracula seems like a father or not, the point is that Jonathan seems very much like a child in this scene, also because he is replaced by the bagged babies: the vampire brides are diverted from the source by the infants Dracula brings to the rescue. So it seems that in terms of this scene of exchange, Jonathan holds down a very early position.

On page 38 and following, you will notice the libidinal excitement Stoker invests in Jonathan's anticipation of the vampire brides' embraces. But there is this one phase or phrase of excitement I want you to hold on to: "The other was fair as fair can be with great wavy masses of golden hair and eyes like pale sapphires. I seemed somehow to know her face and to know it in connection with some dreamy fear that I could not recollect at the moment how or where."

According to psychoanalysis, when your memories or dreams run up against a person or thing you recognize as familiar without being able to make the identification, it is mother who is thus being represented (but also repressed). For example, if in dreams you find yourself in a landscape that seems real familiar to you, but you cannot identify it, Freud says that you are on your way back to the place (where we have all been before) inside mother's body.

Whether or not that equation is convincing, let's see how the rest of the novel obeys its weird logic. So the problem person is the one that is recognized but not identified—it is the one that is identified with and thus not seen—in the room within rooms within the castle. And she is fair-haired. I ask you to hold on to that because the novel's inside view of the two women observes a kind of dark/light contrast. At the light or positive end of the development, the golden lady reappears as Lucy; the sunny ripples of her hair are much celebrated. So what? What is interesting is that Lucy's hair color changes in the course of vampirization: a little observed detail perhaps, but nevertheless it is there. When Lucy is just undergoing vampirization, in chapter 12, Dr. Seward can still describe the sunny ripples of her hair, but when the men are in the cemetery and witness the devourer of children return to the tomb, she is described, on page 222, as a dark-haired woman. Now what is this all about? Why the instant color change?

First, if we are arguing that both figures belong to one problem, or to one scene, back in the castle, what can we say about Mina? We do not know much about Mina's coloring, it is true, but as soon as she is on her way to becoming a vampire, she gets stained by a dark "mark of Cain," the foreheadline of her test results, the positive reaction to holy wafer.

This is a pretty common convention, and I think you are all familiar with it: the stain of darkness, or darkness as stain, is used to mark a woman or personalize her license and status as fallen while lightness is left up there, untouchably associated with innocence.

The vampire women or vamps are a threat, and yet at the same time they do give a certain measure (a fang's length) of pleasure. (All this, by the way, can be and has been taken clitorally.)

Consider all that, and now let's talk directly about the specific phenomenon of "the new woman" (the so-called new woman comes up in chapter 8 around page 94). What is the new woman? Mina writes down in her journal her latest reading of the headlines and features of down-to-the-minute journalism. She has come a long way, and way before she has the baby. She is fully equipped for a workplace that, historically, first opened wide to women with the advent of typing. The male secretaries of calligraphy would not make the switch to the machine; too much time had gone into the training of their art. The change was the first chance women could take; their fingers did the working. Mina's skills make her a shock absorber of what is new. But how is the so-called new woman received by Mina? Mina reduces her to being the sexually aggressive woman. Remember, Mina says, "but I suppose the new woman won't condescend in future to accept, she will do the proposing herself" (95). The new woman—unthinkable, horrible prospect—is the woman who will do the proposing herself. Now this is doubly curious because Mina is the new woman, isn't she? Not the proposing or sexual kind, but she is the one who knows all the propositions of gadget love; she runs the mediatic death cult of the vampire hunt. Even though the men always try to leave her behind, it is after all her skill as typist, as the one who knows the ins and outs of the latest devices of media technology for information gathering and organization, it is her skill that is the match and maker the vampire must meet. She comes in for the skill.

The new woman, then, is another name for a problem split between the typist and the vamp. That is why Lucy, the splitting image of the new woman with the proposition to make, has to be the first victim. But that is also why the novel could not end with her staking. The story had to be repeated. More was at stake. With the second coming of the problem that is part of the solution, Mina too must be punished but, this time stopping short of murder, also saved, cleansed, made safe for motherhood.

Once Lucy has been sacrificed at that limit where the transgression of the old order starts transgressing itself, the vampire hunters learn, under Mina's guidance, to flip through all the channels; they create via total thought control a unit that is (like TV) perpetually on, open—and shut. Once the group members know everything about each other, the vampire can get flushed. Mina, who was all along the toilet trainer of gadget love, assumes the mascot position at the mass or sacrifice. She

undergoes the teen Passion of pack formation through which the maternal and material supplies are sublimated or distilled, but also split
off as the violence of vampirism and vampire hunting.

Jump-cut to an underworld of blood lust that is a multicultural urban coalition that a couple of white college boys visit one night. They are looking to
hire a stripper for their fraternity initiation. *Vamp* opens in the haze of gothic
homoerotic: when the taped voice breaks down and the Satanic ringleader
picks up with his giveaway teen voice, the two fraternity initiates in their
underwear slip the loose nooses from the pain in their necks and interrupt
the nerdy breakdown of the program. But the two friends, who know that
their dorm mates are even worse geeks than the Greeks, offer to make a
deal as an alternative to the low-tech paranoia of the frat boys. Their mission is to bring back a stripper for the fraternity circle jerk. The friends need
a car to get to town, across the tracks to the wrong side. So they have to
visit one of the local dorm dorks, a rich-boy Asian American who runs rentals
and sales on the side as an outlet for the in-group of friends he can't make.
But what if they don't have the cash to rent dork's car? One of the two
once again proposes an exchange or alternative instead (just as with the
frat boys) and deposits "anything" dork wants as barter for the car. (The
other friend again tries to limit the placeholder deposit in the Faustian bar-
gaining to "something" or "one thing.") The East-Asian-American mega-
nerd wants them to pay by being his friends, no, by pretending to be his
friends, how about just for one week. And the trio is off. The "anything goes"
college stud goes backstage at the strip joint to make it with Grace Jones,
who turns out to be the local vampire queen. She starts going for that college meat; he presses the pause button to take off his shirt for her; she
goes monstrously ugly on him and sucks him dry. In the meantime the
friend, the one more careful about contractual relations, less all-or-nothing, has connected with a bimbo waitress who claims to know him though
he can't place her. They set out to look for the missing friend. In a dumpster
the one friend, Keith, finds the other one, A. J., dead. But then A. J. is back: it

was just a joke. A. J. is a vampire: "I love you Keith but all I can see is food."
But Keith reminds A. J. that he is also already one of the boring undead fraternity that he is complaining about. A. J. asks Keith to take him out of the
out-group with a stake. A. J. hands it to Keith and then runs himself through.
The bimbo connection returns as the drop scene that survives this double
death. But the projection is no longer able to stop in these tracks; it's stuck
in the groove, just for the record, of the tensions between couple and group.

The club owner, who snacks on cockroaches à la Renfield, claims to run
an essential service — waste disposal. But what is really a recycling center
has by accident taken in an innocent bystander from the right side of the
tracks. Keith uses his last request — lots of brandy — to set the bar on fire.
As they make their getaway, Keith sees or rather doesn't see in the rearview
mirror (placeholder for the backside) the dork along for the ride, who is
now just another vampire. The color coalition closes ranks, and as the dork
burns up in the car, the couple is on its own. Now she tells him she is Alison,
the girl he played spin the bottle with in fifth grade. Even as he keeps on
saving her from vampire attacks, Keith also tests her (exposing her to daylight, for example) to make sure she isn't one of them. It's just a test, the
one the bimbo connection must pass to go and collect couplification.

Then A. J. is back after all (the staking wasn't well enough done). He
saves the couple from the final surprise vampire attack down in the sewer.
The couple ascends and walks home down the street while the vampire
friend accompanies them underground: "I'm right below you pal." He proposes their ongoing palship: there's a parallel life down there for him: night
school, graveyard shifts. "I can handle this you know"; "trust me." These
Oedi-pals are split-leveled by Keith's couplification with Alison, eidetic substitute for the vampiric mother connection A. J. fell victim to, but only as
the group-compatible replacement and placeholder of the connection or
outlet that has gone under but still gets put through. So the homoeroti-
cism just a displacement away from group membership or best friendship
can be kept on the same skewer as the couple above the sewer. On the
parallel underground track the vampiric relationship to the same sex at

the same time replaces the all-out close encounter with the rainbow coalition of libido and destrudo. The conflict with vampirism, which fills in with the one projective content that always gets the stake, Big Time, gives shelter to the new same-sex friend, vampirized, staked, but still alive, who joins the new woman in the telecommunications underworld of repression. When all the projections come full circle, they hit bottom line, in this case down the line between sexual orientations.

LECTURE FIVE

Celebrations, whether July Fourth or Memorial Day, dedicated to war and war's backfire — the body count — invite us to commune beachside in order to imitate the rockets and special side effects of war's invasiveness just to be sure. But we also thus turn on another primal scene, which opens with the corpses washing up onto the beach in the wake of the Normandy invasion and closes with their fitting in your mouth, not in your hands. Because, back to the beach, we are in the primal past or barbecue repast of mourning; the missing corpses must be consumed. It is the forget-together, all over again. Thanksgiving was made a holiday by Lincoln during the Civil War. Guess what turkey was coming to dinner.

Anyway, we are going to be talking about mourning or the breakdown of mourning and vampirism in due course, but back to media technology, quickly.

We said earlier when we were addressing media technology, the typewriter, the new woman, and so on that through the new media all vital signs could be recorded and stored and that the novel can be read as the transcript that Mina has collected and mediatized. Mina's archive, her typewritten archive in triplicate, is the novel we see before us; the media technologies that brought us the novel were thus able, on at least two counts, to track down and defeat Dracula. Isn't it also the case that this media-technological archive of the vampire hunters (and of their new order) represents a kind of double of vampirism, a kind of new and improved vampirism, and does not so much defeat vampirism as replace vampirism's antiquated recycling system of death and the dead with the live transmission of gadget love, the one we have no trouble listening in on because we are living on in it?

At the end of the novel the new woman has been redeemed, made safe for sex, I mean, motherhood; a baby son bearing all the hunters' and ex-rivals' names marks the spot right in her lap where one year earlier the traveling typewriter was ready-positioned as the group's controlling interest in the future, which, already in the present tense of tension or conflict, took us beyond the Dracula principle.

Through her vampirization, she was turned, during the last stretch marking the close of the hunt, into a medium, first an occult medium bonded via breastfeeding to the Count, then a hypnotizable medium that Van Helsing was able to question by putting her in a trance in time for the Happy Hour, the short time between the vampire's all-or-nothing states of being, out from under the vampire's hold over her. She becomes the vampire's intelligence service, his plant, the instrument of his long-distance surveillance of the vampire-hunting group. But then, finally, to *his* horror, the Count discovers that Van Helsing is able to turn her on as a two-way medium and spy on him: at which point he shuts down his end of the telephonic exchange. The countdown begins with Mina's two-way mediatization and ends by the telegraph that takes over after the Count signs off. Telegraphic communication allows the hunters to find out after all where and when the Count's ship lands. Thus, they lock their pursuit back onto his beam just in the neck of time, the time in which the vampire's bite can hide and bide, but a time that, this time, is on the gadget lovers' side, the side of speedy interception of the eternity that is for the hiding.

To have and to hold the edge in the race against the vampire, the hunters bring to consciousness their own conjugation with the technological devices that have greater range and velocity than the writing and posting of letters and travel by land or by sea. Van Helsing facilitates a consciousness raiser when he informs his fellow ghostbusters that the Count has the disadvantage because during daytime programming he is bound to remain within the "earthly envelope" (309) of his coffin. He can move or communicate only as fast and as far as the very means of transportation that convey him — like some letter inside its envelope.

With the telegraph's instantaneous, or "live," transmissions, the origin of the new media technologies could be attained or retained. At the same time this kind of "live" broadcast that the telegraph introduced was the first literalization or realization of telepathy; so it is no coincidence (even though perhaps, after all, it was an accident) that once the telegraph was introduced, we find societywide preoccupation with the occult (it was the first or primal mode of consumer projection, I mean protection). So the preoccupation with the occult, which is not as ancient or continuous as some of you may think, but as far as our own reception goes, dates from the mid-nineteenth century, begins or is simulcast precisely with the invention of the new media technologies, with the telegraph in the front of the line.

Before the advent or event of the telegraph and the other modern techno media, poetry, literature, you name it, were real concerned about man's transitoriness and mutability. But as soon as the new gadgets arrived, our only remaining concern was suddenly with immortality here and now.

This brings us to another response to media technology, a so-called primitive response, which, in its recognizable otherness, may be that much more acceptable to us. In Melanesia a cult of gadget love arose to consciousness in 1912 under the label "Cargo Cult." This movement coincided with the white man's arrival, who came complete with all the techno devices he brought with him (including, in particular, the telegraph). "Cargo" covers the full range of the white man's sensorium, from canned goods and steamships to walkie-talkies and cameras. The Melanesians first off recognized, by way of the mirror logic of mourning, that all newly arrived white men were in fact their own returned dead. But it turned out that only the unmourned, projected, vengeful dead had returned. These undead phantoms had not come back to share the Cargo they brought with them. The Melanesians knew that their mourned dead, who were still back in the other place they called Australia, a place we too call the Land Down Under, were slaving away to produce the Cargo, through which they were counting on keeping in touch with their survivors. But the white phantom had interfered; he had taken the Cargo, stolen it, kept it for himself; he even intervened in the telecommunications, which he also kept to himself, message after message, setting himself up, then, as far as the reception area was concerned, as the disconnection between the living and the dead.

So what emerges here is a whole sensurround built up not only around media technology, mourning, communications with the dead but also (and more to the point) around the interruption or breakdown of mourning, the breakdown of communications or telecommunications with the dead. The telegraph guarantees the direct connection with the mourned dead, but at the same time an unmourned phantom controls and conceals each live transmission.

Before the white man's arrival, the Melanesians were bound to their own myths and legends about the relations between life and death, which featured voyages for the most part; in one case there was the story of a trip taken by twins separated at birth who then got back together again: it was a successful homecoming and reunion. But as soon as the Melanesians witnessed the effects of the new media-technological gadgets, the round-trip-based rituals were thrashed and thrown away; instead, on one island, for example, they put up poles, mimicking telegraph poles, all across the island; the cult followers now could run from one end of the island to the other, rapping the poles with sticks, beating out their new demand for direct connection with the dead. The Cargo Cultists pounded the imitation telegraph poles while inspired mediums standing by poleside beat their bellies: through this literal kind of ventriloquism the mediums transmitted messages, even songs, which were picked up and relayed by everyone else standing around and humming along. Once our gadgets get installed, we too, whether we know it or not, as whenever we pick up the phone, demand a direct line to our dead. But what we hear, at least on unconscious channels, is the disconnection brought to us by unmourning.

To make room for their returning ancestors or mourned dead (and the Cargo only the renewed arrivals could restore to them), the Melanesians knew that they had to destroy all their current possessions. In other words: the mourned dead can't go home again. Technologization had shifted Melanesian work of mourning down into reverse and reversal. By the date set (and reset) for reunion, every domestic and communal enclosure had to be emptied out, the contents wasted, to serve now as the empty warehouses, hangars, self-storage units in which the restored Cargo could be stockpiled. To rewind the tapes of a completed work of mourning—and bring back ancestors or friendly ghosts who have already been put to rest and put up there in the commemorative mode—requires a matching effort of idealization (and that means annihilation) of the former place to which the ancestors can beam back in all their purity.

Like Cargo-occulted Melanesia, Transylvania is a place entirely of the "trans," of moving across, a place of transference, of switch-over, of long-distance communications or transmissions. At the control panel we find the vampire, the incarnation of telepathy.

And how and where does Count Dracula penetrate the West? What is his double point of entry? How are his signals first picked up close range even while the ship's off on the horizon? First, his arrival is sensed by Lucy. He then enters at the precise point where she picked up his messages: at a cemetery that conveys up front on the gravestones messages to and from the dead that are rip-offs and put-ons. Lucy and Mina learn that the dead buried here were too quickly idealized by their tomb inscriptions: while these dearly departed were still around and in the way, they were only making the unwanted list. But many tombs advertising dead seamen are running on empty. In the place of missing corpses or empty tombs, the vampire makes his entry. Seamen lost at sea, lost without trace or remainder, drop beyond the work (or the representation) of mourning where loss gets lost. The loss without remainder of a vital fluid (blood or semen) is what the vampire recycles. With the vampire you either have the case of some dead body that has been fantastically reanimated, that has returned and continues to exist beyond the deadline, or you have the other case of someone imitating a corpse, someone who—unable to let the dead go—phantasmatically gives the dead extended visitation rights over a body that plays dead but all along retains all vital signs and fluids. Both options describe from different angles of identification the melancholic condition that goes down as incorporation. Remember how Norman in *Psycho* is unable to let go of his mother. It is not only his inclination to run around in her outfits that gives him away (in fact, that alone could represent, instead, work of mourning in progress). He also kills all women who come close to substituting for the original bond with mother. But that could be just another Oedipus complex exclusive. What most compellingly proves that he has gone all the way with unmourned mummy is that he tunes in and turns into a telecommunications device that at the end broadcasts only mother's voice. That the plotline has him murder her first, before unmourning her, points to what he can never do: murder her twice and thus mourn her.

So, it happened during Lucy's sleepwalk that she became a long-distance medium in advance of Dracula's arrival (she picked up the signals of his approach via the empty-crypt transmitters). When mourning shuts down, something like vampirism has already taken its place. The melancholic builds inside himself a crypt where the dead person can be kept alive as undead, and he keeps that crypt of preservation secret because all it takes is for someone, an analyst, for example, to open the otherwise unprotected crypt and let in the light and air, and that is the way it goes, what is already dead must again die, now once and for all. The concealment of the vampire is so important precisely because he remains, on a daytime schedule, as totally defenseless as only the dead can be.

Incorporation is an extreme case of what is always the case. When mourning someone with whom we were real close (especially if that bond reaches back, via lines of blood or transference, into childhood), we are mourning an object of identification. Parts of us were transplanted inside the other person, and the other's bit parts are internally, that is, eternally part of us. So in most mourning rituals, you will notice, identification gets played back — and erased — as in the funeral feast, through which we again identify with the deceased, this time around, however, in the service of an assimilation that excretes what is left over.

Once one realizes, as every melancholic must, that to mourn you must kill the dead, it becomes so difficult to run the disposal. That is why these vampire stakings are such primals.

You will remember that when Mina turns into a telecommunications device during the closing phase of the hunt, she also comes to Dracula's defense. All of a sudden when the men are talking about how they are going to destroy the vampire, that incarnation of evil, she says: Wait a minute. I feel sorry for him; I sympathize with him. How about trying this one out: there is a good and an evil side to him. We are destroying the evil side so the good can rest in peace, in one piece, and come and go into its own.

Mina bears a legacy and a future, a double take that is not superimposable part on part. In the first place she is the gadget lover, the "train fiend," the mother of the group's identification *and* reproduction. But she also inhabits a legacy of mourning. The nonsuperimposable cohabitation of cryptological burial plot and Oedipal plot within technology represents, even in its mixed state, an advance over the vampire's long-distance wavelengths of endless mourning, replication, and deathlike sleep. The vampire's conditions are total and dual. When he knows enough to destroy the vampire hunters' archive at the same time as he turns Mina into his listening post, he overlooks the third copy, the safe text, just as he overlooks the three-way communication that can plug into Mina turned medium. Dracula restricts his remote control over her to the feeding time of communion: she will be his " 'bountiful wine-press' " (304). But the wine press has also already doubled as primal model for the first printing press, which in fact incorporated working parts of the earlier press, and soon became associated in its first reception, as though the melancholic pickling of spirits was now in our typeface, with seeing double, ghostly doubles.

Mina turns the information-gathering service into a mass of typewriting for two good reasons. First, she recognizes the inefficiency of the audiorecords, which do not permit easy access by day or date but must be replayed all or nothing. As typewritten record the information can fit into a filing system that admits the group's overview. But second, she has listened in on the life-size vestigial double of Seward's voice, heard it tremble and his heart beat between the lines. No one must ever hear this unmournable double again. Transferred to typewritten copy in triplicate, the information is in the service of substitution and circulation.

On the way, then, to becoming a complete vampire, Mina pronounces her identification with the Count and opens up another three-way context in what is otherwise the double time of murder or merger:

> "Jonathan dear, and you all my true, true friends, I want you to bear something in mind through all this dreadful time. I know that you must fight—that you must destroy even as you destroyed the false Lucy so that the true Lucy might live hereafter; but it is not a work of hate. That poor soul who has wrought all this misery is the saddest case of all. Just think what will be his joy when he, too, is destroyed in his worser part that his better part may have spiritual immortality." (326)

In addition to the projected part that leads a life of its own—what an unlife of disowned death wishes—there is a part that belongs to the survivors, the part they identified with and with which they must reidentify, this time rerecording in order to erase. In this spirit Mina subsequently invites the men to read the Burial Service over her in-between state so that she (and they with her) can attend her funeral and together put to rest that part of themselves that had already identified with the dead.

Dracula's Daughter is about the family tie that blinds, that makes the heiress tie one on. Vampirism is an addiction, but how the trait is passed down from father to daughter is matter (mater!) for spookulation. Just when you thought you had flexed your willpower successfully, all life long, to keep away the parent's typecasting in irony, you find that you are now on center stage of Oedipal reproduction. You become again the figure of identification you denied, refused to assimilate. You've been taken in. Daughter begins at one of the stations of identification: it is the ending of Tod Browning's *Dracula* all over again, which now continues where on the other screen it left off. What are the legal consequences of Van Helsing's act? He has been caught blood-red-handed. "This is a case for Scotland Yard." "But surely you can't expect to face an English jury with this story. Insane!" "Insane or unbelievable." Van Helsing asks for a psychiatrist for legal counsel, aiming for an understanding beyond hanging or declaration of insanity. The earth moves underfoot: a woman draped in black enters the station. "I've come to see the body of Count Dracula, to see if he's really dead." She takes a shine to him with her magic jewel and hypno-commands him: "You will remember nothing." Count Dracula is one missing dead body. We see the woman lighting the funeral pyre as the dirge comes over her: "Be now exorcised, Oh Dracula." She gets cross with him. "Be the evil spirit cast out until the end of time." Burn, Dracula, burn. "Free forever, free to live as a woman, to take my place among the living and no longer among the shadows of the dead." She celebrates too soon her separation from the undad. As happy hour approaches, she protests too much. "The spell is broken. I can think normal thoughts. Play normal music. Listen! I've found release!" Her Igor-type servant hears between the lies: "That music doesn't speak of release. It speaks of dark shadowy places." "What do you see in my eyes?" "Death." Soon we see that she is back on the street hypnotizing a john, who looks into her eyes. Back home Igor discovers the return of job security. "Hurry, it's almost daylight. I got blood on it again."

Van Helsing: "You can't murder a man who's been dead for five centuries." Shrink: "You can't talk like that." "When you studied under me in Vienna you were more open-minded." "My mind is open and it's scientific, not open to superstition. Arguments like this belong in academic circles. This is reality."

Countess arrives at the social function, posing as a painter. "I never drink — wine. More things in heaven and earth than your psychiatry realizes." These are just a couple of the one-family-liners that the painter-Countess plays back. Hostess wants to know the most: "What is the scientific view of vampirism?" "I don't know, but Van Helsing is the expert." Psychiatrist talks about his work: "Sympathetic treatment can give release from obsession and compulsion." Countess really wants to talk to him. He agrees to stop by her place. "I'm glad you're not Van Helsing. You'd have some occult reading of the lack of mirrors. I need you here, doctor, tonight as a psychiatrist, as a man of strength. Something from the grave takes over my mind and makes me do horrible things."

To Igor: "Tonight I paint and I will need a model." Model removes blouse from the head and shoulders that leave her painting. The first lesbian social in Hollywood vampire films, as though simply any cattle of blood would do. We are refamiliarized with contexts of recognizable cases. Amnesiac girl turns up with marks on her neck. Van Helsing counts on the process of elimination: "No vampire can survive the stake."

To her shrink Countess admits: "I failed the test you assigned. The wordless command came over me." In the meantime Igor abducts doctor's wife. In the hypnosis lab the woman gets the projector turned on her: "Remember. There are pictures behind your eyes. You can see them if you try." Back in Transylvania for the wedding. The Countess knows release is impossible. So she wants his life. Igor wants the forever treatment. The girl's the bait. "Hypnosis?" "Something older, more powerful. I'll take her out of it." "Like the other one who died? Remain with me as one of the undead." "I don't believe in your magic." "Then let your science save me." All right, he gives in: "release her." While shooting arrow into Countess, Igor gets shot. "She's beautiful!" "She was beautiful when she died. One hundred years ago."

Nadja makes a replay for the lesbian social bond. "Nights in which the brain lights up like a big city." They are in New York. "Europe is a village, here it is exciting, especially after midnight." Pause. "Work? No. I'm not really good for anything. My father supports me. Family money, from way back in Romania, like all old fortunes, based on suffering of peasants." Pause. "Hard to realize that everything is superficial in our lives." The date interjects: "Would you like another drink?" Later, just when he thinks the drinks have lubed her, she turns on him and feeds, that's all he's good for.

Visions of Nosferatu-esque shadow plays of vampire stakings. She picks up some broadcast on the air: "My father. My father's dead."

Nadja and her sidekick make appearance at morgue to pick up the body.

On the sidelines we have entered a Jonathan and Lucy plot, one that admits contact with Vampire Hunter Peter Fonda, also known as Van Helsing. He stops by and teaches them a lessening of the murder charge in his staking of the Count: "He was like Elvis in the end, surrounded by zombies, just going through the motions; I didn't kill him, he was already dead."

Nadja wants to change her life. "It's not that easy." "Shut up. Things will be different. He's gone. I'm free. I can live a new life. I'll start over. I'll find someone. I'll be happy." At the bar Lucy asks Nadja for a cigarette. "Upset?" "I'm going to see my brother. I love him. But he wants to destroy me. Do you have siblings?" "I had a brother. He died. He killed himself. He was too young. He didn't know anything." "Young people know everything but they can't defend themselves against it." Nadja gives Lucy some free counseling: "You must dare to dredge up the primary pain. Otherwise you are poisoned." The pain Nadja feels is one of fleeting joy. It is the loneliness of her one night standing with the other.

Fonda tells the story of the children: "The bastard offspring of Dracula are everywhere, they blend in." Most are idiots, but there were two love children, born, not made. "He fell in love once, he thought a new life possible." We see Lugosi's face. "He did restrain himself. But she died in childbirth."

Nadja is back at Lucy's place. They are stuck on each other. Menstrual blood. When she goes home to her minion, Nadja exclaims: "I think I'm in love."

Nadja and Renfield visit her brother, Edgar, and his nurse, Cassandra. "Edgar doesn't have to be sick. I have the disease too. We can save him." To Edgar: "He's finally completely dead. We can start over." "It's too late for that." "No." "I won't infect her with the curse of our fucking family." "As you get older, you'll realize that family is everything."

Lucy to Nadja: "What have you done to me." "I'm sorry, I get lonely." "That's all you can say!?" "Relax, accept."

Fonda visits Edgar. Where is she? "She's going back to her native soil; she's lost a lot of blood. She's in a plane, dying—for a cigarette." We see that she is seated next to Cassandra. Nadja:"I sent Edgar a psychic fax. He's coming now, soon."

Fonda:"Blood is like chewing gum to these creatures."

Lucy to Jonathan:"Maybe we should have children. She's a monster. I hate her."

Nadja gets the stake while Renfield impales himself. The couple is back together again. But Nadja got herself in a fax — into Cassandra's body. Edgar and Cassandra get married."We are all animals. But there is a better way to live."

As I was saying, and as Mina says: Remember, I too could become a vampire, just as Lucy became that nightmare of Lucy. And she teaches the men to separate the good mother from the bad mother, to separate the vampire Lucy from the good mother Mina, who comes into the exorcised or integrated double inheritance at the end and in one piece. It is after she attends her own funeral and commemorates that part of herself that was invaded by vampirism (or which first let it in) that the endless mourning of and for Dracula can begin to run its course and make the deadline.

Now I want to argue — and I have already suggested as much — that vampirism does not really come to a close. The archive has been handed down to us ultimately as the already reproduced (typed-in-triplicate) novel. Mina's gadget love invents desktop publishing in order to keep the recorded voice, the life-sized double, from coming back as the uncanny, and in the place where it was to be kept hidden and forgotten. The novel is the place where all doubling between the media-technological sensurround and vampirism gets introduced. The typewriter, placeholder for our computer, serves as the control panel for this sensurround. And so, driven by this horror of the recorded voice — of the uncanny double — Mina produces the typewritten record that wipes up what is left of the vampirism it flushes.

Which brings us to the very end, that postscript in which the hunters celebrate the anniversary of the first ending. They go East to Transylvania, which by now has been made safe for Great Western tourists.

When we got home we were talking about the old time—which we could all look back on without despair, for Godalming and Seward are both happily married. [To be without the non-pair—the dis-pair— means to be out of range of the horror.] I took the papers from the safe.... We were struck with the fact, that in all the mass of material of which the record is composed, there is hardly one authentic document; We could hardly ask anyone...to accept these as proofs of so wild a story. (400)

We end with a novel that is a "mass"—a pile-up, an artifact of mass culture, and a communion—of sheer typewriting. There are no authentic documents, there is no voice, just as the novel itself has no narrator: it is all citation. Everything has been lifted up into the zone of simulation or unprovability by those fanglike marks of citation. Everything is suspended, no longer vampirically between life and death, but now, and more to the same vampiric point, between quotation marks. This novel cannot prove the existence of the vampire. Nor can it prove the vampire's nonexistence.

LECTURE SIX

The uncanny, that which should have remained forgotten or repressed but instead is back in the place where it was to be kept hidden — already inside the house but as though invading from without — brings us back, over and again, to Freud's most radical gesture, his insistence that everything begins in the home, which family-packs the devil, double, phantom, monster into the forget-together of family reunion.

Freud signs on the dotted line: "The 'double' was originally an insurance against the destruction of the ego" (*SE* 17: 235). But once the earliest dyadic, mirroring "stage has been surmounted, the 'double' reverses its aspect. From having been an assurance of immortality, he becomes the uncanny harbinger of death" (*SE* 17: 235). Both aspects get in our two faces in "The Sandman": the relationship to the robot dolly Olympia is so mirroring dual on the upbeat; the surprise attack of the Sandman's return is styling with double time, with doubling over time, with the compulsion to repeat right on the cutting edge of castration. But these extremes that merger or division go to are on one collapsed downsliding scale. The other notion of substitution comes up in Freud's essay on the sidelines of his discussion of the interchangeability of eyes and genitalia, as in the eye-balling phallus of ancient Rome, the testes in eyewitness testimony, or the fit between Oedipus's sex crime and his eye-for-an-eye punishment:

> We know from psychoanalytic experience, however, that the fear of damaging or losing one's eyes is a terrible one in children. Many adults retain their apprehensiveness in this respect, and no physical injury is so much dreaded by them as an injury to the eye.... A study of dreams, phantasies, and myths has taught us that anxiety about one's eyes, the

fear of going blind, is often enough a substitute for the d
castrated. . . . We may try to deny that fears about the e)
from the fear of castration [on rationalistic grounds], a
that it is very natural that so precious an organ as the
guarded by a proportionate dread. Indeed, we might *~* .__
say that the fear of castration itself contains no other significance and
no deeper secret than a justifiable dread of this rational kind. But this
view does not account adequately for the substitutive relation between
the eye and the male organ which is seen to exist in dreams and myths
and phantasies. (*SE* 17: 231)

So it is the substitutive relationship of parts that gets inscribed upon
the body and taken up by the name's representation and transmission.

Unheimlich, the German word for *uncanny,* as Freud documents in
the opening pages of his essay, is the *un* contaminant of the one opposite basic meaning, which, however, already also means its opposite. If
they are interchangeable from the beginning, then this is one primal
word meaning, like the hieroglyphs of dreams, both one meaning and
its opposite. If you take the German word apart, it has a couple of literal
meanings: *heimlich* can mean secret; it can also mean what is homey, at
home, cozy, belonging in the home. *Heim* is home. And *un* adds negation. But more or less than negation, the *un,* says Freud, functions as a
token of repression. The *un* is the languistic version of the push button,
the industry-saving device that transforms the techno apparatus into
gadgets. Walter Benjamin points out (in the essay on Baudelaire) that
with the strike and flick of the match, the click and dial of the phone,
the pull on the trigger of gun or camera, gadget gives us a shot or shock
of inoculation against the psychoticizing pressures of our ongoing technologization. If the camera thus bestows on the moment a "posthumous
shock," then it is all in a day's work of mourning, group-formatted for
life in the fast-food lanes of mass culture. The shock or shot gives the
lost moment, with all its potential for traumatization, a date, an occasion for you to remember to forget it.

Hanns Sachs kept a psychoanalytic account of the displaced origin
of the machine age. Machines were around way before they were put to
productive use. Originally, in antiquity, machine power was used only

create playthings, which did not overstrain a body-based narcissism. The ancient Greeks, for example, just did not get into the prosthetic applications of technology. Their bodily extensions were their debased body-doubles, their slaves. Their dead were the eternally dying and decaying bodies of lemurs and zombies. But these dead did not introduce the narcissistic crisis of uncanniness. Since antiquity every overinvestment in the body (which is always the mother's body) cannot but yield uncanny returns. When body-based narcissism is in uncanny crisis, we switch into the psychotic mode and relocate projections of the body, now within archaeological repositories (like mummy's tomb or casket), now inside machines (cinematograph, telephone, intercom). Thus, we witness the origin of our technologization (in the breaks the psychotic gets) as the only alternative in the field of narcissism to overinvestment in the body. Through omnipotence of thoughts, the death wish, and the prosthetic extensions and castrations of the body in parts, we graduate to the second and covert staging of narcissism as pursuit of power. Our self-love crawls out of the body bag and gets into relations of mastery between ego and superego, between survivor and ghosts. By the forced sharing of our omnipotence with the first victim of our death wishes—by loving to death and then loving the dead—we open up the corpus of narcissism to a new frontier of wide-open outer spaces of control.

There are different psychoanalyses and different vampirisms. We have been doing one set already around Oedipal plots and secret unburial plots. Now I am going to be talking about the problem of the double down at the pre-Oedipal bottom line of development. It is time to look at Jacques Lacan's remake of "the uncanny" (which belonged in Freud's theorization to the big screen of projection and identification) as "the mirror stage," the small screen on which we will be tuning in vampirism at large but also, in particular, the phantasms crowding such stories as "The Spider" and "The Horla."

When Lacan switches channels from cannibalistic identification to the infant's seeing I, the focus gets fixed on what is primally seen, visually represented and repressed, all at such an early stage. First, I would like to quote from two essays, one citational prop or bookend for setting up, the second to knock it down. The first quote is from André Baz. essay "The Ontology of the Photographic Image":

> If the plastic arts were put under psychoanalysis, the practice of em-
> balming the dead might turn out to be a fundamental factor in their
> creation. The process might reveal that at the origin of painting and
> sculpture, there lies a mummy complex. The religion of ancient Egypt,
> aimed against death, saw survival as depending on the continued ex-
> istence of the body. Thus by providing a defense against the passage
> of time, it satisfied a basic psychological need in man, for death is but
> the victory of time. To preserve artificially his bodily appearance is to
> snatch it from the flow of time, to stow it away neatly, so to speak, in
> the hold of life. It was natural then to keep up appearances in the face
> of the reality of death by preserving flesh and bone. The first Egyptian
> statue then was a mummy, tanned and petrified in sodium. (9)

Now that's a direct hit. Any kind of artistic representation is modeled after the body preserved beyond the limits of mortality. That's just fine as far as it goes. But remember (and here we can return to the psycho-analysis that Bazin already invoked for us) that, according to Freud, the problem we have with death is a problem we have with the dead. We can — or rather we must — conceive of the other's death. Indeed that is just what we wished for on occasion. So it is the other — the other person who must go, who dies — who presents the problem of death for us.

Let us now read, dearly beloved — as you by now gathered together, we are here for the downswing — let's read from the case study of a melancholic patient presented in an essay by Karl Abraham. The patient's dream has come up for analysis shortly after his wife's death in childbirth:

> After some time the husband came back to me and continued his treat-
> ment. His analysis, and in particular a dream he had shortly after he
> resumed analysis, made it quite evident that he had reacted to his
> painful loss with an act of cannibalistic incorporation. One of the most
> striking mental phenomena exhibited by him at this time was the dis-
> like of eating which lasted for weeks. One day this disinclination for
> food disappeared and he ate a good meal in the evening. That night
> he had a dream in which he was present at the post-mortem on his
> late wife. The dream was divided into two contrasting scenes: in the
> one, the separate parts of the body grew together again, the dead

n to show signs of life, and he embraced her with feel-
/eliest joy; in the other scene, the dissecting room altered
:e and the dreamer was reminded of slaughtered animals
er shop. The scene of the dissection, twice represented in
/as associated with his wife's operation. In the one part it
the reanimation of the dead body; in the other it was connected with cannibalistic ideas. The dreamer's association to the dream
in analysis brought out the remarkable fact that the sight of the dis-
sected body reminded him of his evening meal of the night before,
and especially of the meat dish he had eaten. We see here, therefore,
that a single event has had two different sequels of the dream set side
by side with one another, consuming the flesh of the dead wife is made
equivalent to restoring her to life. For it is shown that by incorporat-
ing the dead loved one, the melancholic does indeed recall it to life;
he sets it up inside himself. (435–36)

Now this double image can be grafted onto film (it really does belong in
the movies). Cutting up, dissecting, and suturing together create, through
the editing process, a corpus that is animated or reanimated through
projection.

The melancholic's dream puts on the big screen the alternation between identification and projection organizing the work of mourning,
and guarantees, on the cinematic side of the same mechanisms and processes, that horror movies will always also be self-reflexively about the
film medium. The vampire is double and nothing, image without end,
mirror image without reflection, reanimated still without life. But this
is just the reversed way of saying the vampire does not cast any reflection of its own. The vampire's special brand of unrepresentability was
waiting around for the invention of film.

I guess narcissism for many of us is a kind of forbidden but ultimately upbeat self-relation. Narcissism is love of self; you sit in front of
the mirror and that's it. Remember, according to psychoanalysis, there
are no self-relations. If you think you are enjoying a self-relation, then
something is standing in there, some prop, one that you are overlooking but that belongs to the other and that gets you there. Little one will
acquire his first sense of himself, will enjoy his first self-relation, by getting the look. It may be the image reflected back in mother's eyes or

breasts, or embodied by the mother, in part or as whole. Let's say the breast could be one of the first pictures you take of yourself as a somehow integrated body that is upright bound. It is a self-image that can only be framed from within the standing-upright perspective. Of course, this opening take or double take is delusional at best. And it never really goes away. On this first mirror stage of development we take in impossible fictions or absolute oppositions. But they are back, in a flashback, with each renewal of our wish or vow for total vengeance, victory, control — or whatever.

On this mirror stage mother acts as dummy, screen, double, or extension of ourselves. But these requirements are lifted or contradicted by the introduction of father, who divides the dual relations supporting our little narcissisms. We learn through this interjection of the father's antibody all about doubling, from both sides now. From the point of father's entry onward (and he's cutting edge), we, like Mina's archive, will always be typed or cast in triplicate.

What has father got to do with it? It turns out that little one suddenly picks up on mother's other desires: mother is not being fulfilled in their relationship; she wants something else. *Want* has that double sense in English of lacking something and wanting it. The child discovers outside their dual harmony and heaven that there is something wanting — wanted — right at the heart, the start, of their relationship. And so with this opening of the three-way freeway, you discover yourself always wanting — lacking but also desiring. Missing link

But what goes on with substitution goes double for the ways in which we prove self-identity. You identify yourself by name, signature, and phone number; there is always going to be some part of yourself that represents or substitutes for you, some detachable part of yourself that can stand in for your being identical with yourself. That is part of what is introduced or withdrawn at the close of the mirror stage. Some part of my body can stand for me, will stand up for the whole. But this part is also, in addition, right next to it, its portrait. The signature alone does not count; only with the countersignature does nothing at all increase twofold in value.

You never, up until recently I guess, really knew who your father was: *paternitas semper incertus est.* Who your mother is was always a sure thing. The relationship to father is abstract; it is always up for adoption. But the mother worshipped on early mirror stages must be all-powerful and self-sufficient. She wants nothing because everything is there and in place. And in dreams (according to psychoanalysis) this all-powerful mother is often given in spider form.

Which brings us to Hans Heinz Ewers's story "The Spider." And the reason psychoanalysis can put the spider in the all-powerful mother position (which holds uncanny double occupancy with the castrative externality of the repressed father function) is, I think, given in the narrator's journal, on Sunday, March 13, when the narrator observes spiders mating:

> Then they fell to the window sill, where the male, summoning all his strength, tried again to escape. [This comes after they've finished getting it on.] Too late. The female already had him in her powerful grip, and was carrying him back to the center of the web. There, the place that had just served as the couch for their lascivious embraces took on quite another aspect. The lover wriggled, trying to escape from the female's wild embrace, but she was too much for him. It was not long before she had wrapped him completely in her thread, and he was helpless. Then she dug her sharp pincers into his body and sucked full draughts of her young lover's blood. Finally, she detached herself from the pitiful and unrecognizable shell of his body and threw it out of her web. So that is what love is like among these creatures. Well for me that I am not a spider.

Against the backdrop of this inside view of spider woman as our omnipotent leader who is also cheerleader of all the divisions of castration, a "web" is spun between the narrator and Clarimonda, who faces him across the street, window to window. It is the web, by now worldwide, of the mirror stage. Each gesture in the games they cannot stop playing is always simulcast on the other side. Look at the entry for Saturday, March 12:

> The days pass. I eat and drink. I sit at the desk. I light my pipe; I look down at my book but I don't read a word, though I try again and again.

Then I go to the window where I wave to Clarimonda. She nods. We smile. We stare at each other for hours.

And on Tuesday, March 15, the narrator writes:

> We've invented a strange game, Clarimonda and I. We play it all day long. I greet her; then she greets me. Then I tap my fingers on the windowpanes. The moment she sees me do that, she too begins tapping. I wave to her; she waves back. I move my lips as if speaking to her; she does the same. I run my hand through my sleep-disheveled hair and instantly her hand is at her forehead. It is a child's game and we both laugh over it.

The mirror relation caught in this web goes for the radical regression that keeps on going on automatic all the way back to one's pre-animate beginnings. On Wednesday, March 16, the narrator goes to grave lengths to say how unthinkable it would be to see Clarimonda out on the street or, for example, to be standing right next to her while she purchased something in a store. What is more, when he tries real hard to imagine her outside their web, he hits the bottom line of their on-line relationship:

> I can, of course, put on my hat and coat, walk down two flights of stairs, take five steps across the street and mount two flights to her door which is marked with a small sign that says "Clarimonda." Clarimonda what? I don't know. Something. Then I can knock and . . .
>
> Up to this point I imagine everything very clearly [including her lack of a patronymic], but I cannot see what should happen next. I know that the door opens. But then I stand before it, looking into a dark void. Clarimonda doesn't come. Nothing comes. Nothing is there, only the black, impenetrable dark.

We watch the mirror game take thought-control over him and select the self-destruct program. But notice that there is also a moment of resistance that helps us out. The narrator, the student, does resist, and at the end bites the spider in half. How is his resistance to the bite she puts on him introduced? By phone. The telephone is his one connection to the outside that admits the inspector's paternal voice and words of caution. But Clarimonda finally succeeds in taking complete control when he takes her order to cut the other umbilical cord, the one open to the paternal outside, the public, published space of directory listing, of numbers functioning as names, the first basis for making dates. He falls back on their double bond, the one and all that is left, without any third term to ring interference.

In one of the entries I already quoted we saw that his inability to read—he sees the words on the pages but is unable to make them out, link them together, or connect with them—accompanies his entry into the fatal phase of the game with spider woman. In the entry for Thursday, March 24, we see language reduced to next to nothing, to doubling. He wonders whether the words they keep on repeating to each other are his or hers; their words are like baby sounds resounding in a mother's lullaby. But at the end, he finally writes: he cries out and writes down his name. It is the signing of the name that signals the most powerful moment of resistance. To keep from looking at her, he writes down, tries to write down his last but not least name. But the game of doubling has gone on too long and far, so long and farewell. Yes, the father's name begins to emerge, but it is too late. So, at the end, his surname, too, is cut in half. Not only is the spider cut in half (in his mouth, not in his hands), but the name gets interrupted and divided. What was in parts is already a mouthful, too much; on the other hand, it makes it out only halfway. He writes only the "Bracque" and not the "mont." But the name "Clarimonda" (which is on first-name basis only, the basis of mother and child) bears that missing half of the father's name as "monda" (which adds the lilt of its feminization) and attaches that missing part of the full father's name to "Clari," to "clear," "clarity," to the kind of clear reflecting mirror surface that has reflected back, from doubling to division, the bond and bondage of the narrator's total regression. The father figure, the inspector, brought in by the breakup of the ring, enters mirror stage leftover—but it is too late: "He found the body of the student Richard Bracquemont hanging from the cross-bar of the window in room #7" (204). Cutting his losses, taking her with him down the divide of suicide, looking for some way to get off the hook, it's the hang-up, all over again.

The curse that challenges the student to move in (in "The Spider") is also upon *The Tenant*. The film, which was identified by Hollywood as not such a great career move by Roman Polanski, is a cornerstone projection within the case or crypt that first flashed back upon *The Fearless Vampire Killers*. The new "letter" takes the room of a recent suicide, only to discover a detritus and cycle of identification that, like a perpetual sui-citation, will never let the "living" contents of the flat vary. The figures he sees in the room across the courtyard are like photos, like freeze-frame ghosts in motion in place. In no time he is seeing himself across the way. But when he is all back on one side, he watches a mummy over there start to unravel. He wakes up with his makeup on. He buys a wig. Now he is a TV, like the *Psycho* diversion. Everyone is trying to turn him into Simone Schul, the suicide who moved in and went before him. "You want a clean death!? It was better last time! I'm not Simone Schul." And he jumps. Next the mummy shot, the After picture in the hospital, which was also the Before picture, when he visited what was left of Simone all wrapped up. The flashback is so perfect that he is left out of the picture. We look through his or Simone's mummy wraps. Scream memory. Perfect TV.

A daughter's duties of substitution and mourning give a different spin on the mirror scene of vampirism in Greye La Spina's "The Antimacassar." It is a yarn spun now into a web, now into a saving telegram. And although we are sleepwalked through a straightforward story line, it is precisely on this one-way line of substitution that the plot is arrested. Why is Lucy, the protagonist, so reluctant to replace the missing woman Cora at their workplace? Cora never returned from her vacation. Lucy, who is next in line for vacation, doubles and internalizes Cora's absence by taking her own vacation to the spot of the precursor's missingness, to the spot Lucy is in with the woman who was and then went ahead of her. The strands Lucy follows out are those of Cora's weaving interests — which cannot but represent returns on our investment in the story as text or "fabric." Lucy, in the social register of anxiety, is also on the verge of marriage, the union with the name, with the law of the couple.

She arrives at the house of weaving where Cora was drained of blood by one sick little girl whose hunger Lucy is next in line to satisfy. She thus finds herself marking, under the vampire child's fangs, the spot that now comes out of an unsolved or unresolved blood bonding with her own mother, the vacated, vacationing position she has so much trouble assuming because it would mean taking her place, replacing her in her place. She is struck by the antimacassar, the maxishield of protection that preserves armchairs from the pomaded back of a head, the father's trace inoculatively contained within the woven text covered with what look like ancient symbols. The evil mother figure, the landlady who must procure human blood for her vampire child, notices Lucy's interest and gives away the antimacassar, the one piece of weaving in the house that is not hers: " 'Glad to be shut of it' " (259). Lucy takes it and sends it on to her prospective mother-in-law, a piece of postal networking, of transfer of what is post or past, that establishes her connection with the law even as she overhears, in that mode of hearsay that brings us the primal scene, the blood hunger of a little girl. Lucy dreams of this child's kiss in a state that "mingled antipathy and allure" (263). Following first contact with the vampire, Lucy tries her own hand at weaving or text work only to find out that she's taking dictation: "The weaving grew under what she felt were guided fingers" (265). She recognizes the SOS message woven into her work of transmission. The landlady intercepts the message and cuts through the text. But Lucy speaks in the name of the law when she confronts the landlady with what she now knows. The evil mother collapses back onto the projective apparatus: "Her air of indomitable determination dissipated as she bent her body from one side to the other like an automaton" (265). In the meantime Aaron, a local figure representing the grief-stuck mother's conscience, stakes the child offscreen: "Mrs. Renner slipped unconscious to the floor. She said one word only as her body went from chair to floor. 'Kathy!' Her lips pushed apart sluggishly to permit the escape of that sound" (266). Mrs. Renner, evil landlady or stepmother and mourningsick mother at once, takes the floor and releases the name of her now twice dead child: but the name she releases as sound, as the other's breath escaping from lips that have been "pushed apart" inside out, is given as "word," a circulating, substituting piece of language no longer fixed in the proper or improper place of a scene that could only be concealed and fed. When the name, now word, exits the mad mother's lips, Lucy is paralyzed, as though awaiting her "cue," the stage direction of Oedipalization or assignment of roles. And then she hears her own name, called out by her husband-to-be, and it fills the blank as though the delayed echo of the released child's name: "She found her own voice then" (266). The law of her once and future family line intervenes to tell her that the child was all along long dead (Lucy's first thought while her own voice was up in the air was to charge the ghostbuster Aaron with murder). The legacy of the missing woman, Cora, the antimacassar that Lucy had not kept but forwarded, as though on the same weaving length, to her future mother-in-law, brought in the law of the future couple. The interwoven broadcast of shorthand symbols could be decoded by the future in-laws even as Lucy, in simulcast, was decoding while encoding her own SOS into the text she stitched in time, saved from being at the disposal of a little girl's hunger. There were, after all, savings and benefits to be drawn from those last words of teleguidance the dead woman had to hand to Lucy, her replacement and heiress.

From Dusk till Dawn covers the psychotic foreclosures, the cracked mirror-stagers, but with the post-splatter, post-slasher difference that there are survivors who have worked their way through the disturbance, but not as the couple that was already to be before the interruption of the horror film, as in the earlier Hollywood monster economy, and as in "The Antimacassar," but just as a couple of people who are, however, de-couplified groups of one.

Psycho brother springs his better half, the underworld brother, from jail. Together, with psycho at the wheel, they run over a schoolteacher, all-purpose figure of substitution in the mother's place. They have brought along a hostage from the bank holdup just for insurance. She is a middle-aged maternal type (we first see her x-ray-style inside the trunk of the vehicle like a pregnancy scan). While underworld brother is away, psycho bro rapes and murders her. The underworld brother now must look for a new insurance policy. He advances to the third degree from the psycho's stage of objectionable choice of blow-up-dolly mirror moms: he kidnaps a patriarchal family broken down by unmourning. The father has defrocked himself of the other "father" status of his minister position following his wife's death by car crash. The family's had some bad brakes. The son is plainly adopted. The daughter appears to be by birthright.

The brothers make it south of the border in the hostage family's camper. The group waits at an all-night place, a trucker stop called "Titty Twister." Come dawn, the contact will arrive to buy the loot. The father's truck-driving license (for his RV) gains them all admission into the truckers-only bar. The bar is the extravaganza front for a primeval operation run by vampires. When a striptease act turns on the audience at the same time that it turns vampiric and ugly, psycho brother is the first victim.

Underworld brother convinces the father to give them all the super savings of his greater fatherhood. But then he too is bitten. He makes his kids swear they will kill him when it is time. But the adopted son, with whom the father's rapport seemed all along overdetermined, maternal, blood-bonded via absence and metonymy, just cannot comply with the father's last wish. Vampire father bites the son, who is finished off by the undead pack. He begs the daughter now to finish him off. The mother's blood comes full circle and can be let go with the twice dead father. At the end, the brother from the underworld, who has mourned the lost brother-mother during the all-night close encounter with vampirism, and the mourned mother's daughter are the sole survivors. The brother will not give in to what just crosses the daughter's mind. There is no immediate couplification frame for the future. Now we know that both of them, equal but separate, have broken out of the underworld.

LECTURE SEVEN

Remember that from the Adam and Eve story on down, one of the biggest symptom builders of our history has always involved the first contact we make only through consumerism or sacrifice. The only way to obtain knowledge, self-knowledge, identity, is through consuming and invading the other's personal space. And that means, psychoanalysis reminds us, that we all develop or obtain any kind of identity at all only through identification. Identification is always primally grounded and ground up in acts of cannibalism. It starts out early, one-on-one with mother: we drink her milk, we devour her breasts, and at her breast we in turn see reflected back to us our doubles, those mirror images of ourselves that are at first so reassuring and reinsuring. But it is only the consolation prize for coming in second or losing. The building blocks or blockages of our identity begin as one-on-one doublings not only as visual activity but also at the same time as the acts we are caught in of consumerism, with the mother's body at the front of the line. But then we retreat horrified; there is a backfire, because that same doubling turns out to have already mobilized the divisions of death or the dead. What the dad introduces, then, into the melodrama of absence and presence is another death, the one that can be substituted for and survived; it is the one that does not introduce total eradication. The father embodies this proper dosage of death from the start; he is the antibody who was always in the already position of dead-or-dad-on-arrival. With his arrival or survival we must replace the maternal meat we have been eating with the father's fast food, the symbolizable and generic death we swallow with his corpus.

First it takes two, but then it is Take Two. Vampirism returns from the early stage that had to be discarded, from the now underground world of the maternal blood bond. This is the bond vampires recycle over and again at the same time that they lose it without remainder. The paternal antibody did not take. This is what we saw reflected back in "The Spider": the spider is stopped in parts right at the mouth of the problem, just as the name is visualized on the page, but only in the first part, the parting of a fragment. The name Clarimonda, the mirror staging of the father's name, never made the grade of separation. A certain maternalization of his name attached its mirrorlike "clarity" to a name that in its other or full form — Bracquemont — inflicts breakage or rupture on the "mound."

As soon as you realize that mother wants something, which means that she lacks something inside your duo dynamic, you know that she is not your other and god: Why that dirty little "Horla." Thus, we really get into Guy de Maupassant's "The Horla," which is all about mirror relations and their psychotic crack-up.

Where to begin with the narrator's unraveling in "The Horla"? At the onset he is suffering from a kind of fever. What are the coordinates of this fever state? He feels he is being watched, that his thoughts are known, that he himself is leading the double life of phantom possession. Something has entered him and divided him against himself and opened up his thoughts to total thought control. He is running a race between self-analysis and psychosis, between breakthrough and breakdown. He is on the lookout for analogues for this state of surveillance, now in the inside view of invisible forces offered by a Father (of the Church), now in a demonstration of hypnotism.

But we begin with the narrator's sense of well being, his visual sense of being well situated inside his home, his lookout onto the river. He emphasizes that his home turf has been fertilized with ancestors, the family line, the line of the name's transmission. He appears well placed within paternal precincts. But the association of earth, as of blood, is with the mother, and a house is always also her symbol.

So one day he looks out onto the Seine River and what happens? Suddenly a Brazilian three-master appears — and he instantly falls ill. This three-limbed ship, dare I say it, represents the father's forced entry.

The narrator has been looking out onto the river Seine, which in French could also be made to harbor "breast" (*sein*); he looks out onto this breast with its reflecting flowingness, and suddenly the tranquility is interrupted by the arrival of some three-limbed being. First there is a libidinal upsurge, a salute of jubilant recognition or defiance:

> There came a magnificent Brazilian three-master; it was perfectly white, and wonderfully clean and shining. I saluted it, I hardly knew why, except that the sight of the vessel gave me great pleasure. [That's the end of the entry for May 8; the next entry begins with the connection that goes without saying.]
> *May 12.* I have had a slight feverish attack for the last few days and I feel ill, or rather I feel low spirited. (89)

What first gives him a rise introduces the immediate onset of his illness, the nonstop encounter with the malevolent force of invisibility.

> Whence come those mysterious influences which change our happiness into discouragement, and our self-confidence into diffidence? One might almost say that the air, the invisible air, is full of unknowable Powers whose mysterious presence we have to endure. I wake up in the best spirits, with an inclination to sing. Why? I go down to the edge of the water, and suddenly, after walking a short distance, I return home wretched, as if some misfortune were awaiting me there. . . . Who can tell? Everything that we touch, without knowing it, everything that we handle, without feeling it, all that we meet, without clearly distinguishing it, has a rapid, surprising and inexplicable effect upon us and upon our senses, and, through them, on our ideas and on our heart itself. (89–90)

At first count, his breakdown is crowded with metaphysical speculations or spookulations on the nature of unseen forces; these are the forces that, even though they are invisible, unavailable to our senses, are nevertheless in control. The stage is set for thinking ruled by absolute extremes of presence versus absence. That is why he must contemplate only the most terrific mysteries that seem to have the force of fate or destiny. And as he faces the power of the invisible — of the invisible heir — he calls out for other sense organs through which he might recognize the force that is with him. And this desire for other organs is another way of saying that the organ that is already in place is on the edge of a certain ever-ready position, set to get lost. The threat to his organ requires his primal submission to something resembling fate. The reduction to visibility of all sense data, with which the total threat comes complete, at the same time blinds the narrator with what looks like a blow of Oedipal justice.

But let's look at what happens when the invisible force begins to beam up into the narrator's range and rage of vision. First, the mirror stage is set for eyes too weak to see the hard body that would be his own if the glass of Horla's vengeful invisibility were backed with a reflector shield:

> And I went on thinking: my eyes are so weak [again he is worried about needing new organs], so imperfect, they do not even distinguish hard bodies, if they are as transparent as glass! If a glass without tinfoil behind it were to bar my way, I should run into it. (107)

But a piece of glass *with* tinfoil behind it is a mirror. He asks for a mirror in place of transparent bodies. What he gets is the phantom's self-presentation as the interruption of his own mirror relations.

> Behind me was a very high wardrobe with a looking-glass in it, before which I stood to shave and dress every day, and in which I was in the habit of glancing at myself from head to foot every time I passed it....
>
> It was as bright as at midday, but I did not see my reflection in the mirror! It was empty, clear, profound, full of light! But my figure was not reflected in it—and I, I was opposite to it! I saw the large, clear glass from top to bottom, and I looked at it with unsteady eyes; and I did not dare to advance; I did not venture to make a movement, feeling that he was there, but that he would escape me again, he whose imperceptible body had absorbed my reflection. How frightened I was! And then, suddenly, I began to see myself in a mist in the depths of the looking-glass, in a mist as it were a sheet of water; and it seemed to me as if this water were flowing clearer every moment. It was like the end of an eclipse. Whatever it was that hid me did not appear to possess any clearly defined outlines, but a sort of opaque transparency which gradually grew clearer.
>
> At last I was able to distinguish myself completely, as I do every day when I look at myself.
>
> I had seen it! (109)

The phantom craves water and milk, a fuel of regression on which narrator and the force of invisibility are still running. So I have already said it. Horla is the mother-and-child merger made monstrous, murderous by its perpetually unmetabolized interruption by the three-limbed third party.

What overwhelms the narrator is that Horla represents some new being that is going to make man over — and out. Man is the being who can die any day at every moment. The Horla is the being that will die only at the proper hour and only because it will have touched the limits of its existence. What is it that only dies at its proper hour (and thus does not die)? It is part of the father's introductory offer: the proper name, the legacy, the insurance policy, you name it, whatever proceeds according to the scheduling proper to its death-defying act of signing, signing off.

The Church Father cannot absorb Horla's impact within the symbolizable relations between visibility and invisibility. A second attempt is made, this time by a psychiatrist, who is also a hypnotist, to put him back on the auto-analytic track. A demonstration of the invisible force of hypnotic powers is what the doctor ordered. The hypnotic session consists of one part diagnosis (by immediate suggestion made to and through the narrator's blood relation) and one part intervention-and-modeling demo via the delayed and thus transferential understanding or following of yet another — posthypnotic and long distant — suggestion. Posthypnotic suggestion is the way to go when you get the message while under hypnosis that three days or three years from now you will on one particular day at one particular moment say or do the following. Freud in "A Note on the Unconscious" said that posthypnotic suggestion was one proof that the unconscious exists; the unconscious too is an unseen agency (a foreign body) exercising remote control over programmed portions of conscious existence. So this scene of posthypnotic suggestion that I am guiding you through — you are getting sleepy — reintroduces the substitutive relations that presuppose a gap to be fulfilled within mirror blood bonds that, contrary to popular relief, only cut the losses or gaps that are already also there. The proto-psychoanalyst guiding the demonstration of hypnotic remote control is named

Dr. Parent. The parent, whether we are talking French or English, is always going to be one of two. Parent is what the mother becomes once it is clear that she and little one are no longer alone. "Parent" always implies the triangle that is already set up. But there is the three that breaks company with the duo dynamic of primal coupling between mother and infant, the big three called father or parent, and then there is the three that is a crowd, the ghost pack that disperses the couple formed in the name of father's substitutive teaching.

In the session the narrator is not alone with his resistance; he shares it with his cousin, a blood relative he, for one, would characterize as more of a sister. She goes to sleep under Dr. Parent's mirror stage direction. The narrator is asked to stand behind his cousin; she is given a visiting card to look at — the card one carries to identify oneself with the proper name, a father's name — and the hypnotist tells her that it is a mirror. She looks into the mirror to which the name's personalized license has been reduced — and what does she see? She sees her cousin, the narrator, behind her, looking at himself in another mirror: he is looking at a photograph of himself. And that is the complete circuit of the live demonstration. At this point Dr. Parent introduces the posthypnotic suggestion: he tells the woman in the experiment that tomorrow she will go and ask her cousin, the narrator, for the sum of money needed to help out her husband, who, she will just know, is in debt. Dr. Parent introduces a third term, a husband and father figure, to intervene in a dual blood relation and introduce the calculation of debt or (same currency) guilt. Next day the narrator's cousin carries out the command, asks for the five thousand francs, and the narrator, now faced with this posthypnotic proof that unconscious punitive relations with the father (and I want you to hear the unitive, the union, in the punishment) are already along for the drive of invisibility, withdraws most completely, completes the system of his paranoia, substitution-proofs it. Mesmerism and hypnosis now belong to the advance signs and proofs of the Horla's unstoppable invasion.

He can interpret Dr. Parent's scene only as another intersection crowded with the ghosts that are out to attack him. The gridlock leads him to conceive of his own life as double, and to look forward to the end-in-sight that can be given only by his own suicidal execution of a phantom command. The Horla is not dead, the narrator realizes at the end. "No, no he is not dead. Then, then I suppose I must kill myself" (95).

With Clive Barker's "Human Remains" we leave the bottom line of regression for more personalizable precincts of haunting. From now on we will be learning how to fill out the missing persons reports of unmourning. The vampiric perspective in this story spreads from an underworld of bisexual license, in which clients get their fix of human connection, while the hustler tries to save face, his perfect face, the face that must never vary, all the way to the other underworld of occult and archaeological provenance. An ancient statue that is one of a kind comes alive within one man's lifelong excavation of the past. This man hires Gavin, the hustler protagonist, not for sex but for sacrifice. The statue must be showered in blood draining from cute cut bodies. But the statue, which not only requires this bloody skin conditioning but also the availability of mimetic models to sustain and develop his animation, is struck by the hustler's face, which the statue now too must save and keep safe, in the safe of their incorporation.

Hustler and john are endless mourners or unmourners. The archaeologist crowded his apartment with relics he had stolen while on digs: he thus doubly tampered with the proper precincts or guidelines of commemoration and scientific postmortem. Before he kills himself, he destroys the relics: " 'It's a sickness. . . . Needing to live in the past . . . I stole most of these pieces . . . over a period of many years. I was put in a position of trust, and I misused it' " (32). Then the klepto-, crypto-archaeologist mentions in passing one of the lifted finds by name, one that has, for all these same pages, been sticking in the hustler's mind too: " 'Flavinus lived and died. That's all there is to tell. Knowing his name means nothing, or next to nothing. It doesn't make Flavinus real again: he's dead and happy' " (32). Mourning begins here, but it is too late.

When Gavin was originally hired and first brought to this relic-crowded place, his wandering short attention span tuned in primal wavelengths around the tombstone of "Flavinus the Standard-Bearer":

There was something satisfying about the idea of having your likeness, however crude, carved in stone and put up on the spot where
your bones lay, even if some historian was going to separate bones
and stone in the fullness of time. Gavin's father had insisted on burial
rather than cremation: How else, he'd always said, was he going to be
remembered? Who'd ever go to an urn, in a wall, and cry? The irony
was that nobody ever went to his grave either: Gavin had been perhaps twice in the years since his father's death. A plain stone bearing
a name, a date, and a platitude. He couldn't even remember the year
his father died.

   People remembered Flavinus though; people who'd never known
him, or a life like his, knew him now. Gavin stood up and touched the
standard-bearer's name. (14)

Commemoration dates this standard bearer as ancient history but
also as a history to be taken of Gavin, whose presenting problem, the
father's death, secretly bears the mother-and-child standard or era of
body-based narcissism. First there is reference in passing to the failed
commemoration of a father. But this turn to the father is diversionary.
The thought crossing the hustler's mind that he will retire one day by
wedding some widow fits the Oedipal bill of this diversion. It is not so
much that the father is unmourned as that his mournable antibody function has not kicked in. Doubly missing is the mother, gone without saying. But we catch a glimpse of her each time Gavin looks in the mirror,
and she comes back from the mirror realm with the statue that gives
that face a permanent life or unlife. It is the same face that Gavin can
only identify or identify with in passing and eventually lose. The need
that drives Gavin to turn a trick the night he is brought face to face with
the statue sets out on a detour that is really a shortcut through mirror
relations: "A wave of unhappiness came up from some buried place in
him. . . . He wanted, no, he *needed* to be with somebody tonight. Just to
see his beauty through somebody else's eyes" (8).

   Why is face value so charged? Because the face-to-face with mother
is our establishment of first contact. The connection is at once mutual
and programmed (like the mirror game with spider woman): we smile
gazing into our mother's modeling and mirroring face. The other is in
our face.

The statue realizes Gavin's childhood fantasy by converting an original wound into the wonder or miracle of doubling, countdown, and takeoff:

> "I am a thing without a proper name," it pronounced. "I am a wound in the flank of the world. But I am also that perfect stranger you always prayed for as a child, to come and take you, call you beauty, lift you naked out of the street and through Heaven's window." (28)

This wound starts outflanking Gavin when, opening on the person of the statue, a recollection starts bleeding outward:

> The flesh of its chest had been blown open, exposing its colourless innards. There was, of course, no blood.... Its fingers touched the edge of the wound. The gesture recalled a picture on the wall of his mother's house. Christ in Glory—the Sacred Heart floating inside the Saviour—while his fingers, pointing to the agony he'd suffered, said: "This was for you." (37)

Following his solo reference to the missing mother, to her sacrifice, to the wound of or in their transparency, Gavin wonders why the blasted double is not dead. It answers that it is not yet alive or—if we reread and reverse the message between the lines—no longer dead.

As this face-to-face with the mother takes on independent existence—the natural development of every projection—the paternal function of mourning after separation is attended by the double.

> "What's wrong?" said Gavin.
> "It always makes me cry, coming here." It stepped over the graves towards him....
> "You've been here before?"...
> "—I come to visit Father. Twice, maybe three times a year."
> "This isn't your father," said Gavin.... "It's mine."
> "I don't see any tears on your face," said the other....
> "I will miss him until I die.... Why is it all so painful?" it asked, after a pause. "Why is it loss that makes me human?" (41–42)

Gavin came to the cemetery to take leave of his father, sensing that his own last will to die of catatonic refusals of nourishment or movement would not be respected otherwise. Instead he encounters the mourning the statue undergoes, but not over the loss that has given it its comeback. Gavin runs into the busy street to die, a genre of suicide that always represents destruction via the crash coupling of traffic between parents.

In *Vampire's Kiss,* Peter is one neurotic white male in a new world of advantages and advances. Psychosis or vampirism marks yet another advance, while it advances, up the psychopathology continuum in the speed race between the breakthroughs of self-analysis and ultimate breakdown. Peter's analysis is stuck on a transference that only gets articulated (and never examined) once he is completely solo psycho. Peter's presenting problem is that he falls in and out of love with the women he must have and then just has to dump, trash, some morning after.

We do not see the series of objects binding Peter to the couch right at the film's opening. But we see the hallucinated fantasy woman, and she comes complete with his identified class, culture, and so on. She is the match made in a delusion of therapy heaven. In the fantasy or delusion, the psychiatrist introduces Peter, now the independent client who has taken the cure of self-insight, the one called love, to another client, who has all along been filling the hour right after Peter's session. But the fantasy match catches the raging old flame before Peter has made it home with his invisible placeholder.

The only object this total fantasy choice resembles is the murder victim of Peter's first psychotic attempt at taking blood, just like a vampire, life-size. Otherwise it is objects of color that make the advances on the screen and that darken the door of a difference, a misrecognition, which can be called love, if only in color contrast to the recognition on which Peter's goodpatient fantasy of a true partner in love, the fantasy he keeps on refueling incestuously with the unexamined transferential relationship, is totally based. On the other side of a phone call, a visualization that could be real or could be the peripheral vision of the delusion shows the psychiatrist at home all cozy with a number of color on the side of an erotic transference that self-entitles her to take advantage of class and age difference.

The color bind begins with the woman in love he picks up for a one-night stand that gets stood up or interrupted by a bat attack. What is up next to bat is the dark vampire mistress Peter picks up or chooses in the bar where he is up for another night of mood swinging. She sinks her teeth into their one-nighter, and he has forsaken all others.

But there is a bad mother of color too. It is the Latina Alva, who is in the secretarial position at Peter's office. Peter gets the call from one of the agency's authors, who requests an old contract for translation of his work into a foreign language. The contract was with the German mag *Der Spiegel*, which, in translation, is self-entitled "The Mirror." The scrawl of an author figure across the foreign mirror called up by a voice blasting from the past immediately sets Peter looking for a quick fix in the files. But it must have been less precisely filed away, not under the author's name, for example, but presumably in the huge miscellaneous file of correspondence with the mirror. Already raging, Peter assigns the search to Alva, whose secretarial services he shares with several other colleagues but whose complete attention he demands for himself for this one mother of a task. Alva tries to get out from under this overwork ethic, hoping tomorrow will be the other day the work or the boss are gone away. The escalating conflict between Peter and Alva inside the backsliding dialectic as though between near equals acts out a farce of affirmative reaction. At the end of his corridor war Peter is a psycho and Alva is the traumatized victim of his blind rage rape.

But first, Alva finally finds the missing document. But in the meantime Peter has completely crossed over into his vampiric identity. He does not see what we see: not even his image in the restroom mirror. He is now, at any time, the hallucinated suckee of the vampire woman, who now takes what he must already give at the office. So Peter has only one response to Alva's good news: It's too late, Alva, it's just too late. During the rape that follows the blanks Alva's gun draws (thanks to her overprotective brother), which abandon Alva to violence and Peter to the unlife he hoped her bullets could stop, the rapist hallucinates in the victim's place the form of his victorious vampire mistress. When next he fires the gun into his mouth, his blank stare meets the look of his laughing mistress.

At the disco he murders a woman with those plastic kiddy fangs and drinks his first blood life-size. He gags on it in public, like a dead drunk. The vampire is back one last time to dump him. She beats him to the draw of blanks. But is she just some acquaintance he is mistaking for the hallucinated mistress? He seems psychotically alone with his recognition values. "Just look at her teeth! She's a vampire. She made me one too!" Thrown back out onto the street, he begs passersby for the release, the change, that would be his for the staking.

The hallucination of the session with his matchmaking psychiatrist is the first complete scene we know to be fantasy from beginning to end. In the delusion the shrink announces, like Van Helsing in Tod Browning's *Dracula*, "I guess you two won't be needing me anymore." Peter leaves the street corner he was in while acting out solo his hallucination of the session for three parts. Alva's brother wants revenge. Peter sees another chance for release and places the stake over his heart. Bro won't give no for an answer. If the stake fits, push it in.

In Earl Peirce's "Doom of the House of Duryea," the crypt-protection that diversion covers holds the plot together by pulling one over us. The father is set up as the transmitter of vampirism. He wants to disbelieve that he is the carrier, that he once murdered two of his sons in the trance state of a transmission that fulfilled the family rep or rap. But there is a heartbeat of difference. Ancestor Autiel was found unconscious next to his drained younger brother.

Father is reunited with his first born, the third son, who had been locked in another room on the night of the vampiric legacy's transmission over the dead bodies of his brothers, and was then taken away by his aunt, who has now, in the meantime, passed on. This aunt, the sister of the mother who was already missing on the night that was the night of transmission, protected her nephew by projecting the father as fiend. The son returns to his father's side to reclaim the projection. But the book of denial—INFANTIPHAGI—is inside his father's luggage. The son learns that the vampire, according to the tradition or transmission of his family line or lie, appears completely normal as long as his inherent evil is not combusted by proximity to "the blood of its own family" (203).

> "But the *vrykolakas* cannot act according to its demoniacal possession unless it is in the presence of a second member of the family, who acts as a medium between the man and its demon. This medium has none of the traits of the vampire, but it senses the being of this creature (when the metamorphosis is about to occur) by reason of intense pains in the head and throat. Both the vampire and the medium undergo similar reactions.... Where other victims are unavailable, *the vampire will even take the blood from the very medium which made it possible.*" (203)

When father catches son reading his book—and the appropriated book, let me mention or order on the side, represents the mother—his denial is erased: he now believes the letter of the book his son has thrown at him and orders his own restraining to his bed on this night that is now the night. But when the son wakes up safe next morning, he feels a heavy rawness that he suddenly recognizes from way back when. Then he finds his bound father drained of blood. It was a sibling transmission that was bleeding across generation under the cover of father and son, a subterfuge authored by the mad sister of the missing mother and at the same time withdrawn into a double diversion. It is the mother's vampiric legacy or mediation, preserved in the person of the son under her sister's guidance, that glides beneath and ahead of the paternal position of protection or projection. But the feedback of a maternal medium now draws from the father function. The curse has run its course of fulfillment when mother's son sucks the blood of the father. The son commits suicide. Both bodies are cremated. The story lowers the doom into the grave.

LECTURE EIGHT

Friedrich Wilhelm Murnau's *Nosferatu* was the first film in the genre to cast doubles of Stoker's novel to do the new medium's stunts. Horror was seen first in films based on *Dr. Jekyll and Mr. Hyde*; even the film Murnau made right before *Nosferatu* was a Jekyll and Hyde movie, titled *Janus Face* (which also counted as Bela Lugosi's first time in pictures). The earlier candidate for projection, *Dr. Jekyll and Mr. Hyde,* is a story of doubling gone out of control because, by uncontrollable chance, it had been turned on not by the known formula but by some foreign body, the unreconstructable ingredient in the potion or drug. The doubling trick was something that film kept turning, that kept film turning. Even the first *Frankenstein* film portrayed the monster as the double of Victor Frankenstein. Literature, which is where the phantasm of the double used to be at home, say, in the eighteenth and nineteenth centuries, during the opening era of the uncanny, suddenly released the double and no longer featured it. At the same time film and psychoanalysis were the two new institutions that began attending to the double feature. The phantasm of the double split to another medium (to the first techno mass medium) and to a science (a science of techno media).

Freud first addressed the double while attending the opening up of the soldier psyche broken down by shell shock during World War I. Freud saw the incapacitating symptoms as referring to an internal conflict between two egos, the peace ego and its "uncanny double," the war ego. Freud follows this splitting into his second system, where they are renamed ego and superego. In the essay "On The Uncanny," which also follows the split Freud observed in symptomatizing soldiers, Freud refers to the self-observation or doubling of the ego as one of the sources of the uncanny. And he follows Otto Rank's lead and points out Stellan Rye's film *The Student of Prague*, the primal screen of doubling, which was released just in time for the Great War, during which for the first time, at least in theory, trauma was technologized and internalized as a force of replication. Narcissism was the final frontier Freud opened up through the inside viewing of the uncanny soldier psyche. The war showed Freud the way that traumatic wounding places the ego in double jeopardy by striking the register of narcissism or self-esteem, which gets reformatted in military terms as group morale and gadget love. The war shock of injury or loss that can contain itself only through symptom formation and repetition follows the dotted fault lines to the other shocking moment of intake, that of primal repression, which, Freud states universally, no one gets around, the instance of separation from the mother's body. The study of the double relation thus soon entered the science or institution of military psychology (ranging from absorption of shock on one side and infliction of shock on the other side via psychological warfare). As occult relation, doubling was taken up by the societies of occult research, which expanded double time after World War I, motivated in large measure by the desire on the part of individual adherents or researchers to contact missing sons. Leaders of this expanding science or institution of occult studies contacted Freud on several occasions in the hope of setting up diplomatic relations and immunities between their respective efforts. At the same time, American and German film productions or projects sought collaboration with psychoanalysis, even on films in which psychoanalysis would be illustrated, and thus the new alliance between film and Freud's science advertised. Freud said no, double no. But not because he did not believe in the close connections among all these media and mediums. Murnau entered the stage of theatricality and Oedipus pre-war through a break with his father, which he sealed with the name change to Murnau. Between the staging of a name change and his assumption of film directorial duties there was his tour of duty in the Great War. A few months after his true love died on the Russian front, Murnau took to the skies of the new air force. There he discovered artificial flight as a new manner of perception tried and tested in the lab experiment of the new techno war. Film alone could realize this motion through and across the image. Apparently during his time as a POW in Switzerland, following landing his plane this side of neutrality, he began the ground work for his postwar aerodynamic and cinematic POV by participating in propaganda filmmaking for the German side. I guess a Swiss miss was not the same as landing on the side of the enemy.

The modernist villa in *The Black Cat* is constructed right on top of the crypt of the lost war; the whole unburial plot is still undermined, its detonation only held back. But in place of the long-range guns, the turrets hold mummified women held upright in their Snow White coffins. Inside the traumatized psyche, then, we discover a narcissistic wounding in the relationship to one's own body, which is always also the relationship to the missing body of mother, so near but so far away. All long-range or long-distance relations include the long distant, the undead contents of one's internalization and doubling of traumatic impact, which in fact time travels back to the most primal settings of separation. As Boris Karloff comments to Bela Lugosi when the American announces the sudden breakdown of all access to the outside world, whether by car or telephone, "Do you hear that, Vitus, even the phone is dead."

Earlier Karloff, the architect of the encryptment of the lost-war setting, encouraged the war-neurotic Lugosi, who returns to this site of his own traumatic scene, to view them not as a couple of interpersonal combatants but as a couple of "living dead" leftovers of one-and-the-same catastrophe. The war ego tries to hide his advantage in a postwar era of unmourning. But the peace ego will prove him right by consummating their relationship in a double death that releases the American couple on a honeymoon to the outside of the encryptment they already represented. The husband is a writer of mysteries, a graduate of the Oedipus complex. And even though the wife falls victim to the accident that overturns the taxi and kills the driver, and forces the couple to stay at the villa (where she goes "mediumistic" for a spell upon returning to consciousness), she is also on her way, inside her couple, to meet up with her parents in Vienna.

In *Universal Soldier* the traumatic flashback is to women and children, which is where peace ego and war ego forever part company and lock their double beams onto one track of internal and eternal conflict. Because they would not listen, the war ego wears the ears of his civilian victims: they are all "motherfucking traitors" who deserve to die. The two egos kill each other in combat. But then technology saves them, rewires them, for maternal rescue operations. But when peace ego on a rescue mission sees the hostages, he flashes back to the primal scene of the conflict, and the war ego catches on, in a flash, too. The reporter, who has been fired, humiliated, caught in the cross fire, and who then can be redeemed, complete with her new woman mediatization (when we see her through the TV camera we have reentered the techno POV of the two recycled MIA), presents the outside chance that can differentiate the age of motherfucking treason. But she gives up safety and in a sense sacrifices herself to join the peace ego in surviving the all-out conflict with the war ego. The rewired psycho sarge, who is again all ears, pursues peace ego to his home, thus bringing the lost war home to the home front, home on the firing range. The reporter survives to cover the rerelease of the lost war, making the film the projection reclaimed under her direction.

Witness the vampire always rising up out of his secret crypt in centuries-long anticipation of the film medium, where the sensurround of his unrepresentability fills the screen of doubling. Vampirism in Murnau's film makes ghost appearances as the ultimate double of the film medium. Most dramatically, you will have noticed, but always only when it is ready to cross over into the spirit realm, we see the film (at the same time revealed as medium) go out of control. We see Nosferatu's carriage lurching and jumping forward; we see the film reverse dark and light, negative and positive. The moving picture loses control: but once we get this jolt in the eye, we see better that we are crossing over into some unheard of, some unrepresentable realm, which is none other than that of the film medium. If we are reminded that this is a film, that someone has edited out shots to create that jumpy, lurching motion, and that some-one has treated the film in the lab photochemically in order to reverse light and dark, then we are led to an inside view of medium and vam-pire as occupying interchangeable places. So, when the film reminds us that it is an artificial product put together in laboratories, by editors and other technicians, the unrepresentable somehow gets represented. That is when, when the film seems to go out of control, the "Land of the Phantoms" comes into focus.

But what the first film version of the vampire phantasm also intro-duces, on the sidelines of unrepresentation, is the doubling of Harker's bride-to-be as the photo-portrait he carries with him, which further dou-bles as point of first contact with the vampire. As soon as the Count catches sight of the miniature, it locks him onto its long-distance beam. He is willing to give his eyeteeth to look upon her face-to-face, window-to-window, image-to-image. And he wants to get to gnaw her better. Who else is on eye beam and food drive? That's right, baby. Nina, as image, has been exchanged between the two signatories as though part of the deal they seal.

Nina sees one specter in the Count, on the side-effect lines drawn around her couple, which even across the long distance of a breakup or separation she would save in a warning shout she sends Jonathan's way. But the Count is in the way. Jonathan has met someone else in the person of the Count on whom he counted for delivery from the couple and from Nina's telepathy strings, which get tied instead around her own bond with the vampire. In "The Taboo of Virginity" Freud argues that when the marriage is in crisis, the wife encounters in her husband the same problems she is still having with her mother, while the husband meets up with problems he never stopped having with his father now arrayed along the dotted lines of separation and estrangement from his wife. Observe the way the marriage of Jonathan and Nina is set up and set in motion right from the start of the movie. Nina is always shad-owed by a kind of melancholic anticipation of what is to come. It is not just that she is a telepathic long-distance medium that picks up all the signals of danger, but she is set in grief-stuck contrast to Jonathan, who is such an airhead. He rushes back home all excited that he is going to be gone for several months, without realizing that the future plan he is sharing with her counts her out. So, for Jonathan this trip—which, as we have come to recognize it, is also always into his interior—seems necessarily to be a journey away from marriage. This is repeated in Werner Herzog's *Nosferatu* remake. Right from the start, I think, the partners in the couple are shown in both *Nosferatu* movies to be on different wavelengths. There is something wrong with their marriage; whatever it is, it gets represented by or as vampirism. Let's keep in mind—or let's remember to forget—that in Romanian *nosferatu* is the name of a type of vampire specializing in making husbands impotent.

In her sleepwalking telepathic state, Nina cries out to warn Jonathan. The subtitles in the Murnau film are curiously one-sided on that score, but if you *look* at the film, it is not at all clear that Jonathan hears her and is warned; in fact, at the other end of the telepathic relationship, at the other end of the line, it is the Count who pricks up his ears and picks up the signal, and who instantly turns away from Jonathan (more or less instantly) and starts packing for his trip to Bremen.

Also, as the Count approaches Bremen, on parallel tracks with Jonathan, the film is ambiguous about whom she means when she is rushing out to meet "him" ("I am expecting his arrival"), or when later on in the film she stitches, embroiders, in German, "I love you" on her pillow. The pronouns in the titles do double duty.

Jonathan goes for the incarnation of the blood bond away from marriage with the wife, with the law of the couple, which is the law of the father. He enters the solitary bond of group-centered or mother-centered consumerism and connection. But what he meets up with is the primal father, to whom all exchange of property, from the proper name to all women by proxy, is owed. When the wife tries to save her marriage, her primalized delegate, the father Count, hears her. But then she encounters in the Count, in the place of her estranged husband, the primal mother and medium.

What, finally, do Nina and Nosferatu have in common? The exchange scene gives it all away. Both are images animated by the same orbit, the same holding pattern, the one that has been running circulation and exchange into the unburial ground. The Count's just another motion picture looking for the way out of yet another release on undeath. Nina too, in the exchange scene, comes into focus as the image that has changed hands, an image that, in exchange, leaves her out of the picture. She makes her move after reading the vampire book, the self-sacrifice manual. She takes the how-to lesson to heart and consummates a relationship she has already enjoyed long distance with the Count, bringing it to the conclusion that takes them both out of circulation. This suicide pact between the woman and the vampire plays to the sacrificial assignment that was mission impossible for the German home front during World War I. Murnau allows the image and blood drives to converge in a scene of super savings that cleanses the communion and community of the bad blood from the Eastern plague.

If we examine *Nosferatu* now on two counts, we must psychologize (indeed, group-psychologize) where before we technologized. I am talking about Herzog's 1979 remake of *Nosferatu,* which right away confronts us with its post–World War II take on vampirism: the film opens with its internal scan of a crypt crowded with mummified victims that double as snapshots of a disaster, the stills that the film will reanimate. It is clear that these mummies are unmourned — without the cover or rest-in-peace of burial. One can see by their death-mask expressions (and expressionisms) of horror that they are the unburied body count of catastrophe. Disaster, which befalls the entire group of casualties at the same time, synchronizes death and builds the other group of survivors out of the state of preparedness that also gets turned on by disaster. Group psychology is our shock absorber; it gives us consumer projection, I mean protection. Like the disappearance of the sailors at sea during Nosferatu's journey to Germany, which in both *Nosferatu* films puts through a direct connection to all those soldiers missing in action, this crypt sequence foreshadows the catastrophe that will plague Wismar (the place name that resonates with Weimar).

These mummies are part of the fantasy of undeath, the inert part that the fantasy covers up with the jolts of reanimation. They are immediately juxtaposed to Lucy's horrified awakening—as though they formed the content of her dream vision. Lucy's scream is amplified by whatever plugs her into this crypt of unmourning. The bat we next watch travel forward in slow motion establishes a connection that is really a return. This missing link that is up to bat invites us to view Herzog's version as Lucy's dream.

Jonathan goes for the outside chance of splitting Wismar, the place where the "canals flow around and back into themselves." In Transylvania Jonathan's head shoots up in a salute of recognition when Nosferatu lets him know just how wearying it all is, what they call everyday life, when put to the test of countless centuries ("Can you imagine enduring the centuries and each day expecting the same futilities?"). Nosferatu advertises being alone with one's thoughts. It is an aloneness that is at the same time a syndication of group membership. While waiting his turn to lead the support group, Jonathan identifies with the solo status enjoyed by the leader and the pack. He is the group of one. Cut off from postal circulation in Transylvania, he is alone with his thoughts, which he confides to his diary, *the* group psychological outlet.

Lucy is the wife. As the protector, thus, of the couple (and of the law of the father), she must defend her marriage against the group-psychological pull and appeal of vampirism. To protect Jonathan (or lock him in place), she surrounds him with pieces of holy consecrate. But even this ring of communion left over from the marriage bond cannot stop him from riding off to the next town to spread the plague of vampirism. There is a double survival at the end of Herzog's film. On one side, it is the survival of the society of Wismar, represented as a recycling center that already on its own keeps bringing back what was set aside for the disposal. On the other side, there is vampirism; the two, as though they were collaborators, survive at the end of the film.

It is time to point to a certain difference Herzog lays on the figure of Lucy (this is how Herzog renames Mina or Nina). That is, not only does she have this powerful bond with vampirism, but the bond also goes beyond what is merely symptomatic or projective. Unlike anyone else in Wismar society, Lucy is capable of believing or acknowledging what she sees right before her. She confronts the opinion or nonbelief of those around her:

> "You've read Jonathan's diary—you have seen it with your own eyes."
> "I have an inner knowledge. I believe what I see with my own eyes."
> "Faith is the amazing faculty of man which enables us to believe things which we know to be untrue."

It is as though vampirism or, for that matter, Nazism can take over because belief is always stronger than knowledge. Required to believe only what is believable, you cannot acknowledge or know even what you see before you. Belief always also means public opinion, means journalism, means newspaper reports, means you only know what the other's inquiring mind thinks you know. So, even though the Nazi party was completely open about its intentions, about what it was going to do— it held nothing in reserve or under cover—it was that very openness that also gave it ultimate protection. Lucy recognizes vampirism and will not deny what she sees (and therefore believes) in the typeface and blinding flash of public opinion. What she is up against can be seen when Jonathan in Transylvania decides to go on his own to keep his appointment with Nosferatu: he asks for a carriage with horses or just for a single horse, and the coachman stands there and says, "I don't see a horse," or "I don't see a coach." This business of being able not to see what is manifestly there is a kind of societywide repression or conspiracy that Lucy pretty much alone sees through. All this, contained in her dream, loops us back to her warning waking shout. Not see? Nazi!

LECTURE NINE

Music has a long-standing score to settle with the visual media, in particular with the movies, which started out silent, with music in the background "covering" sound. Even Murnau's *Nosferatu* was subtitled *A Symphony of Horror*. The crossover into the "Land of Phantoms" forces entry of visibility into spheres and fear of the invisible. Thus, the professor looks through a microscope to behold the polyp blown up out of invisibility and identifies it for his students as "almost a phantom."

Points can be made and gained about music claiming one sense for haunting as opposed to another. It is as though the media had all along been competing for the place of the unrepresentable, the last of the phantoms. But when it comes time to represent the unrepresentable, one sense is cut off, shut down, so that in its place hallucinations can be released. If there are zoning regulations for the different senses, then they say hearing must be situated close to the unconscious, since the ear is one sense organ that just cannot be closed. We cannot help but hear. But with vampirism we have to start our genealogy of the senses all over again — from scratch and sniff.

Smell brings us closest to the other. The other penetrates you where it gets the most personal. The smell is what goes most rapidly the way of the repressed; that is why at the tail end of civilization's progress we are all not only deathless but also odor-free. That is why smells are always attributed to those who are under societywide repression — of the body. The vampire's chief attribute, when all else is played, seen, heard, said, is that whiff that gets us closer to the origin, the blood bond with mother, and thus with the body.

Freud argues that all civilization can be seen to begin with man's assumption of the upright posture. Before then, when he was on all fours, he was more closely linked to the sense of smell, and his behavior followed the seasonal, rhythmical pattern of mother's menstrual cycle. Once he assumed the upright posture, man also put on display for the first time the whole hard body, which gave rise to a new visual overstimulation of sexual appetite that henceforth was always on. For that reason the family became necessary because you had to have a constantly available outlet for your sexuality. The emergence of the family has everything to do with the shift away from the sense of smell to the visual sense. Vampirism comes from the repressed realm of smell — from the mother on all fours.

This range of the sensuous brings us to the living end of Stoker's psyche, the story called *The Lair of the White Worm*, with which he signs off. But first we hold on to the stability of a narrative frame and of a family tradition or transmission. Great-Uncle Salten contacts his great-nephew Adam, who lives in Australia, to book their advance preview of the delegation between them. The transmission is Oedipal-static-free. But the great-uncle has been clinging to the end of the line ever since he read the news of Adam's historical research interests with their specific focus on the Roman culture of Britain, the precise mixture, too much by half, of the populace of their ancestral region in what was once known as Mercia. The Salten duo joins the president of the local archaeological society in meeting the challenge of two villains. Edgar Caswall, public enemy number one, arrived in the area at the same time as the Saltens to claim an inheritance that has reached him only by default, complete with tower in the plains view of sky and land. Caswall embodies one of the local strains others are under: he has the Roman look of willpower that has been fortified with occult awareness of how to rule everybody everywhere within hypnotic range.

At the homegrown end of the evil that is upon them there is Lady Arabella March, who is one part society vamp, while the other, greater part goes to the white worm, which comes in and out of its mysterious orifice deep inside the earth with no soul and no morals (and no clothes on). Through their scientific study of metabolism and evolution the ghostbusters come to view the Great White Worm as having, over time, exchanged much of its size for intellectual growth, thus producing, with Lady Arabella at the front of the line, " 'a new class of creature' ": " 'a force which can think, which has no soul and no morals, and therefore no acceptance of responsibility' " (129). But how to kill the snake or devil that is also a woman with legal and property rights? " 'I never thought this fighting an antediluvian monster would be such a complicated job. This one is a woman, with all a woman's wit, combined with the heartlessness of a *cocotte*' " (133). The Lady is a snake, and she leaves fang marks on the necks of children. But how do they know? " 'I feel convinced that the marks on the child's throat were human — and made by a woman' " (60). It is time once more for the magic act of sawing the new woman in half, the better half: " 'We may get into moral entanglements; before we know it, we may be in the midst of a struggle between good and evil' " (57). The split is even easier said than done: " 'I have come to the conclusion that the foul White Worm obtained control of her body, just as her soul was leaving its earthly tenement' " (62). Her husband, Captain Marsh, was found dead, by murder or suicide, after the creature from the marsh moved into the tenement. " 'God alone knows what poor Captain Marsh discovered — it must have been something too ghastly for human endurance, if my theory is correct that the once beautiful human body of Lady Arabella is under the control of this ghastly White Worm' " (62). The Marsh name or legacy has come down to the woman on all fours crawling out of the literalized word in the name, which re-fuses the name.

The fantasy set up at this end of Stoker's writing (syphilis led the way) is pretty recognizable; indeed, the good guys, the busters in this case, have it easy. But they must take out the other outpost of evil, the tower Edgar Caswall electrifies. He comes to madness with one-on-one mesmeric or hypnotic powers that, for him, are a natural; not only are they called part of his racial inheritance, but they also come complete with Mesmer's own treasure chest, which has been handed down the family line.

There are also two good girls, whose hypnotic powers of resistance are also all-natural. One, Lilla, has to go. The one with staying power, Mimi, lets flash the current of love between her and Adam, a safety zone or circuit breaker within a setting overcharged with electricity: "Some sort of electricity flashed — that divine spark which begins by recognition, and ends in obedience. Men call it 'Love'" (35). The new woman arrives and survives riding out the inoculatively insulated or quarantined force of the future of our technologization. The pecking order of a new woman's group-psychological privilege, which is also the danger she faces together with her double, is pointed out to Adam when he admits that he had instinctively defended dovelike Lilla against Caswall's hawkishness. The local archaeologist observes: "'She seems in danger, in a way, from all you young men. I couldn't help noticing the way that even you looked — as if you wished to absorb her!'" (38). She is the power pill the members, or pacmen, of the new group psychology need to swallow to win the game.

The good team drops dynamite down the worm's hole, to which tower and kite were already wired: Caswall does not know it, but his kite will ignite the dynamite (and I'm a poet). When lightning strikes, the reign of the tower comes down in the flash. While laying the detonation (they want bombs to explode), one buster gives his note of caution to Adam, who answers in giveaway juxtaposition: "'But if it has to tear down so many feet of precipice, it may wreck the whole neighborhood.' 'And free it for ever from a monster,' added Adam, as he left the room to find his wife" (157). In the flashback of incorporation we see the peristaltically released fragments, part worm, part woman, which, as a whole mass, "seemed to have become all at once corrupt" (190). The good guys go back home for breakfast, where Mimi, who is a late arrival of Mina, I guess, and a forerunner of Minnie Mouse, waits. She deserves the vacation coming soon of her honeymoon.

Ken Russell's *The Lair of the White Worm* also begins by digging archaeology, but it is already inside, and that means is going without, the uncle-to-nephew frame-up of delegations rebounding from the Land Down Under.

And where Edgar Caswall was evil by default of racial inheritance, mesmeric transmissions, and related caricature attacks that put him in the same spot the snake lady was in, Lord Danton is one of two good guys who falls for one of the good sisters. The visiting archaeologist, the just as good half, shares the goods when he falls for the other sister. It is twice the two of them against the Lady, the Snake plus however many minions can be created or, as the diagnosis goes in the film, "afflicted by a form of vampirism."

A skull ditched in Roman times belongs, if not to a dinosaur, then to some unidentified creature. One of the girls, Mary, sets off the injunction inside her name when she ribs him with what he doesn't know from Adam: "You'd think you found the missing link!" But the local celebration that same night takes better aim: a fake snakelike monster leads the "worm-dance" line across the disco floor. It is all about the Danton worm, named, like Danton Hall, where the party is going on, after Sir John Danton, the dragon killer of believe-it-or-not history.

On the way home from the party Mary fills in between jump cuts the recent or primal past: her parents disappeared last year, were swallowed up, it seems; she still can't believe they're gone. They pass a deserted house that shows signs of light. The officer called in to check it out finds the Lady of the manor back so soon. "But you don't come back till Spring." "It is Spring. Here's the first swallow" (and she gulps down her brandy).

When the Lady visits the dig, she picks up, writhing and lisping with a reptilian measure of pleasure, the mystery skull. As she passes the crucifix in the hall on her way out, she goes completely snakelike, hissing and spewing venom through sudden fangs onto X marks the spot. When the other sister, Eve, takes a wipe at the slime on a cross, she gets a shock from first contact and goes into hallucinatory scenes of live crucifixion rising above nuns getting gang-banged by Roman soldiers out of habit.

Before Lord Danton arrives at the Lady's home to pay a visit of introduction, she has already given the teen hitchhiker she picked up a bite job in her hottie tub; his paralyzed form waits in the ready position for the privilege of dying that the god may live. But when it is Lord Danton at the front door, she tidies up what she bit by pushing the poor stiff under see-ing level (she tells him she is actually doing him a favor). So Lady tells it like it was when the Lord asks if she has any children: "Only when there are no men around." But when she can tell that she almost deep-froze the Lord with another Oscar Wilde quote (there is always one Wilde quote too many), she lies and cries through her teeth: "I loathe snakes." Then, the Lord wants to know, why does she play the Snakes game (the board game she was playing with the hitchhiker before she offered him a bite)? "It's a compul-sion. I'm a bit of a schizophrenic." "You'd have to be to play the Snake game by yourself." The power of psychobabble, a force that is otherwise with us, can be annoying when it is so near missing its definitions. But perhaps that is the preconscious understanding of psychoanalysis already preprogrammed in our mass culture. Any Ken Russell film is psychoanalysis saturated, though no more so than the advertisements of fashionism that libidinize what ter-rifies us most, even or especially along the cutting edge of castration.

That night the Lord has a dream that travels the heir waves. He boards a plane: Lady and the two sisters are stewardesses (there to serve him). An older, paralyzed woman is force-fed during the meal service. She is the missing mother. The missing father is also there, clutching his watch. Stew-ardess Lady and stewardess Eve fight it out in the galley while the Lord sig-nals that he is holding an erection. Father gets up and walks down the cabin aisle. When the dreamer wakes up, he suddenly recognizes the cave that opened unidentified onto his in-flight dreaming. He forms a search party with the archaeologist and the two good girls. The party goers band together and bandy about around the group bond of replication, their se-cret identification with the worm. "What happens to a worm cut in two!?" "That was a long time ago." "No time at all in archaeological time!" "Satis-fied?" "Penis envy?!" "Figure was a hermaphrodite. Could satisfy itself like an earthworm." The Lord, the embodiment of heir power across same-name relations, concludes that the watch, the one memento linking the search party to the missing parents, was what was left over and out after the snake digested the rest of father.

Now that her dad is shit, Eve is on the run, but the run is in the Lady's stalking and capture of her for virgin sacrifice. It is the snake god after all that reused tick-tock technology, like the crocodile in Peter Pan, to remind her of what she lost when the shit hit her father's biggest fan. While investigating the Lady's lair (under the cover of snake-charming music), Mary finds her mother there watching TV, but Mary only interrupts mom's rapt attentiveness to the tube, and even though or especially because the whole scene is a rerun, mother fixes the span of her fangs on Mary. Fangs for the memories!

Back in Danton Hall the mother as snake attacks the Lord while the Lady turns off the sound system blaring the charming music. Lord cuts the missing mother, who has half a mind to bite him too, in two. The archaeologist comes to the rescue playing bagpipes. Lady, who was wearing earplugs, breaks through the holding pattern. But the archaeologist shoots himself up with the antidote.

For her role as high priestess at the sacrifice, Lady wears a mega-dildo while preparing the virgin appetizer. But she cuts the first course short of all formalities when she sees the snake prematurely shooting up the hole. The archaeologist substitutes the Lady for Eve in the fast-food chain of being a snake, and then throws in a hand grenade as digestif. But just when he thought it was safe to go under the fang, the archaeologist gets a call from the nurse: sorry, the antidote he picked up was filled with the wrong prescription. No paternal antibody in this movie. Archaeologist and Lord drive off into the setting son of the Danton line. Lord says, "Let's stop for a bite." "Why not?" I mean, at these points. They didn't shoot up the messenger. Not with father. The mother's pricks of undeath remain the last and lasting intake.

Going down with syphilis, Stoker comes up with the big stink, the invasive otherness, that gives the spots the worm puts us in, and piles up the layered look of historywide and societywide phantasm-delegations:

It was like nothing that Adam had ever met with. He compared it with all the noxious experiences he had ever had—the drainage of war hospitals, of slaughter-houses, the refuse of dissecting rooms. None of these was like it, though it had something of them all, with, added, the sourness of chemical waste and the poisonous effluvium of the bilge of a water-logged ship whereon a multitude of rats had been drowned. (116)

Syphilis and the plague were the two epidemics occupying the transition from the Middle Ages to modernity. Syphilis, which was introduced by the returning Spanish conquerors of the New World, continued to migrate from west to east, which is why each European country gave it the name of the neighboring nation on the western border. The plague, a disease of rodents, covered the continent in periodic waves, displaced with regard to changes in the population density of rats and mice. Not until the end of the nineteenth century did the plague make it to America: by then there were ships that could cross the Atlantic in fewer than forty days, in less time than the period of quarantine that the Venetian authorities had been the first to implement.

In this field of transmissions something new emerged in the 1980s. Because with AIDS everything was different. The spread of the disease did not follow recognizable spatial coordinates or temporal laws. It was there, ubiquitous and omnipresent, and yet at the same time seemed to delimit and target certain marginal groups: drug addicts, homosexuals, prostitutes, and vampires. On August 15, 1989, *Weekly World News,* one of those papers you check out while stocking up for feeding time, ran headlines on the front page next to Lugosi's Dracula grimace: "AIDS is killing off the world's vampires!" The story on page 9, decorated with "Deadly disease beats out wooden stake as Dracula's #1 killer!" and "This virus scares the 'undead' worse than a sunny day, say experts," runs its commentary as follows:

> The world's last vampire hunter has closed the doors of his offices in London and Vienna forever. The reason: The AIDS epidemic has wiped out almost all the vampires in Europe!
> "As late as 1979, Europe had the greatest vampire infestation in its history," Professor W. H. van der Moer said. "Today, less than a few dozen survive, and most of those have fled to the Soviet Union where the incidence of AIDS is less than in western Europe."

The NEWS reported in the mid-80s that the incidence of reported vampire attacks was decreasing at an incredible rate.

And Professor van der Moer agrees that the decline in the vampire populations dates from the middle of this decade.

"The undead were hard hit by the AIDS virus," he said. "Some of the old ones, like the retired 'priest' who lived in the West End of London, had lived for over 1,000 years.

"But even they could not withstand the virus.

"It killed them as surely as a stake through the heart, or getting caught in the sunlight."

Professor van der Moer says the vampire population of Europe, by his calculations, declined from a high of 1,035 males and 679 females in July 1979, to a total today of 18 males and a lesser, but unknown, number of females.

He says the easy availability of drug addicts and male and female prostitutes made them the natural prey of vampires.

"Unfortunately, their natural prey also were the highest risk group as far as catching AIDS was concerned," Professor van der Moer explained.

Professor van der Moer said vampires have been a fact of European life since the Dark Ages — a 1,200-year tradition that seems rapidly to be ending.

"Where there are no vampires, there are no vampire hunters," the 78-year-old Oxford graduate said.

"Like the undead I once hunted, I am the last of the breed.

"The world will never see our like again."

A spokesman in the Soviet Embassy in Washington, D.C., declined to comment on the vampire population of Russia.

Media, AIDS, drugs are three stations of our crossover into live or life transmission. The bio-transmission of drugs goes back to long-standing occult techniques of self-realization and pleasure: medicine men, magicians, and physicians influenced their intake, course, and elucidation. The practice of these paternal "pushers" remained for a long time secret and regional. Not until the second half of the twentieth century were drugs ready for global transmission and in all the right senses: as knowledge, substance, inheritance, addiction.

Vampire fictions and phantasms are along for the live transmission of the epidemic end products of one genealogy of circulation we, needless to say, shared with vampirism. It is all about the T-Cell Count. Brian

Stableford's "The Man Who Loved the Vampire Lady" goes back to the seventeenth century, the source of circulation, and fantasizes an era loaned to the vampiric other, the recycler and transistorizer of every invention away from its point of impact with intervention or change and back onto the tracks of identification. The vampires are beginning to fear the humans, what with "all this play with lenses" that is being shown off and that comes to the point of focus with the microscope (65). The vampires, who see what's at stake, prepare for the removal of the new sight. The bottom line that humanity holds down in the evolutionary race between occult and technological media guarantees that we will leave the vampires behind at their finish line. "Humans remain the true masters of art and science which are forces of change. They've tried to control that — to turn it to their advantage — but it remains a thorn in their side" (65). Now with the microscope the bodily fluids (and with them the boundaries of the proper body or between life and death) reverse the covers of invisibility and give the inside view of vampirism as blood disease: "I think vampirism may be a kind of disease — but a disease that makes men stronger instead of killing them" (66). Vampirism is transmitted through the blood contact sports of sucking and sex: vampire women do not give it to their human lovers (and humans must, by law, never drink the blood of the vampires), nor do vampire women regularly reproduce vampire children. Vampires are always "converts." The women who loved vampire men tend to become vampires. Vampire men, and there are way fewer of these around, are created by men through anal intercourse. This is how the legacy begins: Attila, that hon, gives it to his male friends. Heterosexuality spreads around the original male-to-male transmission. This is the desublimated version or prehistory of the father-and-son transmission framing and filling the story. It is the Laius chip off the old complex, but running way before it was converted into family housing.

The father is court mechanician and is also the longtime lover of the vampire lady, who will soon age him out of her eternal regard. The son is heir to the mechanician position and possible replacement of his father's role in the vampire lady's unlife. What lies between father and son, alongside the transmission of name or knowledge, is the same-sex, same-blood literalization of this adoptive bonding via the missing mother, whose place is held by the outlet between them of vampirism. Self-sex or same-sex designates the original rapport with the missing mother. But the son, upon learning of the primal scene of modern institutions, as organized between the vampires and us, gives the oedipedagogical response: "An expression of disgust crossed the boy's face" (67).

The microscope shows the disease workings of vampirism's black magic and thus the primal, desublimated, unprotected view of male-to-male transmissions backed up against a scene packed with the body and blood of mother. At the same time a plague is spreading from Africa sight unseen that has the power to kill even vampires. As the defender of knowledge's transmission — the sublimated circuit from male to male — the mechanician infects himself with the African disease and carries it to his Vampire Lady. The live transmission beaming the invisible up into the all-visibility that media technologization has begun to advertise holds interchangeable places with the liveness that is now available through the blood's circulation: the live transmission of disease. The vampire's greatest fears are being realized: a new fraternal or group order (as distinguished, in other words, from a patriarchal, parental, or couple-to-couple organization) will emerge in sync with the extension of the senses through technologization. Death itself will have been transformed: it too will be transmitted live, and not even the vampire, outmoded incarnation or limit concept of life and death, can tune it out. The mechanician sums up the conclusions coming soon: "There is the Fraternity, which is dedicated to your destruction; there is a plague in Africa, from which even vampires may die; and there is the new sight, which renders visible what previously lurked unseen" (75). Vampires understood that the otherwise imperceptible creatures inside our fluids carry illness from person to person, but they overlooked the missing link and mediation of technology. Ships arriving from Africa are quarantined to guarantee that the person-to-person connection is not put through. But the Fraternity has bagged the rats, those original totem figures of father that, via their link and stand-in role in the laboratory service of an experimentally escalated evolution of the human species, are by now the mascots of team efforts (like Mickey Mouse). They can carry disease without dying of it. The new sight has put through the missing link. The Fraternity recognized that rats, in sum, recorded and stored the disease. The mechanician goes from rat bite to his vampire lover's sucking. Through his premier or pioneer sacrifice, the Fraternity has thrown the invention — of a new disease — into the evolutionary cycle to see what comes out in the wash.

It is conceivable that everything we think we know about AIDS will prove false. But all those discursive and institutional interventions that went, hit or miss, with the disease's cure or containment are here to stay. When Adrien Proust, author Marcel's father, discovered the plague bacillus, the epidemic effect of the disease had already been brought under control. But the medical and state provisions and preventive measures developed to combat the disease were still in place and in practice: passport control, the census, and state superintendence of physicians and hospitals or lazarettos (named after the island in the Venice lagoon where the disease was to be kept under quarantine).

LECTURE TEN

I read a story in the *Santa Barbara News-Press* that confirms some of the reservations I have been making with regard to phantasms of vampirism and the different kinds of circulation connected with the same non-life. The headline reads, "Postman stored three tons of mail in home":

> Mail carrier John Cade lived in a labyrinth of more than two tons of undelivered junk mail, magazines and letters that he stacked in his ranch home in Boulder, and postal inspectors can't imagine why. Cade, 36, moved into his home in 1984 and apparently started hoarding the mail shortly thereafter. He lived in the house with a cat, some kittens, two ferrets, a boa constrictor and the 6,555 pounds of mail. Postal inspectors who seized the mail last week had to pick their way through corridors of mail stacked in every room. "It was in the bedrooms, the den, the living room, the kitchen, the bathrooms, the basement, in closets, underneath boards — it was everywhere," said postal inspector Jerry Sandhagen.
>
> Cade's bed was surrounded by stacks of mail and the bedroom was strewn with open magazines. . . .
>
> Mail was heaped on the kitchen counters, on top of the refrigerator and overflowing the table. Piles of mail in the yard were used as a backdrop for Cade's archery target, Sandhagen said. The mail included some first-class personal mail, but most was bulk mail. It included stacks of the Boulder Daily Camera, People magazine, catalogs and samples of Prell shampoo and Cascade detergent.
>
> Uncounted would-be millionaires lurk in the bundles of undelivered entries for Publisher's Clearinghouse Sweepstakes.
>
> "We've never encountered anything like this," Morris said. "The postal service needs for the public to believe in it. We can't explain it, and we feel shocked by it."

The Greek god Hermes was the first postman, the first circulator of post, who, when he arrived on his own, brought you the news of your own death. His was thus the first live transmission. His message survives, but in the same time it takes to stay annihilation, it is shadowed, over-shadowed by the death or death wish it passes through, surrounds, and contains. When you send a letter, you already survive yourself as the other you double as: you know where the other lives (station identification). Hermes was also known as a deceiver, a trickster, someone two-faced. As soon as we get into the realm of telecommunications, we face the prospect of death, loss, the post — which means of course the past, the place of loss, of nonretrievability — but also a place of deception and espionage. Arminus Vambery (who is cited in *Dracula* on first-name basis) was not only an expert in the occult and the matching "Oriental" cultures, but at the same time was also a spy for Britain (and Stoker's good friend). He was professor at the University of Budapest, but while he was on location in the Orient he was also collecting information for the British secret service. Back in London, he would appeal to the British authorities that they consider making saving interventions in the su-perstitious East.

Jonathan's trip to and through Transylvania is already something of a fact-finding mission. When he runs up against the vampire, who shuts down postal access, Jonathan is already making his diary entries in shorthand, that is, in code. (Already at this stage the skills of the New Woman or techno feminist have entered the husband's C.V. and now come out to counter the vampire.) Everything we have said about the meeting of man's media-technological range and the telepathic connec-tion that is a natural for the vampire applies to the competing coloniza-tions of long distance by espionage or psychological warfare on one side and the vampire's own diplomacy on the other. Espionage is often enough along for the blood drive in occult literature. Thomas Peckett Prest's *Var-ney the Vampire* and Hans Heinz Ewers's *Vampire* are two bookends that set off the trend. In between, Stoker introduced the rule that would from then on be binding: a vampire can enter a household by invita-tion only. There has to be an inside job that prepares the way for the vampire's entrance. We have rightly held this rule to apply to the desire inside dread. But it also covers certain diplomatic I-Spy relations. The

long distance of telecommunications has always been matched by the
long range of weapons (in fact, the media range of the sensorium is often given an advance in the war effort of overtaking the enemy by surprise). Even with the seeming accomplishment in the Persian Gulf War
of a united live transmission of video and bomb, still at some point prior
to "shoot!" or "fire!" intelligence had to be collected regarding the targets in the enemy zone. This intelligence of the other that is required in
advance of long-range relations corresponds to the invitation the vampire must wait to receive from inside the household he is into invading.

Espionage or intelligence covers the one-on-one relationship; psychological warfare provides the group psychology. Stoker's only other
vampire novel, *The Lady of the Shroud* (which is also the other novel he
wrote in his so-called *Dracula*-style of sheer citation), is far less about
vampirism than *Dracula* was, and far more about the counteroffensive
that must be set up by the Eastern European locals (with a little help
from their friend, the British gentleman-adventurer who has adopted
their country as his own) to resist the covert operations of the Turkish
Bureau of Spies. The British protagonist, who readily turns Counter Spy-
master, sets up the basic three Cs organizing the efforts of war: command, control, communications.

But the Lady of the Shroud, whom the protagonist meets in his castle at night under occult-seeming conditions (she, too, by the way, takes
her invitation ultimately from the narrator's relationship to his own dead
mother), is working overtime as part of the psychological war effort
the authorities mounted to protect the government—against the sus-
piciousness of the natives. Back in the castle he at first takes her to be a
vampire because she follows the rules: " 'she had to be helped into my
room—in strict accordance with what one sceptical critic of occultism
has called "the Vampire etiquette" ' " (76). But, undead or alive, she is
the daughter of the ruler, who is away on some top secret diplomatic
mission. Not too long ago she up and died—or so it seemed. When she
woke up from her coma after her death had already been news-flashed to
the public, it was decided that it would be too unsettling at this time of
war preparedness to reverse right away the news of her death. It is as

though the time it takes to mourn must, once begun, work itself out in any event. At least she wasn't buried alive! So she had to start impersonating a vampire: her ghost appearances at night even make it into the press. Now, the content and cause of this strategy or subterfuge bring us back to the corpus of the narrator's dead mother, where the logic of their connection is stored. But what is also important is that the parallelism of structures of psychological warfare, espionage, and the command/control/communications organization of war can be brought into focus under conditions of vampirism. Mourning keeps on making this retrograde: we are talking projection, not only the ballistic kind but also (same difference) the cannibalistic kind (the projection of death wishes).

But it all began in a past that is also the post. As soon as the first modern national postal service was introduced in Europe by the Austrian emperor, who borrowed system, clerks, and officials from Venice (where the service was already in place in smaller format), espionage was also introduced. The Venetian officials were copying down every bit of mail that looked important and sending copies back to Italy, where a whole secret service industry ran on the sale of information the Austrian emperor should have kept hidden.

To put it one last time, and looking back at the newspaper article I quoted, the postal system, like the return trip, presupposes that when I dispatch something, or when I, myself, follow that route of dispatch, there will be a return. The circle will not be broken. Of course, that very post, that very pastness, that very delay that allows for circulation can also become the crypt of the mailman's nondelivery.

The successful homecoming is what we project in one sense. Bloodsucking fits another sense of projection. What happens when Dracula makes it onto Hollywood's big screen of projection? What happens to the gadget love in Stoker's *Dracula*? Consider Tod Browning's film *Dracula*. The media-technological emphasis of Stoker's take on vampirism disappears completely, and with it, I would argue — just to give you the headline right off — the funereal or cryptological dimension too; concern with the dead and the disposal of the dead gets displaced by problems of sexual repression. If you look at the various Frankenstein and Dracula films made in Hollywood, there is always some wedding night that has been postponed by the phantasm of monstrous invasion, always some consummation or couplification that cannot be carried out because suddenly the monster has arrived. And the monster must be put to rest before the couple can be united. There is always that parting shot, that final shot of reassurance (when we see the couple united) that the phantom has indeed been put to rest. In that case the phantom would be an image or symptom of repressed sexuality; what has to be cleared up is a sexual problem between the partners, and once that is laid (and I mean laid) to rest, the couple comes complete.

Consider the changes that went into the story line before Anne Rice's novel *Interview with the Vampire* could be projected onto the screen. In the film version Louis is driven by (and the entire screen story is organized around) the untimely deaths of his wife and child. What was in the book a radically decontextualized focus, really a foreign body, namely Claudia's emergence and her melancholically explicit relationship with Madeleine, is now the adopted side effect of Louis's extended family of mourning, in which he figures as the widower of his own heterosexuality. But in the novel Louis's encounter with vampirism comes out of his brother's death. The turn to the dead wife for the new and improved occasion for going vampiric is a turn at the same time to the dead father, the guarantor that even the vampire's lips will pray to mourning's disposal service.

In Francis Ford Coppola's *Bram Stoker's Dracula* the complete series of Stoker's gadgets gets into pictures in the context or contest with Dracula's long-distance power (the evil eye beaming across the same horizon that train, shorthand, and telegraph are collapsing). But the wrap-up is brought to us by the love that comes in couples and that takes on aspects of the vampire under the wraps of the mummy phantasm (I am referring to the admixture of reincarnation).

In keeping with Stoker's undercover momentum, the loss that afflicts this couple in Coppola's version is a psychological warfare exclusive: some Turk drops out of the large-scale all-out war on the popular front of projective orientation and sends the totally deceptive news of the Prince's death to his bride, who checks out through suicide, out of this loss in the one-on-one relation. Dracula strikes back—against the heart of Christianity, and releases the blood inside the cross. The flow of this desublimation of the Christian mass surrounds the corpse of the bride and suicide while the Prince enters the vampiric mode so that he will be around when, on the mummy-phantasm track, his beloved beams back from across the centuries via reincarnation.

When the Prince first encounters Mina (the reincarnation of his suicide bride) in the streets of London, he takes her on their first date to a new invention: the cinematograph. Coppola was the first in his medium to go this far with the series of gadgets that are the centerfold-outs of Stoker's novel—all the way in fact to the introduction or internalization of his own medium. But he takes away from Mina's gadget love (she is a schoolteacher in this version, and it was Jonathan's idea that she acquire the typing in order to be addressed as skilled) and re-places it with the rebound, reincarnation-style, of the love that drove one woman to suicide and her man to vampirism. But whenever blood lust inspires the vampire, we too enter the perspective we recognized in the cinematograph scene as belonging to the shaky, sepia-tinted projections of the primal apparatus. It is the perspective Mina shares as she slides into the reincarnation ready-position. Yes, the movie is encyclopedic in its references to the vampire films that have preceded it. And the films we see flickering in the London theater include a shadow play of battle that takes us back to the start of Coppola's movie. The vampire's hunger, the slide back and forth, metamorphosis-style, on the evolutionary scale, and the phantasm of reincarnation are contained in the range of visibility released by the new cinematographic medium.

Evolution admits the power of repeated accident, trauma, or invention. All that is missing in a theory of links across time and the borders between species is the link: the missing link is the monster at the heart of evolutionary speculations, which always admit technologization. The monster is beamed up as a traumatized hybrid—the monsters are us—produced inside some techno lab. As soon as Darwin's theories were out, their fans were hit by fantasies of evolution's extension to the machine world: we were thus the reproductive organs of the machines that were the developing units of our evolutionary history. Cyborg fantasies tell it like it is: we together with our machines form one body organized and disbanded by the live transmissions — of drugs, technology, and disease. In Van Helsing's lecture on epidemiology we hear that Christianity was a setup to defend against diseases of blood and sex through an inoculative treatment that could only backfire: Van Helsing refers to the spread of Western "syphilization." And we are given the inside view of the meeting of vampire and reincarnation when the absinthe they drink together rhymes with absence: the circulation and transmission system that is also on screen has the look of corpuscles doing overlaps with disease, vampirism, drugs, and technology.

I once read in the junk mail a therapeutically correct assessment of the bond between vampire and Mina, in Coppola's film, as classic codependency: this New Age diagnosis marks the replacement or colonization of the unconscious through the time-share everyone occupies as group-of-one and, at the same time, as member of some support group. Codependency means that everyone qualifies for the support of diagnosis, for all-out healing in groups. The group-psychology portrait is included in Coppola's film right inside the internal representation of its technical medium. The motion pictures flickering on the primal screens in Coppola's cinematography feature porno comedies that pull one over the couple by replacing the wife with an "other woman" in the husband's newfound capacity for hallucination, but then beam the wife back, superego-style, into the double occupancy that remains in this state of techno tension with the group outlet of hallucinatory consumerism of objects. It is a case of couples therapy that cinema opens and shuts, at least according to Coppola's primal-time account.

LECTURE ELEVEN

Here is a quote concerning the original reception of Tod Browning's *Dracula:* "Its success was immediate. Two years later the Count was accorded the signal honour, roughly equivalent at the time to a presentation at Court, of appearing in a Mickey Mouse cartoon" (Butler, 42).

How does the film medium press for representation in Browning's *Dracula?* What are some differences between the *Nosferatu* vampire and Bela Lugosi. Yes, Bela is way more glamorous. And it is not only that he is better looking than Nosferatu, the vampire who seems to personify every corpse's excremental survival of itself in the final bowel movement or in the continued growth of hair and nails. But Lugosi's look also involves the way he is staged. How does the vampire enter society in Browning's film? At the theater. Everything about this vampire is theatrical. So the attraction is there. His influence as vampire on his vampiroids (that's the technical term for the victims in the lexicon of vampirology) — does it travel the pathways of telecommunication or telepathy? What I would like to get at is this: never does he exercise remote control in his absence. He always "was there": which is Hollywood's addition of star aura to the vampire legend. In Stoker's *Dracula,* in *Nosferatu* too, we are used to the vampire as incarnation of telepathy or telecommunications, but here in Browning's version it is part of the Count's theatrical or hypnotic presence that he also has to be there, even if only as the bat ("My, what a big bat"). He always has to sign in within every scene that is a demo of his control; so there is a demand for his presence to be accounted for, which follows the Hollywood preoccupation with the stars upstaging any self-reflexive concern with the film medium. This is very much a film about Dracula the star, the person who always has to keep in touch with those he influences.

Lugosi's sex appeal is thus uncanny-proofed by this condition of never being out of sight, out of mind, whenever we at the same time see him do his number on the others. The light shining on his eyes reflects back the camera or projector; it is an image of the film medium that name-tags along with this nameable, identifiable actor, Bela Lugosi. Hollywood's vampirism goes for the stars, overshooting or overlooking the media-technological networkings of vampirism — or of film. And remember: the theatrical is always also the Oedipal.

Why did they put Renfield at the front of the bloodline instead of Jonathan Harker? So that everything is explained, of course. Renfield is now the naive businessman taking a trip. What is the instant impact of his being vampirized? Madness. And what is more, and for the first time in the Stoker-started Anglo-American history of vampirization, the Count, this very kinky Count, vampirizes Renfield, a man he has taken away from his "more normal" zombie brides; so there is this unbounded appetite that leads to madness, which Lugosi's Dracula embodies and advertises. He instantly vampirizes Renfield, taking him away from the three brides. In the novel the vampire followed certain rules of dating. And what makes Lugosi's castle seem so out of place in Transylvania? Like, did you notice the armadillo? I think this film does place the vampire on the Coast. The kinky Count comes from California and goes to or for an England that might as well be the East Coast. In *Dracula* the East-Coast high-strung society meets (and that means invites or projects) Californian kinkiness. (Remember the little animals in their little caskets back in the castle: it's a small world after all.) The Count is also a foreigner; remember Hollywood is the repository early on not only of Californiaization but also of foreign influence, foreign film directors, and their appetites and styles. So everything could also be read in those terms. Certainly he comes from some other place, call it California, and he embodies an appetite that produces madness. The struggle reduces itself ultimately to the one between the Count's foreign accent and the other foreign accent, the un-American one with which Van Helsing opens wide when he speaks the English. It is the accent of the East Coast psychoanalyst licensed to bust the Hollywood-European projection.

Another difference as we slide into the Hollywood films — and this difference might have been included in what I said just a heartbeat ago — is that the vampire hunters no longer belong to a societywide setting of identificatory rebirth but instead are reduced in format to fit a kind of nuclear family. There tends to be one outsider in the film — her name is Lucy — and the outsider has to go. The first sacrifice to vampirism is the outsider, who is not at all protected by father or fiancé. So it is family savings that are at stake in the Browning film, or, more precisely, it is the couple that is being delivered from everything vampirism represents.

Repression is something double, depending on how you drop it. You often get some secret pleasure out of the way you repress something. So this film is clearly all about sexuality at the same time that it warns against it. In the case of denial — I never wanted to sleep with my mother, I don't like sex — repression lets you just say no, and thus appease the inner/outer institution that tells you to repress, and at the same time it lets you name it, touch it, put it in your mouth. If you just remove the no, you of course have said what you do want, or what some part of you really wants.

When Lugosi makes his appearance in the theater, we have this wonderful situation where he announces himself as Count Dracula and the kids exchange glances (did you notice?). Anyway, he is from the start considered weird. However, on the fringe of that reception, that adolescent take on the outsider as somehow weird, there is already Lucy, the young woman unattended by her own nuclear family unit. She is the one who likes to recite poetry, especially the creepy kind. As teen outsider, she is instantly, of course, attracted to the vampire. That is why she has to go. Even when we see a policeman walking beneath her window, we know that nothing is going to protect her. She really is asking for it. And the film does not even explain whether she is ever staked. I mean, she is safer undead than alive reciting melancholic poetry and liking kinky Counts. But even though Minna, too, soon falls under Lugosi's spell, at first she is set apart from her loose friend by the saving power of resistance. She is not taken in, she claims. (It is sheer denial, in the "I don't like" sense.) When Lucy goes on about his attractions, Minna says she is not interested in the Count. Minna says she prefers "someone more normal, like John." (In Browning's take it is not Jonathan any more, it is a more normal name, like John.) Now, whatever it takes — or stakes — to prefer someone more normal like John, that is what this film is all about; it is what Minna is finally taught to do after her closet encounter with vampirism, or, by any other name, with the kinkiness associated with the Count's polymorphous appeal and appetite. But she is on her own. There is no one stopping her from going the way of the vampire, of course, because someone more normal like John does not become top preference just like that. Psychoanalysis as represented by Van Helsing helps her come around to preference for Johns — before it is too late. And Van Helsing's intervention succeeds because he alone believes in her bad dreams. John tells her to think of more cheerful things: Forget about those bad dreams. Put on a happy face. But she puts on her fangs and starts giving him the affection — the infection — John still takes to be normal necking. Heck, they're just a couple of kids in love. But Van Helsing listens to the dreams, observes the formation of hysterical symptoms, like those marks on her neck, encourages her to replay the tape of her recollection — the red eyes and so forth — and is able to tune in her troubled state. Only then can he go down into the crypt, down into the place where she is troubled or where the internal couple is under attack, and destroy the vampire. Minna is released from the spell, and she and John are reunited by the stake Van Helsing originally prepared for killing two vampires in as many blows. So at the end, the couple that has been reunited, reconstituted, walks up the stairs into the Hollywood hygienic future. Down in this basement, we have left behind Renfield (killed by the Count on his way down), the Count, the Count's control over Minna, and Van Helsing. He remains behind; that is very important. Van Helsing says: go on ahead, I have to stay behind to do something. But he too remains in the basement, and his staying behind — his staying power — has something to do with what he says earlier on in the film, that about certain kinds of knowledge it would be better for him to know and for no one else to find out. His kind of knowledge is useful up to a point, but it in turn then has to be left behind, forgotten, never known, if the couple is to make it out of the crypt. But then again the preference for "someone more normal like John," which Minna can embrace at the end, is propelled in part only by another repression. Both vampirism and what Freud called "the underworld of psychoanalysis" must be left behind. Once the foreign-accented complex has been busted, its foreign-accented cure must also be discarded.

At the end of a successful analysis, you of course leave the terminating to the analyst. What was so interpersonal about the analysis, especially in the beginning, gets left behind. The transference work lives on — on intrapsychic automatic. So Van Helsing withdraws into the couple's internal history when he says that he will remain below (just as he has always sat behind the couch of your free association). You two go on ahead. In other words there is still something that he must do, maybe cut off the head or whatever, it doesn't really matter. But it is going to be done in isolation. John and Minna are to go up alone. Remember, we already saw the group triumph in Stoker's *Dracula*; here, through the treatment by the other accented figure, this New York analyst, who at the end has to remain out of the picture if the analysis is to be considered complete, we watch the triumph of the couple.

In *Dracula, the Vampire Play in Three Acts*, we learn that the vampire has been waiting for the airplane connection and extension of the sensorium to spread to our time zone. (By the way, it is a German airplane.) But that also means that the nuclear family no longer has to travel to faraway places (as in the Stoker era) to meet up with vampirism, which is now down in the basement or in the next room. What finally caught up with the play's literal take on the techno compatibility of vampires was the more recent attempt by an airline to push back the bankruptcy that was coming soon. I quote (from the *San Francisco Chronicle*) the occult compromise between depletion of resources or reserves and the recycling of relations with the dead. Listen to the geopolitics of the same old projection. Here is the headline: "Corpses Can Earn Frequent-

Flier Awards on Eastern." And here is the scoop on traveling ghost to ghost:

> In a unique bid to win back business, strike-crippled Eastern Airlines is offering 50 percent discounts and frequent-flier awards to funeral homes that ship bodies on its jetliners. The surprising promotion is Eastern's bold attempt to pack the cargo bellies, not just the passenger seats, of its planes.
>
> "It's just a whole scheme of rebuilding an airline from scratch," a spokesman for Miami-based Eastern said yesterday. "We have been out of many markets for some time, and as we return to those markets we are using price as an incentive to get some of them back."
>
> Eastern's 50 percent offer on shipping corpses lasts until August 31, but it could be extended, the spokesman said. For example, the airline will ship a body for $287.85 from San Francisco to Miami, compared with the $393.75 charged by Delta Airlines....
>
> As part of the latest price-cut plan, Eastern is crediting funeral home operators one free mile in its "frequent-shipper bonus program" for each $1 spent on shipments. This is akin to frequent-flier clubs for passengers, which offer free trips once a certain number of miles is accumulated.
>
> Eastern was quick to note that the frequent-flier awards applied to all its cargo customers—not just funeral parlors.
>
> The airline industry recently has been in a cutthroat competition to win cargo business, and offering frequent-shipper awards is certainly one way to do it, analysts said.
>
> The industry is starting to realize that it is both economical and potentially profitable to transport freight within a hub-and-spoke network. That strategy already has been adopted by companies that fly only freight, such as Federal Express.
>
> Shipping corpses is a key part of the air freight business, one airline executive said. Unlike passenger fares, the rates for shipping bodies recently have been falling, according to Joe Lopez, an embalmer for Bryant Mortuary in San Francisco.
>
> Funeral home executives reacted coldly to the idea of trying to win their business by offering frequent-flier perks. "That seems in bad taste," one said....
>
> Not all the funeral home operators were enthusiastic about the half-off rates, either.
>
> "Sure, it's a bargain, but an airline's schedule is often what matters most," said Joe Valente, an executive at the Halsted N. Gary-Carew & English Inc. funeral home in San Francisco.

Not only flight frequency but on-time performance is crucial, said Valente, whose funeral home ships about 100 bodies a year.

Eastern now has two non-stop flights a day from San Francisco International Airport, both to Atlanta. But with a sharply curtailed schedule, its on-time record is among the industry's best.

The focus of the Anglo-American theatricalization of Stoker's *Dracula* is on madness. In Browning we are asked to look at his eyes, Renfield's eyes, which reflect back his madness and make him the double of the vampire (whose eye beams reflect back camera and projector). The audio portion is what a scream across the asylum grounds. In Hamilton Deane and John Balderston's play, Renfield is strapped to tracks parallel to the ones onto which Lucy (who has switched places with Mina, who was the expendable friend who died of the same illness that now afflicts Dr. Seward's daughter on stage) has been bound: both are saved or cured by the end. Van Helsing says when the vampire is still on his winning streak through the family: "I must be master here or I can do nothing." Once he is master, he arranges Lucy on the couch to entrap the still unidentified intruder: the patient talking and free-associating on the couch is the bait for the return of the repressed. The other trap Van Helsing sets uses Renfield, that "repulsive youth," as master's bait. Lucy is told to "make" her "mind passive"; with that she turns off her vamp behavior and goes back to being the patient who can describe the vampire's embrace. Otherwise she runs "hysterically" from the scene and leaves it up to a hysterical amalgam of "my lover, my father, my dear friend" to save her from vampirism's suction and seduction.

The play thus sets the stage in the sanatorium, which is the economy of focus it hands down to so many film versions. Lucy's "bad dreams" interrupt her upcoming bond of matrimony: she tells John that sometimes she just wants to be alone. But John is sure that the only cure that will come will be along for their honeymoon. Van Helsing's diagnosis reads vampirism, but this time around it could not be the Transylvanian brand: "I will make inquiries by telegraph. No, but after all the thing must be English.... Or at least have died here. His lair must be near enough to this house for him to get back there before sunrise" (29–30).

But after reviewing the outside chance of the Count Dracula next door being an impostor, Van Helsing reschedules the difficulties he is having: "For five hundred years he has been fettered to his castle because he must sleep by day in his graveyard. Five centuries pass. The aeroplane is invented. His chance has come, for now he can cross Europe in a single night" (42). Under the wing of the plane the Count's impostorship, passing reference to the internal theater inside Stoker, finds cover and makes the connection. Another span of wings frames the Count's postponement of his staking through two more theatrical diversions. He leaves a second sixth packing case lying around "as a blind" in one wing of the house, and he wings his power of suggestion over the servants, as in the stage direction placing Lucy's maid's exchange with the Count: "(*On a direct line with* DRACULA)" (38). But then they find the secret passageway to the basement crypt in the home, and the cover is blown. Van Helsing's solo reminder or warning to the audience at the end broadcasts a paranoid vigilance that gives shelter and rings up the group-psychological response crowding the horizon of the horror genre (I am thinking, for example, of the closing lines of *The Thing*): "There are such things."

It is hard to be too precise or choosy about the essence that fueled the writing of the Stoker novel—except maybe by playing back the effect of Stoker's fiction inside Lugosi. Lugosi could not make the divestment from his Dracula part. He wore those vestments to the living end: his final request that he be buried in his Dracula outfit was, at last, fulfilled. While making *Dracula*, Lugosi developed a big pain in his legs, which he covered with a morphine habit.

All this, I would argue, is on phantasm rebound from Stoker's own life.

Stoker had his own problems "standing upright." So did Oedipus. You know: "swollen foot." Only in the service of a theatrical (in other words, Oedipal) role or identification could Stoker stand to the tension. He was the actor Henry Irving's manager for life. They bonded over Stoker's dead faint. When Irving read aloud, at their first meeting, "The Dream of Eugene Aram" (which packs a double dose of undeath), Stoker was back in touch with the helplessness of his first seven years when he could not "stand upright": he fainted dead away. Irving handed him a freshly inscribed portrait (the signature marks the spot right next to the neck), and they were friends forever. Harry Ludlam, Stoker's biographer, comments: "They were moments of deep passion. When Bram had recovered, Irving disappeared into his room and brought out for him a photograph of himself with the inscription hastily scribbled across it, the ink still wet. . . . Something had happened that night between the two men; something that sealed a friendship till death" (44).

What does it mean to be the captive audience of your parents' bedside manner for seven years? It means that you spend the formative years of your Oedipalization locked into one position, that of the moviegoer, perhaps. On occasion little Stoker would be lifted onto his father's shoulders and taken on a minitour, or more frequently his mother was bending over him, telling him ghost stories and related inside views of horror. Live burial was a close-range analogue for his own perpetual bedtime. He would never forget how he was declared dead in childhood many times over — and out.

And finally, as you know, Freud argued that one's sexuality, which is always only an interpretation of sexuality, in other words, of something one never really knows as such, is determined by the so-called primal scene. The primal scene is always a construction or interpretation that every child has of what happens in the master bedroom (which rhymes with masturbation). That interpretation, that image, that construction, which has to be make-believe to get the picture, depends on infantile fantasies, on things heard or overheard, but not necessarily seen. Nevertheless it is the scene we make, and it has a controlling influence over our ongoing rapport with sexuality.

To come full circle, one could say about Stoker's *Dracula* that it includes a whole range of childhood (and extended or bedridden childhood) interpretations of intimate relations. Is it this gender, is it the other one? Is it bloodsucking? It is a whole fantasy of reproduction that the bedridden and bed-driven child, who was repeatedly declared dead and thus declared his own survivor, has about that other world called life and birth. It is right from the start the vampire's perspective on human intercourse.

Complete cryptological treatment requires that full-corpus immersion that does not uphold fine, upstanding boundaries between work and life. Freud's diagnosis of where the wound goes in any vehicle for wish fulfillment can be counted as another way of locating this fall of the wall: all literature having any kind of story to tell is, bottom line, trivial. On the low row, literature shows its lifelines of defense with blinding, blindering openness. That is why the transition to technologization is another easy one to make through open borders. And it works both ways. The crypt in Browning's *Dracula* is hard to make out (in part because of the theatricalization and Oedipalization that have control-released the projection from book to screen): you have to make the transition to Stoker's novel and to his life. The crypt effects that then float to the surface are the same ones Lugosi rides out.

But it is yet another film that brings the disturbance full circuit; the undead projection or ghost will in time, in turn give way to a displacement of the mourning that could never be conducted in its proper place. So when Ed Wood claimed that his post-productions filmed real life, he was right on the shifting line of that continental divide between life and work that is Hollywood. Through the cuts, stopgaps, contextlessnesses, or open wounds of Wood's corpus of projections, we follow the logic of the uncanny through the links and separations between inside and outside. It is *Plan Nine from Outer Space* that I would like to bring into focus. Even the most campy construction, as though its mobilization of immunity against the outside chance of invasion from any other dimension other than the twofold or two-faced kind amounted to an ominous denial (one that Burton's film only turns up the volume on while running it on empty), must soak up the invisible blood of a crypt transmission, the floating or flying crypt, sighted somewhere over the corpora of Stoker, Lugosi, and Wood. What makes the crowd of Oedipal plots and equally prefab unburial plots in *Plan Nine* is the accident of Lugosi's death early on in the filming. But Wood would not let go: he worked the leftover recognition value of Lugosi the vampire through to a posthumously living end. In the movie thus completed with Lugosi as lead in spite of the star's death, unused trial or stray footage of Lugosi (which has the posthumous status of every home movie) gets spliced into the makeshift plot and filled out with the continuity shooting of a body or forehead double who passes for Lugosi by keeping cape raised up to the lookalike eyes and forehead. Except for a couple of shots of the vampire's approach or stalking, there is only one full scene that appears to be part of the film's original schedule with Lugosi live: the funeral procession that has stopped short at the cemetery before the grave of the Lugosi character's dead wife. The once and future icon Vampira fills this role, whose own stolen resurrection in another life is also on the film's inner-outer schedule.

When Lugosi died, then, his or the protagonist's mourning sickness was plugged into the film posthumously by overvoicing footage of Lugosi in the front yard of his bungalow. Wood was inspired to give voice-over to images of the crypt. But the film's contradiction or discontinuity shot was always also in place: although the grieving protagonist follows his wife, who has already been reanimated according to Plan Nine, his corpse is interred above ground, in the penthouse mausoleum, the pent-up house, as outlined by the deceased's giveaway instructions, recognizably those dictated by one anticipating the return engagement of vampirism. When the beam from outer space is lowered on the dead melancholic, he is already—through the accident of Lugosi's own death—part of a series of resurrections and not the model source of nor even the diversion from the posthumous terms of haunting, which his mausoleum and recognition value have, after all, set up. The outer-space government later singles out his second resurrection as target for demonstration to the earthlings of another power—that of beam-induced instant decomposition.

We first see the beams of resurrection interrupting in-flight personnel: the air or heir waves will be cited as that which earthlings can already explode through hydrogen bombing, the penultimate step toward mass destruction of the universe. The beam trajectory of the plot skewers the airplane pilot next to his wife in their couple habitat next to the cemetery receiving the outer-space electrode jolts. The wife is the first intended victim to survive the zombie attacks. Actual Lugosi footage gets folded in around this subplot, which is pulled up before the final encounter with the recycled melancholia at the moment scheduled for his decomposition demo. What we see decomposed and superimposed is what Lugosi got according to the conditions of his own burial: what is left is a skeleton in a cape. Before the melancholic's final appearance on the couple's patio, someone notes that something "started stinking" out there in the cemetery next door.

The outer-space commander pulls the double-death stunt to gain time for further resurrections of new recruits to crowd earth's cities with live proof: "Their own dead will be used to make them accept our existence and believe in that fact." This time around, as one of the undead, the Lugosi figure is the first to go, but only as a diversion from Lugosi's multiple death. The diversion is along for the outer-space collapse of distinctions between the living dead and "the dead."

The outer-space plan follows the terms of Oedipalization: the aliens encounter resistance of human thought, which has only just now caught up with their own special wavelength. Mankind is second in line to the way more advanced outer spacers. But earthlings are just a split second away from inventing and inflicting total destruction. The air explodes with the hydrogen bomb: sunlight will be next; and once detonated, every corner of a sun-centered universe touched by the light will go too. From heir to son, a transmission between the lines of murderousness is proposed between competing parties. Within a movie so crowded with the look and shots of discontinuity, there is one element in the plot that is carefully guarded: before the earthlings enter the space vessel, the outer-space woman turns on a translation machine that gives subliminal access to their easy inter-special communications. Indeed, first contact between species can be made only now in time for the film because humans have finally devised a language computer that picks up and translates the beam from outer space.

But the humans also fear what cannot be construed in terms of thinking. The otherness of these aliens fills the gap or overlap between

Oedipalization and the return trajectory of undeath. "What do you think
the next obstacle will be that the earth people will put in our way?" "Well,
as long as they can think we'll have our problems. But those whom we
are using cannot think. They are the dead brought to a simulated life by
our electrode guns. You know, it's an interesting thing when you consider
the earth people who can think are so frightened by those who cannot—
the dead."

The Oedipal struggle between species doubles the diversion the couples have offered back on earth from the outside chance of controlling
death or the dead all the way to double burial. "Plan Nine" translates
into nine months: outer space doubles reproduction back onto the jump-
start of reanimation. The outer-space men are advanced and archaic; a
certain norm of relations is parodied up above when outer-space woman
is put in her place as close breeder of the evolution of their species. Plus
from their outfits to the bio-blurbs filling the roles, the men from outer
space are coded as nonreproductive. We are talking out space.

At the end the first live people ever to enter the flying saucer come
and go: the outer-space craft explodes in flight. And even while they are
flaming, it is replication that has pulled one over reproduction — replication as the heartbeat of technologization in groups, for example, in
the mode of preparedness: "Take any major disaster and then wonder,"
wonder whether it wasn't a visitation from another planet externalizing
our internal or technological need for self-replication. Or as the aliens
describe human nonrecognition of outer-space existence, "their soul is
too controlled." The closing frame of the narrative guarantees that just
as we laughed at the phone or even at TV, we are now laughing at outer
space, all the way to outer space, the outer limit of long distance and
remote control, the ever expanding frontier of the sensorium and thus
of the point of return of the dead.

LECTURE TWELVE

Around *Dracula* the fastest puns in the West have drawn in the blanks: Batula, Blacula, Spermula, Suckula, and, twice in the seventies, the era of the other's bad taste, Dragula. Once it starts putting itself on, the drag of mourning is not transmittable: but its unconscious makeup will transmit until the look it has is out and over. At the crowded intersection where drive power exceeds most transferential models—the crossing that is jamming with perversion, psychosis, and the psychology of the group or group-of-one—transvestitism (or "TV") nevertheless puts on the one and only mourning show available within a network of melancholic or haunted delegations.

To fine-tune the screen of small differences in mourning style, one could review the cases of H. G. Wells, Stephen Tennant, Rainer Maria Rilke, and Andy Warhol, in which the little boys were caught, under their mother's funereal direction, wearing the clothes and look of a dead sister. Mother, who could not let go of her missing child outside the group context or contest of mourning drag, thus granted the sons her captive audience. These transmission examples are direct. At the remove of displacement skipping one generation of the mourning, the cases of Mary Shelley and Elvis line up. Into our own time the special side effects of Elvis sightings, impersonations, and other brands of return from the past (indeed, from the post, which asked us to comparison shop Before and After Elvis pictures) dive off the crypt flotation device that Elvis shared with his dead twin. The lookalikes were still tied, between the shell and the Colonel, in the race to the finish line, beginning or ending with his relationships with interchangeable women (which came too close to consciousness in one affair with a certain Joyce Bova, a Pentagon office worker who was partner to a living twinship), and catching up with the role he was on whenever typecasting himself as rescuer, the vehicle for him to rise to the most remote occasions (just about any traffic accident in his greater vicinity brought on the change), events endlessly out of real-time context but charged with the headline-sense he had of himself as Elvis, here to help.

The Stoker crypt has not yet yielded a full body shot of loss, the kind that can be rebuilt, let go and put to rest. The internal or eternal coordinates of this crypt's location break down into and between the lines of a "TV" transmission. It was after gagging on "dressed crab" that Stoker dreamed up *Dracula*. The crab that always moves backwards was the mother's loss, which had gained on him.

Less a period than a coma, Stoker's childhood was not early or late but extended for a seven-year stretch, the time it took before he could "stand upright."

Stoker assumed the vertical controls only after the youngest sibling and seventh child, George, was born (who, like all the Stoker sons but the other one, became a physician). Even in the fine-tuned, upstanding mode, Stoker always had to be patient to the siblings playing doctor. But in exchange, remember, primal time and again, it was the last born who outlasted the primal father.

When Irving for his part needed to know how to carry a corpse across stage, Stoker called in brother George, who had served in the Russo-Turkish War, to give the demo — which George agreed to only if, by no default of his own, brother Bram would fill in for the missing corpse. This was the ready position Stoker assumed when he ghostwrote George's memoirs from the war front, *Among the Unspeakables*. Stoker's fave brother forever, George, was number seven; via the logic of his own delayed onset of getting up, Stoker was too. For seven years Stoker had been playing dead, modeling the state he wished on his siblings. In a children's story he organized around the pun "horrorscope" (it is what a child in the doctor's office mishears at the end of a series of -scopes), Stoker does an occult number on seven. In "How 7 Went Mad" seven is lined up for extinction — but in the next line he is the number that is brought back. The next story in this series for children, "The Wondrous Child," focuses on the death wish two siblings hold for the most recent arrival. The imaginary baby, who replaces the real one in their thoughts, dies when the duo has bad thoughts, and comes alive again when the thoughts that count are good ones. Follow the bouncing baby jolted by death wishes: little one comes, like Dracula, from across the sea.

In *The Lady of the Shroud*, the presumed undead princess shows off her vampiric comeback at night on the lake. Her flotation, however, is a device: the coffin that holds her up has been wedged upright inside a boat. The upstanding mode of the princess's well-coffined apparition comes across the sea, to you and me, via the multiple impostures of vampirism.

In 1910, near the closing time of his collected work, Stoker published his casebook *Famous Impostors,* a series of studies that celebrated its season finale with a rerun of rumorological accounts of Princess Elizabeth's sudden death in Bisley: the blank had been secretly filled in, rapid-turnover style, with a lookalike boy ("The Bisley Boy," which is the legend's name or nickname) who was then raised incognito to give continuity shots to the virgin queenship. Stoker concludes, "For convenience we shall speak of the substitute of the Princess as though he were the Princess herself whom he appeared to be, and for whom he was accepted thenceforth."

Stoker's resistance to this convenience story or conspiracy theory broke on the evidence of a young girl's skeleton in Elizabethan rags found in an inside-outside compartment on the Bisley grounds. And then there was the strong evidence of guardedness, which was changed but never interrupted, among those immediate attendants who had been with the queen since childhood: "a staunchness which has caused more than one historian to suspect that there was some grave secret between them which linked their fortunes together" (323). Stoker followed the lead of improper burial to the spot the immediate attendants must have been in before the breakthrough notion of the lookalike contest, which, if they could win it, would circumvent the rage of the comparison-chopping king.

Before Ed Wood Jr. enters the Stoker legacy as finalist in the drag race of mourning, and thus lines it up with the machine delegations that were getting the work done in the cases of Wells, Tennant, and Warhol, there is a cluster of encryptments blocking the way. It is often up to the phantom to mourn over the melancholy delegation that got him there and thus put it and himself to rest. The crypt transmission that makes it into the live mode of "TV" *and* comes out as mourning can be followed emanating from Stoker's case, which does overlaps with those of Tod Browning, Lon Chaney, and Bela Lugosi.

First there was Tod Browning, premier American director of horror. His oeuvre picked up on the narcissistic wounding of mutilated World War I veterans (and, at closer range, the impact of his own 1915 car wreck) as though developing an at once castrative and literal syndication of the psychoanalytic review of the unhappy troopers of the Great War. The rehearsal or repetition of the car-crash catastrophe and turning point was Browning's sideshow specialization in live burial:

> For an admission price of twenty-five cents, you could witness the burial of Mr. Tod Browning (who had unexpectedly "died" the previous day) and receive a return ticket for his exhumation and resurrection by trumpeted nostrum the following evening. A one-day stunt was standard; the two-day burial was trickier, if more spectacular — a freak-show travesty of Easter weekend, and a guaranteed crowd-pleaser. (Skal, 26)

Back in Hollywood, Browning and Chaney became the first Horror couple in the business. But by June of 1930, Chaney's throat and lung cancer started showing up as the static on the line of his first attempts to put himself into talking pictures. The opening of this vocal crypt gave Lugosi his one and only role on the big screen of projection for life. Chaney went down as the man who was to be Dracula: "The MGM switchboard was flooded with offers from fans to donate their blood to the Dracula who never was. There were many transfusions, a final blurring of boundaries between the actor and his public" (Skal, 116).

As closing comment on the one-man transference Chaney had embodied from the mutilations of the Great War to cosmetic surgery on every body up for display or projection (surgical improvement ads surrounded every magazine spread on Chaney's latest horror disguise), Chaney was buried in flag-draped coffin, as if one of the war dead (Chaney, like Browning, had not done the military time usually required for the taps playback).

Just the same, the producer, with a name that means in German "little lamb," was upset by the homoerotic possibilities of the *Dracula* script and spelled out that "Dracula should only go for women and not men!" (cited in Skal, 126). In the interest of the plot's economy—and its Oedipalization—Dracula did have to suck Renfield first: that way madness lay. Murnau, for reasons of his own, established the precedent of same-sex crossover. But in the Browning version, the exceptional, cornerstone status of Renfield's object relations with the vampire turns the high beam on the open-and-shut functioning of this particular transgression. This suffixal coordinate cannot be overlooked when it comes to the long drawn-out drag of mourning from Stoker to Wood. It is the coordinate that displaces the castration complex to the side of diversions away from the crypt. Browning's cinema wears its complex up front: the typical Browning hero is a con man who is crippled at one minimal remove of displacement from the center cut of castration. Dracula can penetrate only via mouth and teeth.

The 1930 blockbuster *Dracula* ran on its own momentum: when Chaney's drag did not make it from silent film to talkie (the cancer caught, mangled, gargled the beaming-up process), Browning gave up on the direction of what was now Lugosi's runaway vehicle. Hats off or hands on to Karl Freund, who, though cinematographer in the titles, performed the directorial duties in effect. Browning pulled himself together, within the two-year span of mourning, to make a tributary offering or opening up of the crypt he and Chaney had shared—with millions of traumatic or war neurotics. *Freaks,* a film that was in turn buried alive until in the 1960s there arose such a libidinal upsurge of freak identifications. One of us, one of us: you're either with us or against us. At first intake, however, it could not struggle to the screen to be borne or abided. The horror this time was too close to the home front, the internal or psychological front of war traumatization. Techno catastrophes of warfare or car crash (as in Browning's case) were on the kind of open-wound display that required a running supplementary of repression. *Freaks* perpetrated a rewind of the internal tapes of traumatization — between the lines of the visible — that was a rewounding. The mutilated victims of techno accident were only the tip of the list of casualties counted in their majority within psychological categories. Shell shock created the bunker of preparedness for the monster movies. But the freaks, who are us and, what is worse, are among us, drove the pointed headlines of monstrosity home. What had been the case in German films from 1913 onward started beaming up onto the Hollywood screen in the late 1920s, just in time for one more time around the blockage of world war. The metabolization, technologization, internalization, or, same skip beat of distance, externalization that trauma (the trauma of war and, by extension or preparation, everyday life) must undergo or undertake was henceforth a West Coast exclusive.

But the reception that finally came together — in short circuit, skirt, and sweater — in Wood's career was still staggered, staggering across long distance in the case of Lugosi, which it took Wood to see through to its opening and shutting. Lugosi was on a role: even when he was the first to be made the offer no one could refuse or put together again, he turned down the Frankenstein parts on grounds of incompatibility with his Count persona. But he was stoked — just one upbeat away from lying down with the Dracula legacy in the crypt mode of motor uncoordination. When Lugosi began to double over with terrible leg pains, which he could only stand by shooting up with morphine, a double addiction began to follow the role of a lifetime: the identification with Dracula's look and the drug habit.

Toward the living end of Lugosi, when drugs and the recycling of the role had him at the disposal of his identifications, he had a couple (and couplification) of breaks or near misses. His fifth and last wife, Holly, who, having revved up for decades within the fan ranks before up and joining Lugosi for his remaining two years of drug freedom, had the bedside track on his unblurred identifications: "He was always act-ing," she told the *National Enquirer* after his death. In intraview she also recognized his fans, who were all along acting out in front of the crypt or screen, which they sealed, consumer-style, with their approval: "all boys — no girls. They wear makeup and hang around funeral par-lors" (cited in Skal, 254). And there was Wood's attachment to Lugosi, the other break that articulated what Holly Wood finally had to offer: a makeshift compromise formation between perversion and reproduction in the name of gadget love or "TV."

We would be skipping a step if we passed on any mention of Wood's own case of transvestitism. It was the occasion for Wood's first movie break, *Glen or Glenda*, in which Lugosi played the sex-change doctor and omniscient Voice-over.

In *Glen or Glenda* Lugosi opens and shuts the cases of "TV" in person and, then, still as host or ghost, haunts the often encrypted, recycled footage with Genesis-style Voice-over "bringing to light" "many startling things." Street scene footage: "people going somewhere with their own personali-ties." Then the turntable between audio and video gets its volume of life in death turned up full blast: a new day is begun; a new life is begun; a life is ended. We are at the scene of a suicide case that is under investigation. The suicide note left behind by the "TV" (played by Wood) leaves funeral direc-tions: "I was put in jail for wearing women's clothing. Let me wear these things in death if I can't in life." The narrative frame or contract between the inspector in charge of the case and the specialist he consults must rise above the contradiction between the whole story, which lies in the "depths of a man's mind," and the shock people still thrill to when they come across headlines of sex change or cross-dressing. This shock, which is also always the inoculative shot that gets us in the ready position for the changes that are already upon us, recalls our earlier recoil, in the name of God, from the prospects for artificial flight or, earlier on, from the outside chance or change represented by car travel (the blank stares of resistance are filled in with ready-made footage of planes dropping bombs and cars jamming on the LA freeways)."Yet, to this day, the world is shocked by sex change."

In keeping with a certain two-timing of evolution, nature makes mistakes: transvestitism exists, as does the wish to be the opposite sex.

Wood demonstrates on the lounger in drag that there are some men who simply think better in their kickback attire — and are thus a "better credit to the community." The collapse or lapsus across the prefix *trans* of transvestitism and transsexualism is protested against too much by half: the main reason a transvestite like the one played by Wood puts on makeup, wig, and padding to simulate a woman's contours is so that he can pass on the street. A recognizable man in woman's clothing is an outlaw. Glen starts out under cover of Halloween. Then one day it wasn't Halloween any longer. But he was never homosexual (another protest match). But while Glen prepares for couplification with his bride-to-be, he cannot but wonder: What about Glenda, his female personality? The bride's commentary: "Here we are, two perfectly normal people." Voice-over: "I suppose German psychology has a lot to say, but the end of study is only the beginning of reality." This little transvestite does not go for the same sex (we see Wood rebuff a homosexual proposition); what he wants is "to eliminate being one of his sex." When he goes on the covered wagon of his straight masculinity, he almost loses his mind. Voice-over: "Beware of the green dragon in front of the door. He eats little boys." Glen and bride-to-be go into couples therapy to treat the "dual personality." Only mourning can cut off the supply lines between which the cross-dressing has been plugging along into outlets available since childhood. Therapist: "Glen is the author of Glenda who has a certain fantasy life and dies only when he wants her to die, when he's ready to let her die." Unlike Ann, the transsexual case, created Frankenstein-style out of Alan's body partings, Glen has a transferential history. His father saw to it that between them no love was lost; so Glen invented the fictitious character to get love he could not get from the dad. Where was mother? The cure is to kill the second character by transferring the investment displaced from and by father to the wife, the happy medium, the all-in-one package. Voice-over concludes: "What of the other less fortunate Glens the world over?'...and snails and puppy dog's tails...'"

But in *Killer in Drag*, Wood's contribution to an adults-only series (Original Imperial Books), the "TV" (also named Glen/Glenda) is not exclusively straight up with a twist (or, for that matter, otherwise a good citizen) but is shown in all kinds of ready positioning: deciding now for, now against the transsexual operation, sleeping with men or women but always as a man in perfect drag, murdering for pay and then, one time only, one last time, to get funding for her way out of the syndicate or, by any other name, the underworld:

> The syndicate had a long arm, but after the operation which would make Glenda a real girl, she could well disappear forever from their grasp. Oh the ecstasy of it. The love of life Glen felt when he realized, soon it would be possible to be the girl he had always dreamed of himself being. (15)

After the first murder, all systems are go for the clean break or cut of crossing over into a new life. Glenda comments on her one-last-time victim or hit: "Dead men don't tell anything, nor do they prove much except that maybe they're dead" (14). But then Glenda leaves her purse behind at the scene of a murder she did not commit: she is framable, and her drag cover is blown in public. "Then it hit her. Hit her as plainly as if the picture were being projected on the windshield in front of her; like on the screen at a drive-in movie theatre" (25). But on the other side, Glenda, like a vampire, has never been photographed. To survive himself, now that he can no longer fall between the crack that Glenda secretly held in place, Glen crosses over into Glenda, a contamination that is happening anyway, as he discovers when during the period of transition out on the lamb, like a lion, he must again play Glen for close-ups and close calls.

The suture marks that show during changeover frame their cohabitation and give a secret away, one that contaminates her person with a foreign body. One of Glenda's calling cards, which she showed right before giving away the surprise attack to one of her hits, was to address the mark in Glen's voice. But her dread of letting that slip show without knowing it has had her on the guard she might let down before the changing. But now she discovers another kind of reversal: "Glen made a mental note that not only did Glenda have to watch Glen's voice, but Glen most certainly had to be careful of Glenda's musical tones" (42). Now caught between the merger of one identity and the segregation between the two, Glen/Glenda can no longer overlook what had been the scheduling of her every day. Glen/Glenda's life had been great, with an emergency exit kept openly secret, vampire-style, but Glen could not get through a single day without crossing over into Glenda's body. During the period of transition or segregation, Glen still needs a proper nightgown to shop till she drops for, to die for: "Only the nightgown was foremost in his mind. Glenda was taking over fast. Glenda was taking over more and more. He'd have to watch that very closely" (48). Glen takes cover in a circus he purchases with his blood money. One of the sideshow attractions, the Half Man–Half Woman, takes Glen to know one. Browning's circus and freak-show past doubles here as one of Glen/Glenda's transitional objects.

Outside the circus, Glen enlists the local hooker's services for sex, which turns out not to be just a drag, even for her. As the law closes in on them, and they can't see the way out for the sticks, the girlfriend suggests the one-way ticket of operation, the original maxi-protection plan. What does it mean that he now answers, " 'I like things right where they are.' Glen took her in his arms again" (93)? I don't think he identifies as straight or gay. It is fetishism (gadget love, by any other name) that now reaffirms what had been an inadmissible ambivalence compelling the stammer and cover of her "anger" within the stereo range of an object or objective in the one-sided service of identity or segregation:

> "Angora," she said aloud. "What a delightful sound. What a magnificent feeling." She opened one hook on her fur coat and let her right hand enter the opening. A pleasant sensation surged through her body as the hand felt the soft angora fur which surrounded her left breast. She squeezed harder — then harder — she rubbed it — the sensation overwhelmed her — She sighed aloud — "Oh what matter — there are more panties in the glove compartment." (15)

In the drag of his hooker girlfriend, the other other woman, Glen/Glenda does finally escape to California. But the underworld aims its assembly line of double agents at the Wood figure's outside chance in Hollywood; Glen/Glenda's "TV" replacement is sent to the Coast to make the hit. The hit, identified already as the shock of recognition that goes down and out with cinematic projection, is the memento mori that melancholia admits or rather never lets go, the reminder that paradoxically addresses its memo to the outside address or chance of immortality now. Glen/Glenda/other woman — the new California persona — waits and watches the hits wash up onto the shore. Being in recovery, in self-storage or survival, the Californian group reckons by the deadline that is to live for the measure of all lack of finality. It is a different way, one that exceeds integration by just falling apart to put on the happy medium's new closure.

In the sequel, *Death of a Transvestite* (also titled *Hollywood Drag* and *Let Me Die in Drag!*), Glen/Glenda gets the death sentence from the law and not from the syndicate, which had sent another drag killer to the Coast to take out G/G. The hired gun moll added drag to his killing habit when he anaclitically discovered the sensations of brushing up against the sweaters of his rape and murder victims. That became the first item in his "collection." Whenever an item of what women wear daily "excited him to occult proportions" (44), the piece just had to be added to the collection over the owner's murdered body. TV killer doesn't just want to do the job but wants to get even by submitting G/G to the final postmortem humiliation that comes with shocks of misrecognition: "He wanted Glenda found on the street or in an alley, and the morgue people lifted the skirt and took down the panties, there would be more than revenge" (94). Revenge is all about the inability to let things pass. And Glenda had always been able to pass, unlike killer TV, a total near miss. Another variation on the dream of Glenda's death: " 'I'd strip her right down and make her look at it in the mirror. I'd make her die looking at the male body she really is. That would be the thing that would put the fear of horror in her guts' " (96). In the showdown G/G goes down in drag. But at the hospital that repairs her, the regulation fingerprinting frames her for the murder she did not commit, for which she now must die, but in drag, the promise she obtained from the warden in exchange for her true story:

> "I wonder if I would have gotten these things if I had no story to tell. . . . But, Warden, you should be able to see now why it is so important to a transvestite not to leave this world in male attire. It's our religion, so to speak. Maybe we live a lie, but also perhaps in death we have come to a truth." (110)

One of the reporters covering the execution gives the closing sentence: "I thought it was a guy they were strapping in . . ." — rather than the dame he watches pull herself up by her own bra straps.

Between the mixed reception of *Glen or Glenda* (or its remix in the mystery version of the split-level housing of Oedipal plotting and un-burial plots) and *Plan Nine from Outer Space* (the countdown of carrying to term without period), Lugosi was entered into the retention span of Wood's makeshift horror series where, over time, and after the time of the live end Lugosi came to under Wood's direction, talk-show host or Voice-over Criswell took over where Lugosi left off marking the outer frame of mourning's metabolization.

Wood came to direct a virtual degenre of occult plus porn flicks, an overactivity he alternated with cameo spots in the group sex scenes that came together in straight porn films directed by some other, in which he was caught with his drag up and on as though the insertion either of some kind of aphrodisiac or just another drop scene. One of Wood's parting shots was the sexploitation film *Necromania,* which brought to consciousness Hollywood's standard diversion and deviation from the crypt of narcissistic disturbance to and through the couples therapy that treats sexual problems between partners and leaves them there in the afterglow of cure-all. In *Necromania* the couple that is shown to be sexually dysfunctional is separated for the duration of the wife's lesbian diversions and the husband's encounter with an "other woman." But the Oedipal plot gives itself away to climax: the husband is healed by the Madame of the clinic who, without leaving her coffin, shuts it tight on top of the two of them going at it. The crypt-enforced position of downright lying is thus married to the upright takeoff and flight of the man's reset erections, set via the crypt-transmitter of techno haunting back on the straight and narrow path. This was a different way: it allowed Wood Jr. (Young Stoker) to live or get around in (rather than work through, survive, or transmit) the crypt of carried-over losses. But rather than drag around the missing corpus at the burdensome remove of projective displacement, Wood over-and-outed the ghostly legacy via the live or life transmission of "TV."

In 1976 Daniel Farson, great-nephew of Bram Stoker, published *Vampires, Zombies, and Monster Men*. It opens with the 1973 investigation of the bizarre death of a Polish immigrant who had been living in Britain for twenty-five years—in fear of the vampire. There were no lightbulbs in his room because electricity was a scare. His apartment was his fortress, and salt was all over the place. One bag of salt by his face, another between his legs, open containers of salt mixed with urine dotted the lines of defense. Out on the window ledge an inverted bowl covered a mixture of human excrement and garlic. These mixed dregs combined bait and trap; garlic and salt was the main course of poisoning, shit and piss for appetizer. It turned out the man had gagged in his sleep on a clove of garlic that when things got out of hand, fit in his mouth. Farson: "So in a roundabout way, the vampires did get him in the end" (8). But this same roundabout—the fetishistic and group-psychological relations with the vampire—was the man's route of detour around and arrival beyond or sur-arrival at the close of World War II. The stigmata that did not close recycled the backflow of that internal wounding of melancholia, that breakdown in one-on-one relations with the dead.

For his own history in the making, in the 1970s, Farson documented the first tours to Transylvania: Pan Am started out in 1972 under an opening title with its fun in the pun akimbo: "Package Tour with a Toothy Grin"; British Airways followed in 1974 with a more proper naming: "Dracula Tour." By 1974 vampire hunters like David Farrant, High Priest of the Occult Society, had their spades called spades when they were arrested for grave desecration. By leaving the drive of group psychology, fetishism, user-friendly psychosis to the exorcist, the ambivalent press of melancholic attachments could be kept out of focus. The 1970s British exorcist Reverend Christopher Neil-Smith reported on one of his cases: " 'He was a perfectly normal person before, but after the brother's death he felt his life was being sucked away from him as if the spirit of his brother was feeding on him' " (15). But the exorcist could rule out such psychological explanations as survivor guilt (a phrase Stoker's great-nephew supplies from his own package of wheeling and dealing with the stereotypes of insight orientation). " 'There was no disharmony between them. In fact he wasn't clear for some time that it *was* his brother.' " Next to "it" Farson adds in brackets: "the vampire."

Vampirism spread up out of dread of premature burial, the readily available accident of burial alive. Great-nephew traces this phantasmic dread back to a rapid turnover under plague conditions. This brings us back, hush-hush, to Charlotte Stoker's bedtime stories.

> In creating his arch-vampire Dracula, Bram Stoker may well have drawn on stories he had heard as a child of a great cholera epidemic that, like the plague, created an atmosphere of panic and increased the likelihood of premature burial. . . . [Charlotte Stoker's] house was besieged by desperate looters among the last survivors in the village, and the story was told that when she saw a hand reaching through the skylight, she took an axe and cut it off. She told Stoker about Sergeant Callan, a giant of a man whose body was too big to fit in his coffin. To make it fit the undertaker took a hammer to break his legs. At the first blow of the hammer the supposed cholera victim sprang back to life, and he was seen around for many years afterward. (36)

Only by the 1970s could someone far from the son give up the ghost in the distant relation. But at closer range little Stoker was just enacting a maternal relation that fit to be tied. It all comes back to him at the commencement of the better half of his life, which he overspent representing the interests of actor Irving. In sync with Stoker's mother, Farson spreads his plague examples of vampirism's primal scene prehistorically across every conceivable time zone. But then there are two examples from the eighteenth century that remain otherwise out of all context. First, a limerick suggesting the currency back then of dread of being locked up in premature interment:

There was a young man of Nunhead
Who awoke in his coffin of lead,
"It's cosy enough," he remarked in a huff,
"But I wasn't aware I was dead." (34)

The other stray example: "In Moravia in the 18th century a postmaster was thought to have died from epilepsy. When some years later it became necessary to transfer various graves, his body was disinterred and it was discovered that he had been buried alive. The doctor who had signed the death certificate lost his reason over it" (34).

It is just possible that the eighteenth-century relocation of graves to fit the new look of the dead was our one and only paradigm shift into modernity. What seconds this downward motion was the techno syndication of the uncanny era down in the trenches of World War I and inside the stricken zones of narcissistic libido that got us technologizing on the double.

Dying in one's grave happens. But other than the evidence of corpses returning to life or disinterred bodies that bear the freeze-frame of their contortionist attempts to get out of the early grave, there is everyone's experience of energy-draining close relations: "Some people can even have this effect on machines, causing them to drop in electric current" (37). Great-nephew finds evidence of a vampiric world in and around this energy drain. Following in Wood's footsteps, he advances the work of analogy—of mourning—via technology and the experience of women: "A century ago people would not have believed that we would be able to sit in our homes, watch a square box, and through it see a man land on the moon. There may well be another, spiritual world around us of which we are still unaware" (42). Occultist Dion Fortune, who explains vampirism via the astral body or etheric double, submits her view of how Hungarian soldiers who were reported to have become vampires made vampires of their victims:

Now vampirism is contagious; the person who is vampirized, being depleted of vitality, is a psychic vacuum, himself absorbing from anyone he comes across in order to refill his depleted sources of vitality. He soon learns by experience the tricks of a vampire without realizing their significance, and before he knows where he is, he is a full-blown vampire himself. (cited in Farson, 43)

What goes down this drain is the haunting alternation between identification and projection. Colin Wilson refers to the stigmata of so-called devil's bites as reflecting the pull of the "subconscious." But whose mind is it? " 'It might have been somebody else's mind' " (quoted in Farson, 45).

LECTURE THIRTEEN

In F. Marion Crawford's "For the Blood Is the Life," which begins with Old Alario's deathbed scene, the father's death comes complete with a prehistory or economy of loss turned to profit:

> They say that he made his money by selling sham jewelry in South America, and escaped with his gains when he was found out. (172)

> His wife was dead, and he had an only son called Angelo.... Angelo was to marry the daughter of the richest man in the village. (173)

But Cristina, who is the other woman — in other words, delegate of mother — is in love with Angelo. She is sent by the neighbors to bring back the doctor for Old Alario, who dies or departs in her absence. Her dispatching holds the place of all other departures. Two workmen employed by the deceased upon his recent return from South America to enlarge his house steal the dead father's fortune out from under the deathbed and proceed to bury it outside in the "gorge." Cristina's search for the doctor crosses the path of the legacy's miscarriage. She is knocked on the head and "quickly" buried (probably alive) where the workers put the money down.

The loss of the inheritance calls off Angelo's marriage. "As for Cristina, it was several days before she was missed": not only is her body missing, but the original dispatch (that sent her to find the doctor) was forgotten. Angelo turns "melancholy and morose" and begins "to have strange waking dreams. He was not always alone" (178). Cristina's interrupted return, which was cut off and secretly buried (together with the missing patrimony, together with her original departure), is now, as interruption, perpetually on the rebound. Angelo "makes love" to a vampiric

147

ghost on the mound of the secret tomb covering both Cristina and the missing patrimony; he wakes up alone, overcome by "a fear unspeakable and unknown" (179). This recurring "dream of terror and delight" (179) turns him into a somnambulistic medium: his lips moving automatically, he mutters the name "Cristina." The populace believes he is " 'consuming himself' for the love of the girl he was to have married when he lost his inheritance" (181). But he is being consumed by the other. Cristina has returned from the prehistory of the inheritance that was primally connected not to substitution, circulation, and father function but to their simulation as counterfeit.

A ghostbuster who has been away since before the time of Alario's death now returns and gets the big picture. He stakes Cristina while the priest, or "Father," he has summoned prays on the sidelines. "Then suddenly a small iron-bound chest was thrown up and rolled over against the old man's knee" (183). The swallowed "chest" or "box" (compartments of the mother's body) can be disgorged once the woman buried deep and alive has been staked. But even as we are reminded that that is all in the past, in the present-tense frame of the story Cristina's ghost ("the Thing") can still be seen by storyteller and his guest haunting the burial mound.

A father's death is introduced into a household from which the mother is missing. The house (symbol of mother) is being altered with money ripped off through the counterfeiting of a work of mourning that never took place. Even when the money is restored to Angelo and he is delivered from the undead blood bond — it's too late. The recovered legacy only gets him as far as South America, as far as his father's own doubling of a prior departure, which he turned via counterfeit into profit and loss.

In Victor Roman's "Four Wooden Stakes" we start out with a narrator who is a detective, who receives a cry for help from a friend — please, for old time's sake, I'm all alone, will explain upon arrival — which the narrator accepts as the invitation to a more social kind of visit. He has just concluded a difficult case, and he seeks a diversion, a vacation, via this mystery that his visit will soon clear up.

The appeal of all detective stories (and this story opens as a detective story or rather at the end of a detective story) lies in the Oedipus complex, our one and only detective story. That is the one we are forever trying to figure out: Who did it? (I did.) So the narrator enters a place of mystery armed with the knowledge of a detective who has just solved a case. He arrives, and we could be back in Transylvania. No one will take him to the address he announces at the train station; there are some dreadful tales circulating about that place; more than one "tramp" has been found near there, " 'so weak from loss of blood that he could hardly crawl, ' " as one cab driver puts it (251).

Now because of what I just said about the detective and Oedipus, and even if I did not say that, please put your Freudian ears on and note that a tramp is not only a bum but also a fallen woman; a tramp is the victim, and the "tramp" is shadowed by a fallen woman's name, which it also calls; the tramp, the victim, loses blood to the point of becoming an infant, hardly able to crawl. So the first symptoms of the outbreak of vampirism mark the spot of regression all the way to the mother-and-infant bond.

He comes armed, then, with this evidence and with his own detective leanings, his tendency, in other words, to supply Oedipal interpretations. When he arrives at the estate, however, the first thing he encounters is not the standard Oedipal plot but in its place a remarkable burial plot. He sees above ground in the midst of the family cemetery a crypt that stands out. One of his first questions as he begins to read and interpret this new case concerns this unburial plot: why, while the rest of the family lies buried in the ground in the usual manner, had certain other members been kept above ground in the mausoleum?

As we enter the estate and open the case, Remson, the friend in need, goes right away into a fit of hysterics, but once he has been calmed down by the detective friend, he tells the story, the story of his case and crypt. And what is the story? It is the will of the grandfather that we see monumentalized above ground and that marks the beginning of the unraveling of the family line. The grandfather's image is the only representation at the front of the line of vampires. We never see the other three. So the representation of grandfather is also a repression. And it is a ready-made lifted from the portrait hanging in the hall:

> At first, owing to the poor light, I was unable to distinguish the general outline and form of the thing; then I saw. It was a man's head.
>
> I will swear it was the exact reproduction of that picture I had seen in the hall that very morning. (257)

Between the vampire bat that goes for the jugular and the hologram re-pro of a portrait there is no other image of the vampire. There is only the detective's denial that the other image that comes to mind has any bearing: " 'Remson, what we are up against, is a vampire. Not the female species usually spoken of today, but the real thing' " (259).

When vampire and horror fictions on their own lay the blame on the one death they bring into focus, you can count on it: another missing person "was there" already before the official body count could begin. Who was missing from the family before the grandfather was a goner? Here is the account (the countdown and body count) given by Remson (or "remaining son"):

> "Five years ago my family circle [the family circle that has now turned into a band of vampires] consisted of five persons; my grandfather, my father, my two brothers and myself, the baby of the family. My mother died, you know when I was a few weeks old. Now..." His voice broke and for a moment he was unable to continue.
>
> "There is only myself left." (253)

So before all the departures that put through the direct connection to vampirism, there was right from the start the loss of the mother, which has kept him the baby of the family up until this point of reunion. Little ones are not so easy to mourn and are themselves unable to mourn. The work of mourning has to be accomplished for the young child, and if the child grows up to be a haunted outpost of telecommunications with the dead, it is because some surviving parent figure was the one who couldn't do a mourning's work. This parent, the delegate who was not able to mourn, deposits the work of mourning that was not accomplished inside the surviving child, who, without knowing it, remains under the remote control of a demand that has vampiric consequences. So the responsibility and the timing are complicated in these cases, as we will see in the next lecture in "Carmilla." But in "Four Wooden Stakes" the grandfather is the figure of displacement. Between grandparents and grandchildren the fantasy of doubling can be shared. Through this elision of the time and agency of generation, the Oedipal static of the parents is overcome between them. As the "trans-parent," the grandfather, with his "long, flowing" hair (255), serves as delegate of a mother-and-child reunion somewhere over the paternal interruption — the cutting of the heir — which is also back within the forget-together of vampirism. We see through the grandfather that the mother's loss was doubled or incorporated when her departure met, right off the bat, with his return from South America. Each delegate of the father's name does not transmit but sucks on the bloodline that makes Remson crawl like a baby or a tramp.

Remember Clarimonda? The spider-woman way back in Ewers's story? Now we are looking into Theophile Gautier's "Clarimonde" to cop another mother of a fix. Did anyone notice the priest's jackhammer-like denials that he never knew from women? So Clarimonde is the very first body, really, that he has ever come into contact with. There is one exception that he will always make, and that is, of course, his mother:

> I knew vaguely that there was something called a woman, but my thoughts never dwelt upon it; I was utterly innocent. I saw my old, infirm mother but twice a year; she was the only connection I had with the outer world. (83)

I cannot overemphasize: "the only connection with the outer world." But in no time the lifeline connection runs for and under the cover of denial as the covert operation of vampirism: "As I was about to cross the threshold, a woman's hand suddenly touched mine. I had never touched one before" (98).

The denial of his ever having been in contact with another body turns up the volume on that one bond that is in fact in place. Beginning with Clarimonde's touchdown, the priest enters (or is it a reentry?) the underworld of his repression of the body — of the mother's body.

No surprises there. Just as our novice priest is about to take the vow of chastity, which is his ticket to a kind of fatherhood, Clarimonde keeps in touch:

> Never did any human face exhibit more poignant anguish. The maiden who sees her betrothed fall suddenly dead by her side, the mother by the empty cradle of her child . . . not one of them could look more inconsolable, more stricken to the heart. (92–93)

Indeed there is something inside him ("like an internal lake") that rises to do the grieving mother's bidding; what had been "so long suppressed, burst out suddenly" (96). But his "father's discourse" restores him to himself. His own fatherhood comes complete with the testamentary appointment to a parish: " 'The priest who occupied it has just died' " (100). But as he moves to replace the dead "father," he comes across the "poor body" again making its final appeal on the edge of death and missingness. He is summoned to a safe place of leave-taking from Clarimonde. But he soon exchanges the bedside manner of fatherhood for the vows of vampirism:

> I strode up and down the room, stopping every time before the dais to gaze at the lovely dead woman through her transparent shroud. Strange thoughts came into my mind; I imagined that she was not really dead. . . .
>
> The perfection of her form, though refined and sanctified by the shadow of death, troubled me more voluptuously than was right, and her repose was so like sleep that any one might have been deceived by it. . . .
>
> I was unable to refuse myself the sad and supreme sweetness of putting one kiss upon the dead lips of her who had had all my love. But, oh, wonder! a faint breath mingled with mine, and Clarimonde's lips answered to the pressure of mine. Her eyes opened. . . . "I waited for you so long that I am dead. But now we are betrothed. . . . Goodbye, but not for long." Her head fell back. . . . a wild gust of wind . . . flew out of the casement, bearing Clarimonde's soul. The lamp went out and I swooned away on the bosom of the lovely dead. (114–19)

Just when he thought it was safe to be dad — she's back. Clarimonde continues to live by drawing on the corporate account the priest opens up for her on his own person.

"I shall not die! . . . I shall be able to love you a long time yet. My life is in yours. . . . I shall drink your beautiful . . . blood. Sleep . . . my god and my child. I shall not hurt you, I shall only take as much of your life as I need not to lose my own." (140–42)

But the nurture or nature of this blood bond is double — or nothing:

For myself, I was so wearied of my double life that I accepted, wishing to know once for all whether it was the priest or the nobleman who was the dupe of an illusion. I was determined to kill, for the benefit of one or the other, one of the two men who were in me, or to kill them both, for such a life as I had been leading was unendurable. (145)

But the Father, as he is called back at the monastery or in our own lives, makes a radical intervention:

"There is but one way of ridding you of this obsession, and although it is extreme, we must make use of it. Great evils require great reme-dies. I know where Clarimonde is buried. We must dig her up, and you shall see in what a pitiful condition is the object of your love. You will no longer be tempted to lose your soul for a loathsome body de-voured by worms and about to fall into dust." (145)

He charges the son to acknowledge that she is a corpse at the father's disposal. The father shows the son that the mother's body is off-limits in the funereal terms and conditions of the son's own system of foreclo-sure. The father saves the psycho priest's suicide commission. But the priest thus loses the whole race between psychosis and autoanalysis and returns to an off-track setting. He finds a kind of stability within the coordinates of his paranoid vigilance: "Such, brother, is the story of my youth. Never look upon a woman, and walk always with your eyes cast on the ground, for chaste and calm though you may be, a single minute may make you lose eternity" (149–50). The priest puts on a new habit of denial. He will have none of it, or more than one woman equals none. I mean "nun."

Seabury Quinn's "Restless Souls" is another loving-to-death or lov-ing-the-dead spectacular. But first let's go over the detective or Oedipal plot on the way to (or is it in the way of?) the burial plot. Back in the terminal of consumerist identification (I mean, in the restaurant), the detective and his sidekick suspect that they are observing a "badger game" in progress in which a woman is setting up the mark to get mugged and robbed in some other place by the brute accomplice. But when they tail the car, they arrive behind the woman and her mark — at the cemetery. (The detective isn't surprised: he observed back in the restaurant that the woman didn't eat.)

> "You know this place, friend...?"...
> "Better than I want to... I've been here to several funerals."
> "Good!" he returned. "You can tell me then where is the — how do you call him? — the receiving vault?" (179)

They find — how do you call him — the mark.

The vampire's name, Alice Heatherton, which they find inscribed on the tombstone above the mark, leads detective and friend to the endlessly grieving mother:

> "Alice was my youngest child. She and my son Ralph were two years apart, almost to the day. Ralph... went to Florida.... Alice died while visiting him." "But... your son, is not he also deceased?"
> "Yes... he is dead, also. They died almost together. There was a man down there,... Joachim Palenzeke... Ralph's superior in the work.... When Alice went to visit Ralph this person presumed on his position... and attempted to force his attentions on her.... Ralph resented his overtures. Palenzeke made some insulting remarks... and they fought.... When Ralph began to get the better of him he drew a pistol and fired five shots into my poor son's body. Ralph died the next day.... His murderer fled to the swamps... and according to some squatters he committed suicide, but there must have been some mistake... because he was seen again! He killed Alice!... Alice was prostrated at the tragedy of Ralph's murder — somehow, she seemed to think she was responsible for it — but in a few days she recovered enough to make preparations to return home with his body.... A sheriff's posse found them both next morning. Palenzeke had apparently slipped in the bog while trying to escape being drowned. Alice was dead — from shock,... and there was a wound on her throat." (187–89)

Palenzeke, who was denied burial in any consecrated part of the cemetery, belongs to the bond between siblings, an underworld bond that is incestuous: " 'they died almost together.' " The sister takes total responsibility for her brother's death and takes the body home (it's hers!). But on the way she encounters the murderer, the suicide, the vampire, the repressed bond. She returns home an undead corpse bonded to another undead corpse. The brother's body is no longer mentioned. But his loss is absorbed by the bad big brother on one side and, on the other, by the mark Rochester, the loving brother, who on the night he enters the story and meets the vampires had decided to kill himself before his sick heart finishes him off on schedule. The love affair between Rochester, an orphan without family, in every sense a mark or placeholder, and Alice Heatherton puts him (and her) back on track and allows mourning to take place.

> "You'd have thought she'd known me all her life, the way she fell in step when we went out of the cafe.... Before I knew it, I was telling her who I was, how long I had to live, and how my only regret was losing her, just when I'd found her." (182)

Rochester is the brother whose mortality Alice must live with. With him she is able to put the bad brother (both Palenzeke and the part of Rochester given to suicidal ideation) and herself to rest. After she has let Rochester die and go, her last request is that the detective stake her. By now we can lip-synch the detective's follow-up refrain: " 'It is not hard to see the living die, my old one, but the dead!' " (203).

In Count Stenbock's "The Sad Story of a Vampire" it is the brother who attracts the attack of the undead. But who introduces the vampire into the household? The father. The father is "totally blind" (121) to the vampire's attraction to his son (which means he is riding out an identification so close that it is at the same time so out of sight). Why is the son right from the start the target? Whom does he resemble? Surprise! The missing mother. Once again the household or economy into which the father invites the vampire is missing a mother. And the son, Gabriel, bears a resemblance not so much to the mother as to his mother's only portrait. He resembles not only the living person but, in the first place, the still life (still alive!) of that person. The narrator's only connection with her mother is through brother or portrait: "Of my mother I re-member nothing: she died in giving birth to my brother" (115). The vampire story will tell how the sole survivor came to spend most of her "useless wealth," the legacy she alone inherits and does not transmit, "on an asylum for stray animals," pets that must be cared for and never eaten. Thus, the narrator, whose work of unmourning (the animal shel-ter) frames the vampire story, has doubly lost her mother: the portrait, which is a token of idealization, extends its range of repression to the matricidal brother, the living on of the mother as idealization and the living proof that she is gone. Idealization can register anywhere on the ambivalence scale: as with pets, who are so cute because they reflect the outside chance of unambivalence, of idealization without murder. Gabriel was the father's pet in a household of unmourning. And he fuels the undeath of the vampire, the loss that lives on.

"One day" father returned from one of his frequent trips "accom-panied by a guest" (or ghost) who "had missed his train" (117). The sis-ter and daughter narrating this story (her name is Carmela) has already made clear, first, that she is not talking some "financial vampire" but a "real vampire," who arrives not by horse-drawn carriage, however, but by railway train (115) — or rather by the missed connection. Second, on the train — of association — that Carmela rides out in her opening work of mourning or not mourning, she gives the rundown of the vam-pire's casualties via an ambivalence she also admits here outside the in-ternal plot: "He desolated our home, killed my brother — the one ob-ject of my adoration — also my dear father. Yet, at the same time, I must say that I myself came under the spell of his fascination, and . . . have no ill-will towards him now" (115). The vampire "killed" her "father," the vintage mourning model that was already broken down when he was the vehicle lubing the vampire's entry into his son, into the living por-trait of a missing mother. The narrator's commemoration of her brother at this point cuts along a refusal to mourn that he had already embod-ied: "One of his peculiarities, when quite a little child, was horror at the sight of meat. Nothing on earth would induce him to taste it" (117). But what the narrator situates "in contradiction to all this" (that is, in contrast to his nature-boy peculiarities) is his pious "custom to serve every Sunday Mass in the parish church" (117). But where is the contradiction? The desublimation of the communion back into sacrifice, a regression basic to mass consumerism, bleeds into the compatibility between vegetarian and vampire:

> Once, when my father was relating some of his military experiences, he said something about a drummer-boy who was wounded in battle. His [the vampire's] eyes opened completely again and dilated: this time with a particularly disagreeable expression, dull and dead, yet at the same time animated by some horrible excitement. (119)

The vampire blood-bonds with the boy he "loves" all the way down to the "life" that is his "life" (121). Within their shared "soul of music" (120), the cone of sublimation that hovers over the bloodsucking (just as the background music of the mass primally covered up the screams of victims of sacrifice), a mother-and-child reunion comes together over the body, once again, of a casualty. The narrator recognizes this scene even without remembering her mother's embrace. The narrator observed Gabriel walking to communion with the vampire, "his eyes fixed as though in a trance! This terrified me even more than a ghost would. Could I believe my senses? Could that be Gabriel?" (121). Or could it be the portrait of the mother, a tableau vivant framed by unmoving eyes. She was found "in the morning, in an unconscious state, at the foot of the stairs" (121). She identifies and identifies with a dead person, and relocates the mass between her brother and the vampire as celebrating and sustaining the unburial grounds for this identification. Following these stations of double-crossing, the mother lives on forever but in some other place. And the narrator shares this immortality as sole survivor. By protecting and projecting cute animals, she creates a reservation for the denial of any sacrifice in her own communion with all the dearly departed.

Fritz Leiber's "The Girl with the Hungry Eyes" takes us back onto the mirror stage but puts the mouth where the eyes are. There is a hunger that is other or more than sex, or "if it was sex this time, it was overlaid with something else" (176). We are talking the overlay—of identification. This hunger beams into focus the same instant it is reflected back societywide. The vampiric vamp is the media image you come to even when you love the one you're with; she has "the hungriest eyes in the world":

> That's the real reason she's plastered all over the country today, you know — those eyes. Nothing vulgar, but just the same they're looking at you with a hunger that's all sex and something more than sex. That's what everybody's been looking for since the Year One — something a little more than sex. (176)

Ever since the Adam and Eve story, consumable knowledge is the "something a little more than sex" that doubles us over with the hunger of identification.

> You know how modern advertising gets everybody's mind set in the same direction, wanting the same things, imagining the same things. And you know how the psychologists aren't so skeptical of telepathy as they used to be.
>
> Add up the two ideas. Suppose the identical desires of millions of people focused on one telepathic person. Say a girl. Shaped her in their image.
>
> Imagine her knowing the hiddenmost hungers of millions of men. Imagine her seeing deeper into those hungers than the people that had them, seeing the hatred and the wish for death behind the lust. [Please note: the hunger of identification takes a walk on the violent side of ambivalence and packs the death wish into sexual love, which "the hunger" thus supersedes.] Imagine her shaping herself in that complex image, keeping herself aloof as marble. Yet imagine the hunger she might feel in answer to their hunger. (182)

The vampiric rules binding the model to the photographer-narrator? He can't make a pass at her, and they can't pass out of the studio, lab, "camera" into living space: "And I couldn't see her anywhere else, because if I tried to, I'd never snap another picture of her" (183–84). So he makes good use of their sessions. "And I started to talk to her all the time. About myself" (184). But the transgressive urge, the unexamined transference, is uncontained and on the rise. During station breaks he also begins to follow her. She goes to some billboard bearing her image, wants to be recognized, identified (with), and then goes home with the fan. Next morning recognition has hit the fan, who turns up in the headlines as another "maybe-murder."

The photographer-narrator takes her arm and accompanies her: " 'You know what you're doing?' " I guess he doesn't, since he tries to feel her up. She makes it clear that sex is not what she wants from him. She is not the substitute. Papa Munsch, who was the first to fall for her image, was also on the lookout for the end in sight of mourning: "Mama Munsch had been dead for two years" (183). But once again: No substitutions please. In his sessions with her the photographer-narrator stuffs the orifices of his hunger with endless talking about himself. One association gives free access to the crypt between them: "I told her about my mother dying of cancer" (184). But by the end he can only run away from his vampire; he closes the studio and even locks away inside it both unopened letters and ringing telephone — the foreclosed post or past, whether of mournful circulation and substitution or of telepathic remote control. The vampire: "I want your mother's death. I want your blood on the cobblestones. . . . I want your wanting me. I want your life. Feed me, baby, feed me" (159–60).

LECTURE FOURTEEN

The burial plot in Sheridan Le Fanu's case covers his young wife, who died after a beloved sister had passed away too. And this double departure of young wife and sister caused Le Fanu to withdraw gradually from society. He had been a great wit about town. And his writing covered a whole range of topics and genres (he even wrote journalistic essays). But from this point of withdrawal onward, he would increasingly write only stories about the occult. He was known in Dublin as the "invisible prince" because he went out only late at night to rummage through used-book stores in search of more ghost story material. Tell me about it: used books, like the marginal ones put out to this day by Time-Life, which no one used to read or admit reading, are your only sources when it comes to underworld work.

Listen to Le Fanu's writing schedule; listen to the way in which he set up a veritable writing machine inside his house after the double departure of sister and wife. In the bedroom he had shared with his dead wife he would awaken at 2:00 A.M. every morning and drink a required dosage of strong tea. He would take a little desk into bed: two tall funereal candles were placed on either side of this automatic writing routine. He preferred to write at the hour when according to his own recipe, the dark powers are strongest and one's own life force is weakest, leaving one especially open to the dictations of the unconscious. He would write and write, often repeatedly coming to a certain refrain with which he crowded his first-run manuscripts from this time onward: "Dark folk who live in souls of passionate men like bats in the dead trees."

At daybreak he transferred the scene of writing to the study downstairs, where he revised the thing that he scribbled and dribbled in the wee hours upstairs. For this break of revision, he took as his main writing prop the desk of his great-uncle, a famous writer, Richard Grimsley Sheridan. And here in the precincts of consciousness he reshaped the automatic writing into stories like "Carmilla."

As he reached the end of his career, he was chased down by a nightmare opening onto a vast mansion in a state of ruin, a condemned site threatening to crush the dreamer trapped in place. And in fact he cried out that the house was falling again (or at last) right before he died.

I have given you a funereal opener that lies in his life. The bond with the dead, at once sister and young bride, may give us another perspective on the same-sex eroticism that, all agree, this male writer imagines and creates between the vampirette and her victim. Listen to Carmilla's proposition to her intended victim:

> "In the rapture of my enormous humiliation I live in your warm life, and you shall die — die, sweetly die — into mine. I cannot help it; as I draw near to you, you, in your turn, will draw near to others, and learn the rapture of that cruelty, which yet is love." (35)

Besides noting the sensuality of the story, also observe how the unusual conditions Le Fanu places on vampirism build on all the other discrete, contextless parts that together give us the look and the logic of melancholic conditioning. Please try to find the missing person. And when we have got her where we want her: can we leave her there? It is so hard to kill the dead!

I want to focus on the secrecy that Laura and Carmilla come to share. Carmilla's secrecy is what angers Laura. It is one of the first repeated occasions for her not only being attracted to the vampire but also being quite turned off by her. The secrecy, mentioned on pages 34 and 35, for example, wounds Laura's heart (even Carmilla says so). And this secret (secret also in the sense of something that must be secreted away because its secretion is precisely hard to contain) will bite and has already always bitten her heart, hands, and throat. We are well on our way through the story before the mystery guest makes three disclosures: her family is ancient and noble, her home lies in the direction of the west (the setting-sun orientation of mortuary palaces), and her name is Carmilla. (We wait even longer before the name of narrator and protagonist, Laura, is mentioned in passing.)

Carmilla's secret is that she cannot lie. Just as she cannot lie in the sense of rest in peace, so she cannot assume a complete disguise or deception. She cannot leave the mirror stage of language and name.

On page 42 we follow the doctor's orders: " 'Life and death are mysterious states, and we know little of the resources of either.' " But the story knows a place for these resources, as when the father offers Carmilla the "resources of his schloss" (26).

Now the schloss word is a weird one. What is so remarkable about the schloss? Why is it never translated in the English story? The story refuses to translate the word *schloss*; *schloss* is a tamper-proof word or name, and that is what turns up the volume on its various meanings. In German, *Schloss*, which means "castle," includes the verb *schliessen*, "to lock"; *Schloss* also means a "lock." So the resources of this castle are also at the same time the resources of locking up.

Not only do we have, as usual, a castle, which always includes hidden passageways, a chapel, a cemetery, a crypt, but we have even inside the language that contains it a word that is locked up, buried, that keeps its secret, that has within it always something secreted away. And yet it cannot hide or lie.

Locking up, like secrecy, is an ingredient in the growing relationship between Carmilla and Laura. Another one of Carmilla's bad habits is her need always to lock her door: " 'I always lock my door' " (33). We soon find Laura adopting the habit too:

> I had adopted Carmilla's habit of locking her bedroom door, having taken into my head all her whimsical alarms about midnight invaders, and prowling assassins.... These wise measures taken, I got into my bed and fell asleep. A light was burning in my room.... Thus fortified I might take my rest in peace. (48)

Rest in peace. Laura has started openly imitating and identifying with a corpse via the habit that Carmilla introduced into the household, the habit of locking up. Both identify themselves with the lock, or schloss, containing the unknown resources of life and death.

On page 48 we are given a definition of dreams. They "laugh at lock-smiths." So dreams penetrate what has been locked up. This brings us to the important dream that Laura has, on page 52. She is in a series of recurring dreams:

> One night, instead of the voice I was accustomed to hear in the dark, I heard one, sweet and tender, and at the same time terrible [note the ambivalence], which said, "Your mother warns you to beware of the assassin." At the same time a light unexpectedly sprang up, and I saw Carmilla, standing, near the foot of my bed, in her white nightdress, bathed, from her chin to her feet, in one great stain of blood. (53)

Now how does she respond to the mother's warning, which includes also a full shot of Carmilla as vampire? She rushes to Carmilla's room, possessed by the one idea that Carmilla is being murdered. "I remember springing from my bed, and my next recollection is that of standing on the lobby, crying for help." They rush to Carmilla's door; it is locked of course; they break it down: "But Carmilla was gone" (54).

Now this is the final recess inside the schloss, this room that is at once locked up and empty. Carmilla now comes into focus vampire-style: she is at once locked up and missing.

What is being incorporated within this story? There are two stories on that score: there is the story of Carmilla or, as she was named back then, Mircalla, which turns on the influence of a suicide, who upon his own demonic return exchanged her one-time death for vampiric come-back. And Mircalla, thus demonized by a stray shot of suicide, lives on mainly because her lover cannot stand the thought of her corpse being despoiled. He could only imagine — and he composed a scholarly paper to prove it — that "the vampire, on its expulsion from its amphibious existence, is projected into a far more horrible life" (85). The prospect of double death, the killing of the dead, raises the stakes right out of the melancholic lover's overprojective overprotectiveness.

So everything about the Mircalla story is filled with stories of lov-ing the dead. It is the lover who hides her remains. How does he hide her remains? He displaces the grave's location, tampers with its address, hides it by mutilating it to some degree, but not entirely; he puts on the "stratagem" of taking a trip, during which her remains are removed, her monument obliterated. But what he really does under this triple cover is lodge with his plaint all the remains in some other place within the same cemetery. This brings us back to the conditions of vampirism — that "amphibious existence." The vampire can never lie, that is the secret; but what material form does that take? The vampire Countess cannot change her name but only rearrange the letters. In "Carmilla," "Mircalla," and "Millarca" the same unchangeable letters are secretly but openly there. Just as she cannot be removed from the cemetery but can only be shifted around within the same burial ground, so the letters of the name can be moved around, but nothing can be lost, nothing can go.

These conditions of vampirism bring us back again to the schloss, which is that other unalterable name, the name that cannot even be translated into English; it is this schloss that houses or encrypts Carmilla. Carmilla is not so much introduced into the schloss as she is in effect made to return. The relationship between Laura and Carmilla is a replay of ancient memories, which they both recall, of visiting or being visited by the other in early childhood. The apparition that put fangs into little Laura's heart, which marked the first appearance of Carmilla as far as Laura is concerned, emerged in Laura's childhood at a time when she felt neglected, abandoned. During Carmilla's return engagement, Laura senses an immediate attraction to the guest or ghost — but she is at the same time repelled. Every time she is drawn to Carmilla, there is also an element of repulsion. There is the saving of appearances, of course, which dictates her speculation that Carmilla is a lover boy in drag (37). But there is a real early mix-up of feelings that comes out with the watch Laura is on with her passionate friendship:

> In these mysterious moods I did not like her. I experienced a strange tumultuous excitement that was pleasurable, ever and anon, mingled with a vague sense of fear and disgust. I had no distinct thoughts about her while such scenes lasted, but I was conscious of a love growing into adoration, and also of abhorrence. (36)

Her agitations and her language were unintelligible to me. From these foolish embraces, which were not of very frequent occurrence, I must allow, I used to wish to extricate myself; but my energies seemed to fail me. Her . . . words . . . soothed my resistance into a trance, from which I only seemed to recover myself when she withdrew her arms. (35–36)

I omitted from the last sentence, just before the slide from resistance into trance, a description of her words: "Her murmured words sounded like a lullaby in my ear." There is one other thing we know about Laura's early childhood, which concerns her governess Madame Perrodon: "She in part supplied to me the loss of my mother, whom I do not even remember, so early did I lose her" (19). In representing a relationship of substitution for a loss, Laura uses the verb *supply,* which takes us in two directions. As substitute with a prehistoric or prosthetic name, Madame Perrodon supplies the loss of the mother, which also means that she keeps the loss stocked with her supplies and, on a regular basis, acts as Laura's supplier, pusher, of that early loss. The supply train of thought shows just how current that loss is in a register closed for repetition. Add one foreign-language governess, and they were a round of mourners and substitutes that went around in translation. It was a virtual tower of "Babel," which the narrator will "make no attempt to reproduce in this narrative" (19). The injunction to translate falling upon the impossible wish to speak one language, word, or name will not be admitted here. We are inside the tower or shaft where a doubly lost mother (who cannot be brought into focus even as a distant recollection) holds the missing place that always admitted Carmilla. This was already the case when the vampire made her first introductions in that eidetic memory from early childhood. Laura felt neglected, abandoned by her lost mother. It was the magic moment of Carmilla's debut as Laura's vampire. And Carmilla is introduced or reintroduced into the schloss household alongside a mother who emerges with her out from under an overturned carriage. It is the exit that is an entrance: it symbolizes birth.

The variations on one name, which we learn later on can never lose any of the name's existing pieces or letters, which must hide and preserve the name within every variation, are first introduced with a portrait, as a portrait, as an identifying mark that can only be doubled but never handed down, translated, or lost. Even though it dates from the seventeenth century, this portrait is clearly a likeness of Carmilla, says Laura. Laura says or thinks, quite excitedly, "It was the likeness of Carmilla," but it is noted in the story that the father is not struck by the likeness. This too is important: Laura, the one who sees the likeness or doubling, sees it for the first time on the occasion of viewing a portrait that comes from Laura's mother's family. It is the portrait of a certain Countess Karnstein. Laura says, "I am descended from the Karnsteins"; Carmilla says, "So am I." Are there any Karnsteins living now? None who bear the name. The father too mentions that his dead wife embodied a missing maternal link: " 'My dear wife was maternally descended from the Karnsteins' " (63). This is a doubly maternal link to a family that is extinct in name but lives on through vampiric doubling of a woman's image. "My mother," says Laura, "was of an old Hungarian family, and most of these pictures, which were about to be restored to their places, had come to us through her" (43). Carmilla, thus restored to her place, comes to us (comes *at* us, growing internal and that means eternal) through the loss of the mother.

In *The Hunger* we shift to the newest media sensurround of "liveness," where the attention span that flips through the channels is short, based on the ego, and thus also, at only one remove, on the body. The ego or projected body wants to join in, in the machine, in that evolutionary immortality in which only parts are replaced while the whole lives on cyborg-style. Sometimes you have media that realize what body-based narcissism (or the ego) wants, on its own, here and now — sometimes not. The pre-TV media represent the breakdown (the literalization and reversal) of traditional relations with the superego, relations, which, from dead-letter office to mummy's crypt, cut to (that is, set up diversions on the way to) the otherwise utterly unprotected tomb of the undead other. That is why the photograph in the film doubles as the memory station-breaking the hold of the video monitors. Its memorial is the Before-and-After picture.

If *The Hunger* is horrific, it is not because someone's mother up and died and the death went without saying; it is because you get what you don't want. The life-without-death policy is underwritten by body-based narcissism but without the perpetual antiaging clause. It is like those ancient Greek myths that give us the origin of insects: the one who asks for the other's immortality forgets to ask for antiaging (such forgetting represents, from within this fantasy perspective, the death wish in reverse). You remember: the immortal other who must, however, age forever turns into a grasshopper, cricket, locust, or in other words, one placeholder of the missing link, which the *fantasy* of evolution must look the other way never to find.

The flaw or fly in the appointment of this new and improved vampirism and new womanism is that it is outright body-based in its narcissism (which simulcasts its phantasm with the newest media receptions). To put the contrast in terms of vampire lit: Dracula is into power and long distance; Miriam is into antiaging forever.

So, death (that is, the dead one) is so repressed in *The Hunger* that even as there is immortality now, the time nevertheless comes that there is aging forever. A lack of sleep signals the switch-over: sleep is a natural reserve of identification with the dead that gives one the breathing space for immortality now. All this is conceived from within the crypt of plastic surgery, health regimes, and cryogenics. We see it first in the film: the science of antiaging joins the vampirism network. Whitley Strieber's novel is not only on live or life's transmission. Here the characters are imprinted upon dead others. And Miriam is not replaced. Sarah kills herself and gets to die forever.

That melancholia is still the diagnosis of choice even on screen is given with the impurity in the blood that keeps the undead living — and dying. The impurity in the vampire's bloodline represents identification with someone dead and gone. Sarah's suicide, which spills into Miriam's blood supplies, reverses the one-way flow of contamination and control. The eternally, internally aging exs are jump-started out of Miriam's crypt, and they all fall down to rest in pieces crumbling to dust. Suicide takes control within a sensurround of live transmissions. But bottom line: the lesbian vampiric transmission of power and persona goes sight unseen. Lesbian vampirism skips the beat of phallic visibility and substitutability of transfer.

In Strieber's novel Miriam learns her lesson but lives on: never again will she choose an equal, one like Sarah, whose strength, her quest on the stalk show of the truth of love, was up to if not greater than the vampire's gift. Because in the plain text Sarah commits suicide. But it is too late. Miriam: " 'It was futile, my darling. You were too much changed for mortal death, and now you've got eternal death' " (304).

But the Teen Age implications are not novel to the film version. We read between the lines and wrinkles of John's sudden aging on fast-forward and forever that the vampiric holding pattern had hovered over prepubescent perfection: "Maturing was the horrible process of losing immortality. John felt his face. Already the whiskers were coming back. He had inexplicably entered the deadly shadow; it could no longer be denied" (40). It is not just that he is lacking the deathlike sleep. But he is haunted by his most recent kill. He is doubled over now with the indigestion of murder and mourning. This morbid concern with what is leftover turns his mortality timer back on.

> Was the hunger satisfied by their being or just their blood? John had often wondered if they knew, if they felt themselves in him. From the way he could hear them in his mind, he suspected that they did. Miriam angrily dismissed the notion. . . . She would not accept that you could *touch* the dead. (74–75)

"Miriam insisted there was no touch with the dead. But she wasn't human, she didn't know anything about the relationship between a man and his dead" (77). But there is a difference between Miriam's melancholic indifference to the dead and John's mortal morbid mourning only to the extent that "one's grief" could be factored out, over and out of the vampire's equation of blood and life, mother and living on. Tom, Sarah's husband-to-be, one of the few or two characters who simply die in the book, has this thought that all share: "Death, for example, always seems like a lie, a game of disappearance, until one's grief makes it true" (58).

Miriam is the daughter of a mother who died to reproduce the line. As with certain insect species, the vampires, who transmit the line most frequently by a kind of parthenogenesis, must nevertheless replenish some reserve or reservation via actual acts of reproductive contact. Her life had meant mother's death. Miriam the vampire specializes in not letting the ex, the goner, go. Each ex thus marks the spot she is in with her own mummy. Miriam hesitated a moment before beginning her task. "'I love you,' she said softly, remembering each person who rested here, each lost friend. Perhaps because in the end she had failed all of them she remained loyal to them" (42).

Thus, even when John first entered the vampiric couple, the transformation was a felt absence: "as if his father had ceased to exist" (10). Upon entering the vampiric compact, Sarah sees her long-gone mother. Her two-year breaking of an addiction to cigarettes, which doubled in the register of mourning as suicidal identification with her father, dead of lung cancer (96), cannot prevent the return of the mother's unending dying, fading fast-forward forever.

> She rose swiftly into red fog. Beyond the fog was the source of the song. Sarah almost wept, she had not seen her mother since she was fifteen. . . . —her mother dying, the memory of her voice fading.
> "Open your eyes, Sarah." (180)

In *Daughters of Darkness* the name recognition of Báthory releases the S-and-M secret of the perfect young couple; it turns out the groom is turned on by battered, even murdered women; the bride at least enjoys telling him that she knows just what gets him off. The Countess invites the couple to drinks and to think about the recent murders of young women, "so horrifying yet so fascinating." She prompts the groom to recount the exploits of her ancestor since he seems to know them so well. He goes into a trance of reciting; the Countess fills in, gives encouragement, strokes him. The bride splits. The groom's S-and-M secret releases another one. The aristocratic and disapproving mother he has been afraid to phone about his surprise Swiss marriage turns out to be a sugar daddy at the other end of the line. The ancient blood of aristocratic mother overflows with the even more ancient blood of homosexuality, which slips between the hetero covers as incest, Oedipus, S and M. The husband goes straight to his new bride and beats her until he can consummate the compromise formation of his secret passions. The Countess gets what she wants, and the two brides of a same-sex reunion soon drink the groom's blood, one per wrist. As they prey together, so shall they stay together. Right away, however, the renewed bride must fulfill duties of protection and preservation. But the light is too bright, the car goes out of control, and the Countess ends up as impaled roadkill in broad daylight. But next scene we still hear the Countess. Then we see the doubly widowed bride hitting on the next couple with a replay of the Countess's lines and voice. In a spot of neutrality, the groom, once a sugar daddy's kept boy, straightens out and performs a substitution, which nevertheless projects the aristocratic mother. Freud says: the man falls in love Oedipally with the woman's pre-Oedipal attachment to mother. Love is misrecognition. The projected mother reawakens in him the Norman Batesian desire to cut losses on the person of the substitute. The bride's disenchantment runs her up against her own primal ambivalence toward mother, the early kind that must choose between good and bad breasts. She cuts off the one breast and takes in the voice. What lives on is the mother's fatal attraction to the young couple, which must be infiltrated by the group-sex trajectory of S and M so mother and daughter (daughter as mother) can feed on the group-of-one son. But the mother-and-daughter reunion of lesbian vampirism counts only one survivor.

In *Vampyres* there is a house — and a mother — without end. It is where one guy's one-night stand-in turns out to be another — an other — gay woman's internal and eternal partner in blood bonding.

    Primal scene: castle, footsteps, lesbian lovemaking, intruder's gunshots.

Man arrives at local hotel in no time like the present. We check in with a couple that is on a camping trip. They drive by a couple of weird women (haven't we seen them before?) in the woods. Another driver stops to give the one woman who is forward (the other is beating behind the bushes) a lift, which lifts the wife's middle brows: why was one of them hiding? Yes, there is the routine of fronting for the couple, which is what a woman does for her man standing by. But even the couple routine wasn't followed through when the woman in hiding didn't come forward for easy riding. The wife dreams of hitchhiking women and of the mansion next to which they have set up camper. She wakes up and sees a big hand. "There's someone outside." Next morning she sees the two women as they cross the cemetery. There is an ambulance down the road, a wrecked car, a bloody, dead, bloody driver.

One of the two mystery women is on a date — the date that's the date. They penetrate the castlelike mansion, room within room. She is no questions, no explanations. When he tires of the tour, she advises, "Too late to go back." "My lucky day!" "Don't ever say that!" Next morning he wakes up feeling weak. There is blood on the sheets. What's with his arm? He walks the grounds and meets the happy campers. The wife treats the cut on his arm, binding the open-endedness, the one-timedness of the date. The mystery woman is back in the evening. She takes her same date from the night before on a date with her partner and her date or prey. We get the idea that this represents the first time one of them has reused a date. She once again drinks to her health from his bleeding arm. The couple of women empty the other date dry as the bone he had in mind but not as a noun. They shower and make love. The woman who has only one-night standing in dating culture tells her partner to kill the reusable date before it is too late. POV suggests: someone is watching. When they walk outside, we see "the wife" stalking them. Our date survivor comes across a new accident victim: he recognizes his double on the date. The wife is at her easel, painting the mansion. The mansion-family women come by. The tall dark one talks over her head, shrinks it down to her discourse of reincarnation: "I al-ways knew we'd find each other; by this sign I'd recognize you." The recy-clable container of "the date" is now the three-way freeway, the blood sup-ply of the lesbian couple. They kiss and make love alongside him, over his near-dead body.

The wife enters the mansion. "They live down there like the living dead," she informs her husband who is along for the tour of date duty. The arm-supply guy is fading fast food. Another date arrives. The guy with the give-away arm makes it to the camper. The husband goes out to start the en-gine. But what follows is the duo that devours him on the spot, damn spot. The wife goes out and is abducted by those two women who, alien or not, come together. The wife has to go. But the guy with the resealable wound is still going and going. The women two go after you. But because of their own daytime programming, they have to let him get away. Coda: real es-tate agent shows a new couple the mansion for sale. Is it true? The two women were murdered in the act. A hard act to follow, at least in terms of resale. Because everyone knows that the murderer, no, the murdered, no, the murder itself must always return to make the scene of the crime.

Carl-Theodor Dreyer's film *Vampyr* is almost impossible to follow, but its non-followability has everything to do with its self-representation as medium, which goes comparison hopping around the other visual media of representation (like painting). And it has everything else to do with the film's built-in interpretation of vampirism within the greater consumerist setting. At the beginning of the film a painting comes into focus; it is just one fumbling stopover within a frame of stability while the course of the film has already been set on losing control of the frame, the space of representation. The film takes its departure from painting and also splits what is depicted within that painting; it is a deathbed scene, a scene in which all the props and coordinates of proper mourning are in place. That is what the painting represents, that kind of double stabilization both of a pictorial space and of the close of a life—and that is precisely what goes out of control in this movie (or in the film medium).

There is a plot here that is not being shown in the usual way. There is a very conventional, coherent plot, which is being presented, however, only in a fragmentary way. It gets projected through the confined perspective of a person attending his own funeral with a view through the coffin window. The fragmentary viewing fits a fixed POV that fits inside this coffin aperture or frame.

In "The Taboo upon the Dead," Freud discusses projection, which is a theory of haunting, of the ghosts who, according to Freud, always recycle death wishes. That Freudian view can be plugged right up into this film. "Projection is projection is projection"; cinematic projection need not be distinguished here from what Freud says about the psychic mechanism of projection.

Formally the film lets roll its projection in three parts. The first part is framed inside and out by the narrative intertitles. The second part incorporates excerpts from the book on vampires that the murdered father has handed down. The visionary dreams of Gray, the dreams that will finally bust the vampire, set the third part apart. Thematically or informally, the film covers a combat zone of two big principles or drives: in one corner, the father in principle and in the other, the vampire. But notice that it is not just life versus death, it is not as simple as that; the father is the only other being with supernatural powers right from the start. He is able to pass through the door even though it is locked. He enters Gray's room and introduces himself to Gray in what is one of the more hallucinatory scenes in the film. And at the end he returns as the big saving face that blows away the vampire's little helpers still left over after the vampire has been put to rest. So there are two supernatural powers in the two corners of this match.

Enter a daughter under attack by a vampire woman. What do we know about this family? Who is missing? It is the mother who is missing. And how is the daughter's affliction treated? First, by the father's death being introduced into the household. The father's death leaves itself behind in legacy form. He drops something off with Gray right from the start; he delivers a book that is all wrapped up and ready to go: he tells Gray that this one is to be read after his death. It is the father's death or antibody that gets injected into the afflicted household in order to abort the unmournable death of the missing mother. Like a father, he becomes more active once he is a goner, more "live" when dead, than the other way around.

Between the two figures of a seeming opposition, we see a lot of contamination. Indeed, whenever vampirism makes an apparition, it is ultimately the boundary between life and death that starts zoning out into the zone that is in between. That is what is so scary. Not that death is battling life, but that with the introductory offer of undeath, life and death no longer hold the line of distinction. You can be dead while yet alive, but there is also too much life in death: the living live, the living die, the dead live, the dead die. Remember that *between* meant originally "to be two": this between state, which is the vampiric state, is at the same time the state of being two, of doubling. Doubling takes over when the borders between life and death no longer hold.

The first phase of intertitles symptomatizes a lack of perspective in the gray area of the protagonist's unknowing initiation. Then in place of the intertitles we see quotations from the paternally delegated book on vampirism. Remember that what the father does in the face of vampirism, in the face of a daughter shadowed by the eternal, internal vampire feeding on the missing blood bond with mother, is business as usual: he dies. It is the undertaking of inoculation. His mournable death is injected into the household to jolt a grief-stuck metabolism back onto circulation and substitution tracks. Through this death, through the legacy of the ghostbusting manual, Gray grows increasingly powerful in the contest with the vampire until, in the third part of the film, his own visionary dreams take over where the intertitles and excerpts left off. His dreaming has prophetic and organizing powers. He sees Giselle kidnapped and imprisoned, which shows the way to her rescue, and he has a dream of attending his own funeral, which sends him out there to put the vampire to rest.

Dreyer had this to say about the inspiration or dictation going down in *Vampyr* (the director required hospitalization for the nervous breakdown that followed completion of this film):

> Imagine we are sitting in a normal room. Suddenly we are told that a corpse lies in front of the door. At that moment the room in which we are sitting has been completely transformed. Every object in the room suddenly looks completely different. The light and the atmosphere have changed, although in reality everything remains as before. We are the ones who have changed, and the objects are as we see them. This is precisely the effect I would like to produce with my film. (cited in Bordwell n 13, 236)

So, with the report of the corpse lying in front of the door, we start projecting a film. These visual distortions around objects that remain the same belong to the projections we instantly start watching once there is news of a corpse in front of the door. The door shut on our side opens onto the corpse's representation. A door frames something; to frame something is already to represent and to bury it. It is the undertaking of representing and burying the announced but unseen, unadmitted corpse that the film coincides with.

We have seen that the film is impossible to follow because it has been submitted to systematic deletions from and interruptions of causality and context. Everything that is shown is shown in sequence, but there are pieces missing, and those missing pieces all refer to a cause that is absent. We are always getting the effects that have been taken out of context but never the picture. Why? What's the point? Why does Dreyer lift out of frame or sequence, out of the narrative flow and the pictorial coagulation of events those other moments that would otherwise contextualize and frame the leftover events, and give them a purpose and us the picture?

Remember the contest between the painting at the beginning of the film and the film's reflection on itself as medium? The film is trying to come up with an understanding of itself as medium, and to do so it takes its departure from painting. It is not superimposable onto the controlled pictorial space of painting conceived from one fixed perspective. Nor does film add motion to the picture and leave it there. Instead, film offers something else again, the in-between zone of doubling, and it is through this zoning dispute between life and death that the survivor-viewer must work it on out.

We do not see in pictures, we do not see within a fixed perspective; in order to do so we would have to be trapped inside the coffin looking out a little window that constrains and contains our view. Only by embodying a camera or projector, without peripheral vision or context, only then, if we had blinders on us, were undead, and, like the vampire, slept with eyes open, could we see in pictures, put ourselves in pictures by precisely leaving ourselves out, over and out.

At one end, then, there is the implicit frame of a painting glimpsed, perused, dislocated at the start of the film. At the other end is the literal frame of the coffin window; looking out, toward the viewer's context or coherence of reading, there is the undead perspective that—fixed in place by shock of loss, by the backfire of identification with the other, who is always the first to go—can only follow the decontextualized dislocations of what passes before your eyes. The frame thus asserts itself in its dislocation, during your coffin break, *as* representation.

In the scene of Gray attending his own funeral, as he looks out he sees the various enigmatic figures of the film cross before his point of view, both lens and picture frame, including suddenly—I think everyone is surprised—the vampire Chopin, who also suddenly appears on screen, that is, through the windowpane. Here we see that it is not so much that the film records and selects from the sequence of events, but rather that the events pass before this limited and fixed-in-place lookout position. So why do I keep on covering this ground? Only to press home the importance of that scene of live burial. Formally the film leads up to it, because its every take on perspective—in perspective—is held together inside that coffin window, and finally—and we will get to this point—psychoanalytically the scene is a breakthrough: Gray begins to reclaim the projection and put the vampire to rest. Only now can he put the bite back on her.

When it comes to Freud's inside view of projection, notice that ambivalence is the operative concept, a real operator. Ambivalence gets caught in the act in a phrase like "helping someone *out.*" *Watch* out! The point is that Freud saw that mourning rituals pack a double dose of the ambivalence our unconscious is always picking up on. These rituals, which up front commemorate the dead who are revered and idealized, advance at the same time defensive measures that must deliver us from their return.

In the subsection from *Totem and Taboo* titled "The Taboo upon the Dead," Freud reviews many funeral ceremonies, rituals, and concepts from both sides of their ambivalence; he looks into the relocation of the dead up in the beyond or out on islands separated by great bodies of water. He says that originally (that is not originally in historical time but originally, primally—as soon as you hear the report of the corpse in front of the door—originally and always) all the dead were vampires. So originally, primally, right from the start, every dead person starts out a vampire.

When Freud shifts his reflections from so-called primitives to his neurotic patients, he starts talking about certain survivors (we all know who they are) who put on a show of guiltification, proclaim guilt and total responsibility, even though they were in fact in the sick room every day taking care of the dying loved one. Freud again takes us by surprise. He says that even though there seems to be no correspondence on the outside between this guilty affect and the deathbed situation, still one must believe the patient who puts out a verdict on himself; indeed that person is guilty but in terms that are not accessible to conscious thinking; at another level—within the unconscious—there had been this wish that the person go, and it is this wish, which was locked up somewhere else, that is the source of the person's guilt.

> It then becomes easy to understand how after a painful bereavement, savages should be obliged to produce a reaction against the hostility latent in their unconscious similar to that expressed as obsessive self-reproach in the case of neurotics. [When Freud speaks about so-called savages, please keep in mind that, like children too, these are the friendly natives, the unbeatable cartoon figures of the unconscious.] But this hostility, distressingly felt in the unconscious as satisfaction over the death, is differently dealt with among primitive peoples. The defense against it takes the form of displacing it on to the object of the hostility, on to the dead themselves. This defensive procedure, which is a common one both in normal and pathological mental life, is known as a "projection." The survivor thus denies that he has ever harbored any hostile feelings against the dead loved one; the soul of the dead harbors them instead and seeks to put them into action during the whole period of mourning. (61)

Ambivalence, remember, is the disposition special-ordered for our close relationships. The persons we are closest to are the ones we also identify with. Which means that there is part of us inside each one of our nearest and dearest, just as there are parts of them inside us. These partings are sweet: that is why they were devoured. But at the same time, the person close to us is also feared. It is not only because we might fear just about anyone, even our near-miss lookalike, who is other than us. But we fear the other of identification also because the body parts that were exchanged were transplanted, which is always a one-way operation. We are afraid we violated the other's personal space when we loved the other—to death.

Freud says that the slain enemy in primal time was no problem; it is real easy to dispose of someone who is totally on the outside. But as soon as the person close to us (the person we have identified with) goes, then we have to perform the rituals of mourning. The deceased seizes vampiric control over us. As soon as the report reaches us that a corpse lies in front of the door, we have to start repressing or representing, encrypting or burying the dead body that is haunting us. It haunts us because we project right away onto the corpse the starring role in a vampire film: the film *Vampyr* is the projection inside the room (inside the camera or projector) of death wishes onto a corpse that cannot lie before us for long but is (on reanimation rebound) aimed at our destruction.

This brings us to the issue of identification and to the scene in which Gray attends his own funeral. What have we always done when it comes time to dispose of the dead? We have consumed the dead. Eating, I told you so, repeats and rehearses the act or enactment of identification; in the funeral feast we rerecord (and at the same time erase) our identification with the dead person. Part of that person is already inside us, and this is the part of ourselves that must also go with that dead person. So at the funeral feast we take in the body, but not to preserve it—that would be the melancholic repast—but to digest it, assimilate it, and excrete what is left. And that is what the dream of attending one's own funeral is also about. What does it mean to attend your own funeral? Though you will be the star attraction at your own funeral, generally you do not attend it or view it; the only way that you can go to your own funeral is as an other. But that means that you have to have already *identified* with the corpse. So, in attending his own funeral, Gray is able to put to rest that part of himself that identified with the departed, and having put that to rest, he can emerge from his dream of live burial and proceed directly to the vampire's grave and destroy her undead corpse.

Having said all this, what does the motion picture say about its difference from painting, again? It is the same difference from the notion of a proper burial to be contained within a frame, within a deathbed scene that will slide right into the grave, that will close up upon itself and forever rest in peace. Instead, we should go to the movies and reclaim the projections that we have coproduced, and through the second course of identification (which is what the funeral feast, the other pop-corn or pop-corpse, is all about), we can see the film we started projecting onto the corpse in front of the door to its conclusion. When the doctor is buried alive in a plaster mill, the grinder resembles nothing so much as the apparatus that goes into the making and showing of a film. The film comes to a close only as the projective machinery shuts down.

From my viewing of the Danish-language original with subtitles, I take it the Danish word for "The End" is *Slut*. Anyway, that was the word at the film's end. The open-and-Slut reading rules many other "Carmilla"-inspired movies, in particular the Hammer versions or virgins, which jackhammer away around the horror and sex connections (which are taken aphrodisiacally). Making these connections was the import of being a British movie back in the 1950s. But as a reading of Dreyer's film, it has been totally preempted. Among the effects of haunting there is always the literal take on or intake of a word or name substitution-proofed through untranslatability.

But let's at least get back to the formal conditions of our blindered date with sex therapy by beginning again and taking on "Revelations in Black," which takes its burial frame of representation from photography. The story appeared in 1933 in the United States, in the year Hitler got a rise out of power in Germany. Carl Jacobi, a name one might find appended to an eighteenth-century treatise on vampirism, is the author of this story, which is about a vampiric legacy of the centrally powered loss of World War I. And the legacy folds out of a book, a text, that falls in three parts, but that in all parts fits the story we are reading. The narrator, whose interests cover what is ancient or of occult pedigree and range from the symptoms of psychopathology to photography, chances upon an antique store. By chance the proprietor's personal possession, the first part of his poor brother's mad trilogy and testament, was misplaced on the rack of horror books. A year has passed since the brother sickened, went mad, and died.

> "Three books. . . . Two others exactly like the one you have in your hand. The bindings he made, of course, when he was quite well. It was his original intention, I believe, to pen in them by hand the verses of Marini. He was very clever at such work. But the wanderings of his mind which filled the pages now, I have never read. Nor do I intend to. I want to keep with me the memory of him when he was happy." (284–85)

Hand-bound books that were, for better or verses, to be devoted to transcription of another's corpus (whose futurism already belonged to fascism) fill up instead with the forget-together of a brother's madness. Three identical books, three books of identification, which go without reading, hold the place of the lost sibling bond: " 'For hours I could sit while he read to me his poems' " (284). But the brother's unread corpus issues a phantom call to the consumer of antiques and photo ops.

The dealer will not sell any of the books to the narrator, who negotiates a rental instead: by volume three, however, which the dealer refuses to lend, the narrator steals the final installment. Possession of or by these books is doubly a legacy of lost brothers; their bond of identification gets mixed up out of equal parts of rivalry over the mother's corpus. The overdetermined property disputes over books always and again reflect the tug of mother's exclusive rights. The female vampire, the sister incorporated within her search for a missing brother, is the only other source to spill across the mad poet's pages in a foreword, penned in blood, which has the book's last word. Fanglike marks of citation admit the blood-red curse on whosoever should enter the precincts of the unread: " '*Revelations meant to destroy but only binding without the stake. Read, fool, and enter my field, for we are chained to the spot*' " (285).

Books have since antiquity, the era of the antique, been under pre-scription like narcotics (the genre to which the narrator will ascribe the effect of this over-the-counter trilogy). Freud advised that every intoxi-cant represented yet another attempt to find the libido-toxin that could restore that first high of an original connection. The narrator reads a "feminine hand," one that has been forward, has drawn blood instead of ink, and, then as now, has taken possession: "Something about the few sentences had cast an immediate spell of depression over me. The vague lines weighed upon my mind, and I felt myself slowly seized by a deep feeling of uneasiness" (286). The narrator is drawn to a scene that literalizes and reconstitutes the brother's wanderings. Comparable to the way POV literalization is foregrounded in Dreyer's *Vampyr*, the mad poet "had seized isolated details but neglected to explain them" (288). The woman in black completes the literalization of what must be seen, taken in, and not framed or named. This woman has, like the books in the narrator's possession, a brother's story to tell: " 'it was to find my only brother that I came to the United States. . . . In 1916 . . . he was re-ported missing' " (290). Two reports followed: one from a grave-digging detail in a prisoner-of-war camp in France; the other from the United States, where he was rumored to be. When she found him, " 'he was no longer living.' " " 'Dead?' I asked" (290). No response.

When he starts in on the second installment of the other brother's testament, he comes across the beginning revelation of the woman's iden-tity as "loathsome creature" (292): "I closed the book and tried to divert my attention elsewhere by polishing the lens of my newest portable cam-era." He fights against the "sensation" that draws him back to the scene inside and outside the trilogy:

> Then it suddenly occurred to me what a remarkable picture she would make. . . . If I could but catch the scene on a photographic plate. . . . And if the result were satisfactory it would make a worthy contribution to the International Camera Contest at Geneva next month. (292)

He goes back to the point of return — and of no return from the return. But he takes with him a camera and the prospect of a contest.

His return means that the vampire possesses him: the shoot will leave behind a second set of proofs that will pull the vampire's covert operations out from under the testament of two brothers. In the darkroom the narrator can develop the scene but no trace of the woman: "No explanation offered itself" (295). But the evidence of the shoot is the placeholder for the context or contest of representation, mourning, and identification on grounds of rivalry. Now he can steal the third book and receive the news that the siblings in the scene that the trilogy opened onto are vampires. He discovers at the same time that the books were binding: they bound the vampires to the spot they could not get out of, not until the same books had led another reader to the scene.

Yet if the books had found their power in chains, they had also opened a new chain operation for their attacks. Those printed lines were now the outer reaches of their web (298).

But this narrator-reader, who is also a photographer, knows how to dispose of "ancient evils": "I seized one of the wooden legs [one of the prostheses] of the tripod in my hands, snapped it across my knee. Then, grasping the two broken pieces, both now with sharp splintered ends, I rushed hatless out of the door to the street" (298–99). He takes the rescue stakes from the tripod, the support of his photography. The outer frame has developed with his desire to compete for the photo prize within a context of identification that shifts internally from rivalry over the mother to the interpersonal columns of substitute objects. The tripod, as three-limbed support, suggests the paternal support of that room, or "camera," with a mirror inside it making up the internal scene of photography. He takes from its support the means of his two-pronged attack, which short-circuits the sibling bonds and melancholic outlets of vampirism. But then, even after the vampires are put to rest, the narrator burns the stolen trilogy, the antique dealer's unread corpus, which, excuse the overkill, already doubled as the undead corpse that no brother can put to rest. This 1933 story gives us a forecast, picking it up as if in some spiritist photograph, of the ghosts otherwise unseen but in attendance of an uncanny interchangeability of bodies that will go up in smoke.

We enter a worldwide web of vampirism — and at the same time the tight place in front of the scream, I mean screen — with Suzy McKee Charnas's *The Vampire Tapestry*. This text or tapestry weaves and leaves one life out of many solo "transmigrations." The medium for each cross-over is sleep, which tides the vampire over centuries to reawaken in the contextlessness of repression of libido or capacity for love under the sole direction of his hunger, hunting, need to feed. In this life the vampire, Edward Weyland, is an academic with research and teaching interests involving human subjects. He keeps his hunter/prey relations with humanity under the covers of the sleep research he conducts with countless voluntary subjects between takes or tests of blood. On an assembly line of donors, whose monitored sleep is expected to leave them groggy one and all, blood supplies last. The timer of his exposure, and of the end of this life within a series of episodes, is first set with the teeth of a South African woman, the widow of local academic life, whose prehistory holds the margin of hunting. Both champ down on their instinctual recognition of a fellow hunter in the midst of prey. The widow makes all the connections, as when she overhears the academic mix of metaphors at the faculty club:

> Later, helping to dig out a fur hat from under the coat pile in the foyer, she heard someone saying, "... walk off with the credit; cold-bloodedly living off other people's academic substance, so to speak."
> Into her mind came the image of Dr. Weyland's tall figure moving without a break in stride past the stricken student. (27)

Don't mind that the curriculum vitae or lifeblood of a student always belongs to the professor's corpus whose teaching is his research. We get an even closer look at this student-professor relationship when, looking through the widow, we attend one of the professor's vampire lectures. It is the session devoted to, brought to us by, the self-help of long periods of sleep, the station identification that permits the vampire during intermission to enjoy " 'mobility in time,' " " 'his alternative to mobility in space' " (36):

> Katje listened intently. His daring in speaking this way excited her. She could see he was beginning to enjoy the game, growing more at

ease on the podium as he warmed to his subject. . . . It seemed to Katje that he mocked them.

"The vampire's slowed body functions during these long rest periods might well help extend his lifetime; so might living for long periods, waking or sleeping, on the edge of starvation. We know that minimal feeding produces striking longevity in some other species. Long life would be a highly desirable alternative to reproduction; flourishing best with the least competition, the great predator would not wish to sire his own rivals. It could not be true that his bite would turn his victims into vampires like himself—"

"Or we'd be up to our necks in fangs," whispered someone in the audience rather loudly.

"Fangs are too noticeable and not efficient for bloodsucking," observed Dr. Weyland. "Large, sharp canine teeth are designed to tear meat. Polish versions of the vampire legend might be closer to the mark: they tell of some sort of puncturing device, perhaps a needle in the tongue like a sting that would secrete an anticlotting substance. That way the vampire could seal his lips around a minimal wound and draw the blood freely, instead of having to rip great, spouting, wasteful holes in his unfortunate prey." Dr. Weyland smiled.

The younger members of the audience produced appropriate retching noises. (36–37)

Retch out and touch the little ones.

The professor's sense of audience scans the watch of another hunter and sets his own teeth on edge of a double pleasure celebrated in the service of disposal of witnesses. The alternate cover of a local rapist's spree of violence, always available, by the way, in any university town, takes up the special pleasure taken in feeding directly from the human cattle, hunted and seduced, the pleasure the vampire, trying to keep with the times, was for some time now having to forego rather than, as now, go for. But that woman shoots, takes back the life, and exchanges her intended prey status for the hunter's aim. But such wounds, of course, lick him only temporarily. But then he is captive of/to an audience of horror shows that now pays to watch ex-Professor Dr. Weyland in his cage giving the snuff-subject a pain in the neck, all in the peephole space between private parts and public access.

> That night when Dr. Weyland reached for the young man Reese had sent, Roger commanded, "Not the arm. The neck. The people paid to see the real thing. Go for the neck."

> For a moment the vampire looked out at them with an unfath-
> omable gaze. Then he took the young man by the shoulders and leaned
> in and up under his jawline. The watchers gasped. (90)

Mark, the boy who takes care of the vampire between feeding shows,
identifies with the vampire's predicament. Mark has a mother of a problem with the public display of the blood bond. When Mark saves him,
the vampire enters the mother-and-child exchange or reunion, and lets
the boy go, go the way of the uncontrollable other.

All this leads to a final season of therapy. The vampire must open a
therapeutic account to restore the functioning of his academic cover
identity. But this relationship will reset this time of his life according to
the mortality timer, the old timer, the half-life of the other. The first
trauma, the failure to take the widow's blood, enters the history the therapist takes down. " 'What does that mean — to take someone's blood?' "
he asks himself. " 'Her energy,' he murmured, 'stolen to warm the aging
scholar, the walking corpse, the vampire — myself' " (119). The therapist
is convinced that she hears academic midlife self-criticism given in the
readily available mix of metaphors of undeath. But soon the therapist
is listening to the "reality," the anti-metaphorical insistence, of the vampire delusion. Speculating on a background of homosexual drives that
up and devastated his ego, leaving it all alone to rebuild itself with conspiracy theory, she questions his preference for male prey:

> "I take what is easiest. Men have always been more accessible because
> women have been walled away like prizes or so physically impover-
> ished by repeated childbearing as to be unhealthy prey for me. All
> this has begun to change recently, but gay men are still the simplest
> quarry. . . . A wolf brings down the stragglers at the edges of the herd.
> Gay men are denied the full protection of the human herd and are at
> the same time emboldened to make themselves known and available."
> (136–37)

The vampire professor does his overlaps between the margin of sexual
socialization and the vampiric cause within a pre-AIDS era of concern.
His therapist is also free and easy to take the relationship of their sessions
too interpersonally, perhaps as a defense against the erotic transference.

Hers is an era of overconcern with the place of reproduction in a client's fantasy life:

> So he had left an enormous hole in his construct. She headed straight for it: "Then how does your kind reproduce?"
> "I have no kind, so far as I am aware," he said, "and I do not reproduce. Why should I, when I may live for centuries still, perhaps indefinitely? My sexual equipment is clearly only detailed biological mimicry, a form of protective coloration." (142)

When the vampire registers a sensual response to the performance of ballet, his therapist overworks it for the copulation at the art of dance. Post-therapy, but still within the living on of the transference work, the vampire has another strong response to art, this time to music. But the therapist's countertransference is way off the mark of the vampire's connection with what the appetizers of art advertise. Thus, in the corner of the scene of music that suggestively gives staying power to the transference interpretation, we glimpse, down in the musicians' area, the flutist closely reading *The Revenge of the Androids* (198). On his own, down the stretch of pages gradually closing in on him, the vampire recalls the science fiction Mark had read to his captive audience—and how those stories had reanimated him almost as much as Mark's blood donation. We are now inside the story the vampire writes in the first person inside *The Vampire Tapestry.*

> The stories, read tonight, provoked me to reflect that in such a tale I would be explained as—a device brought from some other planet in order to take samples of human history. Extraterrestrial origin is indicated by my long life, based on a premise of self-repair and self-replacement, in contrast to the multiple lives and rapid turnover typical of indigenous life forms. (245)

A reception or resistance that could be respelled as "psy-fi" at the same time protects the witness and projects a deadline for the vampire's academic role. Just as with the swap of getaways he made with Mark, in exchange for her delivery of the paperwork he needs to get back into his role, he lets the therapist go, going against his better half of instincts.

She argued, still within the terms of confidentiality, that she was already not safe from him; why must he make himself safe from her?

> "You tempt me to it, . . . to go from here with you still alive behind me for the remainder of your little life — to leave woven into Dr. Landauer's quick mind those threads of my own life that I pulled for her . . . I want to be able sometimes to think of you thinking of me. But the risk is very great." (173)

The therapist gets left behind, alive to her mortality. This was the strength she found to match him. But now there is only the same message of time running over and out on her. She is gagging now on the undertow of her countertransference: "That was the meaning of the last parent's death: that the child's remaining time has a limit of its own" (178). The last parent's death, then, had already admitted the relationship to the vampire, the replicate or identification she tried to charge erotically with becoming a reproductive member of society.

After he destroys the internal psy-fi narrative, the vampire returns to his scholarly work of identity: "Scholarship was the best game humankind had yet invented: intricate, demanding, rich with risk and reward — akin in many ways to the hunt itself. In the present instance he took special pleasure in elucidating a territory with which he was uniquely familiar" (246). But even while he takes his restoration act to another state, institution, and area of research, he has left an identifiable trace for the live-horror fanatics to fan into a blazing trail. He cannot but leave, and leave them to their controlling interest in him. The life and career of Dr. Weyland must come to an end after all. The vampire is getting sleepy.

You will not recognize our relationship in this story. When I snap my fingers, everyone will forget that I lectured on *The Vampire Tapestry*.

LECTURE SIXTEEN

It has been by stuffing projections down the tube during a one-time-only period of medium transition that Stephen King, who was there first, came up with the building-blockbusters of a screen coextensive with the preconscious, a clearing house where it all comes together, the to-be-consciously-admitted and the to-be-repressed, but as everything and nothing, as Everyman, as nobody. With this monstrous rewiring of TV through the circuits of big screen projection, King alone could win the lottery of this clearing, the space of the dread in front of the test tube. *It* translates into English the German word that, by way of cathexis, is known to us as id.

The world or word of King is dedicated to the unread. King recognizes in the way the block of buildings is divided between Jekyll and Hyde "a startlingly apt metaphor for Freud's idea of the conscious and subconscious minds — or, to be more specific, the contrast between superego and id" (*Danse Macabre,* 71). But King gets away with misrepresenting Freud as the preconscious or mass-cultural way in which Freud gets undigested. The second system (ego, superego, id) neither replaces nor superimposes itself onto the first system (conscious, preconscious, unconscious). The visualization of the unconscious as below us, as subconscious, is Jung's contribution. In King's all-out elaboration of a psychoanalytic concept, *It,* or id, comes right out of the toilet and sits in the corner, watching you watching. The flicking of photos into a horror film, the hallucination of death sentences running across the movie theater marquee, are transitional objections to the installment plan of TV. Deathwish static between brothers accompanied the first emergence of *It.* But the suicide or death drive that *It* lets roll is less projective, circuitous, and more of a direct hit. I am quoting now from *It*'s first appearance on a screen as made-for-TV movie:

> "I looked right into the deadlights and I wanted to be there."
> "I made it, I'm in the deadlights, and you know, it's true what they say, we all float down here, and you will too."
> "You'll lose your little minds in my deadlights — like all the others."

King unpacks behind the deadlights the psychic battery image first turned on in *'Salem's Lot:* " 'hauntings' might really be a kind of paranormal movie show — the broadcasting back of old voices and images which might be parts of old events" (*Danse Macabre,* 265). Reruns without end and serializations are the two and the same trajectories of haunting. The members of the *Dark Shadows* cast never disappeared, not without returning as ghosts (ibid., 232). The fact of rerun gives a new release of unlife, "that sort of fuzzy, black-and-white, vampiristic life which syndication allows" (ibid., 229).

'Salem's Lot, town or novel, already has the bad rep of being haunted. Right away we are invited to read all the ingredients of melancholia or haunting off the back of protagonist Ben, who returns to this hometown where, once upon a time, he deposited the unresolved parts of his childhood. Ben was parked here for four early years. And he is still looking for validation. Back then his father died, his mother broke down, and he was sent to stay with his aunt in 'salem's Lot. He is still haunted by the primal scene he came across inside the local haunted house. Somewhere between ESP and psychotic break, little Ben saw the long-ago, long-distant owner of the Marsden mansion, whose evil was legend, still hanging in there, undead tribute to his eternal evil. But what's seen isn't what's heard in passing, isn't the internal scene. Ben split, hit the road and hard times with mom, in 1972, right after his aunt committed suicide. Not as long ago he lost his wife in the motorcycle wreck he survived. Add to these ingredients all the tensions between identification and substitution, and we get the picture already. Upon returning to the scene of the repressed memory or the memory of a repression that has been flashing back again following the wife's death, Ben finds the con-

solation prize just around the corner: a local girl recognizes author Ben Mears from his picture on the back of the book she is reading: " 'I thought I was seeing a ghost' " (8).

In a duet of reminiscence and station identification between Ben and local girl Susan, we learn that the movie house of Ben's past, now a real estate office, has given way to TV's competition. TV is what lies between Ben and his reader, the substitute you can't take home with you. TV and RV trailer parks. It is this transitional objective that Ben aims for when he recounts to Susan his vision at age nine:

> "Probably I was so keyed up that I hallucinated the whole thing. On the other hand, there may be some truth in that idea that houses absorb the emotions that are spent in them, that they hold a kind of... dry charge. Perhaps the right personality, that of an imaginative boy, for instance, could act as a catalyst on that dry charge, and cause it to produce an active manifestation of... something. I'm not talking about ghosts, precisely. I'm talking about a kind of psychic television in three dimensions. Perhaps even something alive. A monster, if you like." (29–30)

It would be so easy to found a vampire colony in 'salem's Lot now that TV has superseded neighborhood get-togethers (256). Ben says:

> "But who knows what's going on in the houses, behind drawn shades? People could be lying in their beds... or propped in closets like brooms... down in cellars... waiting for the sun to go down. And each sunrise, less people out on the streets. Less every day." He swallowed and heard a dry click in his throat. (256–57)

King's down-home-and-haunted all-American TV and RV tempo results from backgrafting the whole network, from the click of the phone to the mobility of automobilic technologies, onto the tubular experience. In other words, King's one-shot, scattershot narratives fill the preconscious right where check-out minds keep feeding time with mixed metaphorization and mistaken identification. The prologue tells us like it is up to the mix: "In America missing persons are as natural as cherry pie. We're living in an automobile-oriented society. People pick up stakes and move on every two or three years. Sometimes they forget to leave a forwarding address. Especially the deadbeats" (xvi). King's melancholic mix, if that is what *It* is, confirms or conforms to Lacan's common-sense view that not mourning is one big error or disorder in thinking. Thus, a fabulous monument to someone's ignorance, the character's or, more likely still, King's, is one of two references to Freud in the novel:

> "I've always considered myself a bit of a free thinker, not easily shocked. But it's amazing how hard the mind can try to block out something it doesn't like or finds threatening. Like the magic slates we had as boys. If you didn't like what you had drawn, you had only to pull the top sheet up and it would disappear."
>
> "But the line stayed on the black stuff underneath forever," Susan said.
>
> "Yes." He smiled at her. "A lovely metaphor for the interaction of the conscious and the unconscious mind. A pity Freud was stuck with onions. But we wander." (245–46)

If only some torture writing machine could forever inscribe upon this royally stuck corpus Freud's "Note on the 'Mystic Writing Pad,'" then indeed some order of burial or closure could at last be filled. Instead, right out of this mix or mess, two figures of TV teleguidance get raised by the local priest: our current disconnection from a working definition of evil comes down to Freud and electricity (305). The real horror, as Father knows best, isn't Hitler or Satan, it's child abuse: and then the abused abuses, world without end (151).

These charged connections, which were already wired through Ben's repressed memory, and which already spilled over onto his encounter with Susan, get rerun through what automatically passes between Ben and Mark, a local boy who is the double of Ben at the time of his traumatization. When Ben and Mark meet three hundred pages into the book, we witness an instant bonding for which the opening connection between Ben and Susan was just the repetition or rehearsal:

> They looked at each other for no great space of time, but for Ben the moment seemed to undergo a queer stretching, and a feeling of unreality swept him. The boy reminded him physically of the boy he himself had been, but it was more than that. He seemed to feel a weight

settle onto his neck, as if in a curious way he sensed the more-than-chance coming together of their lives. It made him think of the day he had met Susan in the park, and how their light, get-acquainted conversation had seemed queerly heavy and fraught with intimations of the future. (314)

They go for a ride and a talk, and Ben flashes back to the accident that killed Miranda. He recalls the beginning of acceptance, a feeling he can only compare to rape (315). Susan, the first runner-up, has become vampire legion (when she is staked, her undead beauty reminds the local doctor of the little girl whores of Saigon). On his Mark, Ben flashes Susan's face, wonders if the kid's a psycho, decides to trust him, and they're off. When Mark runs down the Marsden house driveway, away from the castration threats of head vampire and his minion (287, 334), away from an undead voice that is the soundalike of his dad's lowered boom (292), the connection comes through between this experience and that of the boy Ben many years ago (293):

> As Mark pushed open the door and stepped into the room where Hubert Marsden had committed suicide, something odd seemed to happen in his mind. The fear did not fall away from it, but it seemed to stop acting as a brake on his thoughts, jamming all productive signals. His thoughts began to flicker past with amazing speed, not in words or precisely in images, but in a kind of symbolic shorthand. He felt like a light bulb that has suddenly received a surge of power from no known source. (285–86)

Some elemental force is with the duo now. After the crypt door gives way, they clasp hands, and Ben says to Mark, "I love you" (409). But then under the master's hypnotic beam Mark is forced to fight Ben for top-man position. After Ben knocks Mark out, the boy wakes up crying for his mother. (Earlier, Ben rocked Mark in his arms after mother was murdered [360].) The master, whose face is described as almost effeminate (352), finally gets the stake: no more near miss. The other vampires ask, almost as in grief, how he could have killed the master vampire. Ben is reminded of the bystanders crowding in on the scene of Miranda's death on the road (414).

The photo-identification of Ben by Susan comes off his second novel, *Air Dance*. It is just another dance of avoidance. The only heir around to be conditioned is second in line, the secondary one, who always has to settle for the substitute, second best. But for Ben, that all is still up in the air. A cut in time, that's the feeling he gets, a new beginning, somewhere over this meeting with a fan. It is a cut that will save him in time when it returns with or relocates to his earlier bond with himself as boy, with Mark. The substitute Susan will go the way, away, of vampirism and staking.

"If nothing fires between two people, such an instant simply falls back into the general wreck of memory" (9). But he was only fired up by the advance preview of the Mark coming soon. That is when Susan gets fired, thrown into the eternal flame of efficient mourning. When Ben and Susan first meet, sex stresses out as paranoid project, then settles down to rest in identification. When he plays back across his thoughts his first book's treatment by critics and "coffeehouse friends," he comes, silently, keeping it to himself, to his own defense: "Plot was out, masturbation in" (10). But two pages later he confides out loud to Susan, " 'Sometimes when I'm lying in bed at night I make up a *Playboy* interview about me.' " Back home again, the prison rape scene in *Air Dance* flashes before Susan's eyes when her mother asks to read the book by her new friend Ben.

Suspects in local cases of disappearing children are either ghosts or perverts. This is the busy interchange on which the novel keeps mixing up a sexual angle out of the coordinates of identification. Mark, the portrait of the author as a boy, gets harassed at school for being "queer" (46). His free time is spent building monster models. His understanding of death? It is "when the monsters got you" (139). The monsters reflect the local undertaking of counterfeiting commemorative markers of our ancestors. That's the town's business, at the level of identification. On the projective range, "faggot" antique dealers are the middlemen who must be set up for the scam to go through (50). Under the cover of this projection the vampire and his minion move into the Marsden house.

Two delivery men with enigmatic crates arrive at the Marsden house to drop off the cargo: " 'If there was ever a haunted house, that's it. Those guys must be crazy, tryin' to live there. Probably queer for each other anyway.' 'Like those fag interior decorators.... Probably trying to turn it into a showplace. Good for business' " (86). The homophobic or paranoid setting remetabolizes the whole world watching the set of the Vietnam War. The one with the queer feeling next senses a "strain of fear enter his heart that he had not even felt in Nam, although he had been scared most of his time there.... Ghosts? He didn't believe in ghosts. Not after Nam" (87). Again, it is either ghosts or perverts.

The first person to make the connection to vampirism is Matt, Ben's former teacher, an unmarried failed author and bachelor forever. The local gravedigger, whose name is Mike, has been anemic ever since working on the burial of that boy, the Glick kid, who died of anemia. Matt saw puncture marks on Mike's neck. Yes, he believed in monsters, child molesters, mass murderers, but not, not this. But then he hears Mike next door inviting someone in. "And in the awful heavy silence of the house, as he sat impotently on his bed with his face in his hands, he heard the high, sweet, evil laugh of a child — and then the sucking sounds" (165). When Ben takes the emergency call and, armed with crucifix, accompanies Matt down the sound track into gravedigger Mike's place, the young man is the picture of death, no longer ill-looking or blemished by puncture marks. Ben is struck by the young man's look and is not a master of indifference: "His hair was tousled loosely across his brow, and Ben thought that in the first delicate light he was more than handsome; he was as beautiful as the profile of a Greek statue" (174). Ben warns Matt not to tell anyone about his vampire convictions. The kids will turn his life into a real-life horror movie. " 'They would even get around to telling each other we were a couple of queers and this was the way we got our kicks.' Matt was looking at him with slowly dawning horror" (176). When Mike comes back — he already had the standing invitation — Matt beats him off with the cross. Mike leaves with a curse and gives Matt an all-natural heart attack: " 'I will see you sleep like the dead, teacher' " (205). During the vampire epidemic, a heart attack is counted as the only natural death in town on that night. The only death. That goes for Matt's passing too (400). He is the loser-double of Ben. The close encounter with vampirism brought Ben and Mark together and death-wished away Matt, the malignant prophecy, the double loser, the paternal order as curse.

Between the lines of resistance that anticipate and mimic a Freudian understanding of his own case, King raises his issue by a father in *Danse Macabre.* The father abandoned his little family, beaming back into King's life only as a home-movie ghost (95) or through his mother's alleged sighting of him in a TV newsreel about mercenaries of war (93). But the father had tried his hand at writing science fiction. And he left behind his Lovecraft books. This was the first lesson in horror fiction, which King defines for openers as "looking for the place where you, the viewer or reader, live at your most primitive level" and then taking you back there through stimulation of "phobic pressure points" (4). Before King mentions in passing the horror legacy passed down by the missing dad, he throws the high beam on one traumatic event in his childhood, while switching on the laugh track of resistance to any one-way or one-sided reading of that event's recurrence in his horror fantasies, even though or especially because the death of his friend under the wheels of a train just passing through withdrew once and for all into the blackout conditions of King's ongoing amnesia (83–84).

The mix-up in medium transfer that characterizes the fit King has with his instant readership — the forget-together of preconscious consumerism — releases symptoms in the form of mistaken identification. We tracked spectacular flubs in the representation of Freud. In *Danse Macabre,* King forgets on occasion whose body was up for burial or unburial. He dismisses *Plan Nine from Outer Space* as such a misuse of Lugosi's talents that the actor died of shame right afterwards upon seeing the finished product (212). King, who will never die of shame, is a real good overlooker of the overlap between the actor's death during the making of the film and the projection of and reidentification with the actor's role of vampiric ghost in the film of his posthumous or second death. All in a mourning's work. King takes John Badham to task for tampering with the cast of Stoker's *Dracula*, in particular for the new designation of Van Helsing as Lucy's father: "The changes don't cause Badham to say anything new about either the Count or the vampire myth in general" (135). But the change King notices does turn up the volume on mournings and unmournings in the story. Van Helsing now leads the first staking against his own dead daughter's vampiric ghost. In this version Lucy is constructed as the perpetual patient, whose need for constant care sets up her departure as prefabulated in the medium of death wishes. For the father as for friend Minna, who goes off to act out sexually rather than keep watch over her sickly friend, who was placed in her care right in bed beside her, Lucy's passing gives unbearable relief. On the preceding page King was quick to make change where it matters most. The opening of *Night of the Living Dead*, the visit to the cemetery by Barbara and Johnny, is grounded by King in their mother's grave, whereas the original address belonged to the dead father (134). King cannot misplace the dead mother's role in *Psycho*. But he goes into overidentification when proposing Norman as a werewolf who puts on not the hirsute hide but his "dead mother's panties, slip, and dress" instead. What a slip!

What about the hustle of same sexuality? Homosexuality does appear along for the crypt effects, the Cargo, and the projective sensurround of vampirism. But the bottom line, again and again, in all representations of the undead, even those that get drawn into or out of the open admission of the other fact of life, holds down a fort of separation, the separation from some missing body, a breakup that precedes the emergencies of sexual identification. That is why the homosexual edge in vampirism is still most cutting where its exclusion bears the mark of near-miss inoculations against its coming out. The hard-to-swallow buddy-movie dynamics of murderous consummation over a woman's conveyor belting, abuse, and dispatch can be found lying in wait and then, no longer able to wait, climaxing in exquisite overdetermination in the closet readings of Hollywood. We are considering *Salem's Lot,* the lot of them, one and two.

Two newcomers to the little town soon find themselves the leading contestants in the ring: in one corner the antique dealer and master vampire's minion, who is coded for daytime programming as gay; in the other corner there is the blond author, who has returned to the town where he grew up to write another book, finally the Big One about himself (and on location). His coding is forever up in the air, a near miss or mess. The author's return to the town gets connected up with our first look at the local psychic kid: the two of them are the town's once and future blonds. The author breaks the tension and identifies as straight when he starts dating the young woman he came across reading one of his books. She adds the appetizer of disowning a prior claim already made on her. But the author is into recognition, not into love, that mode of misrecognition that the woman has real bad.

The blond kid, the double of the author in his youth, is a group-of-one fan club of the occult. His best friends, the Glick brothers, are the first to fall victim to the new vampire in town. What friends? They didn't understand the blond's interest in the occult. His father asks him when he is going to outgrow all this. Soon, the kid answers. Soon the two blonds will be the sole survivors of the whole town wiped out by occult powers. The kid's parents aren't even vampirized first; with one swipe the master vampire, who bursts in on the family gathering with the priest in the kitchen to talk some sense into the overly imaginative boy, simply kills the parents.

But first one Glick gets vampirized, then he returns to give it to his brother. The first spreading of vampirism in the town is therefore incestuous and same-sex. And that is how the survivorship gets shared too. The girlfriend and her father are bystander casualties in the fall of vampirism by blond ammunition. As the town is flaming, the author, who set the blaze on the vampires, assures the other sole survivor, his younger double, that the arson he would seem to have committed was the only way to beat the plague: "It'll purify Salem's Lot." Arson? Are you a son? No, I'm the double-strength blond purifier of Salem's Lot. Thanks a lot.

Is it gay or straight, was it TV or film, was it Tobe Hooper or not Tobe? The sequel, *A Return to Salem's Lot,* plugs into the post-Holocaust setting and struggle between ethnicities fighting the good and big one for the rights to survival, commemoration, restitution. At first ethnic otherness, given and taken away, is the doubled focus of the film. But the picture alternates with the Oedipal plot that follows, ploddingly, until it too gets headed off again at the passage of ethnic otherness, a near-psychotic condition that remains, however, always carefully doubled, contained, canned.

After the divorce, the anthropologist father is called in to take care of his acting-out son, too hot a handle for the ex-wife and new husband. Father and son arrive at the town that in name bears the nick of time ("used to be called Jerusalem's Lot") to claim the legacy of the father's aunt.

At night the vampires are out and about. Father begins to figure out that they are killing victims in there. "Something like that. You recognized your aunt? She's one of us. You still haven't figured it out, Mr. professional anthropologist. We're the oldest race of humanity, vampires. You've traveled the world, seen starvation produced for profit. Do you think that world is any better than ours? We're still dairy farmers, but we grow stock for blood. Human blood is still the best, but nowadays with hepatitis, drugs, AIDS . . ." "Sounds like you want me to write this all down." "Two hundred years from now it'll be read. You have credentials. You could write a book to change the views of outsiders." Aunt Clara is just the same as in the anthropologist's boyhood; back then she was already one of them. A seventeen-year-old wet dream from back then is still waiting too: "I stayed the same for you. I was seventeen, you were only fourteen. I wanted to be as you remembered me." He's not fucking going to pass up a blast from this past. So he's the historian. He is initiated into their vegetarian rapport with animal blood (the stock of live supplies is never slaughtered). But whatever vegetarian blood bond with live stock applies doesn't with humans who, when available, are consumed.

"Who runs the stores, etc. during the day?" "Drones, don't call them that though; we breed them like the cows." As he drones on, it is not apparent right away, but the son, he wants to become one of them.

Then this old guy, survivor of the Holocaust, comes to town. Would even a Nazi hang out in Salem's Lot? When the son gives him lip, the service at which he's wanting to prey, the old survivor puts him in another place. Father asks, "Where'd you grab him? It works." "I'm a Dutch Jew but my mother was a Rumanian. I'm used to dealing with people who have sold souls to the devil. And I'm not a Nazi hunter, I'm a Nazi killer." As always with "Nazi," there's a slippage and spread via the adjectivalization. If the Nazi era was on loan, ultimately, to the teen haunt where all, the son especially, feel the gift of its grab, then, with the old guy, we can say that superego has come to town, right in the old nick of the town's name. The father's divorce represents the trouble he is still having with his father.

When they are captive eyewitness to the diversion a bus full of people represents in this small town, father tells son, and himself, not to look. The survivor hunter, the true father, gets two not seeing what they are for or in for with the one son they are: "No, let him look." After it is over, the son embraces the survivor, the superego-sponsored side or point of the trauma of identification.

The final onslaught of vampires pulls up short before the rise of the sun. The son repeats that he still doesn't want to grow up. The old survivor says: Me too. Son gets a rise out of their time-share in being human: "I guess it's OK to grow old." Father turns to father: "He's turning human." "Don't tell his mother." They burn witches, don't they?

In Anthony Boucher's "They Bite" the prospects for vampirization are once again projected societywide. These ogres that continue to inhabit the earth are called cannibals; the super-ogre or super-cannibal is as big as the whole white race (20). Do notice what kind of a figure this Tallant person is. He is someone on the lookout for total control; he has a dream of being the ruler of a new American corporate state that would follow "the war." He will be its phantom ruler.

Now what I like about that, this American corporate state or this state of incorporation, is something that can be observed all around us. Forever and again, we have been building up these phantasmic follow-ups to war, these new American corporate states that absorb the loss we never acknowledged. I totally recall the symptomatology of little children running around in murderous green-beret outfits, the advent of Pacman, and our desperately familiar addiction to the power pills that busted ghosts, or the phenomenon of Reagan, who was very much the figure that would not die, who asked for and received four more years. He asked for our lifeblood, and we gave it to him under the vampiric control of his demand. In an interview with Mr. and Mrs. Reagan, Barbara Walters closed the exchange with what she took to be a nonthreatening question, I guess; she asked what movies had been his faves, and he said — and this is what is so great about Reagan or vampirism, the secret is that he cannot lie — he answered that his favorite film had been *Dracula*, and then he turned to "Mommy" and asked, "And what's that other one? You know, with the knobs?" (he was pointing to both sides of his own neck). So indeed there is such a thing as the state of melancholia, whether it be the haunted state of Germany after World War I, where again unmournable loss produced a kind of phantom control over mass media or mediums, or in our own case where an unwillingness to acknowledge loss produced phantoms of another order. "They Bite" is the story that strikes close to home. It takes place in the Californian desert — and is taken over by the enigmatic force of undigested twentieth-century warfare.

We start out with secrecy, and the secrecy soon has Tallant set up to pay protection to some repressed witness in installments of blackmail; remember, he encounters someone who knew him back then in some war zone in the Far East, and who thinks that Tallant is probably still a spy (he has been running around with binoculars close to some air force base). So they have to make a deal, an exchange, whereby Morgan, this unwelcome guest or ghost from Tallant's past, a past " 'loaded down with secrets for sale' " (59), has to go. The past is instantly up for sale, but the crypts inserted in place of that past cause problems, the kind that finally kill off Tallant too.

This person who finds secrets to sell has taken an address that is crowded with uncanny significance. It is the old Carker place, an outpost of cannibalism. But the history of California, of our California, begins in a certain sense (phantasmatically speaking) with cannibalism. (Disney's *Alive* was one more station of this crossing and identification.) The Donner party moved out West in the mid-nineteenth century as part of the general relocation movement from Back East to build up the population on the Coast in preparation for statehood, which was worth the wait in gold. As could happen with these parties, when they caught the drifts, the Donner one was forced by snow dinner around to eat any Donner who happened to be dead, and then there were, as always, these borderline questions that kept on coming up like a kind of indigestion: Were they dead, or were they killed off first before or as they were being devoured? Every westward move, every inward turn of Western Civilization (remember Jonathan Harker's trip inside Dracula's castle) swallows or internally throws up the corpse. Down in the deepest recess of the West, the white race reaches (and I mean retches) at the finish line of its history, where espionage meets psychological warfare, the rehearsal (or is it the repetition?) of the race to be won: it is the double feature of cannibalism and unmourning.

Well, here and now in California we find this spy, this double agent, who has moved into a place that has already shown signs of being in a haunted state. He goes to a local bar, and it is like someone going to Transylvania and mentioning the wrong place; the locals might as well be crossing themselves then and there. But Tallant gets into the crowd of legends surrounding the Carker place; he instantly figures it the perfect setting for a double crossing and secreting away of the one person who knows all his secrets; he will kill Morgan in this adobe that superstition keeps off limits. If his remains were found, the death would be written off as part and proof of the occult legend.

The "blackmail problem" has been solved very neatly—then he has the dream. There was right from the start a historywide theme operative here: the Carkers, who are described as ogres and hence as cannibals, are seen, remember, as the representatives of the whole white race (which is a kind of super-ogre). In sync with this dimension or dementia of coextensivities, he has a dream—of world power:

> Tallant dreamed of power that night. It was a common dream with him. He was a ruler of the new American Corporate State that would follow the war; and he said to this man, "Come!" and he came, and to that man, "Go!" and he went....
>
> Then the young man with the beard was standing before him, and the dirty trenchcoat was like the robes of an ancient prophet. And the young man said, "You see yourself riding high, don't you? Riding the crest of the wave—the Wave of the Future, you call it. But there's a deep, dark undertow that you don't see, and that's a part of the Past. And the Present and even your Future. There is evil in mankind that is blacker even than your evil, and infinitely more ancient."
>
> And there was something in the shadows behind the young man, something little and lean and brown. (64)

The Carkers stand in for a return of that part of the past that somehow exceeds the whole, the hole of the past's proper interment, the gap in the symbolic order that found no stopgap, no fitting filler or fulfillment in mourning's sign and side effects. The past that was not faced covers the loss of face left over from the Vietnam War. It is the unacknowledgable loss that produced symptomatic effects in fashion, in film (even the first *Ghostbusters* movie describes a shift of fronts for sixties types, even vets). Anyway, the problem of mourning, or not mourning, can be occasioned not only by a specific corpse but also by the loss of a war (which at the same time packs the personalizable losses found in body bags).

But here the "Wave of the Future" that Tallant's dream is about facing is riding out an indigestible past or repast: real cannibalism thus afflicts the metaphorical cannibalism, Tallant's California dreamin' of the future, the wave on which he wipes out.

Tallant kills Morgan and looks up, or looks to the side—it is always a side glance that reveals the Carkers, the living carcass—and witnesses some kind of mummy. He notices a cultlike setup with a trough in the middle of the floor and, on the sidelines, a mummified body, black, like the mail he tried to reroute to the dead-letter office. And what does Tallant do? He turns the mummy find into ready-made profit: "Tallant was already calculating the chances for raising a decent sum of money from an interested anthropologist—murder can produce such delightfully profitable chance by-products—when he noticed the infinitesimal rise and fall of the chest" (65). So Tallant enters this place that is also a cemetery of sorts where mummified bodies are kept; he has already committed murder here; he commits a sort of double desecration in this place devoted to the dead or, as it turns out, to the undead. He thinks of raising money from the sale of the mummified body, and automatically we see the corpse get a rise out of this: it reanimates as something vengeful, vampiric, or cannibalistic that takes stranglehold of his whole world: "His world had become reduced now to that hand and that head. Nothing outside mattered" (66).

Walking into a relation to the dead cynically and out of sync (or unconsciously in sync) with all the processes going down there, he finds himself reduced to a bond with the dead that will not let go, the one with the undead. And at the close, "the female" who arrives, arrives in time to drink the blood that Tallant has unwittingly but on schedule dripped into the sacrificial trough. Only by cutting off his own hand in spite of the face he just cannot save can he try to sever himself from the bond that is there with the dead. He has to hand it to the undead. But even that severance, that cut, only feeds the next vampire in line to drink the blood pouring from Tallant's stump.

Now when the work of mourning breaks down, the corpse bloats with blood and throws up these monstrous reducing plans like the head biting into the hand that feeds it. Vampire stories remind us that the work of mourning is also always the work of representation in mourning. To bury the dead is also to represent the dead. And all the difficulties we have representing death go hand in hand, hand in teeth, with the problem of disposing of the dead, burying them, putting them to rest. In "The Ontology of the Photographic Image," remember, Bazin suggested that the very first sculpture was probably the mummified corpse, and that representational art has always been about overcoming the countdown of time. But if that is the case — and let's pretend it is for a moment — the first or primal pictorial artist must have been the vampire, which slides us into Jan Neruda's "The Vampire," a story about an always sketching guest on the sidelines of family outings. After he is already into the last sketch, and down to the photo finish of the picture he has been taking of a young woman in the party, she and her loved ones find out that this artist is also known to the locals as "the Vampire": " 'He sketches only corpses. Just as soon as someone in Constantinople or here in the neighborhood dies, that very day he has a picture of the dead one completed. That fellow paints them beforehand — and he never makes a mistake — just like a vulture!' "

The corpse to be mourned poses as problem for everyone; the person closest to you who goes and whom you miss was also the object of your close call, the one you already missed (but there was always a next time for your death wish to take better aim). We, too, are very much the vampire artists regarding those whose deaths or corpses we are already sketching even while they are alive. We are always imagining the other gone, or, by the same logic, the dead other coming back.

E. F. Benson's "The Room in the Tower" supports, within the context of dreams, a notion of omnipotence of thoughts that death wishes get first. Over time one is bound to count the casualties of one's own wish:

> It is probable that everybody who is at all a constant dreamer has had at least one experience of an event or a sequence of circumstances that have come to his mind in sleep being subsequently realized in the material world. But, in my opinion, so far from this being a strange thing, it would be far odder if this fulfillment did not occasionally happen since our dreams are, as a rule, concerned with people whom we know.... On the mere calculation of chances, it does not appear in the least unlikely that a dream imagined by anyone who dreams constantly should occasionally come true. (187)

Simply because the dream is the place where we tend to include people we know and see also outside the dream world, over time what makes it into the dream could be happening outside in a material kind of way. That, anyway, is the logic that the narrator introduces to support the possibility of what he is describing here. By the end we will have witnessed serial dreaming complete itself in the material world.

Now the dream that keeps on recurring you all know, I don't have to repeat it. But there is something telepathic about the dream. Because the people age in the series of the dream, or people disappear, until toward the end, the season finale, the meaning of the dream is doubly anticipated by the death of Mrs. Stone. Toward the end he dreams that the family members are dressed in black, but Mrs. Stone is missing; and yet it is still her voice that broadcasts the command or the invitation to go up to the room in the tower. But now it comes from no particular body but rather from some place beside the tower outside in the garden, the spot, it turns out, marked by the tombstone of Julia Stone.

There is something telepathic about the dream, because it still keeps time on the outside. And because, of course, at one level there are so many surprises for the narrator and dreamer; I mean he feels that he has never seen this place before, but he also feels that he is in a position to recognize it fifteen years later. Whenever you find yourself in a place that is at once unknown and yet familiar, you can count on it, it is the place. It is the shock of identification without recognition: it is the relation to the mother's body that has been represented but repressed.

So a certain Julia Stone is the one sending out a dream that also pulls the dreamer into its room or crypt, and in the crypt, in that internal place where someone long dead is not being let go, we find a portrait — it is not just a portrait but a kind of mirror image, a self-portrait, Julia Stone by Julia Stone. Julia Stone was a painter of self-portraits who committed suicide. Her multiple involvement in murderous and impossible self-relations meant that her coffin could not be kept in hallowed ground. Her undead remains were trashed or deposited just outside the control tower from which she teleguided the narrator up to this point of return. The self-portrait is a mirror image backed not with mercury but, as the narrator discovers when he moves and thus holds the painting, with blood. It is a mirror relationship that is at the same time a blood bond to which our narrator returns when he makes it into the room or crypt inside the dream series he has been following for fifteen years.

"Mrs. Amworth," another Benson story, is a rematch of contestants we recognize from *Dracula*. We find already waiting around in a town called Maxley a retired professor who all along specialized in the "physical and psychical" study of the "occult" (236). While still at the university, "he advocated that all medical students should be obliged to pass some sort of examination in mesmerism, and that . . . papers should be designed to test their knowledge in such subjects as appearances at time of death, haunted houses, vampirism, automatic writing, and possession" (236).

Now this professor, this specialist in occult studies, is the one who is going to discover our next vampire, but it is also *his* vampire in a certain sense. This showdown, as in *Dracula*, is inoculative: in the narcissism of small differences effecting the dosage of what must be contained from the inside out we never leave the context of contagion. And, while I will not push this point too far, still at least within this story and as far as he is concerned, I think it is not accidental or incidental that he has been retired now for nearly two years. Two years put the period to the time that mourning can take or not take. Coming to the end of a two-year period of retirement, the professor meets Mrs. Amworth and recognizes not, as some propose, an eligible widow who comes and goes but a vampire who always only returns. In other words, his self-esteem or self-worth (what "am" I "worth") is tested over her undead body. And remember that the university—and how could we forget it—is also known as the alma mater or "fostering mother." The university has always tried to replace the mother (this connection is so important in *Frankenstein*).

Mrs. Amworth lost her husband in India a couple of years ago to an epidemic disease that remained unidentified. The professor free-associates that in the area she called home at that time there was an outbreak of vampirism "a year or two ago" (239). He begins to see a pattern: there was a vampirism epidemic in Maxley over three hundred years ago. The vampire then was said to be Elizabeth Chaston, one of Mrs. Amworth's maternal ancestors.

The narrator, the professor's sidekick or initiate, has a nightmare: "I dreamed that I woke, and found that both my bedroom windows were shut" (242). He opens the blinds and sees "Mrs. Amworth's face suspended close to the pane in the darkness outside, nodding and smiling at me." (The opening of blinds in the dream is a reopening of eyes that were once blinded by some scene—forgotten, repeating, obscene.) At the next window he must again see her face. Panic takes over: "Here was I suffocating in the airless room, and whichever window I opened Mrs. Amworth's face would float in." In the encounter with the vampire he finds himself heirless, fatherless, suffocating in close-up proximity to a suspended face floating in through the reflecting surface. The professor can confirm the reservations made by the narrator's dream: " 'Yes, you did well to awake,' he said. 'That warning came from your subconscious self, which never wholly slumbers, and cried out to you of deadly danger. For two reasons, then, you must help me: one to save others, the second to save yourself' " (244).

When the professor charges Mrs. Amworth with vampirism and draws the cross in the air, she is jolted backwards into the road and hit by a passing car. Her "sudden and awful death" creates a community-wide "shock," which, however, "began by degrees to pass off" (245). Her first death is absorbed with the shock of catastrophe. That is why her first death is not enough: even though she has already been buried once in the story, Mrs. Amworth returns.

This brings us to the point of the staking, which packs as scene a primal charge that is kept current in many of the stories. The double burial institutionalizes (packages and dispenses with) the ambivalence that afflicts every mourner. According to this mourning ritual, the corpse is still alive for the first two years of its interment. It is the time of his death when a husband's ghost can still impregnate his "widow." After two years the remains can then be dug up and the departed mourned and buried one more (one last!) time.

> "If I am right, we shall find her body undecayed and untouched by corruption." "But she has been dead nearly two months," said I. "If she had been dead two years [please note that the professor is once again counting down—inside his crypt] it would still be so, if the vampire has possession of her. So remember, whatever you see done, it will be done not to her... but to a spirit of untold evil and malignancy, which gives a phantom life to her body." (246–47)

Then on the final page of the story comes the second disposal service. The narrator has already been told what will happen so he can look the other way. But he does not repress this second death and looks straight on as the professor drives the pick into the object of worth and only then, without pause, shuts the lid of his own eyes:

> A fountain of blood, though she had been dead so long, spouted high in the air, falling with the thud of a heavy splash over the shroud, and simultaneously from those red lips came one long appalling cry, the swelling up like some hooting siren, and dying away again. With that, instantaneous as a lightning flash, the touch of corruption on her face, the color of it faded to ash, the plump cheeks fell in, the mouth dropped. "Thank God, that's over," said he, and without pause slipped the coffin lid back into its place. (248)

And then day comes. When morning comes after the vampire's staking, it is a good mourning that has been accomplished and can now be greeted and exchanged—or only professed.

> *The Lost Boys* is one videocentric film: the mother, Lucy, works in the video store that is owned by the head vampire; the Frog Brothers are into comics,

which give the advance preview, the primal scene of TV culture. More to the point: their prepubescent share in adolescence shows us the way TV replaces not only adulthood but childhood too with perpetual adolescence. The Teen Age is televisual: it is the live transmission that is always on (even when the set is off). And that is because it is always on disaster alert. That is why the crypt in which the teen vampires hang out is the ruin of a hotel built on the fault that quaked: catastrophe builds the haunt of missing children turned teen vampires. The poster on their wall beams up the suicidal direct connection with the body, the Big One Jim Morrison rode out. Before we witness our first vampire attack, we see the sun set over amusement park rides, which rehearse and repeat the thrill of catastrophe, along a pier that is the place of the missing, the homeless, the uncanny.

You would think that it is time to bring the missing father into focus. It is true that the head vampire tries to take over the father's missing place in one family and make Lucy the missing mother for his own vampiric family pack. Certainly, during the showdown, it is Lucy's father who destroys the head vampire; earlier the dog, totem representation of the father, jumped in to kill one of the teen minions. What is more, the grandfather returns for the kill from a date with Widow Johnson, from an exercise in substitution. He returns from his date with the substitute still driving the car he said he never drives (which thus holds the place of some commemoration, one that works) right into the head vampire, his daughter's internal spook. And that is the point. Bottom-line it is Lucy's mother who is the missing person behind the vampires. The father of her sons is absent because they are divorced: the marital problems a woman has with her first husband she still has with her mother. Then, on automatic repeat, she turns to replace her ex-husband with her video-store boss, only to find that she has again turned on the vampirism, the toxic shock, of her maternal blood bond.

There is also an Oedipal plot and couple format that Hollywood always requires as ground for its projections (like the "grounding" of a teenager who is thus kept from going to his favorite "haunt"). The pop-Oedipal plot functions as a kind of transference neurosis, an artificial, inoculative form of the presenting illness that gets built up in session or in the screening because it, the substitute illness, can be busted or contained. The constructive cure dislodges, by proxy, the blockage that was too big for the two (or four) of us in analysis. The audience can reclaim the projection and return home, which has also been uncanny-proofed for couplification. Up front, which is where the audience gets off, this movie seems to be about conflicts with a missing father — left behind in Phoenix, which (with redoubled force since *Psycho*) names resurrection, and represented or repressed by the vampiric video-store owner who proposes stepfatherhood — and about related tensions with the divorced mother, whose loyalty to her boys is in question. This TV-size family pack of treatable problems covers the disturbance fundamental to the household of return, the house of the father to whom the divorced daughter returns with her sons.

If the vampires hide out in the condemned site of a former hotel brought down by the 1906 earthquake, then that is because, in California, the horror of one-on-one missingness can thus get shock absorbed within the ongoing group prospect of catastrophe — earthquake or nuclear war — the big one we prepare for and survive (even as it is always and already upon us). Preparations are under way in the mode of control release, of inoculative shots and shocks of catastrophe: as in the pop thrills and amusements that crowd the pier together with peer access to drug highs, the comic-strip hieroglyphics of total combat, or the video time capsules that down disaster or horror in the context of rental and return. At the same time we are flying high on a *Peter Pan* reference to adolescent same-sex or unisex bonds with a group's maternal body. *Lost Boys* is the Californian syndication of *Peter Pan*, the fantasy of perpetual adolescence, which was the projective outside of an interior shot. On the outside James Barrie carried the name that calls to "bury"; on the inside he carried his brother David, his mother's other and god, who died at age fourteen in a skating accident. But inside out he grows up to be teen ghost forever. His stature, features, and voice got stuck on the fourteen-year-old model. He in turn could go for libido only by playing fantasy games with equally adolescent types. Missingness blurs the deadline that alone keeps little ones young forever: only the dead die young. Each child who stood model for a character in the Peter Pan fantasy was an early goner, beginning with brother David. It is a death cult that turns on its media message (its connection with the dead) over the body of Tinker Bell. In stage and screen versions, remember, Peter calls on us to save Tinker Bell's fading light and life by proving our belief that fairies exist within the round of applause. This call for live participation or transmission opens onto Barrie's primal scene: backstage he was doubled over in anxious pause for the thought that the lifesaving applause might be withheld. But that is ambivalent. Tinker Bell is the now Good, now Bad internal mother who has not yet been blended in the completed course of adolescent acting out. She is the stimulus/response bouncing ball that leads James always back to David. But the writing career devoted to David also conveyed James's own name (and the patronymic's summons to bury) to another intersection and accident. Barrie's right arm, paralyzed by writer's cramp, folds out along the hook, line, and forward march of father time down Captain Cook's prosthesis (all the way down into the ticked-off crocodile where, for a while, he buried his arm).

In the recycling of MIAs and missing children still-framing this movie's vampiric reanimation (Laddie, the kid on his way to joining the vampire bunch, is advertised on a milk carton), we are back on the wavelength of disowned loss or losses that "They Bite" was plugging into. According to Stephen Kaplan, the director of the Vampire Research Center in New York City, it is true: American bloodsuckers prefer California. The only thing wrong with California, from *The Lost Boys* to *Buffy the Vampire Slayer:* too many damn vampires. Californians keep their buffy metabolism bulimically externalized (or vampirized): one's utter unprotectedness inside consumerism alternates with the good workout, the plastic surgery. All those backyard swimming pools are bodies of water that will decay if not kept artificially cycling, recycling, pumped up, and transfused. It is the motion picture industry all over again: the body must be given postoperative jolts to keep it machine-lean and as good as any live entertainment.

What does it mean to track the course of vampirism today through the techno future, the tech-*no*-future we associate with California? And why is adolescence the designated drive and global conspiracy operating between these two primal scenes? The third scene or front is Nazi Germany, the late arrival of German investments in and inventions of adolescence. Exiles from Nazi Germany helped establish California's pop-psychological culture of healing, an eclectic mix-up still freebased on psychoanalysis. No longer reading the symptoms of individuals or groups within a frame of National Socialism's emergence, these thinkers and therapists turned to the California native and his mass habitat to keep on reading the future of techno haunting on its other coast. The emphasis in these lectures on a quasi-dialectic between the couple and the group—between the East Coast or Europe and California—fits right into the bicoastal genealogy of vampire country, which extends from the vampire's video store in Santa Clara to the sensurround of the Gulf War. The Gulf War, which continued to perfect our aim to achieve the whole or hole in One, was one of the test cases of California criticism. Not only because Saddam Hussein defended his desire to hold onto Kuwait by comparing it to California: the United States would not want to let California go, he said. A European colleague, with whom I watched the war, and who counts as one of the experts on military history, received the first listing of American casualties, right down to the update that our first war dead were for the most part accidental victims of our own fire, as guarantee and omen that we were going to "lose" another Vietnam. But with my post-punk-Freudian Californian ears on, I was able to recognize that the instant replay of losses could only refer to a different set of responses—to the TV set. The introduction of "friendly fire" (which is a Californian concept, if I've ever encountered one) brought sitcom relief from what was threatening to become Vietnam mourning and standstill. "Friendly fire" is the primal-time controlled rerelease of our suicidal inoculative bonding with the shocks and shots of catastrophe. It is the bond of "liveness" and it gives us shelter. I saw it; I was there. Suddenly we were out of the body bag. We were so efficient or friendly that we were even killing ourselves with a direct hit of excess.

Consider the rerun of phantasms to which we were entirely subjected. The warring parties were fighting World War II while both war protesters and victory celebrants hailed the war as a Vietnam repeat. Although the war did not mark the conclusion of Vietnam (we have yet to see that conclusion), it did (at a level that still concerns us) mark a certain season finale of World War II. The media war's live transmission was coextensive with the video control that (right down to detonation) gave us the inside view, second by second, from the point of view at the end of the missiles. Unlike wars said to be in history, this one ran an eternal rerun of all the same phantasms. From portable gas chambers made in Germany and conveyed by the recycled buzz bombs of the Battle of Britain to the singular German response to the opening shot of the war (which followed the leader), World War II was back on. At the level of phantasm reception, therefore, the Gulf War brought a certain closure to World War II (I am thinking of the Patriot System, the first real-time defense against Nazi rockets) — but what was also along for the war drive was a pathogenic denial of the non-overcoming of the Vietnam trauma.

There were ghosts in the Gulf War, for example, an A-6 pilot nicknamed "Ghost" who was cited in *Los Angeles Times* coverage of operation "Jackpot." What hit the pot or spot of haunting resided within the split between the shutdown on the side of one war and the nonclosure of the other war, which is still being fought or acted out in the mode of denial. In the reception area, the Vietnam War was a graft or draft of newsreel or film technology onto TV sets, which filled with projections and identifications and, between them, with the dotted between-the-lines of a suturing that invited the audience to cut straight to the pre-TV, pre–World-War-II crypt. The Gulf War was the full realization of World War II or total war on sets of TV liveness.

The resemblance of the Gulf War (with its smart bombs armed with their own video coverage) to video games was often noted at the time.

But the connection has to be put in reverse: video games were rehearsing or repeating the media war using the same technology. That's TV. Gadget goes to war. The slogan "The whole world is watching," which the liberation of Eastern Europe shared with the defeat of the Vietnam War, missed the point—of impact. Now we have progressed via user-friendliness and friendly fire to a nonrelation or noncorrespondence between the professionalism to which gadget love appeared to have graduated and the teen-age pool of libido applicants. TV's live transmission is "the place"—of this noncorrespondence. We arrived at a renewed structure of submission that turns on the split reception within techno phantasms. What was happening when all the people in the position of the ego ideal—from Madonna to the Persian Gulf pilots—were in their thirties or forties was not that we had in fact made it into the maturity of the Teen Age. Instead the only reserve left in the libido pool for midlife stars (which included all of us who had been professionalizing to the point of running media wars, publishing, or whatever) remained the group of misguided or rather teleguidable teenagers. It is the total split that continued to be pathogenic. That is why the adolescent culture that survived the war was so jacked out. The noncorrespondence between the pool of applicants for libidinization and the successful gadget lovers, who seemed pretty much in control, was calling only for primal submissions.

The technology is one thing, the group psychology of acting out is the other. Take role-playing. Is it Californian? Is it adolescent? The material is saturated with eclectic specializations of kinds of knowledge in the absence of knowing the standard reading and writing lists of passage, both the canon of tradition and the frame of legibility or transference that opens the corridors of transmitter institutions. But if this were another displacement inside the house that repression builds, then adolescence would *always* be the place to go to learn what exceeds the standard, what gives access to the insupportable supports of the standard exchange. But the culture of role-playing is a family romance that both reflects the day-tripper's deprivation and ignorance and keeps the dreamer ignorant and cut off. As with the burning cottage industry of disquisition, treatise, and typology during the inquisition, there are constructs of knowledge that are the vast but empty forms or placeholders of energy coming and gone from the once and future repressed. Back then sexual research and science were discarded, and a false or hysterical or psychotic science or scientology was constructed around all that was left to know anything about in an open season of projection. Given our own ongoing Puritan ideology or ego ideal, nonissues like temperance, abuse, and harassment were worked for all the complexity we deny ourselves whenever we discard the corpus of thought and refuse to address the transference. It was possible for the one member of the staff who did not sleep with the boss but who, given the atmosphere created by the boss's sleeping around, could nevertheless immediately be assumed by all to be part of the harem to file charges of sexual harassment on that account. Now that is what happens when thinking or science goes into the throwaway packaging of repression and gives what is next to nothing real staying power and constructed complexity.

Role-playing is another late arrival of the preconscious culture industry, the one that Jung was so good at capitalizing in Archetypes, in Synchrony. For example, the game book *Vampire: The Masquerade Companion* spills an excess without access of new rules, rites, methods, names, and categories: Prestation, Numina, Psionics, Thamaturgy, Cathari, Monomacy, Inconnu, Assamites, and Golconda. These role-playing game books, which are not to be confused with comic books, which are close to the unconscious, have extended their discourse into a mass of literature that includes serial vampire treatments set in a new world order of mixed-metaphorical and arcane bit parts from mythology and legend. The language is interactive to the extent that the narrative key punches an assembly line of place and proper names, which mark the spot that the reader, his imagination pretrained in game playing, is in and out with the blanks that get filled. All words and syntax between names are short-order, empty, phatic filler for even shorter attention spans.

The underworld of footnotes and marginalia gets plundered for all the names that will never be in history, all the names it takes for every player to have his own new name, but always inside some greater holding pattern or patter of archetypecasting. But the main body of the text is not, in exchange, now supporting the underworld tour. It is gone. The interactive reading or acting out puts footnotes in the mouth of a consumerism that will never graduate to the corpus of knowledge. Just read the spontaneous transmissions that take themselves interpersonally across the Web. It is a final frontier for those who want to feel good about themselves — already and always as adolescents off the track of power transmission or tradition. To feel good about yourself is the easy out of libidinizing what the other has given up on: namely you. Wanting to know only what can already be known without knowing it, E-pals hold forth opinions on whatever is out there. When all culture is the peer review that begins in early adolescence, then we are free — to recycle opinions and die. The glaring plots, names, and omissions of role-playing are all the filler info out there that's fit to redecorate what's no news is good news (at least in the beach and zombie culture of body-based narcissism).

So what is the Teen Age and what do I mean when I say that adolescence is a relatively recent invention? Adolescence as rebellion without cause only begins looking like it is outside the law at the moment it is first invented — as an original and origin. Once, at this same original moment, teen passion goes against the law, institutionalization takes it over as its charge. Goethe, like the other German inventors of adolescence, praised the newfound energy as the source of genius, but that upbeat idea wiped out on the upsurge of other side effects. Goethe's *Werther*, the first best-seller, the original work of what Goethe called "world literature," was also the owner's manual to the new invention of adolescence. But as though without connection, instant copycat suicides crowded out its close readership. Within the close call of reception, we will see Frankenstein's monster consume *Werther* as one of three books he reads (he needs no others) and recycles with the lilt of sheer citationality all the way to sui-cite: *Werther* gives the monster his suicide instructions. What was symptomatized and formalized in *Werther* — the short circuit of adolescence via friendship and suicide, which have replaced love and war and which thus position adolescence out there with the group as the other of the couple—was always part of the program. The adolescent begins outside the law of the couple in a place of tension between that couple (the couple of parents) and the couple he will form. The group he enters to acquire his sexuality (since he cannot take it from his parents) comes complete with free membership in the mutual admiration society of group identification. The way to go from couple to couple can thus be endless. On a group scale ambivalence covers this regressed relationship of the teenage group-of-one to the couple of parents withdrawing into the master bedroom. But you have got to become like the couple you can never come like. "Like," the Californian particle and copula, belongs to the pull and attraction of group identification— "the different way." Every move teen self-esteem makes toward outlandishness or excess has to submit to the likability principle of identification that forever rebuilds the group. The adolescent likes to be different—like everyone he likes—to be like. And that is why in adolescence only the drives get couplified—over the body of the group. We are talking a sadomasochistic distribution of pleasure. Only the phantom or vampire gets off at the prospect of group members waiting around or sleeping around but always standing by at the pleasure or fun their "best friends" are having. So it is that split again (we are back to the split-level distribution of phantasms and technology receptions), it is that split that keeps Californian group formation in the service of the narcissistic object, the One, which heads the group off at submission impasse. The logic of the One—one nation, one god, and (Michael Jackson–style) one race and one gender—is here to serve you in a body culture that sets up the exquisite corpse as model and goal of every workout. It is the memory picture that is getting built, the parting shot that is Forest Lawn's specialization in the field of the death wish. But couplification nevertheless rides the shot that is gone and forces entry into the group-of-one under ongoing threat and charge of child abuse or vampirism.

LECTURE EIGHTEEN

In *Near Dark* we are set up inside a contest between, in one corner, shit-kicker bloodsuckers (what is the difference between this pack and a family of psycho killers?) and, in the far corner, the transference set of family ties with the future through a couple bond between two teens, the couple that must survive the horror of group metabolization and the loss of a mother. Caleb, the son out on the town for a spell, is cast as vampire fledgling by the bite job the blonde he is trying to date-rape gives him. It is the bite that saves him, that takes the bite out of the rest of the white-trash vampire pack that just wants to finish him off. But they can't: "he's turned." When he drinks his blonde creator's blood, he is sexed, vampire-style: he sees and hears the night. But night and nothing can be one word or world. What's there to do? "Anything we want till the end of time. You have to learn how to kill." "I can't." "Do you want to die? Just use your instinct. Don't think of it as killing, don't think at all. It's something you do night after night. The night has its price." The oil derricks pump away as Caleb feeds on her wrist again, right after she has finished feeding. She just cannot wean him, never did, never will. Caleb walks out into the night and finds a mother to feed his infancy. From back home, where mother is dead and gone, father and sister (the father/daughter relationship is the ultimate paternal bond) have set out to reclaim the mother's son. And father can turn Caleb back again, away from the vampiric bonding, just by pumping his own blood through him. Caleb is reborn, again, as the father's son. The antibody transfusions have aborted the funereal maternal relation. But then the blonde joins the family, as future wife: she is transfused back together with her former life —

the life of the substitute, not of the undead mother — via Caleb's restored blood treatment. And this one-time-only fiction or fantasy of vampirism's reversal in the exchange of bad blood for dad blood belongs to the perspective or direction of a father's daughter.

In F. G. Loring's "The Tomb of Sarah," what I think is important, just as important as in *Near Dark,* in Dreyer's *Vampyr,* and in "For the Blood Is the Life," is the way in which the father gets introduced. Here the father's entry represents a successful intervention, whereas in so many other case studies he is introduced too late or, in any event, without effectiveness. The story opens with a son citing or making public the diaries of his father. The opening sentence begins with "My father"; the heir's opener ends with reference to the careful record that his father kept and that the son is now "presenting . . . to the public": "As he kept a careful record of every case he investigated the manuscripts he left at his death have a special interest" (153). The father was a church restorer who somehow also investigated cases.

So in the course of restoration, a tomb is moved, and the side effects of that removal or displacement become recognizable to the father. In fact at the end, he will congratulate himself that "Thank God" he was in attendance; another might not have been prepared to recognize in time the giveaway symptoms of vampirism. What is documented here is the successful introduction and intervention of father, who knows best, in precincts troubled by an interminable or impossible mourning that has reanimated a dead woman. Whereas before the start of the relocation project the vampire's tomb had been "air-tight" (154) — that is, impervious to heirs or fathers — the lifting of the crypt's cover releases a hungry corpse, whose reanimation, however, "Thank God," leads to its staking by father. "The most horrible part, however, was the extraordinary freshness of the body. Except for the appearance of starvation, life might have been only just extinct" (155).

Not only does Countess Sarah's life or unlife return once she has been replenished with blood, but her beauty makes a comeback too. The father must therefore warn the parson not to obey at the last moment the siren of her seductions. The parson is only too ready to leave the safety zone of the garlic circle when she comes on to him. But at the end father and the parson (another "father") face their task unmoved: "We set our teeth, however, and hardened our hearts" (160). Now this setting of the teeth in the face of a phantasm that is all teeth doubles the vampiric image, shares the tension of its threatened release, and at the end when they see her face soften (from wantonness through hatred through panic to rest in peace), it is at the same time their own relaxation they are watching face to face after nursing, feeding, staking. This diary-recorded, testament-related busting of mummy by dad brings relief. Let the dad bury the dead.

The tomb contains the last of a family line. At the other end of the countdown of a father's name, a mother enraged with grief strangled Countess Sarah, who had sucked the mother's children dry. Both the murder and the hunger that the stranglehold would hold in place are advertised by the sculpture of the countess set on top of the tomb to give weight to the inscribed warning that it must never be moved or opened. "On the slab is a magnificent group of figures. A young and handsome woman reclines upon a couch; round her neck is a piece of rope, the end of which she holds in her hand" (154). The regrouping of the beautiful woman's hunger and execution fills in the blanks of what looks like suicide. But they are only blanks, and do not, not this time, penetrate the spot marked by return.

The father's friend, the parson of the church in which the tomb of Sarah was found, is the son's delegate. The father thus requires his obedience: " 'Will you put yourself unreservedly in my hands and help me, *whatever I may do*?' " (159). The parson believes that God is the One who (like a mother) accomplishes everything for you. He asks, " 'Shall we not call rather upon Heaven to assist us in our need?' " Father answers, " 'God helps those who help themselves, and by His help...we must fight this battle for Him and the poor lost soul within' " (159). But before the father drives his point home, the parson is unable on his own to proceed against a vampire that is just beginning to freshen up: " 'Great God!' he exclaimed; 'the woman is alive!... Take your piece of mortar...

and let us shut the tomb again. God help me! Parson though I am, such dead faces frighten me!' " (156–57).

"Father" though I am, he thus says, I am also parson, "part son." When at the end father notes that his intervention came in time to save one more child, found pale and exhausted near the church, he concludes for all his sons, "Now the vampire is no more, no further danger either to that child or to any other is to be apprehended" (165).

A slip that comes from nowhere (and everywhere) in the story falls into place: at the start of the story the parson recounted the legend that Sarah was a "witch or were-woman" (154). But "were-woman" would mean that she was a man-woman, a man who periodically (in every sense: once a month in sync with the moon) turns into a woman. This being is the monstrous aspect of a son's identification with the mother he must regularly become whenever the blood bond calls.

The werewolf has a history of extra-literary activities as long on projection and persecution as the vampire's own sojourn among the living. A crossover between species or evolutionary throwback, the werewolf enters the vampiric domain as doubled or mutated manifestation of the vampire herself. Or the werewolf remains just a sidekick away from the vampire's mastery. Thus, the wolf standing by Sarah in the tomb's representation and repression of all its contents acts as the delegate of transmissions and blood transfusions from the outside world into the vampire's early crypt-bound dependency. To interrupt the chain of monstrous becoming, execution was never enough: cremation was in order to prevent the werewolf's comeback as vampire.

In Marx's discourse of mixed metaphors, the vampire goes to capital while the werewolf gets assigned the role of capitalist driven to replace living labor with dead labor. From the mass of communion through modern mass culture, a three-way of capital, militarism, and Christianity intersects in our investment and interest in the werewolf. The 1865 classic *Book of Were-Wolves* was written by the author of the hymn "Onward Christian Soldiers." Werewolf and vampire were the two monster mascots (as though distinguishable from the all-out recourse to

Mickey Mouse at the same wartime) to line up at the fronts of World War II. In name the werewolf could rebound in German down the lines of folk etymology as "Wehrwolf," Defense Wolf. It was a name or nickname used many times over down the lines of the German military formations. Hitler, whose Adolf name was a variant of Wolf, assigned the werewolf name to the camp he made the center of operations on the Eastern Front. And then in Melanie Klein's wartime treatment of the boy Richard in Britain, we find the Australian warship named, down under, *Vampire,* jamming in the background of overlaps between all intrapsychic conflicts and the war going on around the analysis. Same side, same wartime: copies of Stoker's *Dracula* were distributed to GIs to bring the Nazi menace into focus.

Lycanthropy, the curse of transformation into a wolf, named by the Greeks after Lykon, the host with the most gross-out (he served human meat), was the first occult label to double as diagnosis of mental aberration and delusion. Lycanthropy was thus almost from the beginning a melancholic condition characterized by delusions of metamorphosis into wolf form in which the urge to devour human flesh carried you away. Lycanthropes just as often committed incest with the kids. Like all the other stars on the horror marquee (so sad!), the werewolf was another abused child abuser. In his more consumerist melancholic manifestation, he might kill for the warm rush of blood. But he was best known as late-night raider of and snacker on the contents of graves. A host of psychos were caught dead-handed, in the act of their best graveside manner, wolfing down the recently deceased and buried, but with no outward transformation to show for it. Only bullets of inherited silver were surefire against the werewolf. That about more than covers the identification duty attached to all the totemic animals, which stand in for the dead father. The indigestible chunk the werewolf takes out of the family pack sends out a projective haunting of the encrypted corpus hidden away, unburied, inside. Frank Hamel writes in her 1915 study *Human Animals:* "A more original idea is that certain human beings possess animal doubles and that the soul-animal roams at large while the man remains invisible in his ordinary form, and many of the vampire and wer-wolf stories are traceable to this belief" (4). The mummy's astral body fits right in here too. (Frankenstein's monster, three.)

The Wolfman is not, like *An American Werewolf in London,* a late work that sees through its tradition: it is a readymade washed up out of the unconscious. But it observes the logic of melancholia Big Time. Larry is back from California. His older brother, John, has died young, and now he must be the heir at the head of his generation. It was a hunting accident that brought him back. That's right: a haunting accident. What's more, the older brother's death was part of a destinal and sacrificial program. From generation to generation, it is a death other than the father's that is on automatic repeat. As the father says, in the Talbot line the older brother always has to go so the rebellious one can be brought back into the fold.

When Larry looks through the telescope he brought home with him from California, he brings a blonde babe into focus: "I can figure things out if you give me electrical wiring, tools, etc. but . . ." It is gadget goes to Scotland, which is between a crypt and a haunted place. At the intersection of sex and hex Larry turns to father because he has got to know about two local phenomena: the blonde and werewolves. Father, who already knows the name of the telescoped-out beloved, telescoops the son. About the werewolf legend father knows that like most superstitions it has some basis in fact: it reflects back the condition of a dual personality. That's right: he had two sons and one is dead so that the other one could come back. So, out on his first date with his local sweetheart, Larry meets Bela Lugosi, part-time gypsy fortune-teller, part-time werewolf. Larry clubs the werewolf part to death, but he also catches the disease. At the end the father beats werewolf Larry to the finish line and survives yet another son. In the living end, the family without a mother, now as forever, consists of the primal father, the melancholic dad, and the ghost.

Across the gap of a decade, from cinematic projection onto television, the missing mother belongs to the feeding time of commercials. *I Was a*

Teenage Werewolf is a made by TV movie. On TV we watch ourselves trying to conform to the commandments and agencies of adjustment that are everywhere. The parents of the girlfriend advise Tony: "any job that keeps a teenager busy is good." In other words, "you must be guilty." The school principal confides in Tony once it appears that the psychiatrist has him under control: "I knew if we could just get inside of you, you'd be a credit to your father and your school." The psychiatrist begins treatment with a physical exam: "You're a perfectly normal human being; you can have a normal life." They just need to make a few adjustments and then "you will be you." The psychiatrist then drugs and hypnotizes his teen patient, who is off to the movies, captive audience to horror films screening a primal past, complete with fangs and blood lust. The psycho-director-psychiatrist returns Tony to the maternal blood bond because, as he tells his assistant, he had noticed telltale signs on Tony's body. But later, when the entire team is chasing Tony, who has sought refuge with the psychiatrist, the assistant says, oddly, to his boss, "You can't bring the dead back — save him!" The psycho-psychiatrist-director needs one more transformation for the photo shoot that will document this "first perfect regression." But when the telephone rings, the techno death cult turns on the murderous appetite of the werewolf — and everyone dies, everyone who was part of the missing-mother complex. Only one mass burial remains for the short circuit of this internal return of the insane: "The newspapers will just eat this up."

At first the psychiatrist was able to protect his patient by dismissing the town's conviction that Tony was the werewolf as "mass hysteria": "These myths from the Carpathians passed out with electricity." But with electricity these myths passed into the movie theater, like the internal, drug-induced one he and Tony have erected over the mother's dead body.

Tony's paternal order works the night shift: he has never seen the need for "disciplining" Tony, "not even," father says to son, "when your mother was alive." But with regard to the adjustment institutions he neither identifies with nor projects, he does give genuinely fatherly advice: "Sometimes you just have to do it the other fellow's way."

"Maybe I should have remarried," the father later muses in front of the police: "no one could replace his mother." This is his difference, again, from the police adjustment order that originally counseled Tony to visit the psychiatrist. But maybe he thought about remarrying? That is the unconscious difference. The adjustment institutions advertise inside-out replacement. The psychiatrist and Tony make up a suicide pact that Tony's acting out was already beginning to formulate. The psychiatrist wants humanity to start over, and it is to this humanitarian end that Tony will be sacrificed: "What's one life compared to such a triumph." The ones who cannot adjust or replace are sent to the night shift — or to the psychiatrist, the director of the mythic past, of the unconscious, which is reconceived here as the only place left (the place of suicide) for the outsider. This is a fifties movie: no Europe, no difference, no hope. But it also forwards "adjustment," a developmental concept brought to us by evolution, from the primal past of missing links to the real time of our tech-no-future: hypnosis, film, drugs, TV.

The force field of adolescence has always been occupied by the body that changes uncontrollably into monstrous exhibitionism. Adolescent confusion sets the skin tone: the werewolf's metamorphosis was really an inversion, a turning inside out of his whole surface. Underneath it all the werewolf always wore his pelt. (He was the original turncoat.) Gender confusion dots the landscapes of metamorphosis. The maenads put on pelts to become uninhibited huntresses. Monstrous crossovers between species were also broadcast in gender stereo. (Play which name can be assigned to what gender with the two leading experts on lycanthropy, Frank Hamel and Sabine Baring-Gould.) Animals are not only totemic in stature. They can also serve as group mascots for teen siblings or friends forever. When group blood pumps the blush into cute critters, then it is a reunion, mother and child, dead or alive.

The Thing takes the evolution fantasies all the way — to outer space — from where they return as the homegrown (and that means uncanny) products of vegetarian rejections and literalizations of identification. That is why there is static on all techno channels. The audio portion, conversation overlapping with conversation, is crowded with the paranoid rapid fire and cross fire (friendly fire) of the exchanges. The conversation that never varies (that is, when it comes to the male bonding of identification) turns on one thing: women. At some locale warmer than the North Pole, women wear hardly anything on account of the heat: "very smart of them"; "only dames can do that"; "it's warm in Seattle … the girls there don't wear fur pants." And via ultimate upward displacement, even the "General is nursing secrets like a June bride." Right at the tip of the pole is the pinup-girl member of a research team that is headed by someone who used to be at Bikini (atomic test site and intersection of the woman's body and war). Captain, it turns out, is in love with the one woman around (this is what the men joke about — but they don't compete with him for or over her pinned-up body). It's joking matter or mater.

The other story line: in the all-male group, there is also a journalist in search of a story. Then the story hits: mysterious crash landing: "Russians? They're crawling around the North Pole like flies." The journalist goes to the Pole in search of a sensational story; the captain goes to see his girl, to ask her if they could start over again. Apparently they had one date, which he failed miserably, overdrinking, acting "like an octopus" all over her. But the pinup girl held her liquor and her own and then pinned some message on his back. She made their date public and set off its jocular recognition by the men. (The last laugh is had always about father.)

At the site of the crash they find the tail of an enormous alien craft. When they try to detonate it free of ice and it blows up instead, the journalist charges those in charge with turning "a new civilization into a Fourth of July feast." But they do discover a survivor at the bottom of the barbecue pit — an eight-foot man in ice. They decide not to thaw this remnant — they do not want to risk another explosion: there is in addition danger of germs not yet introduced into our immune systems. So they must break into their defense against the cold and turn the room containing thing into a deep freeze. And thing is guarded — largely against the research team's desire to examine it. Guard: "I could use something to read — a nice horror story." The guards are freaked by thing's hands and eyes; they can't stand staring at its stare, which, as evil eye, represents a casualty of a death wish staring back with looks that could kill. One guard therefore covers thing with a blanket — not realizing that it is electric and on.

Pretty soon they do not know where their thing is. But when thing fights and kills some dogs, it also leaves behind an arm, which gets examined: there is no blood, no tissue in the arm. There is no arterial structure, no nerves: just porous disconnected cellular growth. It is some kind of vegetable matter, some form of "super carrot," and it cannot die — not as we understand dying. In some other place, on another stage, evolution has fast-forwarded vegetable life to the front of the line. That is why thing is superior to us: thing does not have to mess around with emotional or sexual problems. It replicates itself via seed pods beyond pain or pleasure. But can it think? Thinking is the crowning achievement of evolution, they think. Ever hear of the telegraph vine? The century plant? To evolve is to technologize: plants too can network and communicate, can think. The Geiger counter not only registers the alien's approach but also relays information to thing via telepathy or wireless telegraphy. The vegetable being uncoils a certain analogy with celluloid: scene or site of thing's discovery is first viewed as pictures shot in sequence but shown picture by picture on a kind of monitor or viewmaster. The scientific reconstruction of the crash at the same time slows down the film, which touches down or crash lands on itself. But not only can certain plants auto-technologize. Some even live on blood. The dogs, and the first human victims (from the research team), are drained of blood.

Thanks to the pinup girl, who points him in the direction of the professor's laboratory simulation of thing's project, the captain finds out what thing is up to. Wild thing wants to proliferate by dropping pods and watering them with blood. While bathing them in blood plasma, professor listens to his superhuman plants through the stethoscope and hears the wail of a newborn child. (At this point the pinup girl doubles over with morning sickness — and moves toward siding with the captain against the outer-species desires of science.) With the girl's help, the captain knows what the monster, in league, in a sense, with the scientists, hopes to accomplish: to turn humans into livestock, the food supply for its new brood. But now that girl has crossed over from the evil paternal research team, thing can be engaged (in combat or to be married). "What if our boyfriend gets lonely?" they jocularly ask one another. Pinup girl answers: "What do you do with a vegetable, boil it, sauté it, fry it?" Thus they realize that thing must be fried. Their first attempt to burn thing backfires — thing escapes and they lose one room of the compound through fire damage. When they decide to pursue their thing, the girl wants to tag along. At first the captain wants to leave her behind, but she counters woman to captain: "If I start burning up again — who's going to put out the fire." It is as though hers was the mounting animal magnetism that was being measured up the Pole.

They decide to set a trap, an "electric fly trap." The scene of thing's destruction is the scene of ultimate confrontation between the paternal order of science, on one side, and the fraternal order of the military, on the other. Scientist: "Knowledge is more important than life; thinking is all that counts — it's our only purpose." Scientist or professor even attempts to sabotage the military effort of the group, and then, as last resort, appeals directly to thing — and gets thrown to the side: thing advances and is trapped and fried. "That's enough," one shocked soldier begs. The answer: "No! We don't want any part of it left." This total destruction of thing accomplishes, under its cover, the removal of the paternal research unit. It also leads down the aisle the couplification of captain and pinup girl as though their bond in fact represented the future, the joining of the reproductive organs of group protection.

The boys joke about the captain at the end: "He should be tired. He's had two things on his mind." One thing has been destroyed, so the other one is now the marrying kind. The evolution of plant life that thing embodies suggests nature in the maternal or nurturing mode: the maternal body of nature offers itself as gift, as abundance in which one can share. It represents consumption or feeding that does not kill. It is edible, not Oedipal. And yet the super vegetable from outer space feeds on blood. It is the specter of identification: no sex, only blood bonding and destruction; no sexual reproduction, only doubling on contact. It is the group's maternal bond with each group member or ego that must be externalized and ritually killed off so there can be a couple, a future, and sexual love — so there can be death or substitution or reproduction.

The journalist in hot pursuit of sensation has been the harassed, sacrificed impotent clown throughout. He has missed every chance at photographing thing, just as he is readily censored (and without resistance) by the military. Even when thing is destroyed, he cannot take a picture, because he passes out. But at the end he advances to the position of group leader or mascot: he gives the group its mythic history in his broadcast of the news of victory over thing. In this mythic account of the encounter, he compares Noah's ark and the arc of electricity charging couplification to survive near total destruction. The boys pat him on the back; he is the leader even though or because he is an impotent clown or nerd (like Mickey Mouse, like Christ). In the mutual admiration society of groups-of-one, everyone gets a chance at being leader (since there is no leader or father around). And that is what the mascot (the journalist or Mickey Mouse) guarantees. Group identity or identification recycles the maternal bond, which is unconditional, just as it is sensual or sensational. The mascot is the loudspeaker of the group's paranoia: "Watch the skies everywhere!"

The movie calculates a future of couplification out of the paranoid economy of groups. The woman on the screen interpersonalizes or staggers the intrapsychic density of two images confronting the all-male research society in J. W. Campbell's 1938 story "Who Goes There," the plain text for the film. Thing is not the movie's real-time traveler from outer space but a twenty-million-year-old find, also described as a "mummy" (84). And on closer look, which the men just cannot bear, the three-eyed creature has worms for hair. Like Medusa. When the men try to convince themselves that it is safe to thaw out their mummy, the calculation of its evolutionary distance from mankind gives them shelter with the very image or analogy that nevertheless comes back with thing's monstrous head shot: " 'Man cannot infect or be infected by germs that live in such comparatively close relatives as the snakes' " (84).

The group ultimately votes not to destroy the thing but to release it from deep freeze because it is irreplaceably, infinitely unique: " 'Never in all time to come can there be a duplicate' " (86). This is another denial that will come back to foreclose on the team's own sense of self-sufficiency.

The double that moved on up to the screen from literature a long time ago was ghostly and showed and contained all cut and suture marks of the alternating alterations of identification and projection within one psycho-technical economy. But another kind of double, one indistinguishable from any original or copy within a continuum of live transmission, could be admitted in 1938 by literature. But before the work's inner devastation is complete, Campbell's story pulls up short and switches registers to a localizable contagion, one that can be totally blasted. The final mobilization of boundaries has the cinematic fit that alone frames the fifties movie. The thing stays with a threat of contagion that never makes it to advanced mirror stages of psychotic, techno-simulated replacement of all those who used to live here but do not anymore with androids or "miraculated men" (as Schreber, Freud's favorite psycho, saw it coming). In the story, by contrast, we reach the point of simulation from where there appears to be no return. Once the one thing has been electrocuted, they discover, in cross section, its replicative process. It was already turning into one of the dogs in order, they figure, to survive the cold. Imitation is its destiny. Thus, with direct access to the " 'deepest secret of biology,' " it could have " 'become the population of the world' " (99). It duplicates whatever it encounters and replaces it in the same operation. But each time it has imitated the one it was drawn to be like, the original weight — with which it began and begins anew the endless series of its imitative being — is left over, an eternally supplementary weight that lies in wait for the next cloning opportunity.

"And every time it digested something, and imitated it—"
"It would have had its original bulk left, to start again." (100)

Then the men realize that thing's only chance out of there into a world it would make its own is via imitation of humans. Through them the technologies of transport would be at thing's disposal. Thus, they are all, in theory, the missing link (to technology) of an evolutionary leap that is in progress. In practice they realize that the imitation has already commenced. Only the test of blood can distinguish original from a copy so perfect that even thoughts continue in character. But who is to administer the test? Who is human?

Nervous breakdowns brought on by thing, and by thing's indestructibility, have put two madmen in isolation from the group. One madman screams prayers of protection against the imminent destruction of the world (the number-one psychotic fantasy). The group that can only wait and see decides to watch movies for the diversion; sound track plays full blast to cover the wailing prayers next door. But under this cover someone knifes the madman. Another kind of monster is thus revealed, and the murderer thus adds a third M word to their setting. But this murder also breaks the holding pattern of the group. The man who was murdered was a replicate. And that means that his killer is guaranteed human. With one figure certain the calculations can proceed, the remainder carried over, and cancelled out. The blood tests proceed, and when the results are bloodcurdling, electrocution erases another carryover of the remainder. The last thing was the other madman, the first one to be quarantined and for the longest time forgotten. The group wipes out the great thingly hope with only half an hour to spare before it would have parted for the world tour of groupie-fication with the atomic generator it had just finished assembling. The thing—or the supplement without end—had cloned in two men an extreme case of paranoia in one, and a hysterical condition in the other, without any external modeling. The thing's duplication from the inside out selected the internal capacity of these men for delusional formations as its own best defense. That covers the speed race between self-analysis and psychotic breakdown. But the murder that broke through the first defense of a marginal state of madness also opened up prospects for mourning. Thus, one of the men admits that if survival were not their issue, he would not want to see the replicates, the imitations—the identifications—gone forever: "'In some ways—if only we could have permanently prevented their spreading—I'd like to have even the imitations back. Commander Garry—Connant—Dutton—Clark—'" (129–30).

LECTURE NINETEEN

The spiritist connection, which picks up its primal but really recent momentum when it makes first contact with the live transmission of telegraphy, also passes through the return of Egyptoid burial practices that were counting their latest arrival (which is still with us) in the United States, at first as a by-product of the Civil War, originally to keep dead soldiers "fresh" or "live" for their train transmission to the proper place of burial back home. This new alternative to being dumped out of sight at the target site of battle reflected a kind of photographic desire, potentiated through the speed race between train transport and telegraphic transmission, to lose the war dead and have them too back on the home front. This home front was thus the first internal front of what would be from this fraternal or suicidal conflict onward, whenever another war of doubling turned inward, always total media war or, in other words, psychological warfare. The photographic wish deposited alongside this war bond maintains Forest Lawn, where at the Hollywood franchise, the statue of Lincoln holds center stage: he was the first president to be embalmed (after falling victim to a shoot). Discretion was along for the new order of transport and transmission, at least according to legend. The new nineteenth-century postal organization of pre-stamped mail (whereas before the invention of stamps, what was posted had always been COD) maintained post offices as the exclusive reception area where you would go to pick up mail. But when wives were getting the word from the war office that their males were going to be sent back embalmed, the instant war widows tended to carry on or faint dead away. These public events did not contribute to the containment of traumatization. Therefore, to personalize—to keep out of public view, out of public mind — these first contacts with loss and grief, home delivery was introduced during the Civil War.

Forest Lawn is the Elysium or elision of bodies of commemoration: within an as-live habitat the "memory picture" of the deceased is propped and pumped up for the survivors, all together now, to remember — to forget. Once the shoot is over, the contents can spill out and disappear within this Elysian force field of ambivalence. Forest Lawn was the first modern theme park and one-stop shopping mall styling with accessories. In no time the park's picturesque settings admitted weddings and all sorts of family gatherings unconcerned with death. The park's enfoldment of life onto death was a tribute to what the founder Hubert Eaton called the memorial drive. He saw the future and called it the comemoral, a park zone that would contain all the cultural institutions dedicated to the drive to make, leave behind, or read and live with monuments. Libraries, museums, universities, you name it, all would join the Forest Lawn setting, where the dead were in the first place, buried but repressed. The disappearing act that modeled Eaton's big idea in 1917 (but which he did not really realize until it was time for the Great War's Second Coming) could only have been the mass cemeteries, anonymous by default, burying the impression of big body counts of the war or battle dead. What is worse than mass death, the death of all at the same time? Death one by one in the one on one.

Karl Freund worked as cinematographer on some major German Expressionist films; when he went to Hollywood, he was behind the camera of horror movies. The Mummy is his debut as Hollywood director and delegate of the horror legacy of German Expressionist film. Freund ended up with a regular job as camera man for the I Love Lucy show.

Remember the mummy's apartment where Helen goes on the telepathic beam to visit Boris Karloff: she says she loves the Egyptian look that lacks anything modern. But we are being E-gypped. Karloff's pad in which Helen sees deep inside the mummy's pool the whole doubling prequel to her current role in the ongoing prehistory of "the mummy" (both creature and film) has the Egyptoid look of art deco movie palaces in the thirties. And the pool in which the doubling fantasy of reincarnation is realized just because it is a film, that is, a film within a film, takes mirror stage, which, at one remove of self-reflexivity, holds the place of TV, the set of multiple personalities, of self-surfing. I Love Mummy.

The film is the case study of a young woman, Helen, who is first introduced as the "most interesting patient" of the Van Helsing–esque doctor. In her case too psychosis must race autoanalysis to the end, either that of living end or the one that comes with analytic breakthrough. On the way she must pass through the techno mummy phantasm. Her British father is off in the Sudan; her mother is (you guessed it) doubly missing. We only know that Helen's maternal line is Egyptian: it is on this bloodline that the mummy (you know: Boris Karloff) transmits the occult telecommunication intended for his original mummy bride only. But I guess everyone can tune in on the loving-the-dead channel.

Helen picks up long distance the mummy relationship via the blood bond with her own missing mummy. She becomes an occult medium at Karloff's telecommand. In the archaeology camp that struggles with the mummy complex for control of Helen's body, there is a related disturbance; Frank's mother is missing. The father is on the side of the work of archaeology (that's right: it is also the work of mourning). He defends the scholarship of pottery shards against sensationalist discoveries. The doctor was there back then too when the father's team just the same dug up a mummy, which was then reanimated, by accident, while father was outside with the doctor arguing against the power of the occult. Mummy is never just dead and gone.

Ten years later the son is back in Egypt on the lookout only for sensationalist discoveries (I mean, he does not even know Ancient Egyptian). In league with Karloff (the mummy that dad's team inadvertently brought back), the son discovers the mummified princess. When he first meets Helen, he is reminded of that recent primal view of mummy: why, they are lookalikes. This is real clear when Helen is passed out, like lifeless. Helen wonders out loud whether Frank always has to rob graves to get a date. But the date is thus set: Helen must choose between the melancholic crypt of her bond with mummy and the barely veiled (the unwrapped!) substitutive position as souvenir of Frank's mummy.

To expand upon the Oedipal plot until it will cover and not just fall into the burial plot, Frank's father has to go. When the archaeologist dad dies of a heart attack inflicted by the Karloff mummy across long distance, and the Van Helsing figure, part psychoanalyst, the better part scholar of the occult, explains the connection to Frank, the dad's heir, the son just cannot accept it: it was just a heart attack, which is just an "attack," one that always arouses death-wish participation in its wake. It is the evidence of his own death wishes, which are displaced, but only at the one remove afforded by occult and technical media, about which the son just cannot be frank.

But the mummy has already given up a little, and thus shifts the balance toward mourning. Even though mummy wants to kill Helen and, then, in a heartbeat, reanimate her, he has just the same chosen the substitute brought to us by reincarnation over the mummified original.

The double feature of telepathy and technology was all along giving archaeology the inside track. In addition to all that technological filler, psychotic delusions regularly feature journeys through the encrypted underworlds opened up by archaeology and, at the one remove of analogy, by psychoanalysis too. Opened up, however, to a desperate struggle for preservation. The contents of Pompeii and of the Trojan tombs were destroyed only once excavation admitted air and light inside their crypt space. What the archaeologists learned to dig was a fast-forwarding of deferred death that vampire movies always give us as the ending. But there is always also some outside chance that the destruction was not complete. When Freud gives the Pompeii analogy to his patient Ratman, he too senses, for both of them, that he has gone too far too soon. But he reassures himself and Ratman that everything is being done just the same to preserve the underworld as though its secret burial had never been disinterred.

The autoanalytic breakthrough and its alternating state, psychotic breakdown, pull up "endopsychic perceptions" on the psychoanalytic scanner. These are inside views of the psychic apparatus, and of Freud's theories of the psychic apparatus, which get released to the delusional outside (onto screens of projection) as the psychotic's one last inside-out chance at self-recovery. In the cases of Schreber and Ratman and in the *Gradiva* rereading, Freud gave endopsychic status only to those delusions and analogues drawing on archaeology and technology. In Victor Tausk's analysis of the schizophrenic patient Natalija A, the "influencing machine" that persecutes her resembles a coffin that happens to be a repro of a body (especially on the inside: the machine's batteries recall organs). By virtue of its telepathic connection to the patient, and because, quite simply, as the patient admits, it kind of resembles her, the machine is her double: it projects her body back from the stage to which she has regressed: it is the stage on which her body was a so-called body-genital. This fantasy that the whole body is a genital belongs to the "womb complex" (277). This body-genital or machine runs independently of the ego, that is, on or under another's willpower. Libido has regressed behind the stage of identification, and all contact with the outside world has been given up. The two-dimensional externalizations of hallucination and mummification simulate another world out there in place of the one that the psychotic break totaled. Freud's comment following Tausk's presentation of his case study addressed the connection between the influencing machine and the significance of Egyptian mummification; the placement of the mummy inside a shell modeled after the body corresponded to a "later" conception, that of the return of human life to mother earth — a return to the womb through death. In sum, the spiritual death the schizo undergoes on the way back to the womb corresponds to the physical death the mummy must pass through on its way back.

So the archaeology track rides out the two impulses at once: psychotic shutdown around a loss that cannot be recognized as lost or as ever having been around to be lost, and analytic breakthrough that nonetheless cannot but watch the contents of the tomb fast reverse from mourning to dust. The speed race between psychotic implosion or encryptment and autoanalytic breakthrough (often via the close encounter of delusion) passes through endopsychic terrain crowded with the running commentary and interference of archaeology and technology.

By the close of the eighteenth century, many new categories of membership — in childhood, adolescence, the family, the couple — had opened a complete portfolio of investments. But these new living members had to exit too. And their early exitus occupied the one intersection that the membership drive shared with some of the first externalizations of long-distance relations inside new technologies of transmission and recording. It was primal time for the mummy to be projected among the very first double features to preview motion pictures. For his Phantasmagoria spectacles at this time in Paris, Robertson strapped the magic lantern to a moving vehicle that could convey through its transport the advance and withdrawal, the close-up and long shot of the still image. Within the crypt setting Robertson selected and redecorated for his underworld explorations, mummies were shown to come alive upon impact with this double penetration and desecration of their resting place. According to the authorities, they unlawfully trafficked with the dead.

Karl Hans Strobl's "The Tomb of Père Lachaise" is the day-by-day accounting of one author's occupancy within the tomb of an eccentric in life who in afterlife has tagged her special bequest to go to the one who can fulfill all her conditions: double occupancy with her remains for one year in her tomb cut off from the outside but for the silent regular contact of feeding time. With the proceeds from his crypt residency, the author will be able to pursue publication of his magnum opus with the security blanket order of subvention funding to fall back on. These conditions and conditionings are not at all far removed from the terms of any academic leave, also often the taking leave of the senses. He will be undisturbed, alone with his thoughts for the year. During the year, then, he can finally write the work that he has been planning, and planning to publish, for so long now. The study he has in mind, on the decay and finitude of matter, will fit right into his new think-tank setting.

The grantee and gravetop publisher has improvised a color-separation filing system for his mass of notes. But one morning he discovers all the notes just scattered across the floor. They seem difficult to pick up as though owing to some electric or magnetic attraction. Then there is the night that he is jolted wide awake from deepest sleep — "as though my nerves were connected to an electric battery, which gave a signal" (203). He sees some sort of night-light illuminate the crypt interior. But this is just the kind of novelty in the realm of light manifestations that he must study in order to reevaluate all received notions about matter's essence. A breath of air or wind accompanies the emanation of light. Once again the research notes are scattered. This time they stick to the floor by another analogy: it is as though the stone were some frozen mass that was slowly dissolving from the surface on down. The author is convinced that there are "intermolecular forces at work in the marble of this tomb which science has not yet registered" (206).

His next observation in the material world is that he is getting fat. He no longer fits through the small opening that leads to the funeral monument; when he tries to pass through, he almost gets stuck as though in a trap. He is the "prisoner" of his own belly, which is a roundabout way of saying that he gags on the incorporation that has gone down inside him. His captivation by the research project emanating from his entombed setting keeps on growing. When he tries to catch the tomb's rays, divert them, or even measure them, he makes the "uncanny" discovery that they lack any "spectrum" at all (212). They leave "not a trace on the photographic plate" (212). He concludes, therefore, that it is self-illuminating aether, indeed the visible manifestation of the legendary world aether:

> The world aether is nothing other than the transfer of force into matter. Energy is not a characteristic of substance, but is rather what was already there, earlier, out of which substance emerges. Thus the riddle of the decay of matter is solved, the riddle that so unsettles our physicists; matter must decay in order to become once again pure energy.... There is a circulation system of world energy, which first forms matter out of itself. (216)

Now he can begin to explain away the strangely specific disappearance of the nameplate on the tomb for the interval of the late-night illumination and airing: "It seems worth noting that with the return of the bronze plate an unpleasant taught sensation, a kind of difficulty breathing and a frenzied heartbeat, which come over me at the moment of its disappearance, now subside completely" (216–17). He writes down the question, If it isn't the world aether, then what is it? When he wakes up, he finds the answer scrawled in its place: "It is the breath of Katechana" (217). What is more, the handwriting appears to be his own. But then he detects signs of counterfeiting. Then again, if he writes in his sleep, those somnambulistic conditions might alter his writing. Who else could be there?

When he detects small bite wounds along his wrist and throat, he becomes convinced that his fiancée visits him at night and covers him with love bites and bloody kisses. His fiancée has indeed started reality checking up on him. She comes graveside to beg him to break off the experiment. But he cannot give up this grant opportunity. Besides he is still the prisoner of his body. But then, when he makes the discovery that Katechana means, in the deceased's mother tongue, vampire, the author decides to feign sleep for one night. It is Madame Wassilska emerging with the light and air emanating from the crypt. He knows what to do now. He grabs her and bites open her neck. It is his blood he is taking back. In death the vampire spitefully assumes the form of his fiancée. "I am freed . . ."

The Strobl story puts one meglo author under crypt conditions that are at the same time infantilizing: then the strobe lights and disappearing acts can begin. He, who has always only planned to compose his scattered notes or thoughts into a body, begins now, in the vampire's crypt, to build the corpus. His project concerns his own unique ideas about the material or maternal world. His contemplation of the limits of decay imagines the about-face of aetherial conditions for the recycling of matter. He defends himself against the vampiric bond with his project, which is in turn the fantasy about a body of work that comes down to his own egoic projection of his infantile body and thus back up and out as the new, psychotically reconstituted world of matter. But self-defense (even auto-cannibalism, since he emphasizes that it is his blood after all he is guzzling from the cut throat) is the second degree, the cover the author assumes or consumes in cutting down his standing invitation to reenter the world via substitution. Before his body entered and filled the crypt place of his corpus-building research, the author had come up with three motivations fitting for the dead woman's funereal arrangements: she wanted someone to watch over her in case she had been buried alive; she wanted protection for her otherwise defenseless body from grave robbers, necrophiliacs, or lycanthropes; she took great pleasure in imagining her captive audience. Thus, he gives us three stations of thoughts crossing our minding of mummy's wishes, which are our own.

The mummy propped up at the beginning of yet another version of the mummy phantasm in fact concludes the process that began with a death that had to be placed (under wraps) in the reanimation ready position. At the beginning there is a dead person whose loss cannot yet be acknowledged but must be recircuited instead through the emergency sensurround of identification (the contained material loss or mummy) alternating with projection (the astral body, the double, or phantom telecommand). The mummy is the wrap-up of what has gone on before. When we begin with the mummy that must be unwrapped, we are in fact at the end, the living end of a death that could not be mourned. Thus, we must read these fictions and phantasms on rewind. The failed resurrection (or rather the failed union of reanimation and reincarnation) that comes at the end as an end was also in the beginning.

In Stoker's *The Jewel of Seven Stars* reversal wraps up the mummy on rewind: a death, which was at the beginning, gets replayed at the end of the contest between reanimation and reincarnation. The narrator's dream woman, Margaret Trelawny, is at the same time the reincarnation-double of the mummy who is seeking reanimation once and for all. Thus, the narrative proper begins (and ends) with the specter or semblance of Father's death. From and toward this end, Margaret "Forest Lawny" enters and exits the narrator's dream between the lines of the post:

> It all seemed so real that I could hardly imagine that it had ever occurred before; ... And so memory swooned, again and again, in sleep.

There was somebody knocking.... Without premeditation, I was out of bed. Instinctively I... went down to the door. I opened it; there stood a groom.... His hand produced a letter from his pocket.... The letter was in a strange hand, a woman's....

"You said you would like to help me if I needed it.... The time has come sooner than I expected.... An attempt has been made to murder my Father; though he still lives. But he is unconscious.... I suppose I shall realise later what I have done in asking such a favor; but at present I cannot think. Come at once!
MARGARET TRELAWNY." (1)

The father's undeath signals that another death rules the household. Margaret, who asks the narrator to accept the rescue mission of reanimating her "unconscious" father, was the issue of dad's original dead faint. While excavating the ancient tomb of Queen Tera, the father, a patron of Egyptology, fell into a three-day trance in the Mummy Pit. During this unconscious period, his wife back home died giving birth to Margaret, who in the meantime has grown into Queen Tera's lookalike. Thus, when the father returns to consciousness, he cuts straight to the crypt: he leads the group to some underworld site where "The Great Experiment" — the reanimation of mummy — can be conducted.

If the Old Gods had lost their power, or never had any, the Experiment would not succeed. The conclusion: that the struggle between Life and Death, should the Experiment succeed, would no longer be a matter of the earth (32). The struggle between life and death would no longer be a matter — *mater* — of earth or *terra*.

The narrator takes comfort in scientific discussions: "They took my mind from brooding on the mysteries of the occult" (32). But these are the mysteries that otherwise preoccupy him once the date of the scientific experiment is set and draws near: in sync with the coming of the date ("the night of nights") Margaret grows increasingly "*distraite*" and "inspired." The other great experiment — the autoanalysis Freud always analogized with archaeological excavation — comes full circuit on the person of Margaret wired to mummy's dictation:

I was beginning to doubt Margaret!...Margaret was changing....
Her coming back to her old self had something the sensation of a

> new person coming into the room. But now I never knew whether the personality present was my Margaret or the new one, whom I hardly understood, and whose aloofness made a barrier between us.... It was as if she were speaking at dictation of one who could read words or acts, but not thoughts. (34–35)

Margaret Trelawny not only speaks mummy's techno dictation but also speaks out on behalf of Queen Tera's wish to return inside some different time zone in which equality in love might be obtained: she wants to return as the "new woman" (31), the kind of woman Margaret presumably is (or wants to be).

With each "mysterious veiling of her own personality," the narrator registers a "subtle sense of separation" (36). The narrator's share in the mummy complex thus gets separated out as he imagines the consequences of Margaret's "strange dual existence":

> The dual existence! If Margaret were not a free agent, but could be compelled to speak or act as instructed; or if her being could be changed for another without any one noticing the doing of it, then all things were possible. If this individuality were just and kind and clean, all might be well. But if not... the thought was too awful for words. (35)

On the down side of this mood swing, the narrator brings into focus on Margaret's auto-technologizing person the mummy projection or astral body:

> She had been born of a dead mother during the time her Father and his friend were in a trance... effected by a woman mummied, yet preserving an astral body.... With that astral body, space ceased to exist. Vast distances became as naught; and whatever power of necromancy the Sorceress had might have been exercised over the dead mother, and possibly the dead child. The dead child!... How could I believe there was no Margaret at all; but an animated image! (35)

On "the night of nights" the Great Experiment is on: up front it is conducted in a techno-electro laboratory-crypt, but in primal time the consent of the mummy herself is required. For this one time only, Queen Tera must drop her astral projection back onto her dead body. Now that Margaret is mummy's walkie-talkie, she must confirm that Queen Tera will fulfill the precondition—and absolute risk—of the experiment:

"It means that at the sunset the 'Ka' is to enter the 'Ab'; and it is only at the sunrise it will leave it!"

"Go on!" said her Father.

"It means for this night the Queen's Double, which is otherwise free, will remain in her heart, which is mortal and cannot leave its prison-place. It means when the sun has dropped into the sea, Queen Tera will cease to exist as a conscious power, till sunrise; unless the Great Experiment can wake her. Whatever change may come from the Great Experiment, there can come none from the helpless dead woman." She stopped and I could see her eyes were full of tears. . . .

"You believe, Margaret, that Queen Tera has voluntarily undertaken to give up her freedom for this night? To become a mummy till the Experiment is completed?". . .

"Yes!" (37–38)

If Margaret is not the "dead child" possessed one-way by the mummy queen's astral body but is instead her "mother's daughter" (as Father sees her) superimposed onto her dead mummy, then the Great Experiment will replace with the melancholic phantasm of reanimation the reincarnation or substitution over time brought to us by the work of mourning. The original experiment auto-destructs and (reading now in reverse) the father's undeath — the unconscious father — is shot up the melancholic metabolism to make way for substitution and reincarnation.

The father resumes consciousness (or falls unconscious) not only to conduct the experiment but also to give daughter and narrator his blessing — and wound. The dream interrupted or continued by the posted message from father's daughter brings the narrator, like "the country doctor" in Kafka's story, to the side of a wound that cannot close but (for the duration of father's unconsciousness) is periodically reopened. Margaret shares with the narrator (her rescuer and suitor) her recollection of the first time father went all the way into the unconscious:

"There was Father on his right side. The track of blood went across the room up to the bed, and there was a pool all around him which looked terribly red. . . . The left sleeve was torn, showing his bare arm, and stretched out toward the safe. It looked so terrible, patched with blood, and with the flesh torn or cut all around a gold chain bangle on his wrist." (2)

At the wound's reopening, the narrator witnesses the father-and-daughter blood bond, which is, in contrast to the maternal connection, a bond of bleeding: "The former wound in front of the arm had been cut terribly; one of the cuts seemed to jet out blood with each pulsation of the heart. By the side of her Father knelt Miss Trelawny, her white nightdress stained with blood" (7). The bleeding wound marks the terms of the narrator's initiation into matrimony, which must take place prior to joining hands with the wife. In the face of the recurring attack upon the unconscious father's hand (which must thus bleed periodically), the only organizing instructions the daughter receives for absorbing the mysterious flow of events are spilled, I mean spelled out in a letter in "Father's hand" (4). In the midst of directives that will lead from the bedroom (which contains unconscious Father alongside mummy) to the laboratory crypt of the reanimation experiment (and back again), Father includes a couplification requirement: "There should be added one other watcher of the opposite sex. Understood, it is of the very essence of my wish there should be, awake both masculine and feminine intelligences" (5).

Thus, with the father (of the wife) in superintendence of couplification, we observe the "taboo on virginity" bleed into the one on menstruation. Freud:

> Menstruation, especially its first appearance, is interpreted as the bite of some spirit-animal, perhaps as a sign of sexual intercourse with this spirit. Occasionally some report gives grounds for recognizing the spirit as that of an ancestor and then, supported by other findings, we understand that the menstruating girl is taboo because she is the property of this ancestral spirit. (*SE* 11: 197)

Thus, the virgin bride so desirable in our culture, Freud admits, was originally or primally off-limits. Instead, some delegate of Father first ritually penetrated the virgin before she could be handed over to her husband, who comes second.

The legacy of mummy, transmitted from father to daughter or mummy-reincarnation, is that of periodicity. From the number of stars or facets of her magic jewel to the number of toes on her cat's paw to the number of fingers on her own hand, seven was her lucky number. Seven stands for the days of the week and thus for the whole calendar of periodic recurrences.

The hand with seven fingers was, already at the time of mummification, positioned or designed for its separability:

> "Her hand was to be in the air — and in it the Jewel of Seven Stars, so that wherever was air she might move even as her Ka could. This . . . meant her body could become astral at command, and so move and become whole again when and where required." (24)

Thus, the separable hand with seven fingers technologizes the mummified body, which is henceforth "immortal and transferrable at will."

The narrator witnesses such a transfer when after studying the mummy's hand ("The wrist of the hand was stained with red as though dropped in recent blood"), he is jolted back into the present: "All at once, all thoughts seemed to stop. There lay a real hand across the book! I knew the hand — and loved it. Margaret's hand was a joy to see — to touch; and yet at that moment, it had a strangely moving effect" (22). The father behind the woman returns to consciousness and resumes his "grave duties." Another kind of blessing is requested of him: " 'I am to take it . . . that it is in your mind to be a suitor for her hand' " (28). Father immediately calls in Margaret and commands her to show the narrator the mark of the father's prior claim on her hand:

> She threw one look of appeal and, without a word, raised her right hand, so the bracelet of wings which covered the wrist fell back, leaving the flesh bare. An icy chill shot through me.
>
> On her wrist was a thin red jagged line, from which seemed to hang red stains like drops of blood!
>
> She stood there, a figure of patient pride. . . .
>
> As we stood for some seconds, the deep, grave voice of her Father sounded a challenge:
>
> "What do you say now?" . . .
>
> I pushed back the golden cincture and kissed her wrist. I faced her Father:
>
> "You have my answer, sir!" (29)

But the paternal legacy of periodic dating, the upright body's schedule of couple formation, gets replaced by the date of the Great Experiment, one that, once set, starts a one-way (that is, nonperiodic) countdown, which the narrator can only anticipate with dread: "I was almost overcome. The definite fixing of the hour seemed like the voice of Doom" (37). Mummy has only one chance to achieve reanimation; to take this chance she risks all; the one-time offer of reanimation requires that she return from and relinquish her projective or phantom beam and be the corpse she is. Everyone is in the ready position. But when an accident reverses the progress of the experiment, the narrator begins the body count; his mourning has come up and gone down — and out. The sentence that concludes the narrative of a dream, autoanalysis, or psychotic episode: "It was merciful I was spared the pain of hoping."

The narrator's initiation into the hymeneal bond with the wife (and thus with father) is pushed into the past by the melancholic blowout he alone survives. That the wife is always also the reincarnation of mummy along the dotted lines of separation and substitution that father transmits is the lesson the narrator learns, but either too late or at the end of his work of mourning. The wife can get laid — but to rest. We now know what father knows best: that she is one of the mournables.

Seven was Stoker's number, too. It was the power pill he took in by playing dead for the seven years it took to wait out the arrivals of death-wish carriers (his siblings) and revive in time to be mummy's and the dad's last and lasting seventh child. That is why this number is ambivalently held and why the narrator (Stoker's official delegate) gets to be sole heir to the seven heaven of successful mourning.

LECTURE TWENTY

John Polidori, who attended Byron as his personal physician with a bedside mannerism that left too much to be desired, was the first to introduce the vampire into English letters, just a heartbeat away from his most unholy and unnatural act of plagiarizing, improperly burying inside his corpus, what was, in the beginning, Byron's conception. The contamination of twos by the third place set for haunting organizes Polidori's *The Vampyre,* which opens with a double entry. There is Lord Ruthven, who runs on the power of his dead gray eye. Sure, its beam is repulsively uncanny, but it is an opener at all those "thoughtless" London socials that welcome (or should I say invite) Lord Ruthven's grand entrance. And then there is the young gentleman named Aubrey who is marked as eligible, ready, set to go for substitution; he joins these same London forget-togethers, where he too is encouraged to make his propositions and proposals. In another part of the same double registry Aubrey has a sister. They have been orphans since childhood.

Aubrey's inheritance, the legacy of the duo's dead parental guidance, is administered by guardians who, in order to keep the heir conditioned to low maintenance, encourage Aubrey to develop his imagination against his better judgment. What programs Aubrey to fall for the facts and fantasies coming soon of vampiric attack and bonding is the guardian rehearsal or repetition of the pull of the imagination over judgment, a pull that pushes up the sod of the grave absence of parents. This pulls up everything we have already said about the trip through the imagination (that is, through identification), a trip that is necessary but, if unchecked, is doubly bound to go out of control and admit monstrosity. Because of this excess of imagination, a surfeit that makes him accessible only to superficiality, shallowness, sentimentality, we find that he is characterized as something of a tourist, who will take trips again and again in this short novel, trips that promise to take him to the cure but that stop short of autoanalysis and admit instead the phantasm of vampirism.

But when he enters society at the same time as the vampire, Aubrey is on the verge of leaving the automatic course of his imagination. He discovers, as he enters society, that there is no foundation for the makeup of his imaginings. That is how it is put. In exchange for giving up a solo career as what Disney Corp calls imagineer, he is willing to have his vanity gratified by all the young women and their mothers who pay him the protection of compliments. So he is on the verge of entering into something that would substitute for his solitude. But the instant he sees Ruthven, he gives up his outside chances at substitution. In a heartbeat Aubrey's imagination is putting Ruthven into pictures: "Allowing his imagination to picture everything that flattered its propensity to extravagant ideas, he soon formed this object into the hero of a romance, and determined to observe the offspring of his fancy rather than the person before him" (17).

So right here, if you wanted to be literal-minded about it, you could see this whole vampire story as lying inside a family romance brought to us by Aubrey's imagination, which has once again been let loose. As soon as Aubrey discovers that Ruthven is going on a trip, he decides "it was time for him to perform the tour" (18). And he turns around and receives from Ruthven (the double or mirror image with the giveaway dead eye) the proposal he was waiting for, that they take the tour together. The first thing Aubrey discovers about his mysterious other is that he loves to gamble but loves to win only to ruin and corrupt any young man asking for it. Freud pulled back the covers from the masturbatory significance of gambling. Mutual self-sexuality is the first arena Aubrey recognizes for the spread of Lord Ruthven's seduction and corruption.

Then, when in Rome, Aubrey loses sight of his companion and breaks out of his captivated audience. Now a reading project takes over, where Ruthven's attraction left off. Aubrey starts searching for "memorials of another almost deserted city" (21). We are stumbling again over the archaeology of analogues that Freud found so compelling. Aubrey is in search of something like autoanalysis. He entered on a kind of self-help cure, when he tried to enter society and, ready or not, give up his solo imaginings. But the vampire suddenly appeared and seduced him back into the projection booth. And here he is given another outside chance, this time around via archaeology. He goes in search of memorials of another, deserted city. But then he is interrupted by the arrival of two letters: a letter from his sister and a second letter from his guardians. And in this second, less guarded letter the corrupt nature of Ruthven stands out upright. What Aubrey last witnessed at the gambling table gets reorganized around a primal scene of adult sexuality complete with rises and fallings.

> His guardians insisted upon his immediately leaving his friend, and urged, that his character was dreadfully vicious, for that the possession of the irresistible powers of seduction, rendered his licentious habits more dangerous to society. It had been discovered, that . . . he had required, to enhance his gratification, that his victim, the partner of his guilt, be hurled from the pinnacle of unsullied virtue, down to the lowest abyss of infamy and degradation: in fine, that all those females whom he had sought, apparently on account of their virtue, had, since his departure, thrown even the mask aside, and had not scrupled to expose the whole deformity of their vices to the public gaze. (21–22)

Aubrey decides to shadow Ruthven at this point, starts to follow him rather than continue his archaeological research. When he discovers his companion making moves on another innocent young woman, Aubrey manages, he believes, to interrupt the fall. Aubrey goes to Greece, deeper down the archaeological track along which psychosis and autoanalysis race neck and neck. Soon he starts tracing "the faded records of ancient glory upon monuments" (23). But although he has separated from Ruthven, he is not alone: a certain Ianthe accompanies Aubrey in his search for antiquities. This figure, who is described as an unconscious girl, seems to shift him from the autoanalytic occupation back onto the track of the vampire. As she stands by his side, he forgets "the letters he had just deciphered upon an almost effaced tablet" (23). And she holds or diverts his attention by telling him stories of vampires, "the super-natural tales of her nurse": "she told him the tale of the living vampyre, who had passed years amidst his friends, and dearest ties, forced every year, by feeding upon the life of a lovely female to prolong his existence for the ensuing months" (25).

Aubrey makes light of Ianthe's stories, making up as he goes along the first lines of resistance. Still trying to follow out the archaeological project, Aubrey goes off on an excursion during which he will cross ter-ritories known to all to be "the resort of vampyres in their nocturnal orgies" (26). This is the last resort, the one Ianthe and her parents warn him not to visit. But Aubrey, who, loud as denial, refuses to believe in vampirism and thus, as though by chance, promptly finds himself in the night spot, fulfills Ianthe's warning or prompting "that those who had dared to question their existence [this almost sounds like suicide], always had some proof given, which obliged them, with grief and heart-breaking, to confess it was true" (25). In the danger zone of vampiric visitation Aubrey hears "dreadful shrieks of a woman mingling with the stifled, exultant mockery of a laugh" (29). When he attaches this audio portion to the corpse he next finds, he realizes that it was Ianthe who was the one living and dying proof of vampirism that would make him a be-liever. In a trance, he reaches out to touch her and pulls back "almost un-consciously in his hand a naked dagger of a particular construction" (31).

Aubrey soaks the fever linen of youth while trying to call two fig-ures — Ianthe and Lord Ruthven — and put through the "unaccountable" connection. Just as Aubrey starts combining Ruthven's image with that of the laughing vampire who claimed Ianthe, Ruthven arrives to break the fever and knock out the shock of recognition. Now Ruthven, just like a friend forever, nurses Aubrey back up and running. They go on another trip together, visiting places in Greece unknown to them and therefore impervious to a sense of return or recall:

> He proposed to Lord Ruthven . . . that they should visit those parts of Greece neither had yet seen. They traveled in every direction and sought every spot to which a recollection could be attached: but though they thus hastened from place to place, yet they seemed not to heed what they gazed upon. (34)

A trip that is a vacation from remembering, that records only to erase, takes in the tour and return of Aubrey's repetition compulsion, which takes him back to the one scene where his excavations always pull up short of discovery. Once again he is warned not to pass through a certain zone because, this time around, it is the native habitat of robbers. He goes there with Lord Ruthven just the same. Robbers strike, on automatic, and Ruthven is mortally wounded. He is on his way out, it seems, and he makes Aubrey swear an oath that for a year and a day Aubrey will not release the news of Lord Ruthven's death. Aubrey has this death to keep secret, which shakes on the hidden and protected bond between survivor and lost one.

The body remains unburied: "according to a promise they had given his lordship," the robbers place the corpse upon a certain spot where "it should be exposed to the first cold ray of the moon that rose after his death" (36). Determined to bury it just the same, Aubrey goes to the spot and finds the death or dead he has sworn to keep secret missing. Aubrey decides to leave a place that only makes worse "that superstitious melancholy that had seized upon his mind" (37). But even as he proceeds to leave, he stumbles upon a missing prop from the scene to which he keeps on returning. Now he finds among Ruthven's effects the sheath that goes with the dagger he reached out and touched when it was Ianthe's scene. Aubrey's scenes of horror are all connected or, after the fact, are always the same one in which he gets accessorized to murder.

So as he retraces his steps doubled over by the bond of waiting, of the weight of the missing corpse's secretions, he now discovers that the woman he thought he had rescued from Ruthven in Rome has also in the meantime disappeared. And instantly, as though to make the direct connection, he rushes home to his sister's side: "He hastened to the mansion of his fathers, and there, for a moment, appeared to lose, in the embraces and caresses of his sister, all memory of the past" (38). Aubrey returns to some former place, not to remember or recognize his once and future scene but to ride out again the wipeout of every memory of the past.

He is back at his sister's side just in time for their double entry into society. For Aubrey, the entry phase goes against the pull power of his inner life: "Aubrey would rather have remained in the mansion of his fathers, and fed upon the melancholy which overpowered him" (40). But he takes the station break of forced entry to protect his sister and project the vampire beside themselves.

They make their entrance right at the tight spot Aubrey was originally in with Ruthven. And just as Aubrey remembers or recognizes that this was the place where his first entrance had shut him up, Ruthven pops up by his side, a whispered aside that reinforces the silent terms of their secret bond. Even if he were to break the oath, "who would believe him?"

Aubrey takes the short circuit of nervous breakdown. While in recovery, he counts down the year and a day of his owed silence. In the meantime his sister has accepted some other's hand in marriage. Aubrey returns from the leave of absence of his senses in time to congratulate his sister on her wedding coming soon. At this point of return he sees that she is wearing "a locket upon her breast." He opens it up, and what does he find: Ruthven's image. Pinned to his sister's person, Aubrey finds a locket (which resonates with "lock it! keep it locked up!") and opens it to find, once and again, the image that always haunts him. "Morning came," but across the echo chamber of its second sense it was too late, too late or too early to let go. Now that it is high time for the sister's abduction by the third person that's a crowd of ghosts, Aubrey's blood bursts its immediate boundaries and flows inward. As he lies dying, he relates *The Vampyre,* the legacy we hold in our hands. The last sentence announces what for Aubrey had been living on forever after: Ruthven's missingness captions the contextlessness of the corpse. Aubrey's sister keeps on going by the simple name, if it is a name, of "Miss Aubrey." So there is Aubrey and there is Miss Aubrey. Remember that Polidori advertises his work as picking up where Byron left off. What is started but never finished is the incestuous attachment. Byron's affair with Augusta, the incest he knew best, was the monstrous scandal that would accompany him to his burial. Sixty black carriages attended Byron's funeral, but all had been sent empty, the placeholders of all others forsaken or excluded by Byron's incestuous commitment and commission. The vampire named Ruthven in Polidori's story, the one that scooped up By-

THE VAMPIRE LECTURES   255

ron's, has another name in Byron's own uncompletable fragment. The well-wishing surname is announced by the other's masculinized first name: Augustus Darvell. The element that Polidori does adopt from the original is the vow of silence that Darvell exacts on his deathbed from his fellow traveler, who slides following his companion's passing into the in-between state with which Byron's fragment closes: " 'Between astonishment and grief, I was tearless.' " The simple assignation "Miss Aubrey" doubles one name that is itself too much by half. We also overhear in the empty placeholder of a more personalizable label the assertion of a relationship in missingness. She or Aubrey is missing, or someone misses Aubrey, or, in short, someone's missing. If we then read this story in the opposite direction, along the dotted lines of the mummy wrapup or just as Freud invites us to interpret dreams, we find Miss Aubrey's parting company at the beginning, a fatal association that is some kind of sex crime. Next to the corpse without a proper name we find the missingness of the vampire Augustus. Incest is always too ambivalent by half. That is why Augusta is part sisterhood, pure longing for a lost association in presence, and part vampirism. "Miss Aubrey" must also be read as a hit-or-miss injunction. Missing Aubrey has kept him in solitary. Even within the mansion of his fathers, melancholia surrounds and seduces him. What first gets emphasized when Miss Aubrey comes up for a closer description is her own melancholy charm. A charm that, as item of jewelry, resonates with that locket that, unlocked, released the vampiric nature of Aubrey's bond to the Aubrey he misses. Next time take better aim!

The long and the short of it is that in "Return of the Undead" Frank Long and Otis Kline put vampirism where your youth is, along for the transmission from couple to group and back again. In the section of "Thoughts for the Times on War and Death" titled "Our Attitude towards Death," Freud was still working the mourning model for what civilization is worth. Freud says that without the substitutive economy of mourning, which is part of our risk calculation, we would gag and get stuck on irreplaceable relations: inventions (artificial flight is Freud's example), discoveries, explorations, and so on would never have been risked against a horizon of unacknowledgable loss. Love or love of life would also run on empty, Freud concludes: "like an American flirt." America will stand over and again for Freud as the final frontier of a mass psychologization that prays to the lip service of the Christian mass. In "American" mass culture it has always been nice knowing and gnawing on every norm bait of the couplification that must be set up as though a free gift that comes with group membership.

In "Return of the Undead" the medical-student frat bros have gone to the cemetery to raise a prank they are mean to play on their pal Freddy. Tensions between group and couple are firing across Freddy's faint heart: he is the weakling or nerd who occupies the border between outcast and mascot of the pack and, more importantly, has prematurely articulated couple formation with Nancy, the most desirable woman on campus. One of the boys, Cummings, who goes by the acronym of his first two names (M.T.), pronounced or cheered by the team as "Empty," prescribes a "jolt" of shock treatment for Freddy, who is the crybaby, always yelling "for his mama" when the surgery demos draw blood (240). Freddy, who managed to skip the fraternal initiation and the beat of the group for the shortcut of the Oedipal couple, must wake to a mourning hazing: his best friends are digging up a recently interred stiff to prop up in his room for the fright. But this corpse isn't the dead or dad it is made out to be. It does not jump-start Freddy's initiation into the group nor does it realign the group's own capacity for substitution with couple capacity; instead it comes alive in Freddy's stuck place and sucks blood.

In the meantime Empty goes for the "consolation date," a girl "almost as good-looking as Nancy" (248), while checking out books on the occult. And he experiences a libidinal upsurge right there in the library where she works, which he diagnoses as arousal arising from the dread fascination with vampirism. But then he runs into Nancy, who is beside herself, as though divided by the move made to replace her. One of the boys was found drained and dying in the "lover's lane where students petted in shadows" (250). Empty's automatic reflection: " 'You mean — you were there with him, Nancy?' " (250). This tension between them is what is relieved or relived under the vampire's attack. That is why the vampire gets in on Empty's consolation date by refilling with Empty's voice. Nancy must stop the violence against women, who are, all of them, substitutes, with an arrow that it is up to Empty finally to drive all the way into the vampire. Between the two of them the crude consolations of random substitution and Oedipal identification get laid to rest. Now Nancy can faint dead away and awaken, her libido reborn up in Empty's arms. "She felt very sorry for Freddy — poor kid. She had foolishly imagined that she was in love with him. It was just her maternal instinct running away with her, she realized that now" (250). That maternal drive comes back with Nancy to fulfill the Empty place inside the in-group, the place where the group, which does not have a reproducing plan of its own, sets up the couple as its genitalia. The ambivalence reserved for the couple of parents — represented by the out-of-it nerd or mascot and the off-limits maternal figure of nursing care — has been worked through over the staked body of the vampire. The group now has a future.

Blood of Dracula draws its monstrous teen transformations out of the bad blood of new women rising up against the order or spirit that assigns their place and leaves them there. We start out on a dark, stormy night road with parents up front and the daughter riding in the back of the family trust, which has been broken. The girl gives the wheel of the family steering committee a spin and makes that car swerve. The stepmother has put on an address that is all ice and furs. The teen's Hamletian gripe: that her father started the step program only six weeks after her mother's passing. But his work-related move forced him to make up his mind on the spot, the spot he was in with a dead wife and her grieving daughter. Teen spirit: "They twisted your arm — around her!"

Then we arrive at Sherwood School for Girls, a place-name resonant with Robin Hood, which like Little Red Riding Hood, holds the place of adolescent initiation ceremonies of bloodletting in circumcision, penetration, menstruation. After the headmistress assures Nancy, the troubled daughter, that they have fun at prep school too, she gets harassed by her new school-mates. The leader of the pack states the case for or against Nancy: no lone wolf, no oddball will be tolerated; she must join the secret society "Birds of Paradise." Nancy, the lone-wolf-to-be of an underworld organization that the "Birds" group only marks a diversion away from or toward, warns her leader: "I never got an A for obedience."

The teen leader serves her time as assistant to and psychotic trans-feree onto the chemistry teacher, the secret head of the scientific organiza-tion of her narcissism, which nevertheless or therefore requires at least one more human subject for the experiment. Nancy's independence — she even resists the common sex offered the "Birds" through the school gardener — makes her "an A Bomb in her own right," as the assistant characterizes the new girl for the teacher's selection and delectation.

As they prepare the next lesson, the assistant, whose senses are trans-ferentially wired, notices that the teacher's thesis is back on the board. The assistant instantly rallies to the powerful margin of genius scorned. The teacher reissues the call: "We live in a world ruled by men for men. They mock my thesis. But they're convinced they're on the right track. They'll de-stroy the world with their reckless experiments." "But you experiment" — the transference junkie reminds herself and prompts the teacher with just the measure that is a treasure of resistance required to keep them both on one side of their dialogue against the world:

> "Yes, constantly. I'm not against progress. But they search for power in the wrong places. If this continues, do you know what the future will look like: monsters, misshapen creatures of radiation. I'm convinced that in each person there's a power so great that if released it would make the split atom seem like a blessing. There's more terrible power in us than men can create. Once I demonstrate this, the nuclear testing will stop for fear of unleashing this natural power. There could only be total self-destruction. And who wants that?"

She should know the answer to that one. Not every blessing is in disguise.

Nancy has made it through stage one of selection out of the same-sex libido pool of teen applicants for missing-link research. Teacher and assistant test their choice, and she really is, under lab conditions: they stage an accident in class that hurts Nancy's hand. Nancy sees through it all and jumps to the conclusion with full-throttle raging. Teacher takes her aside for special treatment. "For special people there's no way out other than getting even. Remember our ancestors: an eye for an eye. It's OK. Under special conditions. It would be silly to strike out blindly. It should be done with guidance." Yes, Nancy now admits, she trusts the teacher. "That means I trust you too. What goes on in this room must not leave this room." Teacher closes the blinds and puts on a chain swinging with an amulet from the Carpathian mountains:

> "It can heal and it can destroy. Also it can release frightening powers. Look at it. Now go to sleep. But you can still hear my voice, hear me and obey me. Your hand no longer feels the pain. You won't forget that I relieved the pain. But you'll remember that it's important to obey me, always, 1, 2, 3, 4, 5, wake up."

Three guys show up after hours in the dorm and just in time: some of the girls were dancing by themselves, others with each other. While the boys sing the theme song "Puppy Love," two girls do a dance routine; two more join in; by the end of the song they are all in on the musical number. Teacher, disturbed by the music of puppy love, turns off the light and puts on the amulet, sits down by the opened window, and starts transmitting. Nancy picks up the signal, right where it left off. When one of the girls goes down into the basement, she is devoured by the POV accompanied by audio portions of werewolfish sounds. While the teacher, satisfied, jots down notes on the experiment, a team of police and doctors arrives to investigate. "Teenagers, you know how they are; sometimes they lose their heads." But then they find the puncture marks right on the jugular with no blood around to show for it. One doctor recognizes the pattern:

> "In medical school I shared a room with an exchange student from the Carpathian mountains. He used to tell us stories about vampires, as though he believed them, had seen them. It's an old-world sickness that drives them on and on. When I saw that girl it was just as he described it to me."

"Don't let anyone hear you. You'll get the strait jacket. Not one word to the reporters or we'll have mass hysteria."

But what about the transferee, the teacher's assistant and pet (her name, a real stage name, is Mira)? There is jealousy in the transference to be sure, but they pretend they are talking about research conditions. "Mira, research must be based on what I see with my own eyes." "And work with your own hands." Teacher notices the tension and comes down hard on the safety in boundaries of their rapport: confidence must not be violated! Mira answers, back on track: "Never!"

At the Halloween scavenger hunt, gardener and girlfriend number one break up. Under the teacher's spell and being, Nancy comes up from behind. She gets the girl. The Puppy-Love boy tries to get Nancy, just kidding around, but he gets her ghost: the transformer turns her back on, and he is down her drain. Now the vampirologist on the investigative team just has to speak out again, even after they accuse him of being a McCarthy-style witch-hunter. "You can't laugh away murder." "But what's the vengeance motive?" "It's the work of a paranoid. Someone with a compulsion neurosis to kill." The team uses a lie detector's psychogalvanic reflex on the school's charges. First Nancy takes the demo test. Outside the truth booth teacher has grabbed the amulet and started transmitting. She has dropped the cone of her command over what would otherwise be detectable as a lie. After Nancy passes the test, the inspector cannot help but notice the chain of command. Teacher answers, "I'm not the type for costume jewelry."

Then Nancy and teacher are alone with mentor breakdown. "You must kill me. I'm living a nightmare. When I try to remember, all I can see is you." "When you've realized the part you played in saving mankind, it will make you proud." "But what I, what you make me do is wrong!" "Who's to say? As much to argue for one side as for the other. Remember, the deed and the responsibility are mine." "Like master and slave?" "Like brain and arm."

The teacher assigns her Mira a solo stint as her substitute, thereby giving her the transferential blessing, a wounding in disguise that is almost a letting go, an inheritance. "I know you'll make a good substitute." But the so-called substitute gives the salute of their incorporation: "But I'll never be the teacher you are!" It is the salute or salto that made Nancy, with a start at the flick of her wrist, turn the steering wheel out of her father's grip toward murder and suicide. It is the Hamlet-style protest against the stepping-in of fast or easy substitution. Mom's the word.

Nancy's boyfriend pays her a visit and almost pays for it. The first love always remetabolizes the problems the girl still has with her mother. But after she almost bites his head off, Nancy goes straight to the teacher for showdown. "He's not important." "He's the only important thing in my life." "I know, but you can't be upset at this stage of our experiment, especially not risk the future for adolescent love between teenagers." "What I feel for Glen you'll never understand. Set me free. No more lines about mankind. I know what you are. When I was in his arms, instead of feeling what I should, I almost killed him." "You can't defy me. My will is stronger than yours." But when Nancy undergoes the transformation again, this time she goes for the teacher and gets the murder and suicide combo she ordered in her father's auto, the vehicle that is also just a word meaning "self." Headmistress, Mira, and boyfriend burst in: even the lab notebooks have been destroyed, the record of teacher's experiments broken. Mira cannot give up worshipping the record; she is stuck in its groove. Headmistress intervenes to break or replace the spell of transference with an affirmation of the complete destruction, the completion of the destruction: "As it should be. There is a power greater than science." The burned notebook looks like a charred, grilled, spread-eagled vagina or womb.

In *Buffy the Vampire Slayer* the junior highlight of adolescence lowers its beam on the New Woman complex, set in "Southern California: The Lite Ages." But Buffy is not just another cheerleader from the Valley, she is also the late arrival of a long line of maiden hunters reaching back, reincarnation style, into the "Dark Ages." And instructor and father figure from the Middle Age, a specter of transference within the nontransferential settings of TV, must, in lieu of the transferential connection, convince her of her heritage and mission. Her valley-girl resistance gives way to the evidence of her own flashback multiple-personality or channeling dreams about vampire busting, the "gross" birthmark that the trainer knows about even though the family plastic surgeon got rid of it ages ago, the coming out of her superwoman strength, and finally, the final gross-out, the way the "alert system" of period cramps kicks in whenever vampiric bad blood is around.

There is also a subplot of substitution that comes up for Buffy once her Valley friends have left her all alone — she is "so five-minutes-ago" — with her new primal identification. The future heart throb in geek's clothing is a loner from the wrong side of the Valley. After he and his equally out-of-it pal have a first run-in with Buffy still with her in-group of friends at the movie theater, they get blasted on the side of the road. Even though the pal really hates those "rich bitches," thinks they should "be stopped" since "they're not even human," he would still like to "bone them." But then he tells the loner that he's the one he's with: "Another shot of this and I'll have sex with you." What gets metabolized in this out-group are the complex ingredients of Oedipus, the legacy of the off-limits or out-of-it parents. That is why Pee-Wee Herman's comeback in this film is at the command performance of the Oedi-pal wish. By senior dance time Buffy and the loner can face the vampire invasion together as future couple. The instructor was phased out after his own many-season series of paternal guidance. His death signals that Buffy is in the finale, the winning hunter and finalist. He leaves her with final instructions: when the music stops, you will be hearing the all-clear to bust the master vampire. After it is all over, like the closing titles are ready to come up, we see once again the vampire master's assistant, Pee-Wee Herman by another name, the name caught in the headlines of scandal, still dying in outrageous slapstick, like the joke and embarrassment that will never end. The couple reunited over the busting of vampirism is cheerled by the feminization of what is buff; the slayer is under paternal guidance, but it is the kind that is sheer legacy, that switches from life to death, all the way, that is, to live broadcast, and just in time for the staking. Buffy rises to the occasion by crossing tracks away from her stereotype casting (in other words, her best friends) toward the therapeutically correct type who is new-womanhood compatible. The lack of childhood in the Teen Age, which is symptomatized as vampirism, the spectacular withdrawal of same-sex alternatives to boning the one you hate, and symptomatized at the same time, via Pee-Wee, as child abuse, is overcome when the bonds between the out-group and the New Woman reach maturity. But sometimes a repressed memory is just the memory of a repression, the one that keeps us coming to our desire and, at the same time, going away.

LECTURE TWENTY-ONE

All the meanings and stations of the crossing of the Christian mass with the masses celebrate communion in *Varney the Vampyre*. There are two aspects of Freud's thinking about social structures that we might bring back for our discussion of *Varney the Vampyre:* one has to do with the demands of civilization, and the other concerns the role of love when it comes to fulfilling those demands. Before looking into the meeting of demands, let's examine the meaning behind Freud's claim that by putting a check on narcissism, love showed civilization the way. Now narcissism, that could be another word (for our purposes now) for identification. So love puts a check on identification. The leader we follow knows that his position as leader depends Big Time on the good loving that his followers, because they're the ones he's with, give him, and that the other love attachments his charges reserve for each other may teach him a lessening of his own followability. The narcissistic leader (like the leader of the primal horde) demands that his followers be fit to be tied to him libidinally since his love comes in one size fits all. Such a leader prohibits the personalized love relationships that exclude the crowd or the leader making three; he makes successive demands for loving allegiance only to himself or intervenes like the primal father in the affairs of his followers. This follows from what we have all heard about the Manson family. If you want to control a group, you have to fake with group or groupie members one-on-one love attachments, while thus at the same time making over each member into the solo syndication of your group of one.

The demands that civilization makes of us may be the exciting causes of guilt, which thus give currency to neurosis, or the demands are doubly bound to force evacuation of all libido from the outside world down into the psychoticized ego. If demands are to be met in the name of love, then it is in the shadow of love that they stand or fall, the shadow cast by whatever calls on our identifications. From where Freud stands, the injunction to love thy neighbor is a radically unreal demand. Love that does not discriminate drops in value: there are some people out there who do not deserve my love. Freud isolates the injunction to love thy neighbor as the essential gesture of modern group formation or mutual identification in the missing place of love relations with the future.

One way to begin a reading of *Varney the Vampyre* is to flash the high beam on the crowd constituted each time again around the dread of the vampire. One quote in place of the many that mob the narrative: " 'Hurra!' shouted the mob — 'hurra!' and they danced like maniacs round the fire; looking, in fact, like . . . demons at an infernal feast" (231). This infernal feast — we have attended it before — is the internal funereal feasting of identification. When the relationship to the dead father, to mourning, loses its grounding from the burial mound on up, then the group relation goes out of control. The mobs we encounter in *Varney the Vampyre* are set on auto-destruct. The spread of mob violence is framed by the two individual suicides with which dual relations between vampirism and the masses begin and end.

At the group level, melancholia's loss retention may enter junk-mail contests or entertain wearing the labels of identifiable kinds of clothing. But group activity tends to err and air on the manic side: group mania swallows and loses without metabolization or remainder whatever crosses the ego scanner. This group is like the teenager needing to be grounded. The peristaltic trajectory of group mania (which is a way of group-sizing up melancholia) must be filled addictively with more and more fast food and cut losses.

The subtitle of *Varney the Vampyre* — *The Feast of Blood* — digs more than one circulation system. In the nineteenth century, we find among the new inventions of the expanded printing press the "motley mob," whose identificatory forces we see here on a roll and out of control. So what gets labeled a larger-than-life force of evil in this novel is also the same group to which the novel was addressed. Sound familiar?

That covers the alienation or auto-cannibalism of mass consumerism. But by 1847, the year of *Varney the Vampyre*'s first appearance, certain introductions had been made: the telegraph, the group rate of insurance coverage, spiritism, and, in sum, all the new brands of group psychologization (in love as in war) that are along for the expansionist drive of the sensorium. The new medium of serialization for which *Varney the Vampyre*, as "penny dreadful," was designed, cuts through the Oedipally dotted lines of beheadings. In between the two times of *Varney the Vampyre* (Cromwell's England and the mid-nineteenth-century mob scenes), the guillotine had amalgamated itself to the printing press: what failed as machine succeeded as media technology. The fantasy of talking heads cut off from their bodies but still in touch was one of the phantasmic side effects of the machine that failed. Serialization, which cuts losses not lives, builds out of installments the conditioning of the material to be edited for screenplay, shot by shot.

Varney the Vampyre is a power-pressed-together mass of printing serially organized around repetition compulsion in close-up and—in long shot—a mega ambivalence that cannot contain the masses, who, at least from the point of view of those we think control us, *are* us. To get into scenes that just keep on repeating themselves in the over eight-hundred-page work, we must take off from the top with a shredder assault what is so largely empty and just for the diversion. *Varney the Vampyre* is already a work of the preconscious, one that is coextensive with its mass-medium character and typeface, and that therefore beats a retreat from its cryptology and has it too, up to there. This ultimate line of defense, which extends all the way through to its anonymous authorship, where the double distraction of assigning either James Malcolm Rymer or Thomas Peckett Prest the unnamed, unmanned position is all the show, would hold us up in court, in the forecourt.

Now I want to look at the scene that keeps on asserting or inserting itself, like someone's compulsion. Varney the Vampyre is regularly introduced into households each time after he has been rescued from yet another suicide attempt. Varney the Vampyre repeatedly tries to put himself out from under the curse of vampirism. But each suicide is spoiled; he is rescued by one more family; he enters the household and in return for the favor vampirizes the youngest daughter. His victims must be young, female, and beautiful. He goes all the way to the origins of identification to blow up the family, all families. Either every family goes, or the vampire must be allowed to kill himself. So, the primal ingredients we are reading off the back of the serial box are suicide, rescue, the vampirization of a daughter, a transgression that at the same time mocks the father of the household. Why does it get repeated? It fills up at least seven hundred pages. But there is one exception that rules. There is one exception to the series, and it comes right at the start, with the opening incidents afflicting the Bannerworth household. In these opening chapters about the Bannerworth family we first see Varney the Vampyre — but at a distance. He comes into focus only after over a hundred pages because it was all so complicated by the mysteries covering for his identity, his location, his background. But at the other end the family that is being introduced to vampirism is equally crowded with mysterious or unacknowledged elements from the past. Only toward the end of this spread of chapters do we discover, for example, that the father committed suicide immediately prior to the family's first contact with vampirism.

But this suicide is history. It was suicide that got the Bannerworth ancestor into the picture hanging over the bed on which Flora lies just in time to be vampirized at the novel's opening. The ancestral suicide had been buried, according to custom, in his clothes — and thus as his portrait. But it is also the place where more than one thing is hidden away. What is kept from the reader, and from everyone else for the longest time, is that it was not only some ancestor in the past, hundreds of years ago, who committed suicide. The father only just finished killing himself. And father was not only a self-murderer but also an outright murderer who, already in league with the vampire, offed a gambler on whose account he, the father, had squandered his entire legacy. And so, to re-obtain or retain that money, the vampire and the father together murdered this gambler and hid the body and the loot. But the father, in the meantime, got drunk again—took in spirits—and killed himself according to the remorse code. A good portion of the book's opening introduction of vampirism involves Varney the Vampyre's attempts to retrieve the hidden treasure. He goes for the gold under the cover of the classic vampire attack, which is very much a look he puts on; he simply wants to scare the family away from the estate so that he can unbury the treasure unobserved. That is why he matches the portrait of the ancestral suicide when he stages his first attacks. Vampirism first penetrates the family plot under the theatrical or Oedipal covers of a plot to dig stolen treasure. The vampire puts on vampirism to conceal his designs on another system of circulation. A disorder at the level of capital (possession and dispossession of a secret) plugs into a Freudian, consumer projection—as though without symptomatic connection. That is why Marx brings the transformation inherent in capital into focus as transubstantiation. Capital, which lies at the vampiric heart of the bourgeois order (according to *The Eighteenth Brumaire of Louis Bonaparte*), is at the same time, via the analogy Marx worked in *Capital,* the mass or communion in which father and son become one. The transformation brought to us by the vampiric blood bond dissolves the uniqueness of an individual life by releasing its social character or caricature, which runs alongside the transformed life, like, keeping up with another one of Marx's analogies, price alongside commodity. In vampirism (or, in other words and worlds, in the bourgeois order—in mass-media culture) the parallel tracks of price and commodity also release and keep separate Marxian and Freudian ideologies. At the heart of their common disconnection we find massification and serialization in the missing place of the father function.

Vampirism emerges, then, in the place of a weak father, who before the start of this serial that we just cannot put or keep down, had already established contractual relations with the vampire. So we face in prehistory a father who squanders and doubly loses the legacy; the vampire's ghost appearance follows. But the vampire's own primal crime, we learn at the end (just before he succeeds in committing suicide), was to have killed the father inside himself, in other words, his own son. In a scene back in Cromwell's England replayed at the end of the novel, Varney has just learned in audience with Cromwell that he must now enter a career of double agent, both taking money from the Royalists to secure their escape and turning them over to Cromwell's agents, thus getting paid at both ends for betraying ultimately everyone. He goes home and encounters his young son:

> "When we reached the doorway of my house, the first thing I saw was my son wiping his brow as if he had undergone some fatigue. He ran up to me, and, catching me by the arm, whispered to me. I was so angry at the moment, that, heedless of what I did, passion getting the mastery over me, I with my clenched fist struck him to the earth. His head fell upon one of the hard round stones with which the street was paved and he never spoke again. I had murdered him." (856)

The murder of the son — the transubstantial murder of or merger with the internal father — sets off the vampire charge: Varney goes off in a techno flash of transformation and remains down during a two-year trance. When he comes to (in the restoration period), he does not know that he is consumed with blood lust until he has exhumed in the ruins of his former home (at the murder site) the hidden remnants of his capital. The murder (or suicide) that doubled father onto son (and created the vampire) turned over in a household where mother could only be found missing. Varney soon discovers that he requires a certain blood type — "blood of the young and the beautiful" (861) — which he draws from the child's blood bond with mother. This blood-typecasting of the victim saturates the repetition compulsion but not the primal condition or motive force driving the split between desire for capital and blood lust, between Oedipalization and mass identification (or group psychology). And yet the missingness of mother, which comes prior to the murder and corporation of father and son, is covered by Varney's first confession of his primal origin. It was at the instant an original love object fell victim to his human murderousness that Varney got turned on by the serialization of his vampiric existence:

> "I it was who listened to the councils of a fiend, and destroyed her who had given up home, kindred, associations, all for me." (771)

"Oh when will the crime of murder be cleansed from my soul. I killed her. Yes, I killed her who loved me." (771)

"I killed her — I killed her, and she was innocent. Then I became what I am. There was a period of madness, I think, but I became a vampyre." (772)

The consumerist hunger that craves mother while sinking teeth always only into the paternal antibody (which, at the intake of identification, is coded or coated with a "maternal" or friendly aspect) alternates with the patricidal impulse. On this side the vampire seeks possession of capital only always to fall for (or into) the encrypted secret dimension the vampire himself put on to cover up designs on a secret inside another circulation and disposal system. Within the reception of this serialization, Freudian and Marxian takes on what is at stake alternate as each other's concealment — of their common but double origin or identification.

To be released (if only for a season) from the series in which he must obtain a victim and thus renewal always with " 'the pangs of death,' " Varney seeks " 'the voluntary consent of one that is young, beautiful, and a virgin' " (686). The vampiric projections and group formations observe, then, an alternation and serialization of origins or identifications: " 'Those who know about vampires say that there are two sorts, one sort always attacks its own relations as was, and nobody else, and the other always selects the most charming young girls, and nobody else, and if they can't get either, they starve to death' " (745). The two sets of vampiric existence or identification are interchangeable yet nonsuperimposable. The attack upon family relations is paternal in scope (it recycles death wishes that originally targeted father); the thirst for virgin blood draws from the mother's account. But although the voluntary gift of virgin blood would fulfill the vampire's ultimate desire, it is offered only in the series of its withdrawal. At the close of the series (at which point the opening secret is released), Varney kills himself without remainder but with a witness (a third party or pater) in attendance. The one identification has always contained the other in the mode of shock absorption: The one on one (of the maternal relation), which shares its unwitnessed immediacy with mass murder, is contained via the shock administration of vampiric attack as the kind of catastrophe or techno accident that, unlike the selective randomness of mass murder, contains itself. Throughout *Varney the Vampyre* the vampire's attack (which doubles always as the introduction of group spirits to smaller units of social relation) administers doses of the shock that otherwise comes naturally. Shock value begins in the one on one and gets dissolved, in the aftershocks, within the group.

This record of a patricide is a broken one that is stuck in one groove or crypt. This is the time (Cromwell's England) of a regicide (Charles I has just been beheaded). At this time Varney cuts down his son, the father inside himself. He cuts off access to a future conveyed by generations coming soon and finds himself alone, cursed with the series of a vampire's being. In this version of vampirism Varney does not replicate himself or his hunger through his victims, who all just have to die.

Whenever love appears in the novel as somehow attainable, it is right neighborly of all those concerned. When Flora at one point passes on mercy or pity to Varney, it is the best love relation he will never have. The priest makes Varney the offer of "friendship," the one alternative he is given, once again, to catching the stay-away of shunning. Under the double barrel of Christian love, the demand that one love one's neighbor as one's self (or as Christ loves us one and all), we already find ourselves marrying modern group psychology. It is one thing to be asked, like everyone else, to love Christ (or whichever leader is granting cohesion to the group), but the request that on top of loving Christ you should also love everyone else just as Christ does means that you must also identify with the leader, who is also already the object of love. Thus, only mutual bonds of identification get equally distributed among all group members in fraternal association forever. In *Varney the Vampyre*, a threat to the brotherhood is posed or introduced by the vampirization of the sister. But even after Flora has for many, many pages been in and out of danger of becoming a vampire bride, the most horrible disappointment is still to come. It is when her two brothers discover that Flora's suitor had been to them a false friend. What counts, then, for them, is brotherhood and friendship—and suicide.

Sympathy with the vampire's condition at one point produces a reflection — and then short-circuits: "It was sad — very sad, indeed, that such a being could not die when he chose, the poor privilege of all" (806). Suicide would appear to be, then, the most basic privilege of human existence.

The abusive father struck the masturbatory strokes of the child. Gambling — which Freud assigns to infantile autoeroticism and its repression — guides the spirit-fueled degeneration of all the fathers in *Varney the Vampyre* who fall ("'without any previous intention'") not for the desire to win but for the "'desire to retrieve . . . loss'" (304). A casebook of crowd delusions contemporary with *Varney the Vampyre* stakes its claims on the consequences of gambling:

> Money, again, has often been a cause of the delusion of multitudes. Sober nations have all at once become desperate gamblers, and risked almost their existence upon the turn of a piece of paper. . . . Men, it has been well said, think in herds; it will be seen that they go mad in herds, while they only recover their senses slowly, and one by one. (Mackay, xx)

Gambling is like taking a guess or like the bet that one is right, which is all the license rumor needs to circulate as public opinion or, more rapid fire, as the warning shout that turns on catastrophic danger. What is indeed more dreadful in *Varney the Vampyre* than vampirism is the belief in vampirism, the rumor of vampirism's existence, a belief or rumor that will infect the populace, driving it onto its auto-destruct path.

Atomic bomb posters of the forties and fifties advised us, after all was said and done in, above all not to spread rumors. Rumors kill. And during the Los Angeles Olympics, rumor centers were established at the Olympic site; here, too, in Santa Barbara where the Olympic athletes were also housed, rumor centers were established, even here in this university building. Centers that would collect and process and de-demonize rumors that might otherwise run out of control and create panic and lead to self-destructive mob violence. In *Varney the Vampyre* once the rumor of the vampire's existence starts making the rounds, the mob goes out of bounds, annihilating everything in the way of the all-out attempt to hunt down the vampire, who of course escapes: " 'nothing could be more dangerous than allowing any such story to pass current as a wonderful fact. It would receive so many additions and so many embellishments that the mischief it might produce upon the mind of an ignorant population might be extreme' " (831).

The "penny dreadful" mass-cultural mix of ingredients that promoted serialization in narrative form takes on a different shakedown of elements in the popular dramatic forms to which vampirism adapted around the same time. Melodrama covers the points of overlap between the two takes. But a logic of identification specific to drama (*the* Oedipal medium) also always requires a laugh track of drop scenes to be run through the vampire phantasm as the way in that's way out. Dion Boucicault's *The Phantom* opens with a newly wed tavern keeper who, because the woman in the equation has been married before, occupies not the husband but the bride position. The bride, Davy, holds the foreground well into the first act of the play of vampirism. There are thunderstorms, haunted castles, some talk of vampires, phantoms, and wolves, Oh my, but it's all props for conversation that must keep coming back to a man in the bride's position. "Oh, when I consented to become a bride, I had my fears, but I never contemplated such a nuptial proceeding as this" (6). Or again, when members of the party stuck in the castle in the storm inquire after Davy's maiden back home: "No, I'm the charming maiden in this case. She was married before.... I might as well have married Blue Beard" (7). Soon the other turn in the conversation, which was second turn, the subject of vampirism, picks up the frequency. On what does the vampire live? "*Lord C.* 'On human blood! Upon the lives of others, he recruits his terrible existence' " (8–9). Lucy, the soon-to-be victim, picks up bad vibrations from Alan Raby and then gets Raby's point by point. Over Lucy's drained body, Lord C. shoots Raby, who on his way out still makes it all look like mistaken identity. In exchange he asks, last request, for placement under the moonbeam. He gets the treatment and closes this act with a solo address to the moon so soon: "Fountain of my life! Once more thy rays restore me. Death!— I defy thee!" (14).

The stage that has been set for act 2 has been set, during the break, to start from scratch. The vampire, Raby, the Puritan theme of a still recent and primal civil war, and the present tense or tensions of restoration, are the only continuity shots. We open with another wedding that is to take place. There has been a pooling of hard knocks stored up in the bride for the past two months. First, news of Mr. Edgar's death in battle hits Miss Ada, who falls down as if shot, takes a fever leave of her senses, dies. She pressed down a pause button, hysterically pregnant with death. A stranger arrived on the night before her burial. He had the coffin opened up, and out popped the corpse he was able to revive: it " 'stopped the mourning.' " But ever since the jump start of her second chance, when the second hand stopped on the clock face of mourning, she has no longer been the same girl. Just the same, nothing will keep Ada, keep her away, from loving Edgar. But she is still in the trance underlying the apparent death from which the stranger delivered her. The stranger, Raby by another name, keeps her under remote control. Raby returns for their wedding and to lay claim on property that belonged to an earlier Raby generation in the past that is still present tense to the vampire owner who must put on heir's claims. He thus submits another last will from long ago.

The doctor in attendance, Dr. Rees, has been following the stranger's solo occupations by telescope. He observed him moon bathing " 'an unclosed wound' " just over the heart (18). For our ears only, Raby spills what the blood of the wedding night will be good for. But Dr. Rees has been reading up on necromancy. Rees soon gets to the punch line of the vampire's entry, the line about the vampire punching in to get in some feeding time. It is into pure maidens that the last straw breaks through. All together now the group members recollect the local legend about the castle, the curse of Alan Raby, whose phantom returns for visitations always commemorated " 'by the mysterious death of some daughter of his race' " (22). The contesting will gives it all away. It is in Raby's hand all right, but on paper bearing a watermark of manufacture that was introduced one hundred years after his official death. Just as Raby has succeeded in teleguiding Ada to the spot of her sacrifice, Dr. Rees intervenes.

Ada is saved. Raby rushes off to revive his drooping life. Rees shoots the vampire and drops him down into the bottom of the gorge, which, moonlight unseen, will never throw him back up.

The name that ordered the doctor respells the name of an author, Robert Reece, who dropped all the melodrama climaxes but kept all the lube of laugh-tracking consumerism and identification. It is the condensed or canned laughter of punning, bad rhyming, nonstop eating with a spoonerism, and all the multiple senses of the gag. Right from the start of *The Vampire: An Original Burlesque,* from the first dialogue onward, a rhyme is supplied, selected from the discourse of word-to-food directions. Sometimes the sentence gets finished by the hungry other, sometimes, on second helping, by the hungrier self:

> "My breakfast, dinner, tea — mere *supper*-stition."
> "Odd fish I am! — but don't love *salmon* else!"
> "Why drink on Wednesday?"
> " 'Cos I'm *thursday* dear!"
> "Your head is *week*."

This version has Raby too. But while Lady Moonstone is the celebrated author, Alan Raby is the plagiarist: "Still, I must live! So from men, maids, and wives, / Contrive to filch their literary lives." In their duet, Edgar and Alan must draw the fastest pun in the text:

> *Alan.* "Tho' I'm your *cussin,* you need not be *swearing.*"
> *Edgar.* "I'm not the heir!"
> *Alan.* "I see it Sir, with ease,
> As 'air, you're always kicking up a *breeze!*"
> *Edgar.* "Be quick rash *pilferer.*"
> *Alan.* "Yes, I've a *pill for her!*"

The damsels too enter into the mouthful of punning:

> *Jenny.* "I feel so *hawk* ward 'neath that eagle eye!"
> *Ada.* "And at the altar take this *alter*-native: kill him!"

But when Alan mesmerizes Lady Moonstone to obtain her literary notebooks, she must admit instead, under the spell of the truth, that her own book was stolen from Ada. Alan is pronounced a plagiarist and dies. But the moonbeams reach him just in time for him to drop through the so-called vampire trap. He is given a new name. All agree that he must study "adaptation" to get around the plagiarism charge, or else vampirize only foreign authors and corpuses.

What crosses the art of punning is improper burial, represented in letters as plagiarism, which, only by another name, still covers the preservation and open concealment (and non-metabolization) of a foreign body. The primal scene of horror always requires alternation with (and alteration through) some supplemental drop scene, which, languistically, is punning. The wisecracking idiom control-releases the melancholic deposit. Freud suggested that humor was one big way for the ego to submit to the superego's verdicts and, at the same time, get off with the superego's magic wand, the suspension of belief in one's limitations. Ernst Kris argued, therefore, that every caricature, every aggressive bit of doodling or graffiti, allows for more bearable acceptance of father down the laugh track. The horror comics and mags from the fifties were training manuals for pun-filled libidinization of all the ins and outs of the Teen Age. At its more expansive this Age now occupies the larger public spaces, like *People Magazine*. Take a look. It is the tension between the couple and the group that is getting the lube job of punning.

LECTURE TWENTY-TWO

We read at the start of the movie *Gothic* that on a certain datable night in history "two legends were born." *Frankenstein* and Polidori's *The Vampyre* were the two productions to make the finish line of the Geneva contest. The light show of electrical storm activity grounded the perpetually teen contestants at Byron's place and made them captive audience to the public's fear of ghosts. Who can pen the most uncanny tale upon *Phantasmagoria,* the collection of German ghost stories they had just read out loud in group? So *Gothic* covers the Geneva scene, and Ken Russell gets mileage plus out of this one. We also get to see Percy Shelley's textual response; as reported in the "Extract of a Letter" that introduced Polidori's *The Vampyre,* "his wild imagination . . . pictured to him the bosom of one of the ladies with eyes" (8). The seeing-eye breasts lead us back across the bottom line of development reserved for a mother-and-baby reunion. We also see Percy Shelley given over to narcolepsy and thus to panic attacks of doubling between sleep and death: still on the downside of a desire to return to the womb, he dreads falling asleep only to awaken at his own wake—the wake-up service of live burial.

Mary Shelley was haunted. Which is why it is hard to know where to begin when it comes to *Frankenstein,* the work of unmourning with which she identified. *Frankenstein* was her first work, the work through which she kept the promise of her background; both her parents were writers, and she had every reason (it just takes two) to come into writing. But she had to work her way with and through the relay and delay of ghost writing. Under the heiress pressure of the ghost story competition, she was able to break through—but ultimately to the outer limits of a holding pattern. She would never (in her own estimation) write a work of comparable determining force. After this first one, she would publish her subsequent works as "by the author of *Frankenstein*"; she transferred her identity, as we will see, to a place appended to this book, a book she herself identifies in her 1831 preface as a monster, a "hideous progeny" that she bids "go forth and prosper." So there is a direct connection that she is putting through here between her composition of the book and the monster's makeup. "Invention," she writes, "does not consist in creating out of void, but out of chaos; the materials must, in the first place be afforded: it can give form to dark, shapeless substances but cannot bring into being the substance itself" (x).

What she is saying, in effect, is that what some people call creation, whether it be the writing of the novel or some other form of monstrous or show-it-all corpus building, is not something that is produced out of nothing but is stitched together out of preexisting pieces. Consider the way the monster speaks in *Frankenstein*: ultimately in the citational mode. The monster has read and, in effect, incorporated three books. So she too stitches together a novel: she overhears the leading ideologues of the era discuss their own powers of creation, whether the topic is galvanism or one or another metaphysical comforter to cover up death. In her own melancholic or antimetaphorical mode, she pieces together (just as the monster is sewn up out of corpse parts) a monstrous novel primally constituted out of fragments of overhearing and overreading.

And she talks about her having conceived the book. She is listening in on her forbidding company of rivals; they are holding forth, out and about with ideas that are never given a body; she is in the background, overlooked as the one least likely to take in the seed of inspiration and carry it to term. But then she conceives the novel in something like a blast of light in which it writes itself. One image extends coverage to both creations.

In *Gothic*, two points were made by Ken Russell, which at the time tended to be kind of original, I think, and they accord well with the sort of reading we want to pursue. At the end of the film, we see the shape of an infant in the waters of Lake Geneva, the head of an infant that will grow and grow and take over the screen in gathering close-up until it even begins to look like Karloff's Frankenstein monster.

All the imagery recycled in *Gothic* borrows Big Time from a whole spread of monster movies, projections that can indeed be credited to Mary Shelley's account of monster making. Russell has read all the ingredients off the back of the monstrosity package: male bonding between the poets mediated and supplemented by groupie sex, for the time being, and by the prospect, for the future, of woman's technologization. Artificial women are brought to grin and bear up the corner of male-to-male scenes. The battery pack of their replication takes its charge from Byron's crypt: the death mask of his better-dead-than-breeding incestuous object Augusta must be worn by all his libidinal outlets. The gadget love of the poets, articulated with the life or death urgency of the big, meglo questions, runs its currency through Polidori's interest in sleepwalking, nightmares, and related processes of the mind. All around the interest taken in the imagination covers, by implication or exclusion, the prospects of technology. The imagination is all-powerful or as powerful as the electric forces of nature. The test is the dead-raising creation of a ghost. Mary can plug into this current event because she has lost a child. "My fear is that I'd give anything to bring my child back to life again." The double release of blood that spills over two bedroom scenes leaves Polidori claiming to have been vampirized. Their creation is alive. And that, says Mary, superego-style, is the punishment. Punishment? God's already dead! Mary answers, "But haven't we raised the dead?" Because the monster she has created, she knows, will occupy the missing place of the father function and, while unmournable, yet will mourn. She speaks of the monster as the being or beacon that will accompany, guide, see its creators to their death. Leave the mourning to the phantom.

Mary Shelley conceived a whole line of childhood mortalities. But when her first baby girl died in 1806, she had a dream in which her daughter had only been deeply frozen: she rubs little one down in front of the fire until she is thawed and rare to go. This dream of reanimation is on a microwavelength of the monster's jump start in life.

Shelley's dream of her baby girl's comeback is the leader of the projection also because, of course, the baby that dies shares its unnamed status with the monster who is similarly without a name. But the monster's share grows to the point of becoming sheer name: to this day we do not know whether Frankenstein refers to the monster or to the maker, and indeed, I think a majority would vote for the monster being Frankenstein (even, as in the movie *The Bride,* Victor Frankenstein).

In Shelley's hallucinated vision in *Gothic,* she forecasts several deaths; she foresees the death of her son William, who had already been quite sickly during the writing of *Frankenstein* (and remember that the first victim of the monster in the book is named William) and died shortly after the completion of the novel. So in a sense she prophesied the death of William only to see her death-wish reservations confirmed. This produced in her the worst bout of mourning sickness ever.

What are the unusual circumstances surrounding William's being the monster's first casualty in the novel? First, it is the locket bearing a miniature portrait of the dead mother that he wears around his neck that gives the monster the dotted line to fill in as strangulation. The monster has been attracted to William as though the little portrait were a kind of transmitter locking him onto its beam. The monster takes the locket from the dead boy and then, still on automatic, comes across Justine, who looks like the portrait of Victor's mother. The monster plants the picture deep inside the pocket of the sleeping lookalike. It is at this time that the "fiend" is born. Framed as the murder suspect, mother figure Justine follows William as the second casualty of the monster's approach. While traveling to Geneva to mourn William, Victor Frankenstein runs into the monster, who once again makes his entrance in a light show of lightning flashes. It is always in these blasts of light that the monster comes into focus. He comes into focus this time around for the first time as the projective agency of every murder that will take out the members of the Frankenstein family. This is the first time Victor realizes (and it is in connection with the passing of William) that he is bound to his creation by a kind of death-wish bond. And the other

William's death will make Shelley realize for the first time that there is a death-wish edge or prophetic power surge to her own inventions and identifications.

Now you will recall that before the monster finishes William off, William is actually boasting of his powerful father. That seems to excite the monster's resentment, or anyway his reaction. This brings us to the other powerful father, who also bore the name William: the father of Mary Shelley, William Godwin, the famous utopian rethinker and philosopher, whose projects and projections featured the creation of new men, the start of new races. But the race or chase Shelley would let roll between maker and new creation fleshed forward the trajectory of a radically displaced work of mourning where the new race, which is the reanimated lost race, mourns the melancholic maker, who never sets out to mourn but only follows the specter of unmournability.

Just to complicate the matter of the name William yet again: Shelley bore the son that she would name William after her first baby's death. William was the name for a quick follow-up to substitute for her first baby's death. However, there had already been another William in the family; her half-brother had been awarded the name.

What connects Shelley to the name William is some bad ambivalence, but it goes even deeper, all the way into her own prehistory. When her mother and father were contemplating the child that would be Mary Shelley, they were already so sure they would be having a son that they referred to the upcoming child in their correspondence as William. So William is Shelley's secret namesake. William is the name of multiple disappointments beginning with Shelley's own birth. The mother, looking forward to the birth of William, produces Mary Shelley and dies. She dies of blood poisoning by the placenta she retained.

Writing to Jung, Freud points out, referring to Frazer's *The Golden Bough*, that in many so-called primitive societies the belief is current that the placenta is always the twin of the baby; the placenta is therefore cared for after birth until its manifest decay requires disposal or burial. So this is already one origin of what Freud would call the uncanny: every baby is shadowed at birth by a dead double. The mother was poisoned by something that had been retained, or strangled by something that would not let go.

These are the domestic or uncanny conditions for her conception of the double that was at once monster and novel. But please remember something else, just because this novel is openly about the socialization requirement of mourning. The father, Victor Frankenstein's father, is always enjoining his son to enter the "house of mourning"; learn how to substitute, he counsels, marry Elizabeth, get over the mother's death already. And after the death of her son William, her father, the other William, wrote to his daughter — and remember that this death had released in Shelley an uncontrollable upsurge of grieving: " 'Remember, too, though at first your nearest connections may pity you in this state, yet that when they see you fixed in selfishness and ill-humor, ... they will finally cease to love you, and scarcely learn to endure you' " (cited in Knoepflmacher, 113).

Shelley's work of mourning recognizes that melancholia is work too, and that mourning and melancholia are opposed and comparison shopped only in the streamlined modeling of a merely integrative mourning. It is not only denial of his most fervent wish to reanimate the mother that is Victor's guiding spirit: the near-miss relations between the two works, now of mourning, now of unmourning, must be ever displaced from view. Victor tries to get into and also, perhaps, around the inside view of invention as always being only a stitching together of already existing materials or corpse parts. He argues that because he used parts outside any given context and from different places or displacements, he will have in fact created a pure and new being and beginning. But Victor cannot get around his amalgam being at the same time primal or prehistorical because all the component corpse parts belong to the *recent* past. Even though it does not really look like he is reanimating anyone in particular, this is just one experiment on the way, he says, to achieving the ultimate goal, which remains the Big One of reanimation jolting back in one piece the one who has only just lapsed into lifelessness. But this realization of the goal would bring Victor too close to recognition that there was a loss in the first place. Reanimation risks activation of mourning.

If we consider the monstrous issue of corpus building also in a context of or in a contest with assimilation, we recognize that Jewish question that Frankenstein also raises to the undeath power. But Frankenstein does not look Jewish. But just look at what stumbles onto the set and screen of Whale's *Frankenstein* (a set, moreover, that in the details of the reanimation apparatus is for this part a remake of the techno doubling of woman in Fritz Lang's *Metropolis*). It is the golem who models the monster down the runway of a Jewish origin of the horror-of-the-transference genre of assimilation or image making. Where the techno dangers are, that is where saving powers will be too. This Jewish origin or transferential object of the genre of assimilation may go back to the cabala but also refers, via the logic according to which the more recent past is the most primal, to Freud. While the German Expressionist screen was recognizing but not always identifying the spooks from the lost war haunting the culture of assimilation, Freud came up with the formula that modern anti-Semitism, the paranoid take on assimilation as melting plot, came down to resistance to psychoanalysis. In Paul Wegener's 1920 version of *The Golem*, the ultimate backup defense system at the Jewish ghetto's disposal is, when all else fails, creation (against the precepts of Mosaic law) of a robot, an animated or moving picture. Once the letters or digits spelling out one of the names of God—aemaeth—have been keyed in, the golem is on. Sometimes the name is removed to deactivate the golem; as many or more times, only the first letter is erased, turning aemaeth into maeth, which just means dead. The golem is the animated name of God the father walking the thin line where we sign off between truth and death. But golem is also made up out of mother earth. At the same time that it is the name it is also a mass-media image. In the 1920 movie, the golem is built by rabbi and assistant in a household doubly missing a mother. Out of this missing connection and via the transference transgressions represented by use of God's name in vein of a creature that is animated visual representation, the golem emerges first to save the Jews from another imperial decree of banishment. But then, following contact with the Christian world outside the ghetto, golem runs amok, endangering the Jewish community all over again. Within the short span of the film's desperately familiar oppositions—the ghetto is shadowed by the internal alchemy of sublimation, the male-to-male transmissions of writing, reading, inventing, while Christian society promotes a feminine way of words becoming flesh—both Miriam, the rabbi's daughter, and the golem go goyim, go for the outside chance of maternal and corporeal connection. Can you imagine Hitler in the audience watching this movie back in the twenties? I can. First the golem saves the Jews; it's the service that comes with the warranty. The rabbi who has traveled to court together with the golem to ask for the restoration of Jewish rights provides the entertainment he expects the emperor to request. He projects a motion picture of Jewish history, which is of course a movie within a movie. But when the wandering Jew crosses the screen, the Christian audience ignores the rabbi's warning that they all must keep quiet during the show. Their laughter almost brings down the house and should have buried them all alive had not golem been there to save them. Then the backfire of bad news follows the good news of the rabbi's media triumph at court. Assimilation, which suggests a way of fitting in via likeness, by becoming image, belongs in the movies, the ultimate melting pot. Jewish participation in the media industries of assimilation, from Hollywood to the Barbie doll, gets embroiled in the fallout of small differences. How much protection does assimilation grant the Jews or you, even or especially when sitting right at the control panel, right in front of the on/off switch? The Six-Million-Dollar Man was a post-Holocaust testimonial to this question. The problems of assimilation that are raised just like ghosts in the visual media are transferentially linked to this Jewish question, the one that comes down to resistance to psychoanalysis.

Because the wife comes into her own as representative of the father and thus of the couple, she defends the couple formation against the group's invasion, which always finds a willing accomplice in the husband, who never really graduates from the mutual admiration society, the mirror stage of friendship. That is why in James Whale's movie *Frankenstein* the wife and the father (or father figure) struggle to cure Henry of his bodybuilding bond with the solo status of group membership. Only marriage will free Henry Frankenstein from his perverted compulsion to engage in concealed experimentation with building a body out of body parts (a project that is pornographic in its part by part visualization of the body). These experiments are centered on the creation of life. The marriage that his father advertises as the cure-all also centers on creation of life — of a son and heir. Henry's achievement — "the brain of a dead man, ready to live again in a body I made with my own hands, my own hands" — suggests nonreproductive preoccupation with one's own body and sexuality. The father senses that "there is another woman." That other woman is the group, the body of the group — the body of the missing mother. "I understand perfectly well. Must be another woman. Pretty sort of experiments they must be." In the movie the father is so certain that his son's aversion to marriage must be a sexual diversion that is more fully embodied than just what fits in the hand. He overlooks that Henry has an object already, he has a dead mother. Presentation of some bridal decoration to be worn by Elizabeth and that had been worn first by Henry's dead mother is the father's only reference to her missingness. Even the mother's own sign of substitution and marriage is a funereal garland that locks the monster (the monstrous incorporation of her loss) onto the beam of nonsubstitution. In other words, once Elizabeth puts on the label of substitution, the monster automatically intervenes in the wedding. And not until he is torched and Henry knocked unconscious can marriage begin to take place. Except — the story continues as *Bride of Frankenstein.*

When Henry upon returning to life again defends his quest for the secret of eternal life, Elizabeth counters, "It is not life it is death that controls these fantasies ... your insane desire to create life from the dust of the dead." As though his dead mother were returning here too, Elizabeth hallucinates the figure of Death and flips out. Dr. Pretorius enters at this point of crisis: it is "a matter of grave importance," a *mater,* mother, of grave importance.

The monster has undergone his own development down in the church crypt, where he has been hiding out ever since his friendship with the blind man was destroyed by the local ghostbusters. An invisible ray created him, the ray that first put light into darkness, and then a blind man gave him shelter. The monster's total reduction to sheer visibility — to corpse parts — is packed into this belief in the invisible creative ray. Down in the crypt (the crypt of identification), the monster discovers that only another corpse can be his "friend." He at first accepts the offer of a mate made of corpses: "Woman? Friend? Like me? I love dead. Hate living." But he is not just dead; he is the vengeful projection by the living onto the dead. And the reanimated dead bride is another projection — but on a separate track. The original monster declares that Henry and Elizabeth "must live." He and his monster bride "belong dead." But Elizabeth can be accepted at the end only because she has been made superimposable onto the other bride's life. Reanimation is what Elizabeth comes to share with the monster's mate across long distance. Henry says he will not continue with the experiment if Elizabeth is dead (and what would be the point — the threat of substitution would be over and out). Pretorius assures Henry that "she's alive." The proof? "In a few moments she will speak to you through this electrical machine." The telephone gets plugged into her absence. Henry listens and cries out, "Yes, she's alive!" Soon the other bride is electro-animated, and Henry exclaims, as though without connection, "She's alive!" She's "live."

Pretorius's TV test tubes of artificial life transmissions in miniature, as seen on TV, must be united with the big screen of projection to create the techno-funereal Bride. A network of TV, telephone, and cinema introduces a Bride of Frankenstein who not only introduces but also balances Elizabeth's acts of interchangeability with the living dead bride. Because the live Elizabeth must never collapse across the gap of a near miss onto the missing mother. The original monster makes the move to mourn — and to put himself and his sequel to rest. The double Bride of Frankenstein, the now wired Elizabeth, lives on.

LECTURE TWENTY-THREE

I have insisted that every haunting takes nourishment from the blood bond with mother. Now, that claim is not made because you can always identify a maternal corpse within every haunted story. *Dracula* is indeed hard to read as haunted one way from cover to cover. At times in *Dracula* it looks like a father's position is being applied for by phantoms and vampire killers alike.

But the way to go, I think, in Stoker's novel, is to look at the new woman problem and the way it gets covered between Lucy and Mina. And then, if you track back to that scene in Castle Dracula where Jonathan Harker encounters the first rehearsal or repetition of this female trouble, then I think one has to argue that the hauntings do come from a maternal place. I am not saying that this is necessarily his mother or anyone's mother, but, just the same, vampirism is fueled by what it recycles: the maternal blood bond.

Melancholia is not an option for (or on) every case of loss. It is unlikely that Arthur, for example, is going to go melancholic over Lucy's passing. If friends or lovers drop a legacy of melancholia in passing, then they already held, while they were still around, primal positions, those of mother, sibling, or child, within the psychic economies of their survivors. A lover who dies might repeat the loss of a sibling for whom he was doing time not as substitute but as continued existence. In contrast to these primal positions that can never be vacant nor ever refilled, there is the other position that is open (the only real position), which is filled out by the paternal prescription of an antibody, the mournable, symbolizable death that helps reject the hold of unmournable death on the grief-stuck metabolism. And if this father's death proves unmournable, then he did not hold the position of father (as advertised) but was all along superimposable onto one of those irreplaceable relations, whether brother or mother.

Melancholic attachments within the couple are preprogrammed. Within the order of coupling or substitution, there is no reason alive for mourning not to work. That is how you got there to begin with. But if you made it to the couple stage only by superimposing your wife, say, onto your mother, then certain prehistorical or premarital problems are also back in the highest degree attained before getting stuck, even or especially when the wife, whether reincarnation or reanimation of mummy, passes on.

Another thing: profound grieving is not the best indication that melancholic incorporation is going down. Incorporation or melancholia is by definition secret. Doubly secret, one could say, because with incorporation or melancholia you have to hide and preserve the corpse, and that means the inside news of the beloved's death; but that also means you can never admit that you have or had anything to lose. If the doors to your crypt are opened up for public viewing, then someone, and that person will make up a third at the funeral feast, can point out, "Hey, she's dead already" (which is what the father figure does over Clarimonde's dead body). "Let's open up the crypt and see what you've got in there. Say aah." It's that easy. All the vampire killers have to do is reach the crypt before nightfall, open up the coffin, and stake the vampire. That is why the crypt — out of sight, out of mind — must be guarded, bottom line, with the crypt carrier's life.

So, it would be much more typical or symptomatic (though I do not want to make this into a law) for the melancholic to fake the signs of grief to get that much more quickly to the absence of mourning. Victor Frankenstein happens to be a good example of this. Throughout the novel he is enjoined by father and by the homegrown substitute Elizabeth to enter the "house of mourning," but he cannot; they assume that he loves "another." But when this other woman — the mother — died, Victor was first in line to pray to the lip service of efficient mourning.

These are the reflections of the first days; but when the lapse of time proves the reality of the evil, then the actual bitterness of grief commences. Yet from whom has not that rude hand rent away some dear connection? And why should I describe a sorrow which all have felt and must feel? The time at length arrives when grief is rather an indulgence than a necessity; and the smile that plays upon the lips, although it may be deemed a sacrilege, is not banished. My mother was dead, but we had still duties which we ought to perform; we must continue our course with the rest and learn to think ourselves fortunate whilst one remains whom the spoiler has not seized. (43)

Look at him: he is perfectly at ease with the rituals of mourning; let the dead bury the dead, and so on. But look at the new words that immediately follow and jump-cut from the reflection above: "My departure for Ingolstadt . . ." So he gives a brief public broadcast of grief, over and out. But then he leaves for the university, thus doubling the departure of his mother and leaving for the alma mater, the fostering mother. At the university, after his course of studies, he builds a monster in the place of the work of mourning he could not perform. And that is his melancholic trajectory that keeps on restarting after yet another span or index of two years is measured up to no end in sight.

At the public end, we have identification too. Who needs to make a secret of identification? The labels of fashionism are in your face. Which is why we don't see it: Just be. Remember, in "Carmilla," Laura alone was the one who saw the vampire as the double of an ancient ancestor. There are no doubles; there is only the desire for the double; and once that desire has been claimed or has materialized, there is always going to be a witness around who will see that no doubling has taken place. Melancholic doubling is secretive, incorporative, literal-minded, or, once again, *anti*-metaphorical. The metaphorical always promises to pry loose one's attachment to the dead at the limit that is the literal.

Before the addition of the narrative frames within frames, originally the story began with the scene in chapter 4 in which Victor Frankenstein, like some kind of father, rejects any handing down to the monster he has created. That is the primal opener of *Frankenstein*. We have talked some about Mary Shelley's complicated relations with her father. In addition to the narrative frames, which the novel entered or internalized under revision, there is also a framing relationship over time between introduction and preface. There is the introduction written late in her career, the author's introduction in which she makes all the connections I referred to already between the writing of the book and the creation of a monster on which she places bids that it will go forth as her hideous progeny. But the preface, the first prophylactic measure introduced into this relay of conceptions, was dictated by her husband. Throughout her career, Shelley had to dodge the attempts by her various guardians to ghostwrite in her name. The preface attempts to absorb the shock of the readership contemplating a woman letting us in on how it is that the home is where the uncanny is and begins:

> I am by no means indifferent to the manner in which whatever moral tendencies exist in the sentiments or characters it contains shall affect the reader; yet my chief concern in this respect has been limited to... the exhibition of the amiableness of domestic affection and the excellence of universal virtue. (xiv)

In 1831, when Shelley comes back for the last time to this novel to superintend its issue, she writes the author's introduction, which slipping between the lines and cracks, supplies the uncanny infection of undeath that the ghostwriter — like father-in-law, like son-in-law — tried to partition off or portray as the happy face of "affection":

> The publishers of the standard novels, in selecting *Frankenstein* for one of their series, expressed a wish that I should furnish them with some account of the origin of the story. [This is a story that is all about origins: where do babies come from when the mother is missing?] I am the more willing to comply because I shall thus give a general answer to the question so frequently asked me — how I, then a young girl, came to think of and to dilate upon so very hideous an idea. It is true that I am very averse to bringing myself forward in print, but my account will only appear as an appendage to a former production.... I can scarcely accuse myself of a personal intrusion. (vii)

So, she talks about this need to dilate and instantly falls into an appendage in which she feels safe talking about herself. We could read this dilation as the wish or command that is coterminous, co-terminator with the novel that someone "die late," later, or not at all. This book that she reintroduces in 1831 certainly celebrates the fantasy of pushing back deadlines, making death late or not at all; it is also very much about an appendage that she carries with her, one that, like a foreign body or body part, she must carry alongside her or inside her, and that issues upon so grave an idea from the transitive urge "to dilate" the other.

I mentioned previously that Shelley was haunted by the prospect of her fiction's prophetic powers. I talked about William. And then there was the way in which Percy Shelley's death was forecast in *Valperga*; about this latter prophecy she writes in a letter: "It seems to me then that in what I have written hitherto I have done nothing but prophesy what has arrived. *Mathilda* foretells even many small circumstances most truly — and the whole of it is a monument of what now is" (cited in Knoepflmacher, 116). Conceived and written around 1819, the heroine, Mathilda, is cast as about the same age as the author at the time. *Mathilda* is about a daughter who must realize that what her father knows best is incest. She receives a make-up letter from her father after their fight breaks them up: he tells all, about how he had tried so hard to replace his dead wife through her or in her. She dreams of her father's death only to wake up and come across his corpse; she skips society, stuck in the groove of guilt. One turn deserves another turn in the groove or grave: Mathilda meets a guilty party, and she will try if she wants to. They get along and on with it. Hers was after all the happy end of the deal her dad dealt her.

Shelley always submitted her work first to some censor: she gave her work now to her husband, now to her father, for correction or approval. Her father often went ahead and published the work on her behalf and then felt free as her agent to draw income from its publication. But when she forwarded *Mathilda* to him, he was horrified; he refused to cosign or benefit from its publication; on second thought he destroyed it.

At the time of her father's passing, Shelley was working on what was to be her last novel, *Falkner,* a working out and about remorse, mourning, redemption, and the close of mourning. And after that, after this mourning book, and after the death of her father, she would write no more fiction for the rest of her life. Instead she devoted herself for the next fifteen years to two longer-term projects: promotion of the financial security of her son and an edition of her father's collected works. It was heir time, cut with some ambivalence, equivalence, or getting even. The edition everyone was waiting for waited on her; she was to supply her store of biographical data in a supplemental note. But (one thing leading, irrevocably, to another) Shelley never managed to write that note, and up and died without completing it. The nonappearance of *Mathilda* was the act of Godwin that left a gap in his collected corpus, which Shelley reintroduced by promising to fill it and which she kept an open wound between them by never keeping the promise of fulfillment for both of them; she had the last say, the lasting nothing-to-say, at least in her own lifetime.

I have already told you why the death of William in the novel is so important as far as Victor Frankenstein's relationship to his monster is concerned. I am talking about the lightning storm scene, in which he sees the monster again. He calls on the storm to double as William's "funeral," his "dirge," and in that light show he sees his own monster.

> I remained motionless. The thunder ceased, but the rain still continued, and the scene was enveloped in an impenetrable darkness. I revolved in my mind the events which I had until now sought to forget: the whole train of my progress towards the creation, the appearance of the work of my own hands alive at my bedside, its departure. Two years had now nearly elapsed since the night on which he first received life, and was this his first crime? Alas, I had turned loose into the world a depraved wretch whose delight was in carnage and misery; had he not murdered my brother? ...
>
> I considered the being whom I had cast among mankind and endowed with the will and power to effect purposes of horror, such as the deed which he had now done, nearly in the light of my own vampire, my own spirit let loose from the grave and forced to destroy all that was dear to me. (74)

This is what gets *Frankenstein* into lectures on vampirism. A few pages later Victor will continue to be beset by what he calls the "fangs of remorse."

There are two contracts holding the novel together and apart, in parts, two contractual relationships into which Victor Frankenstein must enter, now in name, now in full: one contract is with the monster, who demands that Victor build him a mate—or else he will intervene in Victor's wedding night; according to the other contract (which is with his father), he must marry Elizabeth and thus bring the family, in exchange, back into the house of mourning and substitution. Both contracts are equally impossible; indeed together they describe precisely what is off-limits from deep within Victor's perspective.

Now why is the attachment to Elizabeth an impossibility? Elizabeth herself asks about this impasse again and again, as does the father, on her behalf: "Have you then," the father asks the son, "another attachment?" Father and Elizabeth both want to know: "Do you not love another?" They are worried about this other woman. Well, from *Frankenstein* to *Fatal Attraction*, the other woman is always the mother.

Let's take a closer look at Elizabeth. Why can't Victor go all the way with her? Well, how does she enter the household of mourning? Why is she an orphan? Her own mother dies giving birth to Elizabeth. Elizabeth seems so nice! She is the substitute who is always in the ready position. Victor's mother encourages the two in her father's name. (The Frankenstein home frames a painting depicting a scene of proper mourning in which Frankenstein's mother displays the bedside mannerism of a daughter's grieving over her father, dead on the bed.) She gives Elizabeth to Victor right from the start. Her dying words do tell Elizabeth not only to go ahead and marry Victor but also to supply her place throughout the household of mourning. She asks Elizabeth to be the substitute or the supplement. And right from the start we hear Elizabeth referred to by Victor as his more-than-sister and by Victor's father as his more-than-daughter.

But who can overlook the fact that she is constantly killing everyone off? Of course, we are inside the melancholic son's perspective: she is the survivor and carrier of death. First, she kills off her own mother. Second, she gives Victor's mother, who nurses her back to health, the fatal dose of the death she, of course, survives. Elizabeth also tries to save Justine, but her speech in Justine's defense can only produce the backfiring effect of fortifying the verdict against her. And it is her bestowal of the portrait, her putting it around William's little neck, that immediately puts William on the monster's target range. So, from within a perspective like Victor's, Elizabeth is associated with a murder that goes with substitution or mourning, an association to which he cannot commit as her partner or accomplice.

Toward the end of *Frankenstein*, toward the end of chapter 21, we find the hard evidence for our reading this novel as a work of haunting. First off, Victor Frankenstein gives us his succinct recollection of his entire life as it flashes before his eyes:

> I repassed, in my memory, my whole life — my quiet happiness while residing with my family in Geneva, the death of my mother; and my departure for Ingolstadt. I remembered, shuddering, the mad enthusiasm that hurried me on to the creation of my hideous enemy, and I called to mind the night in which he first lived. I was unable to pursue the train of thought; a thousand feelings pressed upon me, and I wept bitterly. (175)

So these are the events of his life: the death of the mother, the departure for Ingolstadt, and the creation of the monster.

I have already pointed out that even though the monster is stitched together out of separate parts and seems to be sheer invention, still Victor hopes "in the process of time," as he puts it, to "renew life where death apparently devoted the body to corruption" (53). "A parent" is along for the renewal drive of Victor's devotions.

At the end of his course of study, rather than work on a thesis on the assembly line of paraphrase and footnotes, Victor produces the monster, which holds the place of his dissertation. It is to this monstrous degree that what he brings home from the university continues to dictate the terms of Dr. Frankenstein's "free time."

After he finishes his thesis, he just goes back to bed and sleep. But when Victor lies down to sleep, hoping to run the disposal service of dreaming and forgetting, the unmourning that is already in his veins takes over the dream work:

> But it was in vain; I slept indeed, but I was disturbed by the wildest dreams. I thought I saw Elizabeth, in the bloom of health, walking in the streets of Ingolstadt. Delighted and surprised, I embraced her, but as I imprinted the first kiss on her lips, they became livid with the hue of death; her features appeared to change, and I thought that I held the corpse of my dead mother in my arms; a shroud enveloped her form, and I saw the grave worms crawling in the folds of the flannel. (57)

And further on down the page, awake again, Victor name-calls the monster who gets in his face: "A mummy again endued with animation could not be so hideous as that wretch."

Now what is important here is not just the dream of the reanimated dead mother following as the wake for the monster. Remember the display of shallow mourning Victor puts on after his mother's departure, and how he moves to replace mourning with the doubling or incorporation acted out through his own departure, which produces in the end a monster. Then he has a dream of reanimated mother. But most important is that Elizabeth, who is the prime candidate for substitution, Elizabeth, the super-substitute, can be embraced by Victor, in his dreams, only when she is superimposable onto the mother's corpse. And awake he will in fact, at the end of the novel, embrace Elizabeth—only when she is dead. It is when the terms of one of the contracts have been fulfilled or unfulfilled, and the monster destroys not Victor—Victor wildly thinks that the monster's threat places only his life in danger—but of course destroys Elizabeth, whose corpse can then get a hug from Victor.

You will have noticed that the monster, the phantom, or Victor Frankenstein's proper vampire, destroys the entire family. Now that that is done, Victor decides this has to be the ultimate showdown and declares a chase to the extreme ends and poles of the globe. Chapter 24 marks his "resolution" "to quit Geneva forever": "I provided myself with a sum of money, together with a few jewels which had belonged to my mother, and departed" (192). He takes with him a kind of deposit or repository, a kind of account, which belonged to his mother, and which now sets him on his way. But as he leaves Geneva, he doubles back once more, before completely taking off, and visits the cemetery. He goes to the family plot marking the spot where his loved ones are buried: "As night approached I found myself at the entrance of the cemetery where William, Elizabeth, and my father reposed. I entered it and approached the tomb which marked their graves" (192). Now who is missing? Whose grave goes unmarked in the novel? The novel thus names, literally names what goes unburied within the text itself, without saying or naming and without commemoration.

So we can say that after his mother's departure, Victor re-creates the separation, reproduces a separation he cannot acknowledge, and re-produces this separation as one between himself and a monster. And the monster now performs all further separations.

Then again at the close, in chapter 24, Victor asks, "Oh! When will my guiding spirit, in conducting me to the demon, allow me the rest I so much desire; or must I die, and he yet live?" (198). But who is guiding whom? Victor speaks of a guiding spirit conducting him to the demon, but is it not in fact the demon who is this spirit? Is Victor really chasing down the demon, or is it not the monster who tele-guides Victor across the globe? He is the phantom transmitting commands from the crypt inside Victor. Victor thinks he is chasing the monster. But it is the monster who leaves behind little clues and inscriptions, who pauses and doubles back and makes sure Victor is following him.

And at the end Victor of course dies, never having mourned, and the monster returns to the scene and grieves over Victor. Like a mother, the monster mourns her dead son. Then the monster puts herself to rest. Mourning has taken place in a displaced kind of way, the phantom has delivered the mourning rites, and it is over.

Now, I have stressed that the one contract, that he marry Elizabeth, is unrealizable by Victor given his melancholic condition, his original bond with "another." But what about that other contract with the monster? Why can't Victor create a mate for the monster?

What does he say? The mate that he would be creating would not stand in a contractual relationship to him. He has a contract with the first monster, but not with the mate. The mate could do anything. This causes him to destroy the female monster.

How convincing is that really? What does he care for the human race? Victor loves the dead. It is not some law-abiding, peacekeeping contract that he fears the mate will not keep. It is the vampiric death-wish contract that he has with his own monster that he senses may be superseded by the addition of a mate. Remember, his monster, his phantom, tells him: if you make a mate for me, I will leave the target area and will no longer seek vengeance; I will no longer be the agent of your death wishes. And so the creation of the mate, which would release the monster, the vampire, would mean letting his mother go.

To produce a mate for the monster, he would have to produce a woman. He would get that much closer to acknowledging the monster as the dead mother. Remember, the closest he has come has been the dream that already goes pretty far under the covers of Elizabeth.

Victor goes ahead and starts building the monster's mate. This is the second trip, everything about this is seconds. It is the second monster, and it will be the second doubling of a departure. First, it was to Ingolstadt; now it will be to England. He will leave for England, and by the end of the prescribed period of time he will have built a second monster body; it will be a repeat of the first scene of creation, only this repeat is also making preparations for closure.

Everyone in the house of mourning is pleased that he is off to England. They do not know that he is off to build another monster. They think he is fulfilling the terms of the other contract leading to marriage to Elizabeth. (Indeed, the two contracts address two phases of the same task.) Everyone says, "Oh, this is great; you seem to be doing better just thinking about the trip; the trip to England will restore you to yourself." This is the language that is used again and again: you will be restored, and in turn you will be restored to us; you seem to be returning to yourself; the change of scene will restore you to yourself. But if there is going to be any restoration to himself, it will be more like self-storage. In chapter 20 Victor decides that he cannot go through with the other contract, the funereal contract; he cannot create the mate for the monster, and so he destroys it:

> Yet, before I departed, there was a task to perform, on which I shuddered to reflect; I must pack up my chemical instruments, and for that purpose I must enter the room which had been the scene of my odious work, and I must handle those utensils the sight of which was sickening to me. The next morning, at daybreak, I summoned sufficient courage and unlocked the door of my laboratory. The remains of the half-finished creature, whom I had destroyed, lay scattered on the floor, and I almost felt as if I had mangled the living flesh of a human being. I paused to collect myself. (162–63)

This is where Victor collects himself; he picks up the mangled corpse parts comprising the self that incorporations built.

Victor's theoretical study of reanimation went on against and on the account of the father's disapproval. Why is he interested in these metaphysical life or death issues? How does he begin his interest in reanimation? On his own he picks up alchemical books and related treatises and shows them to father, who says that they are just so much trash. At the end Victor reflects, and this is why this deserves some emphasis: if only my father had said more than that, I would not have taken this fatal path. So he blames the father for his creation of the monster — which shows that everything about that move to create is a form of dependency on transgression against the father. The father simply says these works are rubbish, do not read them. And then Victor consumes nothing else. This move is syndicated twice over: Walton also decided to become a mariner and explore the seas against the deathbed wishes of his father, and Victor's best friend, Henry Clerval, follows his course of study against his father's injunctions.

Victor's first libidinal experience as a fifteen-year-old is the blast he gets watching a tree get blasted by lightning. It is again a flash (or flashback) of lightning; whatever goes down in the novel goes down with a blast. At the end of the novel, or again and again toward the end, each time Victor reaches another low in his melancholic development or non-development, he will say that he is blasted. "I am like a blasted trunk." Beginning with that first shot of the blasting annihilation of a tree, he is set on a certain course. He is always, when he hits the low point, again that blasted trunk. "I am blasted." And at the end it is even the narrator out in the frame who gets blasted upon listening to Frankenstein's story. This, then, was Victor's premier libidinal turn-on:

> I beheld a stream of fire issue from an old and beautiful oak which stood about twenty yards from our house; and so soon as the dazzling light vanished, the oak had disappeared, and nothing remained but a blasted stump. When we visited it the next morning, we found the tree shattered in a singular manner. It was not splintered by the shock, but entirely reduced to thin ribbons of wood. I never beheld anything so utterly destroyed. (40)

Here we have an image of utter destruction, total loss, remainderlessness, complete missingness (so gone that it is not recognizable as lost), a loss that gets lost, a loss of loss. This image of total destruction is just the other side of his retention span.

The experience or experiment leads to his overhearing (for the first time with his ears on) conversation turning on the subject of galvanism and the modern sciences. Turned on by electricity, he gives up the exploded systems that ruled his "imagination" and that he had grown attached to through his father's dismissal of them. At the university he again manages to recombine both courses of study as he moves from professor to professor. What he accomplishes, then, is the merger of the new science with the metaphysical (Promethean or Faustian) desires that go for the big issues of life or death. The new science at first puts him off because he is told that one must work piecemeal; there are no sensational discoveries, we do not care about the big issues, we make progress but it is by small degrees of real accomplishment. But then the second professor shows him, in effect, that through that kind of work, the modern sciences are in fact getting closer to realizing the bigger-than-life science fantasies of the old metaphysicians. Waldman takes Victor, at the end of chapter 3, to the modern laboratory, and recognizing its power, raised to the power of science faction, Victor sees what from that point onward would be the tenure track of his "future destiny."

Teenage Frankenstein opens just like Jekyll and Hyde (and like Freud's career) with a scene of public resistance to the pioneer's research in technological and occult media. Professor Frankenstein, who is visiting the United States from England, begins with the example of eye transplants, the focus either of substitution or radical intervention in a whole body of replacement parting. A resister cannot but accept the evidence of the eye operations, but only as the limit of successful interventions: Why, even his high school sophomore son wouldn't believe the rest of Frankenstein's proposed workout.

All alone with his sole supporter, a physicist, Frankenstein plans his assembly of a human being out of selected parts. Frankenstein turns to technology to accelerate beyond evolution's reliance on the process of reproduction. The forced marriage of selection according to criteria of perfection can be interrupted any time by "throwbacks" and the genetic calculus of "risks" and accidents. His perfection of the "adaptation of selective breeding" as a happening event that is present tense "will create a perfectly normal human being," a generic "youth," as opposed to the name-brand monster his ancestor built long time ago.

So, the genetic controls imposed on the coming of future generations, as in selective breeding, do not turn on the same continuum with Professor Frankenstein's vision of selective being. The ancestral doctor had built his monster in the place of, as the displacement of, mourning for the dead other. The professor switches from the egoic span of retention to the other span, the ego standing at short attention, wanting immortality now, for itself, with a future without replacement others. To admit and at the same time to control the coming event or advent of the other, however, means to eradicate the other, an impulse farthest from the mind of both melancholic ancestor and the follow-up heir to all the haunts of adolescence. That is why the death or dead with which the professor's work can begin arrives with the crash of coincidence or accident. That is also why death's entry weighs in on a group scale. Two cars full of teenagers collided head-on, face to effacement. By one more chance, one dead body was ejected to the sidelines of the wipeout.

Back in the lab the professor asks his cohort to describe the bagged body. "Dead." "Dead! That's what a lay man would say" — someone, that is, who would lay the body to rest. "In this laboratory there is no death until I declare it so." But the professor would control not just death or the dead but even the teenager he wants to create fully conditioned through pain and pain relief to recognize and obey him with gratitude. Once the remaining replacement parts arrive from the site of a mass in-flight death of the high school wrestling team, the project can be completed. What a waste. What waists!

The pull of the professor's own deferred or perpetual adolescence is reflected not only in the unburial plot but also in a subplot he stumbles upon not so much in America as on his way back to Europe, between America and England. The woman who has fallen for him, and who now empties out with depression at the prospect of being left, left behind, left empty, attracts the professor's couplification proposal. But first she must join his research team as his assistant who keeps any interruption from reaching him in the basement lab where he works with his physicist colleague on the teenager, whose workouts they soon superintend. But via her supplementary exclusion upstairs by the front door and by the phone, she becomes the interruption. She won the first round by folding her in-house memo that they are a couple into his group-bound bonds. She takes their date, including the date coming soon of their marriage, out to Lovers Lane. But why? says the gadget-loving professor, it is "a private preserve of teenagers." She says they'll "turn on the radio and do what the teenagers do."

Down in the crypt lab, professor is bringing up babe. Verbal exchange or control must begin right away between master and creation because when it comes to building a teen and coordinating his sensorium, "time is of the essence." Professor knows that the teen has a tongue because he himself stitched it in place: "no malingering now." The phrase the teen bod finally echoes gives us the forecast: "Good morning." And the built body is in fact soon in tears. "It's actually crying. Even the tear duct functions. The world will be astounded. It seems we have a very sensitive teenager on our hands."

Tear here: upstairs the bride-to-be stages another intervention along the dotted line where she thought she had already signed. She warns that she has ways of finding out what he is up to down there. He slaps her and interrogates her. "It just slipped out; words sometimes do. I don't ever want to know." Jump-cut: when the professor drives away, she has a duplicate lab key made straight away. Her covert operations for couplification take her downstairs, where she opens the locker and the teen gets in her face.

The two Hollywood plots — marriage versus the same-sex or, same difference, unisex group bond — which are linked and separated by one tear line, now overlap in the space of one tension between the couple and the group. Because down in what is now a fitness lab, the teen interrupts the workout to protest his under-life. Even the monster teen wants to circulate. But even after the professor has shown him his current hamburger face and promised him the savior's face of every teen only in time, still he cannot but play back the tape of the bride-to-be's covert operation and break out right away to the street. He peeps through a window at a teen girl, who, at first sight, starts screaming. He breaks in to quiet her down but silences her once and for all. The professor can now use the delinquent creation's disappointment in the face of his first date with couplification to lay down the law.

Upstairs the fiancée is back ring-sizing up the professor for the setting of the date — with the station break she represents. When he throws the jeweler out of the house, she comes back with her preemptive strike: "I saw your monster." She tells him the story of her key transgression, forging it into their more perfect union. She knew he could only want a wife strong enough to love and undertand him fully. "Your secret is safe. Now two of us are guarding it." No, she makes three.

He tells the teen, who is wanting a face to save, that the woman who opened his closet is now betraying him to all those who would hurt him. When she is back from the ring shopping — he had put on such a happy face about her resourcefulness and sent her on her way, any old way she would have it — he tells her that she can now help him with his machine creature project, whereby their more perfect union will be forged. But when she and teen are brought closer together, she is finished. It is the professor and teen bond that her threat made stronger. The face that's wanted is the reward. They drive around comparison shopping for just the right look. Together they make a move on a couple of teens making out. The girl sees the monster and screams. The monster, she saw, was looking only at her guy. Everyone agrees it is a handsome face, and once it is on the creation, he cannot stop gazing at it in the mirror. It is his "new toy." But even though he now can pass as normal, he can also be recognized as missing. The professor suggests to his colleague that they take him back to England for the big debut. But how to supply passport, name, identity? Whatever was assembled can be disassembled and then reassembled. The monster is to be tricked up onto the operating table, strapped down there, and then cut down to size of component parts. But he's rough trade. He panics. Or he kills the professor. When the colleague and the police try to catch monster teen, he backs up against the apparatus and electrocutes himself. The colleague gives the voice-over and out: "I'll never forget his face after the accident, never." The audience is left face-to-face with the disfigurement that cannot be forgotten but only finally released by the closing shot of what is left of the professor.

LECTURE TWENTY-FOUR

At first it looked like vampirism's drag race of mourning had reached a finish line by the seventies at the latest. In *The Rocky Horror Picture Show*, the Hollywood sexological reading of couplification and the Hammer reading of horror as aphrodisiac for that James Bond enforcement of sexual desire had conjoined on a last laugh track. But then there was AIDS, and then, beyond repression or liberation, death was back in sex, with sex, and as big as, if not bigger than, sex. We were forced back down the channels occupied by death or the dead, the channeling of identification. Vampirism renewed its wow of dread, horror, and fascination. The unmournable body count kept piling up. But at the same time the new take on vampirism took us beyond mourning to the fantasy of immortality that can accompany a disease like AIDS. With AIDS it is as though there is nothing else, nothing that is not attributable to the one diagnosis on the horizon, that can get you anymore. In exchange for a certain death there is a deferrable deadline. This characterizes our current age of recovery. Quitting toxic habits now guarantees, on the installment plan of this diagnosis, more life. In the future we will all have deadline diagnoses that we will start living with and deferring from adolescence onward. Our fascination with vampirism is back, but with the difference that we are vampires struggling to survive our immortality, which is threatened only by our own suicidal impulse or control.

Techno-body Frankenstein, by contrast, just kept plugging along, making its dreadful plug for a future that is already upon us. We have more than half accepted the cyborg destiny of our bodies among replaceable parts. The emphasis on health, organic food, and so on as early as in adolescence fits an era of recovery that goes with diseases of deferral. But it also shows concern for the cattle of organ replacement. The accident victim with organs to spare is not all he or she can be if not raised on healthy food and smart drugs. Now survival already carries the status of immortality. When calculations of the survival of so-called nuclear holocausts during the eighties brought down the Cold War oppositions, we were already shifting away from the total war scenarios of opposition to the double strategy of deferral and survival. For the survivor, castration gives way to the sitcom conflicts of the Bobbits. Soon a zipper will be added to the dotted line, along which even the absolute cutoff can be recovered.

The Frankenstein phantasm appears to have lost much of its uncanniness, its surprise attractions. It crossed over into science fiction, joining the cyborg at the front of the line of a certain techno and, technically, perverse capacity for getting around both the need to mourn and the eternal backfire of melancholia. We have been living on the first stage of techno bodybuilding for some time now. Beyond the prosthetic fillers that crowded the public's fear after World War I (and monstrosity fiction, especially in visual forms, ultimately aided the assimilation of deformed and shell-shock-shaking vets), the further literalization of identification and resulting unbindings of our body's boundaries is with us now too with every organ transplant, every marrow escape.

In *Son of Frankenstein* the first writing on the wall is EINGANG VERBOTEN, the German interdiction not to enter an off-limits place. The film does not see or pass beyond this point of entry because it is the police beat it skips onto the screen, the booth or crypt of its projections. Tonight Frankenstein's son arrives to collect his heritage. One leftover from the traumatic past of father is Igor, crippled survivor of his public execution, whose evil eye is feared by the villagers, who persecute him.

On the train we see the Frankenstein couple: the son of Frankenstein, raised in England, has an American wife; he left behind a full schedule of classroom and faculty meetings. "Strange countryside." "Not much like America is it?" "I'm glad we saw London and Paris first." The son cannot blame the father. As all the prequels proved, it was his assistant who made the mistake of inserting a killer's brain. "Why, most people call that misshapen creature of my father's…" The conductor interrupts to call out: "Frankenstein." Now it is a place-name too.

The local inspector arrives to offer protection (he pulls his prosthetic arm up and back down with his free hand to give the salute). "Protection from what?" "Your name." "Should I change it to Smith?" Frankenstein asks in a huff intended to bring the house down. Inspector assures him that even if he were to go generic, he would never get rid of the branding. The inspector encountered the monster back then. That was no superstition: "One doesn't easily forget an arm torn out by the roots." But he dismisses any bid for sympathy; bringing up his missing arm gets him over and around undue curiosity that the prosthesis otherwise attracts. The American wife meets the inspector on his way out. He shakes her hand with his left, which leaves her staring at the prosthesis on his right. "Wasn't he strange," she reflects behind his back. Frankenstein junior: "He said if the villagers bother us, he'd give a hand."

In Paul Morrisey's presentation of Warhol and Frankenstein, the titles scroll down while little boy and little girl look at the lab animals. They dissect a doll and conclude the lesson by guillotine. Cut. The blonde Baroness drives onto the screen with the two kids in a cart. She likes to catch the local peasants where they breed. She finds Dalessandro making out on the job. "Such trash!"

Frankenstein extols the Serbian ideal to his assistant: the local Serbian peasants are direct descendants of the ancient Greeks. He is still looking for one last part: the perfect nose or nasum. As a child he was not allowed to play with the peasant stock. So instead he watched them secretly, transgressively. This is still his research. In the name of science and following ideals from antiquity, he is building a strapping peasant couple who will be new by virtue of their physical perfection, fine-toned by a voyeur's long-standing rapport with parts, but also on account of his telecommand over the species to follow.

The Baroness has removed the children from school. The tales they heard about their parents there are in part true (they are brother and sister) but for the most part merely resentful lies. They, the two sets of Frankenstein siblings, are just different. And she insists on beauty.

In the lab the corpse collage of the perfect woman is raised up from the formaldehyde bath.

At table the parents or siblings quarrel about their mother in front of their children.

Baroness catches Dalessandro in the sex act again. She orders him to report to her in the castle next morning.

Baron tells his assistant that behind the nose job, they need the head of a male with one idea on his mind. So he can right away start keeping ahead of the breeding assignment with his zombie bride. They will go to the local whorehouse to find their man. Baron remembers that he went once in a perfect fit with the other guys. "It was terrible. Overdeveloped women with large breasts, shapeless. How could such a creature even compare with my creation or even with my sister. The man who can make love to anything goes to such a place." Tonight Dalessandro is one of the regular customers. His friend is along because Dalessandro cannot believe he plans to enter a monastery. But the friend is just not interested. As instructed by Dalessandro, he watches his stud pal in action but not, it seems, in order to identify. The friend does have the perfect nose. But Baron is mistaken when he takes him to have the single mind. They clip off his head.

While Baroness interviews Dalessandro for the positions she has in mind, her brother-husband cuts open the stitched-up abdomen of his made-by-hand bride, his hand job, and inserts his hand to cop a feel of her internal organs. When the coming is gone, assistant Otto lowers the table with the strapped-down blow-up dolly. "Soon I will give you life. Soon you will give me the right children, the children I want." Otto, who was instructed not, that swine, to look, must now help the Baron down from table. "To know death, Otto, you have to fuck life in the gall bladder."

When Baroness shows off her new servant at dinner, Baron presents a couple of new guests. He thus doubly takes the advantage. Baroness now feels she has been too modest in her own acquisition. Not only does Dalessandro recognize his friend's head, but the zombie at table cannot keep his eyes off the Baroness's new top man. Soon it is as plain as the nose on his face that the perfect man isn't into the perfect woman. Baron decides to transplant Dalessandro's one-track mind. In exchange for handing over her new stud, who is dangling from the meat hook, Baroness gets to try out the nose job. He follows her orders but then the emergency brake doesn't work. Her crush gets taken literally and takes her out. While the Baron's away, Otto unzips the perfect woman and messes with her organs. But he doesn't know how to put her back together again. The perfect man won't take nose for an answer. He kills the Baron, and then he disembowels himself. Dalessandro is left hanging. The other sole survivors, little boy and little girl, now come into the lab to graduate from their play preparations for experimentation to new work on Dalessandro's body image, which comes life-size. The whole film is one last spasm of 3-D resistance to—and, Big Time, libidinization of—our new start as rip-off of parts to spare.

We can no longer afford to take fright at the prospect of spare parts and their interchange between bodies. It is part of the family pack. Now you can have another child just to have the compatible marrow available for insertion into an older child mother will not let go. But there is horror in the transferential fine print in a contract one generation takes out on the next one. We no longer put our trust in the next generation but raise it to open wide and drop all inserts into the midlife laps on the immortality track.

Youth has perhaps always been a fantasy produced in midlife crisis. But this once punitive fantasy is no longer administered by the superego. It is now on an eco, I mean ego trip. Once when there was time, a salesman pitched a life insurance policy to me, arguing that this was the chance of my midlifetime, because rates dropped as one grew older and thus, according to the risk calculations of insurance, I had already survived a host of possible catastrophes and accidents. The older you get, at least up through midlife, the longer you live. Once you make it to midlife, the insurance-ego body counts down to immortality over the accident victims of the Teen Age, whose replacement parts are fresh for a change. Until our own clones replace them, teenagers are the cattle, free-range and organically nourished, supplying the new organs at the disposal of the middle generation, in which all the investments have been made.

On a TV scale of assimilation, from *Nightstalker* to the 1995 series *Forever Knight*, a New Age yawned over the abyss of total supply wars. Vampires had worked through their blood lust, and now could control-release or even substitute for it.

> *Pale Blood* begins with a vampire flying into Los Angeles, going to meet the local detective, who will implement his expertise. They meet on Melrose, in front of the store Metropolis; one of the mannequins in the window is not so much dummy up as just plain dead. While taking her employer to his subletting, the detective, who is a total vampirism groupie, warms up to live consummation of their correspondence. But his letters were businesslike. She says, "I like to read between the lines." But what she takes between or behind the lines she swallows whole. What if it is a vampire stalk show? "I've seen all the vampire movies ever made. Vampires need to kill to live." "I think people see too many movies. Why couldn't they just take enough to live and let the quarry go?"
>
> While investigating the wide scene of the storefront murder, the vampire picks up a video artist's surveillance. "But why are you taping now? Nothing's happening." "You'd be surprised what editing can do." The artist leaves, makes an about face. It is about paranoid face-saving: "It's a documentary, and don't rip me off."
>
> Two call-girl types, extras for the video, wait for the artist. Under the vampire's surveillance, one chick's out of there; she'll meet the other one at

Drac's. The vampire follows. In the bar scene the close-up of his face (features without the framing outline of the head or hair) looks unisex, androgynous, really feminine or maternal. He takes the chicken to his sublet and sublets some blood at her breast while they make it.

The detective, a dilettante for daze, has been trying to communicate with the spirits of the murder victims. But it is the vampire, in his separate place, who has been picking up bad vibes. While video artist plays back and edits close-ups of both girls, he notices the fang marks on one pair of breasts. He explains to the vampire's one-night stand his masterpiece in progress (the room with a view covered from all corners by hidden cameras looks like a surgery, stainless table and cutting-room floor): he wants to shoot the vampire feeding; then he will be the famous artist. He made all those murders look so vampiric in order to attract a live one. "They're so lonely." He straps her down, punctures her jugular with the metallic simulacrum of a vampire bat's fangs, and pumps her blood down the tube. "I actually know how to do this better than he does." When the vampire follows his vibes to the artist's lab, she is already dead. Video artist enters sipping wine: "Sorry about that. I take the blood out but I don't drink it." But why did he kill her? To bait the master. But the vampire hasn't killed in ages: now it is mad men who have taken over where he left off bloodletting. The artist shoots the vampire and gets back inside the control room or camera to watch his catch regenerate on the spot. Now it is the detective's turn to pick up visions leading her to the artist's studio. The artist locks her up all alone with the lonely, hungry vampire. But then, just as the vampire's struggling up hill against being turned on by her and turned back into a killer, it turns out she is one too: she suckles him at her breast. Fortified by this boost of same-type blood, the vampire breaks through doors but not without knocking out the artist. The knock-off artist ends up in an asylum watching a staticky screen with fellow inmates, whose attention he orders to the details of his nonexistent video. "I actually have footage of him changing and taking off as a bat." Then, just like Renfield, once his declaration of independence is interrupted by the sudden appearance of the vampire couple, he immediately protests his loyalty all alone on his asylum bed, while the vampires openly enjoy having made him walk the prank.

In *Subspecies* Romanian direction stakes the re-claim on vampire projections shot on location. Wherever! Radu kills his father on castration rebound: at this open and cut origin, Radu first loses three fingers. Then it is fingers three, come, come to me, and turn into little devils. They help him reverse the father's order, his era of peace with the mortals via the bloodstone, the little bit of essence of blood that goes a long way. No time like the present: American college girls go to Transylvania to meet up with former exchange student. Stefan, a zoologist, is staying at the hostel too. He's cute! Where the coeds are, he'll be there too. Stefan turns out to be Radu's younger brother. Radu: "Our father was fool. So are you." Radu starts sipping from the blonde American race of arms. Stefan wants the brunette (she made him want again). Radu: "She has your mother's eyes." Stefan may be a vampire, but he lives in the way of his father, the way of feeding-free vampirism. The father even took a mortal wife, Stefan's mother. Eventually only the brunette is not a vampire. Radu is killed but not before leaving his mark on her. "Will I be all right?" "I don't know." "I don't want to be like him, I want to be like you." "I can't do it." Oh yes he can.

At the start of *Bloodstone: Subspecies II*, we get the recap of Michelle's love for Stefan. The demons in the meantime push and pull Radu back together again. After the stake's been removed, we watch his arteries wind their way back up into his embodiment. Radu drives the stake into Stefan. Michelle is saved by the crack of dawn from which Radu cannot but hide. She makes it to Bucharest and calls her sister from the hotel. Radu enters his crypt away from crypt: this is where witch-mummy holds down her end of the raw deal they give the world. In the hotel room Michelle crawls into the tub to sleep. The maids come in to clean and find the corpse. But once the sun sets, she comes alive. She goes to a music club, makes out with a guy, almost goes vampiric on him, but then pulls back, horrified. Radu wants her for his fledgling, his free bride. "Pain and suffering are our pleasure. Fledgling! Savor the taste of your sister's suffering. There's a vein here that feeds her leg. When I open it it will pump blood like a fountain." The sisters almost make it out of there for good. But the sunrise stops Michelle undead in her tracks. Mortal sister will wait until dark. The blackened mummy gets Michelle.

Bloodlust: Subspecies III continues where *II* was stopped in its reels. Radu to Michelle: "First learn patience. We have all the time in the world. There's no love between the living and the dead. What you feel is hunger, hunger for life, the living. Some day the sadness you feel will be a sweet memory. I killed my father, my mother, my entire bloodline for you. What will you give me?" "Forgiveness for what you've done to me." "There isn't enough forgiveness in the universe for what I've done. See the fear! Drink! The sweetness of his agony?" She'll do anything if he only spares her sister's life. "Your sister's life in exchange for your absolute devotion!" Michelle shoots Radu, sun lights up, Radu gets his fill of trees. Out of his blood loss little demons arise and gather round the bloodstone.

It would appear that increasingly the mass of murder, the late survival of the Christian mass, is under investigation by vampires on a diet of killing, in declared distinction to all that murder. But first the suicidal impulse must be relinquished between self and other. In *Dance of the Damned* and its remake, just two times two years later, *To Sleep with a Vampire,* the vampire seeks out humans of the night who have lost the will to live, feels their impulse, and gives it to them, the externalization of what suicide hides inside a so-called self-relation. But the death wishes along for the ride on death drive catch up with the disposal service. It is the vampire, finally, who is self-destructive: what goes around comes around between self and the projection of the death of the other.

One newspaper article occasioned by the publication of Anne Rice's *The Vampire Lestat* highlights the loss generation heading the vampires (and us) off at the impasse:

> In her books, Rice said, she tries "to really envision an immortal mind." In other works, "the concept of the immortal is really boring.... They're

usually looking for a lost love. I think that if these creatures really could live forever, or even for a couple of centuries, they would have to have something on their minds other than a lost love."

We have not been able to rid ourselves of what Rice calls a "lost love," a yearning for a lost love, which causes that mourning sickness that leads ultimately to an inability to survive what not only from the vampire's perspective is our immortality. Because of mourning or not mourning—because the other always goes first—we are immortal. Louis in *Interview with the Vampire* reflects on little Claudia's undead status:

> I was going to say, "for as long as she lives." But I realized it was a hollow mortal cliché. She would live forever, as I would live forever. But wasn't it so for mortal fathers? Their daughters live forever because these fathers die first. I was at a loss suddenly. (283)

But that is why, as in Louis's case, we are suicidal—because the other is the first to go. We are suddenly at a loss.

The Vampire Lestat lets roll a mythology or history of vampirism that takes some direction from Nietzsche's *Genealogy of Morals*. I just want to say something—and this is really going to be crude and simple—about that. It has to do with the discussions in *Interview with the Vampire* between Louis and Armand, and between Louis and Claudia. What is Louis's problem? I have already addressed it in general terms, his inability to survive his immortality, to affirm life. He is also burdened by various notions of evil and so on, and this is what one has to unpack to read and interpret this novel: What is Louis's problem—with evil?

It used to be, one might say in pre-Christian days, that the world was justifiable only as an aesthetic phenomenon; only as surface, only as art, only as fiction did we perceive the world. And therefore our pursuit of knowledge, which followed out a detour of sidetracks, served life before truth. It was possible to see our relationship to truth by way of Caution! Detour! Don't look directly at the sun, go around via some reflection instead, the shadow side that may as well be more fictive than true. Truth, that is, the direct stare at the truth, burns eyeballs. It is what burns vampires along the one-way transmission from the mother or queen of the damned vampires. In the world as aesthetic phenomenon what is good is what resides, upon reflection, within the good fit between form or build and fiction or function.

Beginning with Christianity, says Nietzsche, and I think Rice says it too in *The Vampire Lestat,* the pursuit of the truth at any cost predominates, takes control of the pursuit of knowledge, at which point the pursuit of knowledge, the pursuit of happiness, and the pursuit of the good go their separate ways. Evil is out there, tanned, behind sunglasses on the day that the pursuits follow one heartbeat and truth-beam and thus separate out. In *The Genealogy of Morals,* the model for what I have been calling our genealogy of media, Nietzsche says that on all the stages of the rehearsal for the twentieth century, we find reformulations of the drive to get at the truth at all costs, and this drive is not the one that serves life. It is the one Freud would later call — and it was getting late — the Death Drive. Nietzsche's warning in *Genealogy of Morals* is that life itself faces cancellation of its politics or policy by the drives, wills, and legacies that control our every move historywide or even societywide. Atheism or the age of science counts down as another sequel to Christianity's direct hit; Christian pursuit of truth at any cost — at all costs — leads necessarily to the discovery that there is no God; in other words, it follows the leader all the way to the murder of God. The declared or discovered death of God is what Christianity's own telling the truth (on us) was leading up to. It is what we had to forget but also ultimately get when we opened up the credit line of Christian belief.

The so-called death of God is the headline Nietzsche scored. It is not that he put out a contract on God and then declared Him dead; he simply pointed it out — "Look, God is no longer a functioning concept; God is dead." If God is dead, the same goes for man as we have known him: man as the center of the universe, as the other half of the relationship to God. Now that man is over, over and out, one has to conceive the overman or the superman, the being who has not yet existed, but who would, in the future, be strong enough to affirm life, even or especially in spite of there being nothing out there to guarantee that life has meaning. Life sucks. So start affirming it. The experiment is on.

What was God doing out there? He was the anchorman of meaningfulness. Follow the bouncing happy face: it is because even though man suffers Big Time, the greatest anguish is not the suffering as such, but suffering that cannot be turned into meaningfulness. So we invented God to have a constant witness to our suffering around. Never, even in the remotest corner of existence, could my suffering be lost, wasted. There would always be that dictator out there whose playback and record functions allowed him to take note, take dictation, and learn. It was thus guaranteed that my suffering would always have meaning. Guilt, self-flagellation, torture, witch-burning, confession, you name it, were first downed in major festivals of meaningfulness that were successful (they worked!); but come the twentieth century and even the nineteenth century, they were running on empty because the greatest spectator of all had been found missing within a more scientific and more *unconsciously* Christian Europe. Consider the images of the theater in Rice's first two vampire novels. The "Théâtre des Vampires" stages this whole search, from the eighteenth century onward, for a new spectator of our same old suffering. This brings us to the related question: How do we get off?

What I will say now could be historical, in terms of centuries, or it could apply only to the development of an individual; but let's say that as history accumulates, one's reliance on language becomes increasingly that much more pressing, increasingly, also, in the sense that we are fed signs, images (for example, in our own mass-media sensurround); we are fast fed a buffer zone of symbols or signs. And this applies in particular to our pleasure.

Remember pleasure is everything. The pleasure principle rules absolutely, even when it is outdistanced by the death drive. Pleasure, because it is at bottom masturbatory, is everything, and yet pleasure comes into its own only via a detour, via the other, in the first place, but also, same place, via language. Pleasure pops up on the margin of breast feeding as the first breathtaking (breast-taking) access to excess. The vampires know while trying to survive their immortality that pleasure is not obtained directly from any body; the body is just a metaphor or analogue for the pleasure that one can have (and eat it too). The body is limited; this is the limit vampiric pleasure addresses and exceeds; it is what sadomasochism is all about. The body is only one limited image of the greater pleasure to be had through the imagination, and through language, the bestfuck buddy of the imagination. So, vampiric pleasure stresses theatricality, seduction, and a good deal of talk. But there is a catch to the vampire's pleasure, a catch in the throat: the vampire's hunger consumes the vampire himself, who is stuck on loss and downs it, goes down with it.

Beginning right at the beginning, what is Louis's problem? Everyone must have hit on it because it is as though these lectures have led up to this, were running along only so that we could recognize it—and then go beyond it. What is Louis's problem? Why does he turn into a vampire?

Around page 8, we learn right away that the first occasion for his being vampirized was his brother Paul's death. How does that work? Why is that the occasion for his becoming a vampire? He puts the blame on himself, and he runs around asking for death at someone else's hands: and up pops the vampire. Louis has every reason to feel responsible for his brother's death. He calls that part of himself that put his brother to death an egotist. It was this egotism that kept him from believing that his brother might be having visions for real. Now it fuels his grief, this terrible grief, which leads to his being vampirized:

> I did not escape my brother for a moment. I could think of nothing but his body rotting in the ground. He was buried in the St. Louis cemetery.... [notice the corpse is inside an idealized Louis; on page 108, for example, we are reminded, in connection with this place-name, that this is all going down in Louisiana] I lived like a man who wanted to die but who had no courage to do it himself.... And then I was attacked. It might have been anyone—and my invitation was open to sailors, thieves, maniacs, anyone. But it was a vampire. (10)

What happens to this egotism, which, remember, is defined as a refusal to believe in his brother's capacity for visions, as a refusal to believe in the supernatural? What happens upon vampirization? Just think of the rest of the novel. He changes, doesn't he? It is not just that he becomes a vampire, but he becomes his brother. Whereas before he had been the egotist, the one who did not believe, he becomes as vampire the great visionary and believer; he becomes the tortured visionary brother.

To make the transformation complete, he must go all the way, beyond just turning into another vampire, and must be reborn as one vampire within a vampire couple, one that keeps eternally, internally alive (or "live") the disconnection between the brothers. It is Lestat who, in this first book, is entirely the egotist. He is what Louis was the instant (freeze frame!) he killed off his brother.

Right from the start we hear that Louis is overwhelmed as vampire by the horror of the death of the other, of the death that he quickly says is always the death of his brother (15). The death of the other horrifies him, and yet in vampirizing his victims, it is his own death that he claims as his own experience:

> Killing is no ordinary act. . . . It is the experience of another's life for certain, and often the experience of the loss of that life through the blood, slowly. It is again and again the experience of that loss of my own life, which I experienced when I sucked the blood from Lestat's wrist and felt his heart pound with my heart. It is again and again a celebration of that experience; because for vampires that is the ultimate experience. (28)

That also means that this loss of one's own life, which takes place when one is taking another's life, means that one has become the other, one has become the brother, and this transformation is what Louis's relationship to vampirism animates. He will be rejected by his fellow vampires for having adopted this unusual rapport with vampirism, in other words with killing and immortality. Armand will point out, "You are strange, Louis, in that you always die when you vampirize." Translation: you are so caught up in the other, so caught up in the lost love, that you are always only repeating that departure, that loss, but you never experience the kill. As Lestat puts it to Louis, "You're dead to your vampire nature" (82). The kill, remember, is the vampire's term for life; killing is what must be affirmed. Can we distinguish killing from murder?

Murder is what leaves the corpse lying around. Murder is whatever does not feed on, does not consume the life that has been taken or lost.

In other words, murder does not admit disposal. A certain relationship to killing is what Louis is not able to master. After witnessing his first killing (a demonstration by Lestat), Louis walks, "a zombie," to the scene of his brother's accident or suicide and asks Lestat to kill him. So, suicidally, ambivalently, he becomes a vampire (and takes on his identity with his brother).

How does Claudia emerge in that case? For one thing, Rice's novel is revving up for the range she will achieve with *The Vampire Lestat:* the public address system of the problems vampirism embodies not only in individual or personalizable terms. So what she really offers us here is a whole scanner of melancholic scenarios, and Claudia of course stars within the melancholic phantasm of the missing child (the one, the little one, that still haunts us). But notice that it is always from within the perspective of Louis that these melancholic phantasms come into focus. Claudia, created by Louis and Lestat, is, on her own, on the side of killing. There is no attachment in her to some lost love. That she is always found within the same scene of recycling the loss of the mother was seen first with Louis. Louis's melancholia organizes this book; he is a sort of Everyman, the case of modern man — modern man destined for suicide because he cannot survive his immortality, cannot relinquish the lost love, cannot kill, can only murder and ceaselessly mourn.

On page 73, Louis senses a death wish (he in fact calls it a death wish) against himself, which always also means against the other: and he hears the child crying. For years he has not gone in for the kill, but now suddenly he is attracted to the child who cannot abandon her dead mother lying beside her. This upsurge of his murderous impulse, which stops short of killing her and leaves her to die, is turned by Lestat, and that means within the couple, into the birth of their vampire child, Claudia. All this, by the way, is accompanied on the surrounding pages by dreams of the dead brother.

We have, then, in *Interview with the Vampire* vampirism reduced to Louis's perspective, which holds down a convergence between vampirism and humanity. For the first time in the history of vampire literature, we are on the inside of the vampire's perspective, but in the first novel what has beamed up into the vampiric zone is still very much mixed up back there with what is human, all too human. Remember the impossibility Victor Frankenstein ran up against when he tried to build the second monster? It is as though melancholic bodybuilding keeps going all the way toward complete restoration of the corpse, which must then, however, be recognized and released as lost. Claudia already externalizes the melancholic bond of disconnection between the brothers. That is why she can push for Lestat's destruction without pushing herself into his place. Instead she turns to Madeleine to contain from every side of a double loss an unmourning that is, again, not her own. The fully reconstituted or completed loss that began its outward trajectory with Claudia's vampirization is now in the ready position to be released. It would be tempting to chart a progress of mourning pictures that issues for Louis finally in a closing shot of mourning. It is true that around page 307, when Claudia dies, when those scenes of mother and daughter embracing come to close around this final rest in peace of Claudia and Madeleine, these figures are referred to as dead, simply dead, as though a kind of double death had been accomplished. Claudia dies alongside her "mother" as she would have long ago but for Louis's melancholic intervention. Louis feels close to his own destruction; again and again we hear "it is over." He sleeps, on page 310, in a used coffin in a graveyard — in a drop scene of identification. He gives himself over to his grief and gives grief by burning the theater of the vampires to the ground.

Interview is the acknowledged work of mourning that Rice dedicated to her dead daughter, Michelle. Her child died of leukemia, a blood disease. Out of three years of slap-happy alcoholism, the tapping sounds of typewriter keys announced the unstoppable creation of the vampire novel. With its release, Rice, like Mary Shelley, allowed herself to draw benefits from and thus fully mourn the loss. That is the hardest thing you will ever do, benefit from the loss of the other. The benefits package is addressed up front to the survivor of mother in *Frankenstein* and to the survivor of brother in *Interview*. But both testamentary addresses are set up, close call, still as diversions away from the undead children admitted on the margin outside the main contexts of these works of mourning and unmourning. But these same works run on the crypt battery power of children two mother-authors could not mourn, not directly, not openly, but only by this long shot of placing their address as sideshow beside the final show-and-tell of unmourning, which the reader arrives at only after recognizing its open concealment. The reader is given detours that seem to prove that this is where to go for bust.

The trappings of Rice's melancholia are there in the vampire novel; they are set by Madeleine's inability to mourn her daughter and her follow-up willingness to become vampire, the eternally maternal protector of Claudia, who in turn can never die. There is at the other end Claudia's own original scene of remaining beside her dead mother, whose death she does not recognize. And the scenario of disconnection between mother and child is recycled through a cult of dolls, statues, miniature realms. Claudia discovers Madeleine in a toy store crowded with doll-sized replications of the same dead daughter. When Louis next interviews her for the position of Claudia's mate, he goes all the way to the bottom line of ambivalence:

> And cruelly, surely, I said to her, "Did you love this child?" I will never forget her face then, the violence in her, the absolute hatred. "Yes." She all but hissed the words at me. "How dare you!" She reached for the locket even as I clutched it. It was guilt that was consuming her, not love. It was guilt — that shop of dolls Claudia had described it to me, shelves and shelves of the effigy of that dead child. But guilt that absolutely understood the finality of death. There was something as hard in her as the evil in myself, something as powerful. (271)

When Louis goes ahead and turns Madeleine into one of them, he confides to Claudia: "'What has died in this room tonight is the last vestige in me of what was human'" (275). If the last mortal piece of Louis can die when he creates Madeleine, it is because the terms of a contract that will let her go, go the way of the dead other have now been fulfilled. What does the last remnant of Louis's humanity release between self and other? Madeleine is the total mourning-sick monster, the monstrous death-wish gagster that was so long inside Louis. She wears about her neck the locket of her dead child, whose death, which

completed the control system of her own death wishes, must go unacknowledged. Louis, the one to know one, recognizes right away that her
locket also spells out the injunction, "Lock it," keep it locked. This locked-
upedness, the need to keep locked up the dead child, is what programs
her relationship to Claudia. It is what programs a whole culture of here-
to-eternity services for the missing child. Once she enters undeath,
Madeleine builds a doll-sized mortuary habitat for Claudia, Madeleine's
eternal and internal little one. All the props of the death cult exchanged
in Rice's novel between Claudia and her dead mother or between
Madeleine and Claudia (who is the placeholder of Madeleine's dead
daughter) belong to melancholic phantasms that we are still gagging
on. The unmournable death of a child is the big one that still haunts
us: the missing children, the abused child, the little phantoms on the
milk cartons and on the postcards.

One last or lasting shot in the dark, this time a film that failed so spectacularly that it succeeds as see-through symptom. *Casper* was supposed to be
consumer-friendly, going on and on, on amusement park rides forever. But
it stopped dead in our tracks, flip-flop. The way down into a dead father's
underworld lab was already coasting along the success anticipated for
friendly or efficient mourning. But the reanimation of one girl's recently
dead father through another, long-distant father's legacy of renewal of life
originally set aside for his own undead son, Casper, was too much by half.
The beaming back for a brief visitation by the idealized dead wife (with a
greeting from Casper's equally angelic father) finished us off. It should have
been a horror movie. The gift of reanimation associated with a mourned
dead father (by contrast, the uncles or brothers are unmourned ghosts) is a
legacy only to the living, to the girl with the dad who just died on her. At
the time of the reanimant's invention, Casper was the undead unmournable child. Father and son do not describe all the ingredients in a reanimation formula. Where is Casper's mother, in life as in death?

"We almost lost each other," the resurrected father tells daughter after
a brief span of absence, retention, blackout. First the daughter must jolt

father's memory, turn him around to face the other way, away from the ghost gagsters, back to his living will. Ghosts are defined in the movie as those dearly departed who forget us. Casper and the girl's dad faced off at the film's beginning across the TV barrier: Casper takes to the father's advertisement of therapy for ghosts. Ghosts are dead people who just cannot let go because of their still unfinished business in this life. What a clean break with the projection! When the mournable wife returns to tell him that their daughter needs a father, his therapy needs are met. He understands now that he was always looking for her in his therapy work with ghosts. The returned father sends daughter off to the party space of substitution. But her prince will be Casper, whose ghostliness is granted embodiment for a brief spell, as consolation for his sacrifice. The girl and her ghost split the party scene of substitution, the girl whirling about deadline contact with the ghost's lost body.

The daughter never witnesses the beam-back of her Angel of a dead mother. The high point of loving the dead, girl and boy dancing just a turn away from giving up the ghost, keeps down the caption of the laugh track. "It's my party and I'll die if I want to, die if I want to. You'd die too if it happened to you!" In the chilling scene of the paternal ghost's nonrecognition of his daughter, the avuncular noise screen of pun power and gags gets plumbed by the vacancy it tries to fill. The undead uncles, who, like stand-up comics or channelers, occupy a host of marginal identities, are right on the rim, dying to fall in, of the psychotic melting plot. The uncles or brothers celebrate their comeback or rejoinder within a perpetual drop scene of maternal identifications.

Before the psychohistorical flashback that Bazin gave us—photography's origin in mummification—can get out from under the ground, there are two downbeats to skip along the way. First, there was the stopgap of dead babies for whose commemoration the new institution of photography was immediately pressed into services. Then, there was a follow-up catch, another catch in the throat, associated with spiritist photography, which improved upon the seances that began gathering everywhere telegraphy had just introduced the newest technology of live transmission. Through the occult and technical medium of ghost shooting, Sir Arthur Conan Doyle sought the return of a son who had gone down with the body count of the Great War. The time traveling and underworld sojourns of photography are, by now, part of the legend. But the real time traveling of what Freud called the transference is the psychic ready-positioning internal to and eternally along for this swift passage in photography's history or ontology. The transference concept first struck Freud in the wake of his recognition of the haunting or possession that had taken hold in all his adults-only friendships (with Fliess, for example, and, then again, with Jung). What we saw first with Freud was that your relationships here and now can, via transference, follow like sleepwalk the up-and-down course of more primal scenes of relationship. In Freud's case it came down to his boy-bonding with Oedi-pal John, his half-brother's son. But in the fine print on the legend, we can make out in this original relationship, in its junior highlight, a teen screen that was dropped between the first shock of Freud's relations with loss, the death of his baby brother Julius, and all the rest of Freud's life in relationship.

Julius died on the mother, who passed the unmournable corpse, the mummy's legacy, on into Sigmund for safekeeping. In his correspondence with Fliess, Freud dropped mention of the "seed of reproach" deposited inside him on the occasion of Julius's death. It was the primal source of volatility in all his same-sex relations. But little Julius could be mentioned only in passing, in passing on to the teen passion play of relations with John. This rough trade-in in no time served as the only address under which Freud's idealizations and demonizations of his fellow men could be registered. But (just look at *Casper*) the dead infant or child can only be reanimated as young teen idol, and what a doll.

Freud had, then, been working on the transference all the live long way. But when it came time to give theorization and staying power to the new concept beyond his original shock of recognition of the ghost or revenant, Freud picked for his formulations a point of overlap between photography and the printing press: the transference was the photo image or "cliché" of earliest relations that kept coming back with each "reprinting," within all subsequent relationships that ended up being with always the same ghostly other.

Inside the holding pattern of schooling a longer attention span had to be inscribed letter by letter upon each new candidate for society membership. This little one who was now in training, in transition, during an otherwise nonfunctionalized period of time came to be and to be known as the child. Little one now came complete with name and ontological status—and thus with equal rights to proper burial and mourning. Pre-literacy the rapid turnover of infant and child mortalities could still pass without mention or commemoration. The next born received the vacated name, and the parental couple kept on breeding ahead on their assignment in the face of the matter of fact of life of small chances for survival for little ones. But the childhood mortality rate did not start its decline until well into the era of childhood's invention. The inevitable pileup of dead babies and children who now had to be commemorated but who, it turned out, were unmournable introduced a death cult right in the typeface of our first techno culture. The outer space of tension between the allegorical and functional opens up over death-cult childhood. The pupil was focused first. But there was now, even with earliest infancy, in the zoning, the measure, of what language animates in the speaking and nonspeaking alike, the I, old enough to live, to be called by first name, old enough to die, to be buried with the name call, the role that was now personalized, stationary, even or especially for the littlest corpse.

The mummy only comes life-size. The first modern work of art would have required in the newer spirit of typeface alteration in scale, a move Theodor Adorno associates with the sublimational essence of art. Art, I guess, relies on or tests your capacity for taking one size to fit all the other ones. Thus, the small world after all of toys indeed represented one of the first artistic arrangements between what you see and what you forget. By the advent of techno modernity, doll sizes were all over the place and were set to blow up soon into androids and fuck dollies. But where the toys are, whole scenes of object relationship can be set on loss. Toys indeed had just one available model at the time of child-hood's invention: only in mortuary palaces and necropolises had there been a simulation industry of functional parts of everyday life reduced in scale and durability for exclusive use by the dead alone. Behind the lines of doll accessories and all the other props of childhood's all-out miniaturization (always in the flimsy material of make-believe) of adults-only life, the small underworld after all of toys emerged.

Doyle's reflections on the visitations by the war dead to the home front pick up, down in the footnote underworld where his biography begins, a paternal frequency that was no proof against loss. Doyle's fa-ther, who was an artist, once drew a picture of hemlock. When I saw it, my free association went by way of the Faustian delegation of the pa-ternal legacy of one part medicine, one part poison that amounts to the paranoid reversal of the mother's gift of nourishment. Doyle created Sherlock, unmarried junkie and buster of Oedipal crimes that are all kept in some other safe place, save for his own partnership with Watson, who squeaks through the legacies like an embarrassment. The superego asks, "What son?!"

LECTURE TWENTY-FIVE

For the Rice trilogy, Nietzsche is our teacher. Nietzsche, in one of his anti-reactive modes or moods, gives us ultimately a mixed message about the hold of ideas and ideals over our material life.

> Ideas are worse seductresses than our senses, for all their cold and anemic appearance, and not even in spite of this appearance: they have lived on the "blood" of the philosopher, they always consumed his senses, and even, if you will believe us, his "heart." These old philosophers were heartless; philosophizing was always a kind of vampirism. . . . Do you not sense in the background, for a long time concealed, a vampire who, having begun by sucking out the senses, is left in the end with the mere skeleton and clatter of bones? I mean categories, formulas, *words*. . . . In sum: all philosophical idealism to date was something like a disease. (cited in Rickels, *Looking after Nietzsche*, 100)

This disease, which is now called philosophical idealism, now called vampirism is what we are going to be talking about. At that popularized end of Nietzsche, the baby booming of survivalism of all that fits, I mean that's fit, which is where the stakes of misreading prove to be life or death, Anton LaVey in his *Satanic Bible* devotes a whole section to psychic vampirism, the guiltification power of misfits, not unrelated, again, to the Nietzsche program — nor, in the miasma of middlebrow readings, to the Nazi pogrom.

On page 89 of *Interview with the Vampire* evil is declared to be a point of view, a perspective, one of many. Among the moral or extramoral imperatives that get bounced around between Nietzsche and Rice, the concept of good versus evil is a good one — to start with. The claim that evil reflects one way of looking at acts, speech, as allowed or not worthy already has the Nietzsche look.

Nietzsche argued that exchange and revenge are the oldest thoughts of mankind. Why is man so into the exchange value of revenge? Against what does he seek revenge? Well, ultimately, at the outer limit, according to Nietzsche in *Thus Spoke Zarathustra,* man seeks revenge against the "It Was" of time. The history of mankind can be played back as the scene of man gnashing teeth or fangs before this "It Was" of time's passing, which counts Father Time as always coming first and you as always in second place. It is no accident that Chronos got mixed up by chance with Kronos and castration.

But the revenge against time still fits right into the terms and contracts of family life. We are up to our eyeballs in all the Oedipal consequences. Nietzsche's example concerns what he calls the greatest revenge in history, the invention of Christian rights. This was one successful slave revolution of the tallest moral order. A whole hierarchy, tradition, and transmission could in effect be reversed. This reversal of charges is still with us — and with our spirits.

According to Nietzsche, good and evil are the headlines of Christian or slave morality. What preceded good and evil were the concepts of bad and good. Originally, when we had a more noble morality, whatever was good was well constituted with regard to aesthetic or functional rather than moral categories and properties. What is good, in this view, is well made; it functions well, serves its purpose, and so on. What was called bad, or *schlecht* (in German), was simply whatever did not function well, fell short, was aesthetically displeasing. These were not moral categories in the moralistic sense that whatever was bad (on the scale of the good, the bad, and the ugly) had to be internally (and that means eternally) condemned.

What happens then, according to Nietzsche's version of the one on one, is that the bad ones — in other words, the losers — had their revenge when they called what they were, which was real bad, good, and whatever was good — or well made — evil. They could not afford to get mad, so they got even. They turned it all around, just like children who must join and identify with the ones they cannot lick by a turn of the "and," by identification and projection. This was the primal revolution, and it took place within morality (and that also means, for our purposes, in the unconscious). The difference between good and bad gets reversed (or projected), and the concept of evil is introduced as the target of inner/outer condemnation. Through reversal (or projection) and internalization, whatever is good in every one of us is called evil: Christian love or mutual mass identification sacrifices a good deal of what is vital to the violence management it runs. Suffering is directed inward, against all that is odd, against ourselves: It is our fault. We are still riding out the aftershocks of that one.

Let's put the reversal back inside Freudian contexts of pleasure. In a world of aesthetic distinctions between functionally good and bad specimens, one could feel good being good. What the Christian revolution accomplished for violence control it organized against pleasure. Now you felt evil when you felt good. But, by an inversion that is still very much with us, that also means that being evil is what is so much fun, what feels so good, our flashes of guilt notwithstanding. Guilt just does not provide adequate protection against the pleasure mankind must take in being evil. This pleasure, more often than not, is a masochistic pleasure we take in the sadistic broadcasts of accusation and punishment that our conscience, the superego, issues from inside us, against us little fun-loving egos. We, the egos, are not allowed to get off, except via the superego's punishments.

We have asked ourselves, What is Louis's problem? The usual, please: melancholic retention of an at once murderous and idealized relationship. It is egotism at one end and visionary vulnerability at the other. He cannot survive his immortality, affirm the kill, affirm life; he cannot travel up the devil's road. Why? Because, like us Christians, secular, suckular, or otherwise, he cannot consume or commune without there being at the same time a sacrifice, a murder, an identification. He has that case of indigestion Nietzsche considered as the founding disposition or

dyspepsia of our culture: Christian resentment or revenge. The rese.
ful type (we know the type) cannot affirm life because he is at a loss,
the loss he cannot acknowledge but can only gag on. He has to get even,
overcome the loss or lack through equalization: the equal opportunity
of revenge.

How could good be turned into evil? First, you have to make the
good or well-constituted types swallow the inside view of themselves as
evil. You have to make everyone turn self-love into the fuel and futility
of self-criticism. The intake or insight is lubed societywide and in every
individual through the installment plan of guilt or, better yet, of a guilty
conscience. A whole history or program of internalization is required
so that the surprise witness, a God now on the side of the opposition
between good and evil, can be internalized, introduced as guarantee that
the good prototype will condemn itself as evil stereotype. The inside
view is that life is no longer, in the old sense, strong, good, or attractive,
is no longer enough in its own right, no longer self-sufficient or functional when it fulfills its conditions. Life gets dropped like a kind of excrement of death (that is Nietzsche's phrase). The violence that is out
there between masters and slaves, parents and children, professors and
students gets controlled up to a point through identification and projection. Violence control passes through us as mass culture. It is what
the Christian mass is all about. It is the mass identification that aims to
be a near miss in the target area and era of replacing (doubling and
containing) mass murder. In other words, Christianity had to cover its
ass, I mean mass. First it turned on the all-out urge to get even, but
then it had to control-release the same power surge in the masses to
keep them from going into the auto-destruct mode.

Nietzsche restricts his take on Christianity to appreciation of the
mass hygiene it accomplished for quite some time (although he gives
Buddhism the higher score on this count). With the new Christian morality, a mass culture could be invented, one in which the masses would
become a body, the body or bond celebrated in the Christian mass. How
is mass culture constituted? Nietzsche says: out of and only out for re-

ngefulness or violence that can go out of control at any
y Nietzsche gives the ascetic priests of early Christianity
r redirecting, rerouting mass resentment. So that man-
destroy itself, a priest was necessary to control mass
vengetulness. The devaluation of the present and of materiality and the
pustulation, I mean postulation of a better afterlife were part of the
service dedicated to these ends. But at the end of centuries of saying no
to life, we are left (leftover) with nothing. Remember, I talked about the
witness and man's addiction to finding his suffering meaningful. That
is the only way suffering can be survived. The suffering that is truly unbearable is meaningless suffering. Man's desire or drive is to seek meaning. Or you could call it will itself; man wills; he is a willing animal. And
the aim of that will is always some kind of meaningfulness. Now at the
end of this history of saying no to life, man is unwilling to cease willing, unwilling to cease seeking meaning, and so he wills nothingness
instead. After centuries of finding meaning in everything, or in something or other, man goes for finding meaning in nothing. So Nietzsche
warned that as a result of this history, monsters of nihilism would arise,
thus giving us his forecast of Nazism and every other mass cultural event
that would be in sync with total war, war that is strictly speaking suicidal. Nihilism, conceived as suicidal impulse, is the final outgrowth of
internalization: the witness has gone down and out. That we all go at
the same time, this synchronization of all our deaths at once, is part of
the witness protection program, the witness identification and projection program.

Now away from this historywide or societywide perspective and back
to the family. We started out by saying that man's vengefulness is directed ultimately against time itself or against the "It Was" of time, which
means sequential time, time that moves according to the one line that,
by law, can never be crossed or reversed. Nietzsche puts it along these
lines in *Zarathustra*: it is immensely difficult, if not impossible, to be a
child, an heir, always secondary to the father. The father is that higher
authority who will always have come before (also when it comes to
mother). Linear time is our losing streak. How can the father's author-

ity be reversed? How can the father, or father time, be overcome? Well, Nietzsche's counterthought was, what if time isn't always giving us a line? What if time is also at the same time always on the rebound, surfs up, or Eternal Return of the Same.

The Eternal Return builds up in the maternal bond with your own body (which *is* her body). On our own person we encounter the return of the same by feeling or listening to the pounding of the heart, the cycling of our blood, the rhythm of our breathing. But we must listen to it from a distance inscribed onto the body as limit, as off-limits. Eternal Return asks the overman in or among us, all of us over-and-out men, to stand up and affirm life in spite of the suffering without meaning, witness, or end. We are all bad, poorly constituted, when encountering an unmournable loss. But is the projective idealism of good versus evil the only way, in truth, to go when we cannot let the goner go? Where there's will there's a way to say to the big picture of all that happens to us, Thus I willed it. This affirmative "action" thus says to life, just as you have endured it, up until now, disappointment after disappointment, final exam after midterm: Come again, return, and return eternally. That is the extent of my affirmation.

Freud's revalorization of mourning picks up its own eternal and internal flame from the Nietzschean challenge. Freud admits that mourning is the hardest thing in life to do, but it is now more than ever the most necessary task if life—not the life of some family but the life, Freud underscores, of civilization—is to continue. Mourning, we have seen, exists as an isolatable experience and one goal away from the melancholic impasse. But mourning also cannot help but overlap with melancholia. Each either contaminates the other. The injunction to mourn and substitute makes sense. But our egos do not want to go and do not want to let go. Our mass-media sensurround of technological expansionism and internalization celebrates the melancholia and mania of this refusal, this re-fusing with a loss that gets lost, over and over again.

So the work of mourning must even mourn over the merely substitutive, integrative, and murderous moment in every work of mourning. Thus, we both mourn and unmourn. And we rise to the occasion of affirming the eternal return of the same life over and over again, just for the sake of affirming life in the inevitable fuck face of death. We learn to *live* with our ghosts rather than only die with or for them.

So we can say that since the beginning of time, we have been following out a couple of time schemes. There is the time scheme of the father, the order or command performance of substitution down the line of time—and this time scheme seems to have been the predominant model or measure of civilization's advance over the ages. But we also have flashbacks to maternal cyclical conceptions of the blood type celebrated in the earliest periods of prehistory. But there is no turning back once we have started coming down the line, the line of tradition, of transmission of the name, the line of literacy, the line of mourning. Nietzsche's point about the eternal return was formulated, like his notion of the overman, as an experiment, one to be performed for our survival. That is because, again, the witness cannot be guaranteed. For us today it is impossible to give the witness credit or, same word, belief. We have come too far down the line, the direct line to the truth. And the truth is there is nothing out there giving us the meaningful context, the paranoid comfort, of being watched. Our legacy of father time seems to have promoted several dangerous phantasms at once. Phantasms of total exchange, for example. What would a total exchange look like? An exchange without remainder, an exchange without difference, an equality without difference? At the other end of our preoccupation with exchange and revenge it is getting even, wipeout, that rules us absolutely. What could it mean to dedicate everything to nothing? It would end in mass suicide, the mass the Christian mass had sought to control only by control-releasing it, the mass that in secular culture music and theater sought to control in the group experience of witnessing, and the mass that mass-media music, like Lestat's Death Rock, would recover down the corridors of simulation, liveness, and solitary consumerism.

When three's a crowd—of ghosts—we are talking about a repression of the disruption of exchange, a foreclosure of the moment of station break and word from the sponsor, which otherwise constitutes the possibility of exchange. How does exchange take place? Exchange requires two to play the requested hit of reciprocity. You give something so that you will also get it or something else back in exchange. The gift is given so that you will receive it or its equivalent when it is your turn. But there are no real guarantees that this reciprocal exchange will come full circle. So if you just think about it for a moment, every exchange takes place in the name of something else, in the name of some other, a third party, a third personal pronoun even, and thus in the name of God, the Law, the father. So there has to be some guarantor, in the name of which the gift is exchanged, to insure that the exchange will be reciprocal. Now in the register of pronouns, we can recast what we have already said about the so-called mirror stage: "You" and "I" describe the relationship between mother and infant. Between "you" and "I" a third person must emerge: the Law, the father: he, she, it. So right from the start the exchange of pleasure or satisfaction that goes on one-on-one (in other words, with the mother's body) must address itself, in the first place, to father, the Law. Instead of pleasure, instead of feeling good, feeling good about ourselves, instead of feeling good being or doing good, we face instead, right from the start, the Law of pleasure and the Law of the good. That means that right from the start there are no objects, no bodies for our direct enjoyment or pleasure; our own body, remember, is not our own — it belongs to mother — mother's body is the only one around (but it is off-limits). There are only words, the delegates of the law, the messengers of time, only words to which materiality has already been sacrificed. The material or the maternal must by law be sacrificed to words.

In other words, we are left facing the Law; right from the start we face the Law, we are before the Law. And of course the mother is excluded. What remains up to this point is sadomasochism. What is the aim or desire of the other in demanding our sacrifice of pleasure? It is the way pleasure, shoved right up against the Oedipus complex, gets distributed. It is then always the other, the third party that gets off. And what does the other, the father, the father-god, the Law — what does this other enjoy? He, she, it enjoys our lack of enjoyment. The only joy taken is taken in evil or in the fact of this life — that we don't get no satisfaction. The superego, whatever you want to call it — god, father, the Law — the superego is sadistic. You and I, body and ego, are masochistic. And that is the Law of pleasure.

LECTURE TWENTY-SIX

Reflecting the transition from the feel for killing as affirmation of life to the consumer-protected search for substitute measures for sucking unto death or even for surrogates for the blood is the life, the vampire heroine in *Innocent Blood* protests, even while caught in a compromise, her innocence too much by half. Yes, she feels guilty about her feeding times. That is why she restricts her diet to asshole crooks. But her volunteer disposal service goes beyond the call of the past or part that is played out, the casting call of bit-part players, and takes on and in the whole underworld. The vampire's etiquette fits the isolated one-on-one encounters she formerly specialized in: don't play with the food and don't leave any around and left over. She follows the rule when she finds a Mafia boss, but his garlicky blood knocks her attack out of whack. She infects him but must flee his gunfire before she can finish him off. The boss dies and is reborn bored with what he once thought was food. He holds down his new intake at the home of his lawyer, played by Rickles. The doubly underworld leader grows pangs and fangs of hunger, goes for raw meat and, next step, for what is behind the good smells emanating from the host. Rickles gets vampirized. But his comeback in the hospital is just in time for the nurse's rounds. She pulls the curtains for him, and it is a slice of light that blasts him into sludge, forever dead. He never got to feed. He was vampire just for a morning, for mourning.

The cop joins forces with the vampire, who is not a cold-blooded killer like the underworld mobsters, and then joins her in bed, where his intercourse turns on the orgasmic light show in her eyes for the first time without recourse to feeding.

In the wake of the Rickles wipeout, the undead boss starts re-creating his "family" in the transference of the scratch that gave him his restart to the necks of kin. But even after the duo forces the new underworld into rest, the vampire cannot take the killing any more, can only take it in. She walks in the sunrise to die. But she cops the surprise of unlife when her police pal tells her he loves her. But: "I take lives." "If you were perfect, you wouldn't still be single." She makes it finally to Voice-over, the narrative's articulation without seeing or feeding: "He made me feel alive. So, I said, why not?" Her own sexual comeback replaces the need to feed. Or, in other terms, the distinction between what is good and not so good to eat is no longer so blurred. Via the suicidal turn inward of the passion for precision-loving and killing, the vampire gets re-released as the new species of friend.

We are reaching an end.

What we have been pushing is an inside view of nihilism as the direct hit of Christianity, as the outcome of a belief or credit system that has its own inflation and depression built right into it.

Lestat says that he does not believe in anything, which is quite different from believing in nothing. He also clarifies or classifies in conversation with his mother that as far as the notion of the good goes, he recognizes that being good for him is being a good vampire, being good at killing. The vampires who have gone before him and who have made him their heir speak always in terms of aesthetic qualities and categories. Remember with what care Marius stipulates that Christianity has nothing to do with vampirism; vampirism is older, it dates back to the aesthetic order.

When we stopped, undead in our tracks, in the previous lecture, I was talking about revenge and exchange. I was talking, in effect, about revenge and thus, in exchange, about nihilism, our big problem, the problem of modern man, something that Gabrielle evokes again and again. She is the heroine of Eternal Return. She has visions of the nihilism to come; she is the one who has an almost visceral response (as in, Gag me) to Christianity and its delegations, all the way down to nihilism. The problem to be overcome, which the vampires pose as the problem of viving one's immortality, is also at closer range the problem of killin time, of course. Killing time is what is bringing our era right down to the finish line.

Before we get back to that point, let me tune in *The Vampire Lestat* for a moment because it manages to play back the whole history of vampirism (which happens to be the genealogy of our own unconscious) right down (on page 265) to the relocation of graves in the Age of Reason. The coven, which inhabits an underworld in which all of Christianity's reservations are confirmed, is doomed in any case, Armand finds out, because now in the eighteenth century Paris has decided to relocate the graves and move the stench of death to the outside. And the Théâtre des Vampires, the last stage of Christianity (which opens, ultimately, onto nihilism) was erected upon the former catacomb space of belief in God and Satan. Please notice that the coven's move above ground founds the theater's displaced sense of audience.

Armand, as leader of the coven, does not really believe in the props and superstitions that he uses to keep the people in line; he believes (rather like a hygienist, like the ascetic priest in Nietzsche's analysis) that people need certain accessories in order to survive. His task too is to lead his people to a measure or mode of survival of their immortality. So Armand (on page 288) cannot live without guidance, or rather he recognizes that what he identifies with, as the masses cannot do without opinion or faith. Thus, he stages resurrection rituals for his vampire followers, who through live burial get an inside view: knowledge is obtainable only through that consumerism that adds suffering or sacrifice for the delectation of some eternal, internal witness who likes to watch the suffering.

Gabrielle and Lestat point to the complications that arise when one is on the other side of this belief, when one chooses to live without belief or guidance, or tries to live in recognition of the missingness of God. Gabrielle puts it this way: "If God does not exist, if these things are not unified into one metaphorical system, then why do they retain for us such symbolic power. Why does the symbolic power or the effect problem to be overcome, which the vampires pose as the problem of surviving one's immortality, is also at closer range the problem of killing time, of course. Killing time is what is bringing our era right down to the finish line.

Before we get back to that point, let me tune in *The Vampire Lestat* for a moment because it manages to play back the whole history of vampirism (which happens to be the genealogy of our own unconscious) right down (on page 265) to the relocation of graves in the Age of Reason. The coven, which inhabits an underworld in which all of Christianity's reservations are confirmed, is doomed in any case, Armand finds out, because now in the eighteenth century Paris has decided to relocate the graves and move the stench of death to the outside. And the Théâtre des Vampires, the last stage of Christianity (which opens, ultimately, onto nihilism) was erected upon the former catacomb space of belief in God and Satan. Please notice that the coven's move above ground founds the theater's displaced sense of audience.

Armand, as leader of the coven, does not really believe in the props and superstitions that he uses to keep the people in line; he believes (rather like a hygienist, like the ascetic priest in Nietzsche's analysis) that people need certain accessories in order to survive. His task too is to lead his people to a measure or mode of survival of their immortality. So Armand (on page 288) cannot live without guidance, or rather he recognizes that what he identifies with, as the masses cannot do without opinion or faith. Thus, he stages resurrection rituals for his vampire followers, who through live burial get an inside view: knowledge is obtainable only through that consumerism that adds suffering or sacrifice for the delectation of some eternal, internal witness who likes to watch the suffering.

Gabrielle and Lestat point to the complications that arise when one is on the other side of this belief, when one chooses to live without belief or guidance, or tries to live in recognition of the missingness of God. Gabrielle puts it this way: "If God does not exist, if these things are not unified into one metaphorical system, then why do they retain for us such symbolic power. Why does the symbolic power or the effect of divinity continue even in the wake of a recognition that he is gone" (288). Gift giving is an at once cultural and grammatical example of the reference to a third power. Already built into the economy of our grammar, there is always going to be a third party, a witness, a guarantor who will cosign each and every one of our exchanges, or as Nietzsche put it to us: "If we are in fact to be rid of God, we must first slay grammar." Or, put differently, as long as there are fathers, families, incest taboos, and unconscious commissions of incest, "the effect of divinity" (as Gabrielle puts it) will continue. God is not just some extraneous idea or hallucination that can be wiped off the horizon; he is already one of the family, part of the language that is for or against him. Together with the third-person position of divinity, it is dematerialization, our blocked but hungry relations with the body, our body, the mother's body, that is also the preconditioning for our being in language, signs, images, media.

The recognition in *The Vampire Lestat* and in Nietzsche that God is dead is not the end of a problem but only the beginning, because if He can be said or seen to be dead, then the divine corpse out there on the horizon contaminates all circulation systems with its decay. How are we to be rid of this corpse of God?

On page 381, after Lestat has separated vampirism from Christianity and from nihilism, Marius praises Lestat as someone who is on the way to the "overman." Remember, the overman or superman is the experiment—almost a laboratory experiment—that will produce a being who, in the wake of God and of man (as God the Father knew him best), will have the strength to live without belief support systems and will be able to affirm life, even suffering, without witness or any other related guarantor of meaningfulness.

That is why to begin with we created gods, superegos, and all the other internalizations and externalizations that keep us in check and keep us for a time from checking out. Because we cannot stand to suffer pointlessly, we would rather will nothingness, will our own mass suicide, than suffer without the other taking notes or all the pleasure. Suicide, mass suicide in particular, serves as ultimate example of trying to get meaning out of nothing (or meaning for nothing).

So the innocence of Lestat (the innocence that Marius describes on page 381) has to do with his godlessness, his not giving in to false grief for something supposed to be lost. False grief covers the way time or history has been conceived all along in terms either of nostalgia's rewind or of the fast-forward march to some afterlife-sized paradise. False grief for what is supposed to be lost: that is something Lestat has moved away from, toward an absence of the need for illusions.

I have already talked about Gabrielle and Lestat's advocacy of Many Eternal Returns. They conjure up a truly realized evil, not really in order to advocate it, however, but in order to pose the problem that I keep coming back to: the problem or project of the overman, which requires, it turns out, a thinking through of crime, of transgression, of what Lestat calls the Devil's road. Only by thinking through to the outside of the family, to the outside of a society based on the family, is there a chance for some other option, some way around this nothingness. And you will find on page 335 and again on page 509 Lestat's prediction that mankind is out to destroy itself, something he has read in "stories of the ugly nihilistic men of the twentieth century."

Pleasure in the order of time, the ordering around by the father, the takeout orders of substitution, of mourning, and so on—what we have based or staked our civilization on up to this point—all that has made what is left of pleasure masochism at our end and sadism on the side of the other, the Law, the superego.

The order of Law and language is driven by our exclusions or repressions, is driven by the unconscious. Remember—and remember to forget—that whatever we repress is never lost but becomes a kind of secret fuel (destrudo is one of its names) stored in what is called the unconscious; repression drives us. We do not get done with anything by repressing it, we simply put it in the fuel tank that propels us in certain directions that we do not, consciously, control. We leave the driving to the unconscious.

What continues to gather momentum as we are fueled by our own repressions is the drive to sacrifice. In talking about our culture as fundamentally one of revenge and exchange, I already brought us before the altar of sacrifice where mass resentment or vengefulness is kept from destroying at random everything in sight.

Remember how in *Vampyr* and in many other texts that we talked about before, it was the father function, the dead father, the symbolic father, the guarantor of the Law, of language, of abstract thought, it was this figure who kept our metabolism from shutting down grief-stuck. It was he who dislodged the corpses that we might otherwise hold on to and, by modeling substitution and mourning, kept us going, kept life going, kept a kind of desire going. But now at the Nietzsche and Rice end of things, we find that it went, all right — speeding toward a mass grave. The paternal order has reached a dead end: the end of Dad.

Now on the sidelines of paternal culture (and we have already become acquainted with this subculture, but we have talked about it in different terms, keeping to the terms of successful or unsuccessful mourning) again we find vampirism, but we find it affirmed by Rice as a place where an alternative may be coming soon. Now consider (around page 440) how vampirism comes into being according to the vampire mythology in *The Vampire Lestat* (and in *The Queen of the Damned,* which fine-tunes and gives in stereo, via the twins, the prehistory and origin of vampirism that was first revealed in *Lestat*). The primal vampire parents (Those Who Must Be Kept) started out as the mortal proponents of burial and preservation of dead bodies through mummification, which they introduced over and against the more primal corpse disposal system of cannibalistic funeral feasting. But already there was a division: one peaceful community governed by inside-out connections with spirits devoured their dead only; it was their communal sacred duty: The people of the Nile valley, in contrast, were cannibals through and through, not only consuming their dead but also hunting down their enemies for nourishment. The time came that it was the first time a king of the Nile valley people had to marry outside the family (and even outside his people) to continue the royal line of descent, which was not

only an incestuous one but also the female kind (which, same difference, is the maternal one and only). This new bride from the outside
introduces the ban on cannibalism of the dead or alive. The dead were
to be embalmed and wrapped up as quickly as possible to keep their
mourners from getting to the flesh. It was now to be believed that the
preserved body was the deceased's ticket to a better life in the afterlife.
Thus, the lack of consumption of the dead was not meant to represent
disrespect but rather infinite, that is, idealizing respect; mummification
puts the corpse up there and untouchable, out of reach of the death
wishes that threaten its safekeeping. Spirits soon pose a problem to the
new regime: Death-wish management is at an all time low. The royal
couple is murdered, and their dying bodies are taken over by the hunger
of spirits or demons turned up full blast by mummification, by the interruption of the cannibalistic feast. These royals were the first techno
bodies. But Akasha just had to be everybody's mummy.

Vampirism comes about through the hunger of demons. Demons
are on the loose; demons have always been on the loose since the beginning of time, and they crave a body. That is what drives them. Demons —
craving a body, craving a pleasure that is perpetually denied them —
invade the blood supplies, which thus become contaminated with a
demonic hunger for the always missing direct bloodline to the body.

Given all that we have said so far, we can also say that these demons
are also always us. These demons are creatures of language without bodies. Demons that are driven by a desire for a satisfaction they will never
get: there we are. Vampirism achieves a pleasure that is purely intellectual, and this intellectual pleasure aims at that infinite pleasure obtainable
through language's alliance with the imagination. On page 378, Marius
defends speech, for example, as the greatest mortal gift, as a kind of
model of the dark gift. What is lost as the demons enter the body is
everything that otherwise makes up a body. What is fueled by the de-
mon-run blood is the brain and the heart. That is how it is put.

In this vampiric subculture (which seems more like a remake of our
situation, a bringing to consciousness of our condition, than it seems
an alternative unlife style) still something is lost. The body is lost; that

is quite clear in the discussion of the demon invasion. The body is left behind. But which body? It is the body as limit, which is not run up against but crossed over. Vampirism thus seeks to obtain the greatest pleasure, the release of all pleasures, by erecting one Law, it seems, and that Law requires that incest be committed. This is the counter-Law of vampirism. And it is aimed against the family. Our society, the defective paternal order, is held together by one Law, the prohibition of incest; the vampiric counter-Law commands incest.

The body, your body, every body, is the maternal body. The body is the mother. By declaring the mother off-limits, the body has been declared off-limits. Which is why it is the limit—of pleasure. But vampirism, by making incest into the law, leaves behind the body-as-limit, the body-as-off-limits. Once the ultimate requirement has been fulfilled, the injunction to get it over with already, a whole range of pleasure where no bodily pleasure had gone before is opened up by the alliance between the imagination and language, which inhibitions (trained or rehearsed on the body from early infancy on down inside the Oedipal family pack) have kept unconscious. That is why vampirism does not follow some policy issued beyond or before language of back to nature (or back to the body). Once you have entered language (and we always do enter and will have entered language), there is no way back. There is no way the inevitable phrases *and* phases of our early development can be surmounted. Even though the infant does not speak, little one is spoken. That is one way the superego gets installed. The radical solution or satisfaction is to inhabit language's forced entry to the point of getting the most out of it, even maybe of getting around or beyond it, but from within. So how do you get as much pleasure as you can from being within language? You get beyond the body as limit or as off-limits, and you achieve the deliberate, conscious reception of the truly pleasurable alliance, the one that comes between the imagination and language: That is what the vampiric kill is all about. And that is why from our point of view it translates into an affirmation of life and even of substitution beyond the longing for or the murder of a lost love.

At the time of Lestat's Théâtre des Vampires the family unit, and with it the Oedipus Complex, was being put on as one of our modern stagings. The family has values because it is so exclusive. Since the Age of Reason, the age or stage on which Lestat builds himself up as the over-antibody, everything considered outside — illness, madness, asocial status, crime, melancholia, you name it — gets kept outside with regard to the family. And how is this family unit held together? Well, it is held together by incest, that is, it is held together unconsciously by the incest taboo. What is the point to an unconsciously desired or committed incest? Its point is that it holds the family together through guilt, through the various accumulating guilt accounts of the family members. Repressed desires drive the family's holding patterns. For vampirism, then, incest is not kept unconscious, is not repressed, is not allowed to function as a repressed desire; in fact it does not even serve specifically as a desire. It is the Law, simply. With incest as the Law the paternal order has been undermined at the same time as it has been achieved: the vampiric affirmation even embraces substitution but without fulfilling it as filler. Every body is made infinitely available to everybody else. The body that is unlimited is at the same time let go from one busy intersection between flights of fantasy and language. Vampiric blood fuels the pleasure to be had unbound by the body as limit. That is why vampires are polymorphously perverse. There are no sexual orientations along this maternal line. There is not even bisexuality. There is, in short, for vampires no sexual identity (the other cornerstone of the family unit or unity).

I wanted you to see the trajectory that Rice's vampirism is trying to plan and program. She aims to think through problems that are as old as culture, problems that seem increasingly to come due in a century — at least according to *The Vampire Lestat* — doubled over with desire for its own destruction.

On pages 344 and 355 we find examples of the family nevertheless intruding on vampirism. Nicky's fate, remember, to be amputated before being destroyed, was already forecast, Lestat sadly recognizes, when his father threatened to cut off his hands when he played the violin too much. All this playing with hands refers ultimately to the fiddling about of infantile masturbation, but I will leave that on the side. In any event, we have here the total castrative paternal scenario, which jump-cuts from incest to destination or destiny even within vampirism. Lestat's lament: "When will there be a beyond, when will we reach beyond the family unit?" Or when he loses Gabrielle, around page 355, he wonders "Hadn't I already lost her? Hadn't she already been off-limits before I welcomed her to vampirism? Isn't this always and already the same familial broadcast that I seem in my vampirism only to be able to reissue?" (I have been paraphrasing here.)

Everything we have said about where vampirism wants to go means that vampirism must also try to rethink violence control, identification, and sacrifice — from the other side. The usual scenario is that violence control works up to a certain point and then, down the line, it breaks down. The law of the father, the law of the couple and of the family line, breaks down and no longer functions. What happens then when the law breaks down is melancholic conflict, reciprocal violence, civil war, sibling against sibling, double against double. But this kind of war also always grows and exceeds itself until it becomes total war (which, like nuclear war, always amounts to mass suicide). But in order to control the violence that is always there, social units and unities continue to depend on the sacrifice that is part of identification's program precisely because every identification is an inoculative or introductory offering and ordering of violence.

Why is it that rock music or modern mass music is turned up as the one crowded channel Lestat wants to tune in and turn into? We should be pleased, having already been programmed to recognize it, that on pages 515 and 550 Marius puts the living dead couple, the origin of vampirism, in a crypt packed with the most advanced extensions of the human sensorium. And it is through the technical media, with music video at the front of the screen, that Akasha is turned on, reanimated.

Music has always been the primal mass medium. But what would a history of music that would line up with the histories we have already talked about look like? In the eighteenth century, the Age of Reason, the Age of Lestat, music sets itself up as a secularized alternative to the Christian mass (which had included, as with all sacrifice, its own musical accompaniment). But when Lestat comes back to life, we are in or on a later stage of music, the stage of what can be called a culture of repetition, where even Lestat's live concert has the status of a recording. Everything is recording; that which is spontaneously performed in person is only "live" in quotation marks — those marks that the vampire makes on the neck, right below the earphones.

Music has always been a form of noise control, control, that is, of the audio portion and equivalent of violence. With every scene of sacrifice imaginable, what plays in the background? Music, of course. In the foreground, musically covered, are noisy grindings and screamings of torture machines and their victims. By the virtue of what it accomplishes against or with noise, music, which is always background music, covers and controls the scene of sacrifice and helps push back the automatic escalation of unlimited violence.

So music represents and originates with scenes of sacrifice, and increasingly in the age of musical repetition, we are all locked via earphones and walkmen onto the boom of this scene of sacrifice as solitary (maybe even autistic) participants in a network of relations of identification that are increasingly individualized and purchasable. In the era of representation, music filled air time as communal event; it was an event in which audition and performance were accomplished together as a group. Now every performance is the playback of the already recorded hit. And while each consumer of music is thus isolated, each one is also a group of one. The overisolation of each listener is the franchise expansion of the group. And we, solo, between our earphones, jacked into the audio portion of scenes of violence and sacrifice, only have time left — to purchase these recordings. And our purchase power piles up recordings we will never have time left to listen to. It is a form of stockpiling. We stockpile recordings; we stockpile, in other words, our social relations — the social relations that come complete with the sacrificial or identificatory bonding of violence or noise control that is what listening to music accomplishes or contains. One ultimate model of this stockpiling was the Cold War nuclear stockpile. Only mass suicide could release us from an accumulation of violence controls that we would never have time to listen to or obey. Even though some of the terms of the contract have been renegotiated, suicide is still the live broadcast that heads us off at the impasse underneath a weight of waiting around, killing time, never catching up or getting even.

At some removed point of every Californian's circle or network of friends and family, there is always an overlap with the orbits of serial killers, mass murderers, Hollywood and rock stars, channelers, witches. Every time the chopping spree of modern mass and serial murder has come up for report and discussion in these lectures, there have always been "I was there" near-miss victims in attendance who almost got into the killer's car, almost went with the local flight that was detonated, almost were raised in Jonestown. But in the drive-by encounter or nonencounter between Wilson and Manson, a high beam gets thrown onto the difference between a group in which violence control more or less succeeds and the one where the members go down with the group's spectacular failure. British analyst Wilfred Bion once remarked that the natural-born leader of the group is always its biggest baby or, in other words, a psycho. Manson tried to hold his family together by externalizing all tensions as mass violence, a violence that would contain itself by spreading, by coming out in the wash of blood. Thus, the misspelling in blood of the Beatles title Helter Skelter as "Healter Skelter" at the murder site lets slip the all-out purpose of healing or controlling the violence at the heart of every group formation. Uncontained by the noise control of the music culture that would not admit him and his guitar—like Hitler, Manson just wanted to be an artist—a deranged father or brother raced to the finish line on death drive, the drive that always takes over a group when all else fails. It is the insurance policy of groups.

As leader of his band or family, Brian Wilson took down inspirations or hauntings across a distance that his brother Dennis occupied, libidinized, and brought back as materials for Brian's embodiment-building of songs. Dennis was a self-destructive surf bum. Brian, whose intake of toxicity was ultimately inoculative, and sacrificially so, survived on the life he was granted through his seeing eyes, his brother. Brian was terrified of water, surf, the beach. But he metabolized those same materials as mediated by his brother in the terms of the latest in technicity. The other inspiration took flight above the beach. Look at any history of surf pop (look at *Beach Blanket Bingo*): all the surfer musicians were into aerodynamics, the horizon of their training, their careers, in California. But after Brian broke with his abusive father, he broke down in-flight, en route to the Land Down Under, under a sudden excess of fear of flying. This was his psychotic break. What followed was the team effort of keeping him low maintenance, in the more or less steady state of ongoing recovery. And then brother Dennis could die, by drunk drowning, in realization of his brother's biggest fears for himself, which are, as always, in first place fears or wishes for the other.

As technical medium rock music starts out by playing back the tapes of total war. It made music out of radio frequencies aired first during World War II. The basic vibes of rock culture were first used to guide and track the transmission of bombs filling the air time of the Battle of Britain. As the Rolling Stones admit it in their sympathy, as rock musicians, with the devil: they were indeed already there "when the Blitzkrieg raged." At the close of *The Vampire Lestat*, Lestat's rock lyrics issue open invitation to total warfare on one devil of a wavelength.

The legacy of war transmitted through rock culture turns on *The Queen of the Damned*, both Rice's third vampire novel and the figure of Akasha, the undead matriarch of vampirism. In the war of suicide the Queen proposes, taking her inspiration and new re-lease on life from Lestat's music videos, even vampires must explode, just like nuclear incidents. With Akasha we thus encounter a return of revenge culture, the returns on a culture of exchange, even right at the heart of the worldwide web of vampirism. Re-released from a crypt of concealment and preservation, Akasha launches her own solution to the problems life poses in the register of meaningfulness, one designed to bring peace (that's right: rest in peace) to humanity. She wants to be the witness because she needs to believe that the accident that turned her into a vampire was meaningful, for the good: " 'For surely such a thing cannot happen without a reason' " (365).

Not to be outdone by Hitler (who was a vegetarian lover of dogs and who saw himself as the ultimate humanitarian), Akasha is a humanitarian too and an idealist through and through. And that means that what she has in mind is so ideal it is dead. She proposes a show of godlike power that will bring down the house of witnessing. The power of destruction is aimed at all those interruptions, triangulations, mediations that we associate with paternity, and that for her, vampire mother of the mirror stage, come down to violence or castration. That is why, at the end, the work of mourning over a dead mother (which Akasha had repressed or held back just a heartbeat before becoming, by this accident, the first vampire) is released when the twin mourners are reunited over Akasha's decapitated body. The mourning ritual that Akasha had prevented, the funereal feasting on the mother's brain and heart, can at last be consummated, this time around with the brain and heart of Akasha, the mother of the twins' rebirth as vampires.

Akasha thus ends up the corpus she would not let the twins put to rest when she first severed their bond with the mediums or demons. Akasha created the myth of Osiris and Isis and the conveyor cult of exquisite mummies, the dual legacy of immortality and mass suicide, in order to package in some meaningful way the so-called dark gift—the power and the poison of ambivalence.

Akasha became the undead mother, monstrously reanimated by the demon death wishes. It therefore is no accident that Akasha is turned into a vampire. She needs divine witness protection against admission of her own ambivalence. She just has to believe that her gods intervened to save her from the attacking demon and that they in turn divinized her. Six thousand years later she is out to stake her claim as goddess over the condemned body of the impure or violent half of humanity. But even at its origin vampirism, the instant it started replicating itself, produced a breed immune to Akasha's good will to meaning and power. Khayman, on whom Akasha performed the scientific experiment of her vampiric ability to confer her new status on others, passed his undeath on to the twins, who accepted the dark gift in order to counter or contain, in the slow time of inoculation, the unmourning-becomes-suicide drive that Akasha embodied.

For six thousand years one twin, Maharet, who, before becoming another vampire in order to contain the toxic spill at the origin of the vampire mummy, gave birth to a daughter named after the mother she and her twin sister had been kept from mourning, has been reorganizing humanity around the Great Family, her own ongoing allegiance to human living on through substitution and procreation (and death). The family she raises out of her mortal bloodline grows interrelated and thus coextensive with mankind. So, it is this family that Akasha threatens at its substitutive heart. Her nonviolence is pure violence: to create absolute peace on earth the contaminant that is violence must be removed. This desire for purity *is* the suicidal impulse. Because pure violence, like nonviolence, is the attempt to separate violence from life. And that is violence. Her ultimate wish is to get rid of death. But she cannot perform that service. All she can do is increase the dosage of death as though thus controlling the factor of risk and randomness that is the hallmark of the other, of the future, of life. It is the sacrifice to end all sacrifice, the war to end all wars, all over and over again. But each attempt to bring violence full circle short-circuits and marks the origin of the greatest violence in the backfire of the most radical measures of violence control.

But Akasha is destroyed, and the vampires survive the closing of her rule of vampiric transmissions. The twins perform the mourning ceremony and thus restore their blood, which flows through humanity, to the vampiric line, originally one of unmourning, now the other one of mourning work. The blood bond that linked all vampires to the demons inside Akasha was a one-way techno circuit. As Maharet explains, " 'We are as receptors for the energy of this being; as radios are receptors for the invisible waves that bring sound. Our bodies are no more than shells for this energy'" (385).

A hard shell is made thus for linear time, the time that puts us on the line, the deadline, the one that lines us up into oppositions. Akasha rides out the invisible waves to the front line of total war: gender versus gender, mother versus father, blood drinker versus breeder. But the energy system Maharet describes might also be reconceived as a web of more circular kinds of connectedness.

At the end, Maharet asks Akasha to give humans and unhumans alike the one thing she *can* give, other than death. She cannot give life and cannot take death away. Why doesn't she give time, rather than kill it? But she cannot give herself up to the randomness, the uncontrollability, of the other. She can only give them the line about purity or mass destruction. But the stranglehold of linear time that has her on the line cuts her off too at the instant that it comes full circle with the twins. What we, vampires and nonvampires alike, are given at the end of *The Queen of the Damned* is time. Nothing more or less. Certainly nothing changes: the violence that is life, that is in life, continues in Lestat's rule-busting power surges.

So, we are left with time, and that means with the relationship to the other, who is the future, the time that comes toward us. It is the time it takes to think or take pleasure in making imagination and words come together. The time it takes to come full circle, to heal. Because that is the one time that one must take one's time to take the time it takes. It's the time of mourning. And now it's time.

REFERENCES

Abraham, Karl. "A Short History of the Development of the Libido, Viewed in the Light of Mental Disorders" [1924]. Pages 418–501 in *Selected Papers of Karl Abraham*, vol. 2, trans. Douglas Bryan and Alix Strachey. New York: Basic Books, 1960.

Abraham, Nicolas, and Maria Torok. "Introjection-Incorporation: Mourning or Melancholia." In *Psychoanalysis in France*, ed. Serge Lebovici and Daniel Widlöcher. New York: International Universities Press, 1980.

Adorno, Theodor, and Max Horkheimer. *Dialectic of Enlightenment*. Trans. John Cumming. New York: Herder and Herder, 1972.

Ariès, Philippe. *Western Attitudes toward Death: From the Middle Ages to the Present*. Trans. Patricia M. Ranum. Baltimore: Johns Hopkins University Press, 1974.

Attali, Jacques. *Noise: The Political Economy of Music*. Trans. Brian Massumi. Minneapolis: University of Minnesota Press, 1985.

Barber, Paul. *Vampires, Burial, and Death: Folklore and Reality*. New Haven: Yale University Press, 1988.

Baring-Gould, Sabine. *The Book of Were-Wolves: Being an Account of a Terrible Superstition*. New York: Causeway Books, 1973.

Barker, Clive. "Human Remains" [1984]. Pages 3–43 in *The Mammoth Book of Vampires*, ed. Stephen Jones. New York: Carroll and Graf, 1992.

Barrie, J. M. *Peter Pan*. New York: Signet Classic, 1987 [1911].

Bazin, André. "The Ontology of the Photographic Image." Pages 9–16 in *What Is Cinema*, vol. 1, trans. Hugh Gray. Berkeley: University of California Press, 1967.

Benjamin, Walter. *Illuminations: Essays and Reflections*. Trans. Harry Zohn. New York: Schocken Books, 1969.

Benson, E. F. "Mrs. Amworth" [1920]. Pages 235–48 in *The Dracula Book of Great Vampire Stories*, ed. Leslie Shepard. Secaucus, N.J.: Citadel Press, 1977.

——. "The Room in the Tower" [1912]. Pages 187–98 in *The Dracula Book of Great Vampire Stories*, ed. Leslie Shepard. Secaucus, N.J.: Citadel Press, 1977.

Bierman, Joseph S. "Dracula: Prolonged Childhood Illness, and the Oral Triad." *American Imago* 29, 2 (summer 1972): 186–98.

Bordwell, David. *The Films of Carl-Theodor Dreyer*. Berkeley: University of California Press, 1981.

Boucher, Anthony. "They Bite" [1972]. Pages 58–66 in *Wolf's Complete Book of Terror*, ed. Leonard Wolf. New York: Clarkson N. Potter, 1979.

Boucicault, Dion. *The Phantom: A Drama, in Two Acts*. New York: Samuel French, 1856.

Bova, Joyce. *Don't Ask Forever: My Love Affair with Elvis*. New York: Kensington Books, 1994.

Browne, Nelson. *Sheridan Le Fanu*. London: Arthur Baker, 1951.

Butler, Ivan. *Horror in Cinema*. London: A. Zwemmer; New York: A. S. Barnes, 1970.

Byron, George Gordon. "Fragment of a Novel" [1816]. Pages 1–6 in *The Penguin Book of Vampire Stories*, ed. Alan Ryan. London: Penguin Books, 1988.

Calmet, Augustin. *Dissertations upon the Apparitions of Angels, Daemons, and Ghosts, and Concerning the Vampires of Hungary, Bohemia, Moravia, and Silesia*. Trans. London: M. Cooper 1759 [1751].

Campbell, John W., Jr. "Who Goes There?" [1938]. Pages 76–135 in *The Science Fiction Roll of Honor*, ed. Frederik Pohl. New York: Random House, 1975.

Charnas, Suzy McKee. *The Vampire Tapestry*. New York: Simon and Schuster, 1980.

Couffer, Jack. *Bat Bomb: World War II's Other Secret Weapon*. Austin: University of Texas Press, 1992.

Crawford, F. Marion. "For the Blood Is the Life" [1911]. Pages 169–84 in *The Dracula Book of Great Vampire Stories*, ed. Leslie Shepard. Secaucus, N.J.: Citadel Press, 1977.

Deane, Hamilton, and John L. Balderston. *Dracula, the Vampire Play in Three Acts*. New York: Samuel French, 1960 [1927].

Derrida, Jacques. *The Post Card: From Socrates to Freud and Beyond*. Chicago: University of Chicago Press, 1987.

Doyle, Arthur Conan. *The Case for Spirit Photography*. New York: George H. Doran Company, 1923.

———. *The History of Spiritualism*. London: Cassel, 1926.

Dresser, Norine. *American Vampires: Fans, Victims, and Practitioners*. New York: W. W. Norton, 1989.

Ellis, S. M. *Wilkie Collins, Le Fanu and Others*. London: Constable and Co., 1931.

Ewers, Hans Heinz. "The Spider" [1908]. Pages 190–204 in *Wolf's Complete Book of Terror*, ed. Leonard Wolf. New York: Clarkson N. Potter, 1979.

———. *Vampir. Ein verwilderter Roman in Fetzen und Farben*. Munich: Georg Müller, 1922.

Farson, Daniel. *The Man Who Wrote Dracula: A Biography of Bram Stoker*. London: M. Joseph, 1975.

———. *Vampires, Zombies, and Monster Men*. Garden City, N.Y.: Doubleday and Co., 1976.

Freud, Sigmund. *The Standard Edition of the Complete Psychological Works.* Ed. James Strachey. London: The Hogarth Press, 1955. Cited in the text as *SE.*

Gautier, Theophile. "Clarimonde" [1836]. Pages 1–51 in *Tales of the Undead: Vampires and Visitants,* ed. Elinore Blaisdell. New York: Crowell, 1947.

Glut, Donald F. *The Dracula Book.* Metuchen, N.J.: Scarecrow Press, 1975.

Guiley, Rosemary Ellen. *The Complete Vampire Companion.* New York: Macmillan, 1994.

———. *Vampires among Us.* New York: Pocket Books, 1991.

Haining, Peter. *Ghosts. The Illustrated History.* Secaucus, N.J.: Chatwell Books, 1987.

Hamberger, Klaus. *Mortuus Non Mordet. Dokumente zum Vampirismus 1689–1791.* Vienna: Turia and Kant, 1992.

Hamel, Frank. *Human Animals.* London: William Rider and Son, 1915.

Heidegger, Martin. *The Question Concerning Technology and Other Essays.* Trans. William Lovitt. New York: Harper Torchbooks, 1977.

Jacobi, Carl. "Revelations in Black" [1933]. Pages 129–45 in *Weird Vampire Tales,* ed. Robert Weinberg, Stefan R. Dziemianowicz, and Martin H. Greenberg. New York: Gramercy Books, 1992.

Jones, Ernest. *On the Nightmare.* New York: Liveright, 1971.

Kayton, Lawrence. "The Relationship of the Vampire Legend to Schizophrenia." *Journal of Youth and Adolescence* 1, 4 (1972): 303–14.

King, Stephen. *Danse Macabre.* New York: Berkeley, 1982.

———. *It.* New York: Signet, 1987.

———. *'Salem's Lot.* New York: Signet, 1976.

Kittler, Friedrich. "Dracula's Legacy." Trans. W. S. Davis. *Stanford Humanities Review* 1, 1 (spring 1989): 143–73.

———. *Grammophon Film Typewriter.* Berlin: Brinkmann and Bose, 1986.

Knoepflmacher, U. C. "Thoughts on the Aggression of Daughters." Pages 88–119 in *The Endurance of Frankenstein,* ed. George Levine and U. C. Knoepflmacher. Berkeley: University of California Press, 1974.

Lacan, Jacques. *Écrits. A Selection.* Trans. Alan Sheridan. New York: W. W. Norton, 1977.

La Spina, Greye. "The Antimacassar" [1949]. Pages 257–67 in *Weird Vampire Tales,* ed. Robert Weinberg, Stefan R. Dziemianowicz, and Martin H. Greenberg. New York: Gramercy Books, 1992.

LaVey, Anton Szandor. *The Satanic Bible.* New York: Avon Books, 1969.

Leatherdale, Clive. *Dracula: The Novel and the Legend.* Wellingborough: Aquarian, 1985.

Le Fanu, Sheridan. "Carmilla" [1871]. Pages 7–85 in *The Dracula Book of Great Vampire Stories,* ed. Leslie Shepard. Secaucus, N.J.: Citadel Press, 1977.

Leiber, Fritz. "The Girl with the Hungry Eyes" [1949]. Pages 173–87 in *Blood Is Not Enough,* ed. Ellen Datlow. New York: Ace Books, 1994.

Long, Frank Belknap, and Otis Adelbert Kline. "Return of the Undead" [1943]. Pages 239–56 in *Weird Vampire Tales,* ed. Robert Weinberg, Stefan R. Dziemianowicz, and Martin H. Greenberg. New York: Gramercy Books, 1992.

Loring, F. G. "The Tomb of Sarah" [1900]. Pages 153–65 in *The Dracula Book of Great Vampire Stories,* ed. Leslie Shepard. Secaucus, N.J.: Citadel Press, 1977.

Ludlam, Harry. *A Biography of Dracula: The Life Story of Bram Stoker.* London: W. Foulsham, 1962.

Mackay, Charles. Preface to *Memoirs of Extraordinary Popular Delusions and the Madness of Crowds* [1852]. 2d. ed. New York: L. C. Page and Co., 1932.

Marx, Karl. *Der achtzehnte Brumaire des Louis Bonaparte.* Berlin: Dietz Verlag, 1988 [1852].

———. *Das Kapital.* Vol. 1. Ed. Institut für Marxismus-Leninismus beim ZK der SED. Berlin: Dietz Verlag, 1969 [1867].

Masters, Anthony. *The Natural History of the Vampire.* New York: G. P. Putnam's Sons, 1972.

Maupassant, Guy de. "The Horla" [1887]. Pages 89–111 in *The Dracula Book of Great Vampire Stories* ed. Leslie Shepard. Secaucus, N.J.: Citadel Press, 1977.

McCubbin, Chris W. *GURPS Vampire Companion.* Steve Jackson Games, 1994.

McLuhan, Marshall. *Understanding Media: The Extensions of Man.* New York: McGraw-Hill, 1964.

McNally, Raymond T. *Dracula Was a Woman: In Search of the Blood Countess of Transylvania.* New York: McGraw-Hill, 1983.

McNally, Raymond T., and Radu Florescu. *In Search of Dracula: The History of Dracula and Vampires.* Boston: Houghton Mifflin Co., 1994.

Melada, Ivan. *Sheridan Le Fanu.* Boston: Twayne, 1987.

Neruda, Jan. "The Vampire" [1920]. Pages 229–32 in *The Dracula Book of Great Vampire Stories,* ed. Leslie Shepard. Secaucus, N.J.: Citadel Press, 1977.

Noll, Richard, ed. *Vampires, Werewolves, and Demons: Twentieth Century Reports in the Psychiatric Literature.* New York: Brunner/Mazel, 1992.

Peirce, Earl. "Doom of the House of Duryea" [1936]. Pages 345–59 in *Tales of the Undead: Vampires and Visitants,* ed. Elinore Blaisdell. New York: Crowell, 1947.

Polidori, John William. *The Vampyre: A Tale by Dr. Polidori.* Pasedena: G. Dahlstrom, 1968.

Prest, Thomas Peckett (or James Malcolm Rymer). *Varney the Vampire: or the Feast of Blood.* New York: Arno Press, 1970 [1840].

Puig, Manuel. *Kiss of the Spider Woman.* Trans. Thomas Colchie. New York: Knopf, 1979.

Quinn, Seabury. "Restless Souls." Pages 174–207 in *The Phantom-Fighter.* Sauk City, Wis.: Mycroft and Moran, 1966.

Reece, Robert. *The Vampire: An Original Burlesque.* London: E. Rascol, 1872.

Rice, Anne. *Interview with the Vampire*. New York: Ballantine Books, 1986.
———. *The Queen of the Damned*. New York: Alfred A. Knopf, 1988.
———. *The Vampire Lestat*. New York: Ballantine Books, 1986.
Richardson, Maurice. "The Psychoanalysis of Ghost Stories." *The Twentieth Century* (Dec. 1959): 419–31.
Rickels, Laurence A. *Aberrations of Mourning: Writing on German Crypts*. Detroit: Wayne State University Press, 1988.
———. *The Case of California*. Baltimore: Johns Hopkins University Press, 1991.
———, ed. *Looking after Nietzsche*. Albany: State University of New York Press, 1990.
Róheim, Géza. "Nach dem Tode des Urvaters." *Imago* 9 (1923): 83–86.
Roman, Victor. "Four Wooden Stakes" [1925]. Pages 251–61 in *The Dracula Book of Great Vampire Stories*, ed. Leslie Shepard. Secaucus, N.J.: Citadel Press, 1977.
Ronay, Gabriel. *The Truth about Dracula*. New York: Stein and Day, 1972.
Ronell, Avital. *The Telephone Book: Technology — Schizophrenia — Electric Speech*. Lincoln: University of Nebraska Press, 1989.
———. "The Walking Switchboard." *Substance* 61 (1990): 75–94.
Sachs, Hanns. "The Delay of the Machine Age." Trans. Margaret J. Powers. *Psychoanalytic Quarterly* 11, 3–4 (1933): 404–24.
Schreber, Daniel Paul. *Memoirs of My Nervous Illness*. Trans. Ida Macalpine and Richard A. Hunter. London: W. M. Dawson and Sons, 1955 [1903].
Senf, Carol A. " 'Dracula': Stoker's Response to the New Woman." *Victorian Studies* (autumn 1982): 33–49.
Shelley, Mary. *Frankenstein or, The Modern Prometheus*. New York: Signet Classics, 1965 [1831].
Shepard, Jim. *Nosferatu. A Novel*. New York: Albert A. Knopf, 1998.
Skal, David J. *The Monster Show: A Cultural History of Horror*. New York: Penguin Books, 1994.
Stableford, Brian. "The Man Who Loved the Vampire Lady" [1988]. Pages 60–79 in *The Mammoth Book of Vampires*, ed. Stephen Jones. New York: Carroll and Graf, 1992.
Stenbock, Count. "The Sad Story of a Vampire" [1894]. Pages 115–22 in *The Dracula Book of Great Vampire Stories*, ed. Leslie Shepard. Secaucus, N.J.: Citadel Press, 1977.
Stoker, Bram. *Dracula*. Toronto: Bantam Books, 1981 [1897].
———. "Dracula's Guest" [1914]. Pages 215–26 in *The Dracula Book of Great Vampire Stories*, ed. Leslie Shepard. Secaucus, N.J.: Citadel Press, 1977.
———. *Famous Impostors*. New York: Sturgis and Walton, 1910.
———. *The Jewel of Seven Stars*. London: Jarrolds, 1966 [1903]. Citations are from abridged edition, N. Hollywood: Fantasy House, 1974.
———. *The Lady of the Shroud*. London: Rider, 1909.

———. *The Lair of the White Worm*. London: W. Foulsham and Co., 1911.

———. *Personal Reminiscences of Henry Irving*. London: W. Heinemann, 1906.

Strieber, Whitley. *The Hunger*. New York: Pocket Books, 1982.

Strobl, Karl Hans. "Das Grabmal auf dem Père Lachaise." Pages 192–254 in *Lemuria. Seltsame Geschichten*. Munich: Georg Müller, 1921.

Summers, Montague. *The Vampire: His Kith and Kin*. New Hyde Park, N.Y.: HP University Books, 1960 [1928].

Tausk, Victor. "On the Origin of the 'Influencing Machine' in Schizophrenia." *Psychoanalytic Quarterly II* 3–4 (1933) [1919]: 519–56.

Taussig, Arthur. "Bram Stoker's Dracula." *Film Analyst* 10 (1992): 1–9.

Toufic, Jalal. *Vampires. An Uneasy Essay on the Undead in Film*. Barrytown, N.Y.: Station Hill, 1993.

Wolf, Leonard. *A Dream of Dracula: In Search of the Living Dead*. Boston: Little and Brown, 1972.

Wood, Ed, Jr. *Death of a Transvestite*. N.p.: Angora Press, n.d.

———. *Killer in Drag*. N.p.: Angora Press, n.d.

Woodward, Ian. *The Werewolf Delusion*. New York: Paddington Press, 1979.

Wright, Dudley. *The Book of Vampires*. New York: Causeway Books, 1973 [1914].

FILMOGRAPHY

An American Werewolf in London (John Landis, USA, 1981).

Andy Warhol Presents Dracula (Paul Morrisey, USA/Italy, 1974).

Andy Warhol Presents Frankenstein (Paul Morrisey, France/Italy, 1973).

The Black Cat (Edgar Ulmer, USA, 1932).

Blacula (William Crain, USA, 1972).

Blood of Dracula (Herbert L. Strock, USA, 1957).

Bloodlust: Subspecies III (Ted Nicolaou, USA, 1993).

Bloodstone: Subspecies II (Ted Nicolaou, USA, 1993).

Bram Stoker's Dracula (Francis Ford Coppola, USA, 1992).

The Bride of Frankenstein (James Whale, USA, 1935).

Buffy the Vampire Slayer (Fran Rubel Kuzui, USA, 1992).

Casper (Brad Siberling, USA, 1995).

Dance of the Damned (Katt Shea Ruben, USA, 1988).

Daughters of Darkness (Harry Kümel, Belgium/France/West Germany/Italy, 1970).

Dracula (Tod Browning, USA, 1931).

Dracula (John Badham, USA, 1979).

Dracula's Daughter (Lambert Hillyer, USA, 1936).

Fatal Attraction (Adrian Lyne, USA, 1987).

The Fearless Vampire Killers (Roman Polanski, Great Britain, 1967).

Forever Knight (USA/Canada, CBS television series, 1992–93).

Frankenstein (James Whale, USA, 1931).

From Dusk till Dawn (Robert Rodriguez, USA, 1995).

Glen or Glenda (Edward D. Wood Jr., USA, 1953).

The Golem (Paul Wegener, Germany, 1920).

Gothic (Ken Russell, Great Britain, 1986).

The Horror of Dracula (Terence Fisher, Great Britain, 1958).

The Hunger (Tony Scott, USA, 1983).

I Was a Teenage Werewolf (Gene Fowler, USA, 1957).

Innocent Blood (John Landis, USA, 1992).

Interview with the Vampire (Neil Jordan, USA, 1994).

The Lair of the White Worm (Ken Russell, Great Britain, 1988).

The Lost Boys (Joel Schumacher, USA, 1987).

The Mummy (Karl Freund, USA, 1932).

Nadja (Michael Almereyda, USA, 1994).

Near Dark (Kathryn Bigelow, USA, 1987).

Night of the Living Dead (George Romero, USA, 1969).

Nightstalker (John Llewellyn Moxey, USA, 1971).

Nosferatu (Friedrich Wilhelm Murnau, Germany, 1922).

Nosferatu the Vampire (Werner Herzog, West Germany, 1970).

Pale Blood (Michael Leighton, USA, 1992).

Plan Nine from Outer Space (Edward D. Wood Jr., USA, 1956).

Psycho (Alfred Hitchcock, USA, 1960).

A Return to Salem's Lot (Larry Cohen, USA, 1987).

The Rocky Horror Picture Show (Jim Sharman, USA, 1975).

Salem's Lot (Tobe Hooper, USA, 1980 for CBS Television).

Son of Frankenstein (Rowland V. Lee, USA, 1939).

Subspecies (Ted Nicolaou, USA/Romania, 1991).

Teenage Frankenstein (Herbert Strock, USA, 1957).

The Tenant (Roman Polanski, France, 1976).

The Thing (Christian Nyby/Howard Hawks, USA, 1951).

To Sleep with a Vampire (Adam Friedman, USA, 1993).

Universal Soldier (Roland Emmerich, USA, 1992).

Vamp (Richard Wenk, USA, 1986).

Vampire's Kiss (Robert Bierman, USA, 1989).

Vampyr (Carl-Theodor Dreyer, France, 1932).

Vampyres (Jose Larraz, Great Britain, 1974).

The Wolf Man (George Waggner, USA, 1941).

Laurence A. Rickels is professor of German and comparative literature and adjunct professor of art and film studies at the University of California, Santa Barbara. He is the author of *Aberrations of Mourning, The Case of California,* and the forthcoming *Nazi Psychoanalysis,* and the editor of *Looking after Nietzsche* and *Acting Out in Groups* (Minnesota, 1999). He is currently concluding an *Occult Quartet* of vampire screenplays, the first of which, *Take Out,* is in production. He is not only a theorist but also a psychotherapist.